D0855681

The Making of Tocqueville's *Democracy in America*

Mary Mottley, Tocqueville's future wife (ca. 1830)
(Courtesy of George W. Pierson)

Alexis de Tocqueville (ca. 1830)
(Courtesy of George W. Pierson)

The Making of Tocqueville's
Democracy in America

BY JAMES T. SCHLEIFER

The University of North Carolina Press
Chapel Hill

Manufactured in the United States of America

First printing, May 1980
Second printing, August 1981

Library of Congress Cataloging in Publication Data

Schleifer, James T 1942–
The making of Tocqueville's Democracy in America.

Bibliography: p.
Includes index.
1. Tocqueville, Alexis Charles Henri Maurice Clérel de, 1805–1859. De la démocratie en Amérique. I. Title.
JK216.T7193S33 321.8'092'4 79–9976
ISBN 0–8078–1372–9

TO ALISON, KATE, AND MEG

Contents

PART III

Tocqueville and the Union: The Nature and Future of American Federalism

PART IV

Democracy, Centralization, and Democratic Despotisms

PART V

Democracy, the Individual, and the Masses

PART VI

What Tocqueville Meant by *Démocratie*

Illustrations

Foreword

Tocqueville? In this second half of the twentieth century—in our age of social anxieties and national self-questioning—thoughtful people have been turning more and more to the complex but extraordinarily illuminating work that the young Frenchman, Alexis de Tocqueville, composed about us almost a century and a half ago.

This work was entitled *Democracy in America* (*De la Démocratie en Amérique*), and it appeared, as we know, in four volumes. The first two volumes, published in 1835 and translated in England and republished in an American edition in 1838, described and analyzed the American experiment with a clarity, balance, and penetration that were astonishing, and with an overall approval that surprised and delighted American readers. Overnight they became classic and were printed and reprinted, with editions for use in our schools. The second two volumes, only finished and translated in 1840, seemed to focus on equality, or egalitarianism in the modern world, at least as much as on American democratic self-government. Obviously they were philosophic and more remote. Less obviously, we were not culturally ready to assimilate Tocqueville's pioneering projections into the psychology and sociology of the masses. We regarded ourselves as exceptions, as under a special destiny. So volumes three and four were accepted, but much less read.

Then times changed. After the Civil War, as nationalism replaced federalism, and as industrialism took over and the cities grew, Tocqueville's institutional descriptions of what had been an agrarian republic (volumes one and two) became more and more out of date, while his anxieties about the democratic masses (volumes three and four) appeared to have been refuted by the dazzling expansion and prosperity of the nation. In 1888 James Bryce published his *American Common-*

wealth. And in short order this new classic replaced the old *Democracy* in schools or private libraries.

So Tocqueville was almost forgotten—but has now been revived.

A part of the Tocqueville revival (which began about 1938 and which bids fair to continue for many years) was the rediscovery of the *Democracy in America*, and especially of the second two volumes. What Tocqueville had had to say about American materialism and money-mindedness, about the cultural shallowness of an activist and problem-oriented society, about the instincts and jealous mediocrity of the masses, about the tyranny of the majority and suffocation by sheer numbers, about what wars might do to substitute centralization for freedom, or about the risks of despotism from a democratized bureaucracy, or about the loss of private energy in a welfare state—indeed about an astonishing range of contemporary discomforts and anxieties—rather suddenly and irresistibly, after the Great Depression and World War II and the disillusionments of our worldwide responsibilities, came to seem prophetic, and not only prophetic but challenging and profoundly instructive. So the *Démocratie* has been partially or wholly retranslated in two important new editions, has reentered the curriculum in our colleges and universities, and is resorted to and quoted by writers of all parties and persuasions (see the able analysis by Robert Nisbet, "Many Tocquevilles," in *American Scholar*, winter 1976-77).

A second element contributing to the Tocqueville revival on both sides of the Atlantic has been the recovery, publication, and study of a fascinating variety of Tocqueville and Tocqueville-related manuscripts. This began with the discovery of the existence of the U.S. travel notes and diaries and letters home of Alexis de Tocqueville and his friend and traveling companion Gustave de Beaumont. These were first used in my *Tocqueville and Beaumont in America* and have now in considerable part been printed in the *Oeuvres complètes d'Alexis de Tocqueville*: a still-growing edition which since 1951 has been in the process of republishing all of Tocqueville's works, together with his published and unpublished papers and conversations and letters. Recently the head of the editorial working committee, André Jardin, and I have also brought out Beaumont's *Lettres d'Amérique, 1831-1832.* And over the years a collection has been forming at Yale which includes not only the many other surviving Beaumont documents but copies of lost Tocqueville materials, and the original drafts and the working manuscript of the *Democracy* itself. So there has come into existence, or been recovered, a wide and informative range of materials on the background, circumstances, composition, and reception of Tocqueville's masterpiece.

Rediscovery of Tocqueville—recovery of his papers—yet there has been one thing missing. Critics and commentators have reread him. Scholars and students have been focusing on particular aspects of Tocqueville's life, his experiences in England or the revolution of 1848, his religious beliefs or his social and political thought—almost to the point of generating a small but flourishing Tocqueville industry. Yet up until now no one has had the courage to tackle the great volume (I should say the formidable mass) of Tocqueville's difficult and sometimes almost indecipherable notes and drafts and essays and working manuscript for his celebrated masterpiece—to find out how and why it was put together. This study of the manufacture, or rather of the creation, of the *Democracy* is what James T. Schleifer has attempted, and with impressive results.

The first clear gain for students of Tocqueville and of his *Démocratie* is a many-sided enlargement of our information. Schleifer shows not only when Tocqueville wrote the different parts of his book —and where and under what influences or pressures of circumstance— but what books he read, or used, or rejected—whose conversations and ideas most influenced him—whom he consulted for substance or for style—how his four volumes began and grew and gradually shifted in focus—but also what difficulties the author encountered and what frustrations. With Schleifer's aid each of us will make his own discoveries, both great and small. I found Tocqueville's (here documented) use of the *Federalist Papers*, and his borrowings or rejections of James Madison, particularly illuminating. Schleifer will surprise many by his demonstration that Tocqueville paid considerably more attention to the American economy than I and others have supposed. Schleifer not only confirms Tocqueville's multiple meanings for his key themes of democracy, individualism, centralization, and despotism, and demonstrates the confusion that sometimes resulted, but points out the benefits that Tocqueville realized from this practice. Finally, we profit from the fact that, in the process of tracing the evolution of particular arguments, Schleifer has uncovered and translated a variety of passages in the notes, the drafts, even the working manuscript, which have never before seen the light—passages often lit as if from above by one or more of Tocqueville's telling phrases.

A second general order of gain is in our understanding of Tocqueville's mind: of how he thought and worked. Schleifer's acute and penetrating analysis brings out unmistakably both Tocqueville's pluralism (what Nisbet calls the "composite" character of his book) and his instinct for generalization or penchant for ideal types. Schleifer shows Tocqueville often balancing—opposing his themes—juggling painfully with opposites—or almost playing with paradoxes, and returning to play again. We watch Tocqueville fumbling, and sometimes recovering his fumble. We are initiated into Tocqueville's hesitations and ambiguities and can identify not a few confusions. We encounter some troubling reflections that were later omitted—and some prophetic early convictions or stances which up to now have been identified only in the mature Tocqueville of 1848 or later. So gradually the perceptive reader will come to recognize that many passages in the *Democracy* carry a greater freight of meaning than has hitherto been supposed. For if Tocqueville finally decided against certain theses in his drafts, or seemingly rejected some alternative interpretations, the fact was that he might be carrying the unresolved paradoxes still in the back of his mind. Sometimes sheer fatigue may have been responsible for an omission, or we can watch (in Schleifer's nice phrase) "postponement lengthening into a kind of abandonment."

It should be said that Schleifer has not been able, in so dense and cogent a study, to trace all the themes in Tocqueville's quasi-rationalized, quasi-intuitive analysis of democracy-in-America-and-egalitarianism-in-the-modern-world. But he has identified the materials, demonstrated the method, outlined the evolution of a number of key ideas, and illustrated the rewards—in short, he has shown the way, encouraged further work in Tocqueville's unpublished manuscripts, and brought over the horizon for the first time the possibility of a great annotated edition of Tocqueville's *Democracy*: an edition this classic deserves and workers beyond the field of Tocqueville scholarship will be grateful for.

Is not the original *Democracy* enough, naked and undisguised? It is indeed much, and by itself perhaps more than we deserve, or have the humble patience to digest. It may not be "the greatest work ever written about one country by a citizen of another," but it is surely one of the master keys to an understanding of modern mass society. So to understand it and Tocqueville better is gain for us all.

I am reminded of the *Federalist Papers* and the *Debates* of the Federal Convention. Our Constitution is sufficient by itself? It alone governs? Yes—in the wording and the finality of its pronouncements. Yet only through interpretation. And it may be recalled that after many years of taking the Constitution at face value the Supreme Court was finally able to read the *Debates* which had taken place in the course of its drafting—and our Justices have not been so innocent, indeed they have been the wiser, since. For the *Debates* and the *Federalist Papers* showed what the fathers of the Constitution had been thinking about and so clothed that document with deeper and wider meanings. They gave our Constitution—our ten commandments so to speak—a setting and a depth in history—to the enlightenment and benefit—of the whole nation.

So now we are able to go behind the naked and often cloudy or inconsistent pronouncements of the *Democracy* and come closer to what Tocqueville perhaps really meant. For we can hear Tocqueville's debates with his contemporaries and, more importantly, we can watch him debating with himself. To those of us concerned for the human condition, and not obsessed with Freud or infected with the virus of Marxism, this can be a most rewarding exercise. For Tocqueville was a man of honor, with an intuitive intelligence that came close to genius, who cared profoundly for the dignity and freedom of man.

G. W. Pierson

Preface

Alexis de Tocqueville's first journey to America ended on 20 February 1832, when the *Havre* sailed from New York for France. But his nine-month visit had been only a preface to a second voyage that would consume the next eight years: the writing of the *Democracy in America*. Until now, the story of that mental return to America, that lengthy time of reconsideration and introspection, has remained largely unexplored.[1]

For the undertaking of such a project, most of the necessary materials are readily available. The Yale Tocqueville Manuscripts Collection, housed at the Beinecke Rare Book and Manuscript Library and sum of the successful collecting efforts of Paul Lambert White, John M. S. Allison, and, especially, of George Wilson Pierson, contains the bulk of letters, notes, outlines, drafts, and other papers relating to the young Frenchman's work on America. Even the original working manuscript in Tocqueville's own hand is included among the Yale materials. The collection offers, in short, an invaluable opportunity for a detailed retracing of the gestation and final shaping of Tocqueville's classic work.[2]

The accessibility of the original documents and working papers solves only one of the difficulties presented by any attempt to reconstruct the growth of Tocqueville's book. Beyond the mechanics of his writing process, his sources, his ideas, and his methods must all be reconsidered.

Scholars have long been aware that the ingredients that went into the making of the *Democracy* were numerous and diverse. The book owed something to the influence of Tocqueville's milieu, particularly the intellectual and political setting of early nineteenth-century France. It showed the marks of Tocqueville's early life and education.

It was based on the intense firsthand experience that he and Gustave de Beaumont had had of Jacksonian America. It drew also on the letters and essays of helpful American and European acquaintances, a long list of printed materials, the opinions and criticisms of family and friends who read early drafts, his experiences in France while writing the *Democracy*, and his personal beliefs, doubts, and ambitions. Yet the tale of the *Democracy*'s making demands a general reevaluation of these sources and raises several more specific questions as well. When and how did particular men, books, or events affect the *Democracy*? Were Tocqueville's readings and conversations on various topics adequate? How did he reconcile conflicting opinions and information? Which sources were ultimately most important? Do his drafts or working manuscripts reveal any new and unsuspected roots?

The re-creation of Tocqueville's mental return to America also enables us to trace various ideas from germination in early notes to full maturation in Tocqueville's final drafts. How did his thought develop? When did particular concepts first appear and how did they evolve? Did certain notions undergo unusual stages of development? Do his unpublished papers disclose any ideas which were forgotten or abandoned along the way?

The retelling of the second voyage offers us as well an opportunity to reexamine the techniques and approaches that characterized his research, thinking, and writing. Did he, for example, rely on any special methods to stimulate his thinking? Exactly how did he organize the task of composition? Did he have favorite ways to resolve the troublesome quandaries that arose during the drafting of the *Democracy*? Did he follow any particular patterns of thought?

With these and other questions and possibilities in mind, the following volume begins by discussing the actual writing of Tocqueville's masterpiece and then focuses successively on many of the major themes of the *Democracy*. The general movement is from some of the more tangible bits of Tocqueville's book to some of the more elusive concepts which form the core of his work. The closely interrelated nature of Tocqueville's great themes will quickly become evident; his key ideas appear and reappear in many different contexts and break through in unexpected places. But this volume in no way claims to unravel all the threads of the *Democracy*. Certain major strands are only just touched: the link between *démocratie* and materialism, for example, and the role of religion in Tocqueville's thought.[3]

A word or two should be added about the long quotations that appear below. Some of the passages are not directly quoted from the original papers, but from French transcriptions made decades ago. During the late 1920s, in the days before photocopying was possible, many original papers from the Tocqueville family château were copied for Yale by the local schoolteacher, M. Bonnel. Whenever originals are now available, I have used them. But in some cases, the originals disappeared long ago, and the Yale versions have acquired an unexpected value; in other cases, the original papers are as yet unpublished and thus still unavailable to anyone not working on the new edition of Tocqueville's *Oeuvres complètes*.[4] So often I have had no choice but to use the Yale copies.

An explanation is also in order about the problem of translation. For Tocqueville's travel diaries I have relied on the versions of either George Wilson Pierson, from his *Tocqueville and Beaumont in America*, or George Lawrence, from *Journey to America*, edited by J. P. Mayer.[5] Because of different sources and the individual preferences and styles of the translators, the Pierson and Mayer works occasionally disagree. Mayer's volume is a convenient English form of Tocqueville's travel diaries and is based, where possible, upon existing French originals. Pierson often used duplicates as a starting point and so occasionally reproduced errors first made by the copyist. But in addition to extensive selections from the American notebooks, he also offers valuable English versions of a variety of letters and other papers relating to Tocqueville's book. (For these I have also sometimes relied on his translations.)

For the *Democracy in America* itself, I have almost always quoted from the more recent paperback edition, again translated by George Lawrence and edited by J. P. Mayer.[6] This edition, though flawed by occasional errors and awkwardness, has the virtue of more consistently modern English throughout. In a few cases, I have reproduced the older Phillips Bradley edition.[7] My choice has depended on the accuracy, clarity, and felicity of the two translations. Once or twice I have also attempted an entirely new translation of a significant sentence or passage; these are always indicated.

Apart from excerpts from the American notebooks, some miscellaneous correspondence, and the published *Democracy* itself, the translations appearing in this volume are my own. I have translated all materials presented below which directly relate to the development of the *Democracy*: outlines, drafts, marginalia, original working manuscript, "Rubish," and other papers. So the responsibility for fairly rendering the meaning and tone of Tocqueville's own words is mine.

I would like to acknowledge my debt, first of all, to my fellow *tocquevillien*, George Wilson Pierson, who, by his careful readings of my manuscript at its various stages, by his perceptive comments and suggestions, and by his own high standards of scholarship and style, has left his mark throughout this work. His advice, support, friendship, and inspiration have been invaluable to me.

I am grateful to various other members of the community of scholars: especially André Jardin, for his ready help, meticulous example, and warm friendship; Doris Goldstein, for her interest and encouragement along the way; and Joseph Hamburger and Edmund S. Morgan for their willingness to read and comment upon the final draft of this volume.

I owe thanks to several institutions: the Yale University history department which, in 1972, honored an earlier dissertation version of the first three sections of this book with the George Washington Egleston Prize; the Society for French Historical Studies and the Institut français de Washington, which jointly granted that same manuscript the Gilbert Chinard Incentive Award for 1974; the American Council of Learned Societies for a fellowship in 1974-75 which allowed me, for several months, to devote my full time and energy to this book; and to the College of New Rochelle, which, though small and of limited financial resources, supports the scholarly work of its faculty in many ways and helped me particularly by bearing most of the costs of preparing the final typed copy of this manuscript and by defraying the expense of large unanticipated permission fees.

And finally I am grateful to the staff at the Beinecke Rare Book and Manuscript Library, especially Miss Marjorie Wynne, Edwin J. Beinecke Research Librarian, who has for some years been closely involved (with George Wilson Pierson) in overseeing the development of the Yale Tocqueville Collection; and to the Public Services staff behind the main desk. Their assistance to me over the past decade has been unfailingly gracious.

Tocqueville specialists should note that a fuller typescript version of this book has been added to the Yale Tocqueville Manuscripts Collection at the Beinecke Library. In that uncut manuscript, interested scholars will find some additional textual material and more numerous and detailed notes.

Part I

Tocqueville's Second Voyage to America, 1832–1840

CHAPTER 1

The Writing of the First Part of the *Democracy*

When Tocqueville first thought of writing a book about America has never been entirely clear. In 1831-32, the official mission of the young *juge auditeur* and his traveling companion, Gustave de Beaumont, was to examine and report upon the American prison systems, but even before leaving France the two friends had determined to study more than criminal codes and penitentiary schemes. "We are leaving with the intention of examining in detail and as scientifically as possible all the mechanisms of this vast American society about which everyone talks and no one knows. And if events allow us the time, we expect to bring back the elements of a *bon ouvrage*, or at least of a new work; for nothing exists on this subject."[1]

Beaumont had also admitted to broader schemes. "We contemplate great projects; first we will accomplish as best we can the mission given us . . . ;[2] but, while doing the penitentiary system, we will see America; . . . Wouldn't a book be good if it gave an exact idea of the American people, showed their history in broad strokes, painted their character in bold outline, analyzed their social state, and rectified so many of the opinions which are erroneous on this point?"[3]

During May and June their letters from the New World continued to mention plans of a joint study. Gustave even boasted to his brother, Jules, "We are laying the foundations of a great work which should make our reputation some day."[4]

Perhaps by temperament Tocqueville was more cautious. "I hope that we will do something good here. However we must not flatter ourselves yet. The circle seems to expand as fast as we advance. . . .

[During the next nine years, the expanding nature of his American effort would haunt him more than he imagined.] Besides we have not yet written a line; but we are accumulating a great deal of material. . . . It is true that the said mission forces us to devote to prisons an enormous amount of time which would be better spent elsewhere. However that may be, we do not lack either ardor or courage and if some obstacle does not happen to stop us, I hope that we will finish by bringing forth the work that we have had in mind for a year."[5] The travelers had evidently contemplated a mutual work on America since at least the summer of 1830.

Yet the predicted birth never took place. Between June and September 1831, their epistles ceased to mention the project, and when in October news of their plans finally reappeared, Gustave and Alexis had decided to write separate books. Perhaps a major reason for their decision was a growing awareness of the immensity of the original design, for the simplest way to make an overwhelming task manageable would have been to divide it. Whatever the causes, by late September 1831, the hoped-for *ouvrage nouveau* had become two.[6]

Tocqueville and Beaumont, laboring under no illusions about the time required for understanding the United States, had hoped to remain in America longer than nine months, but by November 1831, the French government was pressing for an end to their mission and a quick return to France. Forced to leave before they wished, their thoughts were brusquely turned toward the future.

In March 1832, the two investigators landed once again in France, where both official pressures for prompt submission and personal desires to begin their own books on America urged them to complete the prison report as quickly as possible.

With his usual enthusiasm, Beaumont plunged into the task at hand, but Tocqueville, despite his best efforts, fell into an unshakable inertia. All their hopes for the future depended on their American projects, and yet he could not make himself work, and from Paris confessed: "I begin to believe that I was decidedly stricken with imbecility during the last months that I spent in America; we believed that it was an attack; but every day the ailment takes more the character of a chronic malady; I am still where you left me."[7] A week later he admitted that his mind still refused to stir. "Do not wait to see *my work* during your absence. I have not done anything, or as little as possible. My mind is in lethargy and I absolutely do not know when it will awaken. So bring enough courage, ardor, enthusiasm, *and so on* for two."[8]

In desperation, Beaumont accepted this advice and shouldered the great burden of writing their report. Meanwhile Tocqueville was dispatched to inspect *les bagnes*, the infamous French prison ships.[9] Aware that six weeks had already been lost and that his colleague could easily waste several more, Beaumont pleaded: "It is absolutely necessary to come out of the state of moral sluggishness in which you have been for some time . . . ; though for the moment you are a proud lazy-bones, I feel that I will never *work* well except when we work together. Think of our *future* and of the way in which we should be occupied."[10]

Travel and his friend's sarcasm finally drove Tocqueville into activity, and by 16 November 1832, Beaumont was able to announce to Francis Lieber: "Our report on the penitentiary system of America is finally finished, but it has taken us a good deal of time. . . . It is now in the hands of the printer. Ten pages are already pulled."[11] *Du système pénitentiaire aux Etats-Unis et de son application en France*, which had consumed over eight months, finally appeared in January 1833.[12]

Two additional events soon intervened to delay any work on Tocqueville's *grand ouvrage*, however. During the last months of 1832, Louis de Kergolay, a childhood friend, became involved in legitimist plots against the July Monarchy and found himself in prison awaiting trial on charges of disloyalty. Alexis, trained as a lawyer, decided to defer his book in order to speak in Louis's defense, and in March 1833, his skill and eloquence secured an acquittal.[13]

The second postponement—a brief visit to England—was more of Tocqueville's own choice. No one knows exactly why he wanted to see Britain during August and September 1833, but perhaps Beaumont's phrase "John Bull, father of Jonathan"[14] gave a clue to his intentions. Apparently, he expected to find in England some American roots as well as an invaluable comparison with what he had seen in the United States. In any case, the episode prevented initial efforts on the *Democracy* for two more months.[15]

Full-time labor finally got under way in October when Tocqueville installed himself in a garret above the Rue de Verneuil and threw himself into America "with a sort of fury."[16] But where to begin? He had already prepared methodically for his American work. Each night in the New World the traveler had entered full accounts of his conversations and ruminations into makeshift notebooks.[17] He had frequently commanded his correspondents to preserve his letters carefully, for they were intended not only as friendly epistles, but also as substantial records of his observations and reflections. The Frenchman had even arranged some of his journey diaries topically and alphabetically.[18] Now he unpacked his notebooks, gathered his letters, and sat down to reread.[19]

Reexamination of his American papers evidently convinced Tocqueville that an even more thorough organization was necessary, for one of his first activities was the compilation of an elaborate index to his own materials. The "sources manuscrites," as he labeled the catalogue, consisted of a list of sixty-four topics, followed in each case by page references to conversations and comments in the travel diaries.[20]

Of some interest are the subjects and episodes that he chose to include at this early stage. The entries consisted largely of specific and easily grasped bits of the American experience, like *Convention*, *Duel*, *Jury*, *Washington*, *Virgin lands*, *Canals*, *Roads*, *Banks*, *Tariff*, *Towns*, *Press*, *Town-meeting*, and *Pioneer*, mixed with a few words or phrases that ultimately became organizing principles for the entire book: *Centralization*, *Equality*, *Sovereignty of the people*, *Public opinion*, *Union: future*, *Federal organization*, *General character of the nation*. In addition, the "sources manuscrites" underscored the particular significance of certain American spokesmen. The names of Joel Roberts Poinsett and John Hazlehurst Bonval Latrobe, for example, appeared frequently and under many different headings.

In further preparation, Tocqueville drew up lengthy bibliographies of printed sources which were available at the Bibliothèque de l'Institut. "Sources. Nature of books upon which I can draw. Books at the Bibliothèque de l'Institut" itemized titles on the following: *Indians*, *Statistics and Generalities*, *Historical*, *Books on law*, and *Legislative documents*. Numerous unclassified works were cited as well, and many of the individual entries included the writer's brief but revealing critical remarks about the book's reputation and worth.[21]

Having accomplished these preliminaries, Tocqueville had next to sketch some tentative grand design for his work.[22] One possible plan soon appeared in his notes:

Point of departure (*point de départ*)

Influence of the point of departure on the future of the society.

Homogeneous ideas, *moeurs,* needs, passions of the founders of American society.

Influence of the extent of territory—of the nature of the country, of its geographic situation, its ports, its population, immigration from Europe and, in the West, from America itself.

The point of departure has engendered the society as it is organized today, *fait primitif*—after which come the consequences formulated as principles.

Political society (*société politique*)—Relations between the federal and state governments and [between] the citizen of the Union and of each state.

Civil society (*société civile*)—Relations of the citizens among themselves.

Religious society (*société religieuse*)—Relations between God and the members of society, and of the religious sects among themselves.[23]

Setting the stage by describing the *fait primitif* of the American republic seemed an excellent way to begin, but although Tocqueville would concern himself with the history of the United States in the second chapter of the 1835 *Democracy,* "Concerning Their Point of Departure and Its Importance for the Future of the Anglo-Americans,"[24] nowhere would he devote a separate section to the American environment and all its facets and ramifications. The first chapter, "Physical Configuration of North America," would suggest the size, fecundity, isolation, and relative emptiness of the continent, yet many physiographic features would not be mentioned until much later, and his often brilliant observations about the profound and far-reaching effects of the *nature du pays* would be scattered haphazardly throughout the book.[25]

Nevertheless, this early statement did announce what would become a permanent feature of Tocqueville's thinking and writing process: the crucial importance of the concept of the *point de départ.*

The author would also deviate from this early outline by reducing the projected tripartite scheme to two: *société politique* and *société civile.*[26] Although this distinction was never entirely satisfactory, it became the permanent dividing line between the first and second volumes of the 1835 *Democracy.* The *première partie* would examine the principles and governmental and administrative structures at the base of American political life. The *deuxième partie* would discuss how certain essentially civil institutions, such as the press, jury, legal corps, or religion, influenced that political life.

Under *société politique*, Tocqueville developed the following plan for his first volume: "*Political society*. The constituent principles of the American federation. Succinct picture of this constitution. Then observations: How it differs from all federations. Advantages of a federal system when it can continue to exist. Manner in which the federal government operates. President. Its obstacles. Future of the Union."[27]

Further thought raised some questions: "Perhaps it would be better to begin by the great principles which dominate all of society in America. The sovereignty of the people among others before descending to the . . .[28] government. The scale should be turned around. Establish the general principles of all the laws. Then take the town, then the State. Get to the Union only at the end. One can understand the principles of the Union only by knowing the United States. . . . The Union is the *résumé* of a group of principles which find their development only in ordinary society.[29]

"On the sovereignty of the people (its history, its development; triumphant and irresistible march of *Démocratie*), generating principle of all political laws in the United States.[30] Its strength; its counterweight, in the *moeurs*, in the judiciary. Sovereignty of the people applied to the governments. Electoral rights. Towns, states, associations, conventions. Sovereignty of the people applied to the direction of ideas. Liberty of the press. Sovereignty of the people applied to the sanction of laws, jury. [One might wonder if Tocqueville was not, at this point, contemplating a book entitled: *De la souveraineté du peuple aux Etats-Unis.*] Finish political institutions by a portrait of the Republic in America. What facilitates it, its future, not *aristocratic, tyrannical.*"[31]

This early blueprint of Tocqueville's first volume disclosed—in addition to an already deeply rooted unease about America's future—two intriguing aspects of his proposed organization during the last months of 1833. First, the very order of chapters in the first half of the 1835 *Democracy* was intended to illustrate a basic premise of his thinking about American political structures. An exposition of the underlying principle must come first, he had decided. One *idée mère*, sovereignty of the people, hid behind all of the political institutions of the United

States. Then, perhaps remembering Jared Sparks's thesis that town institutions predated both the states and the Union and provided the essential forum for the exercise of democratic liberties,[32] he envisioned a progression from the smallest political unit, the town (*la commune*), through the states, and lastly to the federal government.

Second, at this stage Tocqueville evidently planned to include chapters on the press, associations, and jury with the first volume of the 1835 *Democracy*. These institutions reflected the central principle of American society as clearly and as directly as did the administrative and governmental framework of the republic. Later, however, these subjects would be shifted to the *société civile* and consequently to his second volume.[33]

Tocqueville's outline of the first part concluded with the following paragraph: "Finish by reading documents, books, almanacs, or other things in order to find facts that I can spread throughout the work in support of these ideas."[34] Tocqueville here suggests that his method, as many readers have observed, was heavily deductive. From personal experiences, reflections, and earlier readings, he first arrived at general principles and then searched for additional facts to support his initial observations.

Among the first objectives of his research in these materials was the compilation of a factual basis for his discussion of the rise of equality and for his chapters on the history of the Union. Three draft pages presented an assembly of events, discoveries, inventions, and laws from French and European history that demonstrated the steady growth of equality. Here were the bones of Alexis's eloquent "Introduction."[35] The same source contained brief but numerous notes on American colonial history drawn from various literary accounts and official documents of the first settlements. Here were at least some germs of his chapter on the *point de départ*.[36]

Tocqueville's schedule during all of these preparations was extraordinarily disciplined.[37] Almost simultaneously, Beaumont received a welcome progress report. "My ideas have expanded and become more general. Is it good or is it bad? I await you to know." Tocqueville also announced that he planned to complete a draft of his first volume by January 1834—an astonishing pace. But he admitted that such dispatch had exacted a price; his "American monomania" had undermined his health "which suffers a bit from extreme intellectual application."[38]

By November 1833, with a provisional table of contents in hand and certain points of fact established, he was finally ready to begin the actual composition of his *grande affaire*. With a line, Tocqueville methodically divided each sheet of paper in half lengthwise. At first he wrote only on the right-hand side of the page; the left half remained clean and available for later corrections. Also on the left he sketched brief outlines or summaries of the unfolding chapters, entered an occasional date, noted his own unguarded observations and questions about the work, and recorded some reactions of those who heard or read the manuscript at various stages of development. The text, overlaid with accumulated comments, effacements, interlinings, and symbols of many varieties, and all in a hand which Tocqueville himself labeled "rabbit tracks," is at first glance almost totally indecipherable. Only after a considerable apprenticeship do most of the many hundred sheets become legible.[39]

As Tocqueville drafted his chapter on the *état social* of Americans,[40] he encountered a problem which would plague him throughout the *Democracy*: what did the terms *état social* or *démocratie* mean? A tentative definition of the former opened the draft. "I will speak so frequently of the social state of the Anglo-Americans that it is above all necessary to say what I mean by the words *état social*. The social state, according to me, is the material and intellectual condition of a people in a given period." But a comment on the manuscript indicated that one critic found this effort "vague, indefinite" and suggested "perhaps examples instead of definitions." Apparently in response to this advice, Tocqueville deleted the two sentences.[41]

Turning to the second term, *démocratie, "le point saillant"* of American society, he began by distinguishing *démocratie* from the dogma of the sovereignty of the people and examining its relation to *état social*. "Democracy constitutes the social state. The dogma of the sovereignty of the people [constitutes] the political rule (*le droit politique*). These two things are not analogous. Democracy is a society's fundamental condition (*manière d'être*). Sovereignty of the people [is] a form of government." After a rereading, however, he reminded himself in the margin: "Note that in this chapter it is necessary never to confuse the social state with the political laws which proceed from it. Equality or inequality of conditions, which are facts, with Democracy or aristocracy, which are laws—reexamine from this point of view."[42]

A page of the original working manuscript, opening paragraphs from the chapter entitled "Concerning Their Point of Departure . . ."
(*Courtesy of the Yale Tocqueville Manuscripts Collection, Beinecke Rare Book and Manuscript Library, Yale University*)

Was *démocratie* a social condition (*égalité*), or a form of government based upon that social condition? Tocqueville had implied both. His reexamination now led to the deletion of his original statement, but no substitute was offered, and the issue remained unresolved.

It was not unnoticed, however. Someone demanded in the margin: "Explain what is meant by *démocratie*," and after the publication of *Democracy*, readers would continue to object to the confusing use of certain key terms, especially the word *démocratie*.[43] An early attempt to provide meaningful definitions had failed and, in this case, Tocqueville's reaction to frustration was unfortunate; he temporarily abandoned the search.

After perhaps three months of concentrated effort, and as he came face to face with the problem of describing and analyzing America's political institutions, Tocqueville realized that he needed help on his project. Alone and busy writing the *première partie*, he could not hope to peruse and digest the stacks of printed matters which he had collected. He also required someone well acquainted with the United States who could suggest additional resources and discuss troublesome questions. So at the American legation, he asked for the names of some eligible aides and perhaps posted the following notice: "Someone would like to meet an American of the United States who, having received a liberal education, would be willing to do research in the political laws and in the historical collections of his country, and who, for two months, would be able to sacrifice to this work two or three hours of his time each day; the choice of hours will be left to him. Apply to M. A. [Alexis] de T. [Tocqueville] rue de V. [Verneuil] N° 49, in the morning before ten o'clock or in the afternoon from two to four."[44]

In reply to his inquiries, Theodore Sedgwick III and Francis J. Lippitt, two young Americans, agreed to assist him during the first months of 1834, and both ultimately rendered valuable though quite different services.[45] The first gentleman collected books for the author and satisfied various specific points of information about the United States. After reading in the *American Almanac* of 1832 about the varying rates of growth among the states, for example, Tocqueville penned the following reminder: "Ask Sedgwick the reason why certain states increase so infinitely faster than certain others?"[46] Far more important, however, were the lengthy conversations which Tocqueville and Sedgwick shared and which offered repeated opportunities to test and develop ideas on a variety of topics, including some as important as federalism and American *moeurs*. Apparently Sedgwick listened and responded with considerable energy and intelligence, for one unexpected result of their experiences during January and February was a new and enduring friendship.

Lippitt was not as fortunate. His task, composing summaries and brief explanations of shelves-full of books and pamphlets on American political institutions, remained essentially that of a clerk; he even concluded his employment still unaware that the aristocrat who came each day to examine his work and occasionally to question him was engaged in drafting a book on the United States. Nonetheless, the more mechanical chore which Lippitt performed was essential, and his condensations and interpretations would perhaps have a significant influence on Tocqueville's book, particularly on certain ideas about the states.[47]

The help given by the two men speeded Tocqueville's work, and in March he told Nassau Senior of his intention to publish his first volume on "American Institutions" separately, probably in June of that year.[48]

But by the summer, he had abandoned this plan and was in the midst of his second volume. An early outline cited the following major chapter headings: "Of the government of the Democracy in America. What are the real advantages that American society derives from the government of the Democracy? Of the omnipotence of the majority in America and its harmful effects. What tends to moderate the omnipotence of the majority in America and to render the democratic republic practicable."[49]

The significant omission from this scheme was Tocqueville's last chapter on the future of the three races in America.[50] The gap supports the suspicion, later felt by many readers of the *Democracy*, that the last section of the 1835 text was primarily an addendum, certainly one of interest and value, but nevertheless more an appendix than an integral portion of the work.[51]

In July, efforts to master these topics drew complaints from the author. "This second part makes my head spin. Nearly everything remains to do or to do again. What I now have is only an incomplete rough sketch and sometimes not one page out of three of the original manuscript remains."[52]

Tocqueville's father, M. le Comte Hervé de Tocqueville
(Courtesy of the Yale Tocqueville Manuscripts Collection, Beinecke Rare Book and Manuscript Library, Yale University)

Gustave de Beaumont at thirty-five
(*Courtesy of the Yale Tocqueville Manuscripts Collection, Beinecke Rare Book and Manuscript Library, Yale University*)

DE LA

DÉMOCRATIE

EN AMÉRIQUE,

PAR

ALEXIS DE TOCQUEVILLE,

AVOCAT A LA COUR ROYALE DE PARIS,

L'un des auteurs du livre intitulé :

DU SYSTÈME PÉNITENTIAIRE AUX ÉTATS-UNIS.

Orné d'une carte d'Amérique.

—

TOME PREMIER.

PARIS,

LIBRAIRIE DE CHARLES GOSSELIN

RUE SAINT-GERMAIN-DES-PRÉS, 9.

M. DCCC XXXV.

Title page of *De la Démocratie en Amérique*, 1835
(*Courtesy of the Yale Tocqueville Manuscripts Collection, Beinecke Rare Book and Manuscript Library, Yale University*)

At that time, he also began negotiations with his future publisher. Fearing that Gosselin might take some advantage,[53] Tocqueville dispatched detailed descriptions of each meeting to Gustave. On 14 July he wrote: "Gosselin asked me what the title of the work would be. I had as yet thought only lightly about it, so that I was quite embarrassed. I answered however that my idea was to title the book: *De l'empire de la Démocratie aux Etats-Unis*.[54] I have since given it some thought and I find the title good. It expresses well the general thought of the book and presents it in relief. What does my judge say about it?" He went on to warn Beaumont: "More than ever I am resolved to arrive at your place toward the fifteenth of next month [August] with my manuscript under my arm and my gun across my back. So prepare yourself in advance for all the exercises of mind and body. . . . While waiting, I work as hard as I can in order to have a great deal for you to read."[55] "My judge" was to play the critic, listening to Tocqueville's draft, challenging his ideas, and suggesting revisions.[56]

Others too would hear the complete work during the late summer and fall of 1834, but oral reactions alone did not satisfy Tocqueville. He had his manuscript copied in a fair hand, then sent it to certain members of his family and friends, and requested each recipient to criticize it as thoroughly as possible in writing. He titled the collected comments "Observations critiques de mon père, mes frères et Beaumont, sur mon ouvrage" and used them to make his final revisions during the last months of 1834.[57]

The first two volumes of the *Democracy in America* were published in January 1835, less than three years after the return from America.[58] Tocqueville had accomplished almost the entire task between October 1833 and the end of 1834. Much of his speed resulted from personal discipline, single-minded purpose, and an ability to sustain an *existence toute de tête* for weeks at a time. But circumstances had also favored the project. He had enjoyed almost a year and a half of relatively sound health and of freedom from both professional and family responsibilities.

In 1835 Tocqueville hoped that the final portion of his work would follow within two or three years, yet the last two volumes were not destined to appear until April 1840. In the next half decade circumstances turned sour, and one obstacle after another arose between the author and his goal.

CHAPTER 2

An Expanding Task Resumed

Most of the 1835 *Democracy* had been written in what Beaumont called "une mansarde mystérieuse" high above the bustle of the Paris *sixième*. Despite protestations in 1834 that he disliked the country and the country gentleman's "vie de pomme de terre," Tocqueville would draft much of the second part of his work [1840] at Baugy, a small estate owned by his brother, Edouard. The château, located near Compiègne, was little more than a country house, but in the winter of 1834-35 Alexis was quickly captivated by its quiet and comfort. At Baugy, Edouard and his family reserved for their guest "a type of castle tower, or, to speak more modestly, pigeon roost that has been arranged expressly for me above the château."[1] "There," Tocqueville told Beaumont, "they showed me Alexis's room and next to it that of Gustave. The entire thing, which is quite small, makes a pleasant whole; it is a small aerial world where, I hope, we will both *perch* next year."[2] Suspended, in his *pigeonnier*, between heaven and earth, Tocqueville would be able to write in undisturbed solitude.

In the spring of 1835, however, despite the charms of this country nest, he refused to settle down to begin the final parts of his work. Tocqueville often acted on the basis of personal beliefs, firmly held, and he was convinced that no author should hurry into print immediately after a great success. But there were also two other reasons for his refusal to resume the *Democracy*: travel and romance.

In April, he and Beaumont sailed to England where, ever since the short visit of 1833, he had hoped to return. Much across the channel remained to be seen, pondered, and compared with his American experiences. If the United States was, for Tocqueville, the symbol of an advanced democratic society, England seemed the epitome of a successful aristocracy, and the 1840 *Democracy* was destined to present

Alexis de Tocqueville, lithograph by Leon Noël
(*Courtesy of the Yale Tocqueville Manuscripts Collection, Beinecke Rare Book and Manuscript Library, Yale University*)

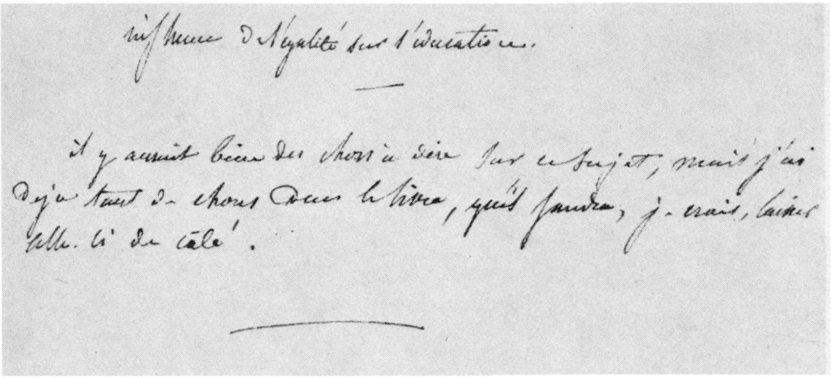

influence de l'égalité sur l'éducation.

Il y aurait bien des choses à dire sur ce sujet, mais j'ai déjà tant de choses dans le livre, qu'il faudra, je crois, laisser celle-ci de côté.

From the "Rubish," the nearly empty jacket for the abandoned chapter on the influence of *egalité* on education
(Courtesy of the Yale Tocqueville Manuscripts Collection, Beinecke Rare Book and Manuscript Library, Yale University)

many more three-way comparisons—France, America, England—than had the first two volumes of the book.

But he also had personal motives. About 1828, he had met a young Englishwoman, Mary Mottley, who, though lacking great wealth or notable birth, had attracted him by her qualities of mind and spirit. Now, despite his family's stubborn resistance, Tocqueville resolved to marry Marie. A second trip to Britain offered an opportunity to meet Marie's family and to make final arrangements for the wedding.[3]

The companions traveled together until August, when a shortage of funds forced Tocqueville to return home. Arriving in Paris in August with the intention of resuming his American enterprise, he wrote to M. le Comte Molé: "My only project at this moment will be to do what I have always intended to do if the book succeeded: to develop a last segment of my work on Democracy."[4]

The letter also stated that whereas his 1835 volumes had tried to illustrate the influence of *égalité des conditions* on the laws and political institutions of America, the *dernier développement* [1840] would examine the effect of *égalité* on American ideas, *moeurs*, and civil society.[5] "I do not know if I will succeed in portraying what I believed I saw; but at least I am certain that the subject is worth being examined; and that, out of it, a skillful writer could draw the material for a volume."[6]

In August 1835, he meant to write only one more volume, and his focus was still primarily on America.

During the last months of 1835, ensconced in his tower at Baugy, Tocqueville repeated the process of 1833 and drew up a list of subjects which he believed were important enough to become chapters.[7] This list included three topics on American education: "(1) On academic institutions under Democracy; (2) On the necessity for *corps savants* in Democracies; [and] (3) On education in the United States and in democratic countries in general."[8] An additional note declared: "The influence of Democracy on the education of men, or rather their instruction, is a necessary chapter," and indicated that this required piece would be placed among the chapters on American ideas. Tocqueville even titled a chapter cover: "Influence de l'égalité sur l'éducation," but the jacket remained empty and would eventually be relegated to what he called the "Rubish" of his 1840 volumes.

In a comment scribbled later below the title, he would write: "There would have been many things to say on this subject, but I already have so many things in the book that I believe it will be necessary to leave this aside."[9] Evidently the sheer size of the last part of the work discouraged him from introducing his ideas on American education, and although the 1840 *Democracy* would include a chapter entitled "Education of Girls in the United States,"[10] no comprehensive discussion concerning the influences of *démocratie* on education would appear. At least one critic has noted that the lack of such a general treatment is one of the *Democracy*'s important weaknesses.[11]

At the same time, Tocqueville considered a chapter on the effects of democracy "sur les sciences morales," and another, closely related, "sur la moralité humaine" which he proposed as his last, for it was an "idée capitale et mère" and "Everything about man is there." The plan was finally abandoned, however, because the discussion would be "too vast, too thorny. Probably refrain from doing it."[12]

During these first months of work, Tocqueville was still thinking in terms of a single additional volume. A preliminary plan proposed: "Two great divisions: 1. Influence of *Démocratie* on ideas; 2. *id.* on sentiments." But then Tocqueville wondered: "Where to place manners, customs?" He was apparently leaning toward some separate consideration of *moeurs*. Yet another possibility also occurred to him at this time: "Make a third division of what is not democratic, but American."

Rear view of the Tocqueville Château (ca. 1930), showing the round tower room where Tocqueville wrote sections of the 1840 *Democracy*

Tocqueville would never find an adequate way to distinguish between democratic and American traits, but at least he had recognized the problem raised in his work. A final sketch avoided this last complication and simply concluded: "3rd volume. Division to make perhaps. Effects of *Démocratie* 1. on thought; 2. on the heart; 3. on habits." He had now fixed the basic organization for much of the 1840 *Democracy*.[13]

As 1836 began, Tocqueville ceased work and hurried to Paris where his mother lay critically ill. On 10 February, he sadly notified John Stuart Mill that Madame la Comtesse had died.[14] The consequences were unexpected. In the division of property Alexis was awarded Tocqueville, the ancient family home in Normandy, long uninhabited and badly in need of repairs. This battered and dubious portion soon won his affection; by 1837, his feelings for the old château would eclipse even his attachment to Baugy.

Tocqueville returned to the *Democracy* in the spring of 1836. Earlier, at the request of Mill, he had submitted an article to the *London Review*, and the Englishman, anxious to secure regular contributions, now pressed him for a second essay. But Tocqueville pleaded the increasing demands of his American work and declined. He also mentioned for the first time his intention of publishing two additional volumes rather than only one.[15] The scope of his enterprise was steadily widening.

Defending his decision, he wrote to his English translator and friend, Henry Reeve: "Instead of a single volume, I will be *forced* to publish two of them. . . . I hold to presenting myself in the smallest possible format. But in the end, there is a limit to being concise, and I have not been able to squeeze what I have to say into a single volume." The spring of 1837 would probably be the date. "At that time I believe that I will publish the two new volumes separately, leaving to a later time the correction of the first two and the coordination of the whole."[16] This was another in a long series of mistaken estimates.

"America" so possessed Tocqueville's mind in the early part of 1836 that the subject poked into his correspondence even when he wished to write of other things. Having inadvertently mentioned America in another letter to Reeve he apologized: "Pardon me, my dear friend, there I go falling again into this damnable Democracy which I have on my nose like a pair of glasses and through which I see all things.

A bit more, and the only thing left to my family will be to have me declared incapable of managing my affairs and led off to Charenton."[17]

Whatever the risks, Tocqueville kept his "spectacles" snugly on his nose throughout April, May, and June. In May he left Paris and perched himself once again at Baugy where he testified that he did only three things: sleep, eat, and work, adding that in ten days at his brother's house he had written more than in a month at Paris.[18]

His only complaint concerned the difficulty of his task, which seemed to expand in direct proportion to his efforts. He also sensed a slow but troubling movement away from the concreteness of the American experiences and toward the abstraction of general ideas about *démocratie*. "There are moments when I am seized by a sort of panic terror. In the first part of my work I confined myself to the laws, which were fixed and visible points. Here, it seems that at times I am up in the air, and that I am most certainly going to tumble down, unable to stop myself, into the common, the absurd, or the boring." Revealing his own self-doubts, he added: "Those who are full of self-complacency are a thousand times happy; they are insufferable to others, it is true; but they enjoy themselves delightfully."[19]

Tocqueville's health was always precarious, especially under the stress of long periods of concentrated work, but in July 1836, it was Marie's constitution, as delicate as her husband's, which interrupted the *Democracy*. It almost seemed that when one wasn't ill, the other was. The couple decided to visit the spa at Baden, Switzerland, where they stayed for the remainder of the summer.

Not until October did they return to Baugy. Four months had been lost,[20] and Tocqueville's mind, so long away from the *Democracy*, turned once again to America only with the greatest difficulty. As a result of the break, he told Beaumont his work would not appear before the end of 1837.[21]

He had attempted to complete his chapters concerning the influence of *démocratie* on ideas before leaving for Switzerland. So now, the section on *les sentiments* demanded his attention.[22] Overcoming his inertia, for the next three months the author spent at least eight hours a day at his desk. He rose daily at six, worked until ten, and then stopped for three or four hours in order to eat and exercise. By the middle of each afternoon, he was back at his desk. As he told Reeve: "I have never worked at anything with as much enthusiasm; I think of my subject day and night."[23]

Yet progress did not match his fervor. The *Democracy's* increasing complexity continued to surprise and trouble him. "I would never have imagined that a subject that I have already revolved in so many ways could present itself to me with so many new faces."[24] The possibility of following an earlier triumph with a mediocre book also haunted his thoughts. Such doubts drove him to a thoroughness so extraordinary and painful that frustration finally settled in. Tocqueville found some comfort, however, in his surroundings, which he described as almost ideal for work, and he also drew assurance from a conviction that at least what he did write was good. Only one thing was missing. "I lack only a *good instrument* of conversation," he told Beaumont, "I need either you or Louis. The system would then be perfect."[25]

Tocqueville often tried to clarify his ideas by exposing them to the rigors of friendly criticism. For the 1835 volumes, he had relied primarily on the critical abilities of his family and Beaumont. But during the writing of the second part of the *Democracy*, his list of "good instruments of conversation" changed considerably. Although, between 1835 and 1840, Gustave remained Tocqueville's favorite judge, Edouard, who was often available at Baugy, probably rose in his esteem. And even more important, Louis de Kergolay's stature as reader and commentator grew to the point of rivaling Beaumont's.[26]

Louis de Kergolay (1804-77), born only a year before Tocqueville and his oldest and probably closest friend, had decided to pursue a military rather than a legal career. He had become an officer in 1829 after study at both the Ecole polytechnique and the Ecole d'artillerie et de génie, and his background, intelligence, and prominent role in the successful siege of Algiers in 1830 seemed to assure a bright future. But the July Revolution suddenly intervened. Unlike Alexis, Louis refused to take an oath of loyalty to the new regime and, after his involvement in an unsuccessful legitimist plot of 1832, retired from all participation in public affairs.[27] During almost forty years of internal exile, Kergolay would publish a few articles, travel occasionally, lead the life of a country squire, and, according to both Tocqueville and Beaumont, largely waste his fine mind and high abilities. Until Alexis's death in 1859, he and Louis, despite profound political differences, would maintain an exceedingly close friendship.

One result of their relationship was now an effort, both in person and in writing, to keep Kergolay abreast of the development of the *Democracy*.[28] "There is not, so to speak, a day that I do not feel your absence," Tocqueville wrote on 10 November 1836. "A multitude of ideas remain obscure in my mind because it is impossible where I am to throw them out in a conversation with you and see how you set about to combat them, or, accepting them, how you give them a new twist. There are three men with whom I live a bit every day, Pascal, Montesquieu, and Rousseau. A fourth is missing: you."[29]

This letter, in addition to underlining Tocqueville's growing reliance on Louis's intellectual companionship, also touches on one of the most difficult parts of any attempt to reconstruct the making of the *Democracy*. Particularly after 1835, readings not directly related to America entered increasingly into Tocqueville's thinking and writing process. He began to study and restudy a much broader range of works than he had found either the time or the need to read while he worked on the first half of his book. Letters and other materials indicate that between 1835 and 1840 he consulted, among great works of philosophy or political theory, the writings of Plato, Aristotle, Plutarch, Thomas Aquinas, Machiavelli, Montaigne, Bacon, Descartes, Pascal, Montesquieu, and Rousseau. Of other seventeenth-century French authors, he read La Bruyère, Charles de Saint-Evremond, and Madame de Sévigné; and from the eighteenth century, Fontenelle, Jean-Baptiste Massillon, and Malesherbes, as well as the famous *Encyclopédie*. During this brief period he also apparently read, more miscellaneously, Rabelais, Cervantes, the *Koran*, and various books by his contemporaries, especially Guizot, Lacordaire, and François-Auguste Mignet.

But demonstrating any firm and specific connection between these extensive readings and the last volumes of the *Democracy* remains nearly impossible. Unlike the 1835 drafts, which, as we shall see, often referred explicitly to many American works, the 1840 manuscripts only rarely hint at how a particular writer or book might have contributed in any precise way to the shape of Tocqueville's *grande affaire*. So almost all claims to influences on the 1840 *Democracy* by one author or another must continue to rest on the grounds of parallel ideas and other broad similarities.

In December 1836, Tocqueville returned to Paris. He continued to work, but lost a great deal of time to social obligations. Such demands did not, however, prevent the reiteration of his intention to publish by the end of 1837. In January, he even announced to Nassau Senior that his manuscript would be complete by the summer. "I do not know if it will be good; but I can affirm that I cannot make it better. I devote to it all my time and all my intelligence."[30] But such dedication would still not be enough to enable him to meet any of his proposed publication dates. During 1837, illness and politics would repeatedly mock his plans.[31]

That summer was the first which Alexis and Marie spent at the château in Normandy. Illness marred Tocqueville's first days at his "vieille ferme," however. And his recovery was not complete enough to allow work. He worried increasingly about the *Democracy*'s retreating publication date. "Time passes in a frightening manner. But what do you want? Above all one must live, if only to have the strength to complete this great work. If the result of my work is really good, it will make an impression whatever the period of publication; if it is bad or mediocre, what do greater or lesser chances of a temporary success matter? That is what I constantly tell myself to calm the inner agitation which besets me when I consider all that remains for me to do in order to finish."[32]

For John Stuart Mill, Tocqueville described his difficulties in great detail, and familiar specters crowded the account. "My plan has much enlarged," he wrote; "and then difficulties seem to grow as I advance and the fear of doing worse than I did before increases. I can not ignore the fact that people expect much from me; this idea constantly torments me and makes me bring to the least detail a care which, I hope, will serve the work, but which renders its writing slower." He noted also that various incidents vexed him, including his recent illness and the circumstance that would consume most of the fall of 1837: "I live here in the *arrondissement* where I want to present myself at the next election, which necessitates visits to my neighbors. . . . the result of all this, my dear Mill," he concluded glumly, "is that I can not, without deluding myself, hope to appear before next February *at the earliest*."[33]

In August 1837, "le bon Gustave" arrived in Normandy to hear parts of Tocqueville's manuscript. Beaumont had just returned from a long voyage to the British Isles where he had gathered materials for his projected work on Ireland. The former traveling companions undoubtedly spent long hours that summer walking through the fields that surrounded the château and thrashing out ideas for their books.[34]

The August meeting also probably included talk of political plans. Their letters during 1837 had turned repeatedly to tales of parties and politicians, and by September the friends wrote of little else except political news. As early as May, Tocqueville had speculated about the possibility of new elections, so when elections were finally called for November, the authors put their books aside and campaigned eagerly for seats in the Chamber of Deputies.[35]

Since they had decided to run as political independents, bound to no man or party, Tocqueville even rebuffed the overtures of Molé who was then head of the government. Such lofty attitudes proved their undoing, and the election results sent two other men to Paris. Shortly after their defeats, Alexis wrote to console and encourage Gustave. "Here we are finally free, my dear friend, and I can not tell you with what joy and enthusiasm I throw myself once again into my studies and into my work. . . . The future is ours, believe me. Never was I so convinced of it."[36]

For the early winter of 1837-38, Tocqueville returned to Paris. There he had hoped to lose himself in his *monomanie*, but the capital once again upset his plans; a call to jury duty consumed the last two weeks in December. "I truly begin to believe that it is not written on high that I will finish my book."[37]

In January, he fled to Baugy and was finally able to reestablish the ambitious work schedule which he had followed in 1836. Yet once again dissatisfaction with his draft tormented him. "Have you ever been fully satisfied with what you write?" he asked Beaumont. "The thing has never happened to me that I recall. Always somewhere above, below, to the right and left of the mark, never fully on this ideal mark that each has eternally before his eyes and which always recedes when someone wishes to reach it."[38] Tocqueville made this admission of discontent while simultaneously drafting several chapters concerning the influence of democracy on *moeurs*[39] and sketching various ideas which he hoped to include in his preface to the 1840 volumes.

Having already determined to publish his last two volumes separately and to postpone a projected attempt to coordinate the 1835 and 1840 parts of the *Democracy*, Tocqueville was troubled about the possibility of repetition or contradiction between the two parts of his work. He now resolved to mention that danger in his preface and, on 5 November 1838, wrote: "Point out—to myself as well—that I was led in the second work to take up once again some subjects already *touched upon* in the first, or to modify some opinions expressed therein. Necessary result of such a large work done in two stages."[40]

Yet most judgments apparently needed no modifications, so Tocqueville also decided to point that out. "It will be necessary to show how recent events justify the greater part of the things that I said." He believed, in particular, that the accuracy of his remarks about "The Indians; Texas; The Negroes; The need to have troops in the cities; The ultra-democratic tendencies" had been confirmed.[41]

As for those opinions which did need correction, Tocqueville felt that only one was serious enough to mention in his preface. In 1835, he had predicted "the weakening of the federal bond," but in 1838, in a "note related to the preface of my *grand ouvrage*," he confessed, "admit my error."[42]

He also resolved to acknowledge the changing focus of his work. The scope of the 1840 *Democracy* had not only expanded, but had also shifted away from America and toward general considerations about the effects of *démocratie*. Tocqueville anticipated criticism of this transformation, but hoped that an attempt to forewarn his readers and to demonstrate his own recognition of the shift would remove at least some of the critical sting. In a fragment entitled "Explanation of the object of the work," he declared: "The first book more American than democratic. This one more democratic than American."[43] Yet at some time between early 1838 and late 1839, Tocqueville would inexplicably decide to delete each of these ideas, and not one would appear in his published preface.

By March 1838, the chapters on *moeurs* were nearly complete, and Tocqueville began sketches of the final section of the *Democracy*.[44] He told Reeve that he wished to publish by the winter of 1838-39, but cautioned against relying too heavily on such estimates. "Each day I see myself mistaken in my calculations. . . . I never know . . . in advance if what remains for me to do will take a little or a great deal of time, if it will consume much or little paper."[45]

His caution was well considered, because calculations once again failed to allow time for illness. After three months of feverish work, his brain refused all service. Mentally and emotionally exhausted, he tried in vain to persuade Beaumont that he was not actually sick, but Gustave easily saw through his protestation. Finally, in the hope that a break might restore his energy, he reluctantly decided to abandon "America" temporarily, and after putting some final touches on the chapters on *moeurs*, he and Marie left Baugy for Paris. From there they soon continued on to Normandy where they anticipated a quiet summer.[46]

Tocqueville planned to draft the last major part of his book while settled snugly in his tower at the château, but a multitude of annoyances once again made any writing impossible. He was besieged by "people, *boring* but *useful* to receive," who allowed their visits to become five-hour sojourns.[47] When visitors failed to appear, Marie, who was directing extensive renovations, kept the old house in tumult. Tocqueville quickly grew impatient with the noise and disorder and lamented: "The charm of embellishing my property does not yet move me: perhaps that will come to me as to so many others I see who easily console themselves about all the miseries of life by making an English garden. But it hasn't happened yet, and while waiting, I am chased from room to room by a throng of workers who, under the pretext of soon rendering a stay at my house very pleasant for me, begin by rendering it uninhabitable or very nearly."[48] Not until July was he able to get back to his *grande affaire*.

Finally, on 19 October 1838, Tocqueville happily announced to Beaumont that he had written "the last word of the last chapter." He restrained the impulse for celebration, however, because he realized that the chore of rereading and revising both volumes still remained. Beaumont learned that his friend would remain in Normandy at least until January. "I fear the distractions of Paris and I am willing to expose myself to them only when I believe myself almost the master of *mon affaire*."[49]

But the *Democracy* was not to be mastered even now; the task of revision proved immense. The first two chapters, for example, were in such terrible condition that Tocqueville destroyed them and started over.[50]

From October to early December, Kergolay was at his side, and as Tocqueville confided to Beaumont: "He has been very useful to me in my work."[51] Louis's suggestions were apparently decisive on at least two separate problems that arose during the rewriting.

In December, as Tocqueville reread the first of his 1840 volumes, he noticed that most of his section on *les idées* assumed an awareness of the later chapters on *individualisme* and *jouissances matérielles*.[52] Should he have put the chapters on *individualisme* and *jouissances matérielles* first? He considered reorganizing his first volume, but Kergolay evidently dissuaded him. As Tocqueville remarked in one of his drafts: "L. [Louis] thinks that whatever logical interest there might be in beginning with the two above chapters, I should persist in placing the chapter on Method at the beginning. That, he says, opens the subject very grandly and immediately presents it from a lofty perspective."[53]

During the reworking process Tocqueville also pondered the fate of a small chapter written some time earlier. He could not decide where to place the piece or even whether to include it at all, and he apparently leaned toward deleting it.[54] As he noted, however, Louis's enthusiasm for the essay helped to save it from oblivion: "L. [Louis] thinks that this piece must *absolutely* appear in the work, either in its present form or by transporting the ideas elsewhere. I believe, as a matter of fact, that he is right.[55] The two friends did not know that they were weighing the destiny of one of the *Democracy*'s most famous chapters: "Why Democratic Peoples Love Equality Better Than Liberty."[56]

Tocqueville was anxious to complete the revision of at least his first volume by the middle of January 1839. At that time he planned to leave for Paris, where he counted on the critical abilities of his "cher aristarque," Beaumont.[57] "You are for me," he told Gustave, "not only a good judge, but the public personified. The spontaneity of your impressions and the lively and total way in which you express each one of them, the ideas and the passions of our times that you always bring so vividly to the work submitted to you, make you, my dear friend, the most valuable of all critics to me. I have some sharp misgivings about the destiny of this book. I admit that, only with difficulty, would people persuade me that it contains nothing of good. But I fear that in its entirety it is boring and tiresome. That is what you alone can tell me; and about that I burn to question you."[58]

Beaumont's services as "bon instrument de conversation" were crucial, but his aid to Tocqueville went beyond the friendly obligation to evaluate the drafts of the *Democracy*. While laboring over a discussion of American attitudes in the chapter "How Democracy Modifies the Relations between Master and Servant," Tocqueville suggested to himself: "To do a good job, a small portrait in the manner of the *Lettres persanes* [Montesquieu] or *Les Caractères* of La Bruyère should be inserted here. But I lack the facts." To the side, however, he wrote: "Perhaps Beaumont's notes will furnish them."[59] Whether he was referring to Beaumont's own travel diaries or to the extensive appendices of *Marie*, we do not know. But there would be some intriguing parallels between certain remarks in the 1840 *Democracy* and words of 1835 from the notes of *Marie*.[60]

In "*Rubish* of the chapters on sociability,"[61] Tocqueville once again reminded himself of Beaumont's materials: "Good qualities of the Americans. Sociability. Defect of susceptibility. See Beaumont. C. n. 6. [Cahier number 6?]."[62]

Still another example of his reference to the writings of his former companion occurred as he drafted the section entitled "What Sort of Despotism Democratic Nations Have to Fear."[63] Returning briefly once again to his *idée fixe* about the crucial connection between inheritance laws and the progress of equality, Tocqueville mentioned in the margin: "See Beaumont's piece on property in England and especially on the immense role played by testamentary freedom. 2nd volume of *L'Irelande*."[64]

So apparently Tocqueville made at least some use of the papers and books, as well as the advice, of his former companion.

At the beginning of 1839, Tocqueville's health, which had been unsteady all winter, worsened, and he resigned himself to the possibility of further postponements.[65] But by February, energy returned. A call for a second election persuaded him, however, to devote himself to campaigning. This time he succeeded, and in March 1839 he became the representative from Valognes. Once in the Chamber, he began almost immediately to make his mark by writing a report on the abolition of slavery in the French colonies.[66] Throughout all of these activities, work on the *grand ouvrage* necessarily remained suspended; "America" simply had to wait.

Finally in August 1839, Tocqueville returned to his two volumes and assured Reeve that a polished version would be in hand before the next session of the Chamber, which presumably would begin at the end of December.[67] Late in August, Jean-Jacques Ampère arrived in Nor-

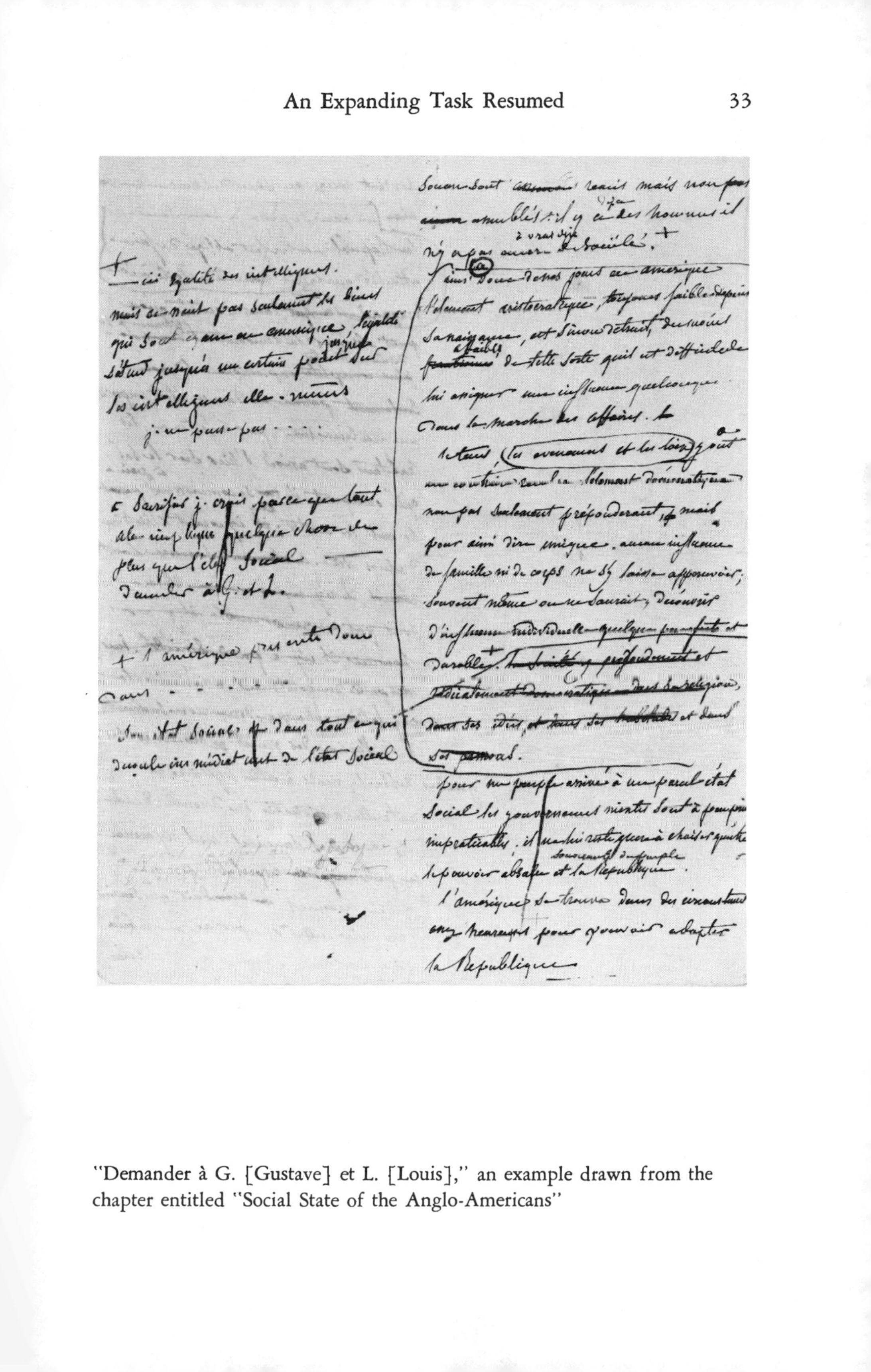

"Demander à G. [Gustave] et L. [Louis]," an example drawn from the chapter entitled "Social State of the Anglo-Americans"

mandy and read parts of the developing draft. The visitor's criticisms were so astute that Tocqueville extracted his promise to read the entire final manuscript.[68]

About the middle of November, Tocqueville reached Paris and announced to John Stuart Mill: "I arrived . . . at Paris to have printed the work on which I have labored for four years and which is the sequel to the other; it is *L'Influence de l'égalité sur les idées et les sentiments des hommes*."[69] By now, America had apparently receded well into the background.

Only last readings by his friends stood between Tocqueville and publication. He had already warned Beaumont that his manuscript "would pass through your eyes or ears, as you wish, and you would be able to judge it all in one breath. I ask this last effort of your friendship."[70] A few days later he added: "You will see even on the manuscript some traces of the importance which I give to this task. You will find in many places phrases such as this one: *To include only after having read it to B. and to L.*; or this other: *Propose these two versions to B. and to L. and make them choose*. Unfortunately one of my two counselors is missing. So try to double your wisdom."[71]

At least three chapters now bore citations similar to those mentioned in Tocqueville's letter: "How American Democracy Has Modified the English Language"; "Concerning the Way in Which the American Governments Deal with Associations"; and "How the American Views the Equality of the Sexes." Of these, the second would not appear in the 1840 text. Apparently Gustave, the single available critic, approved only the other two.[72]

In addition, on the title page of the section entitled "Why Some Americans Display Enthusiastic Forms of Spirituality," Alexis had written: "Small chapter that I should retain only if someone expressly advises me to do so."[73] Possibly here too, since Kergolay was in Tours, Beaumont alone had the final say.

By the early months of 1840, all evaluations and changes were finished, and Tocqueville submitted his book to the printer. In April 1840, the last two volumes of the *Democracy in America* finally appeared. Now he might well have repeated his earlier expression of joy: "My book is finally finished, definitively finished; *alleluia*!"[74]

Part II

How to Account for America? Tocqueville Looks at Some Particular *Causes Physiques*

CHAPTER 3

An Hypothesis Weighed and Rejected

During the first fifty years of American independence many Europeans admired and envied the prosperity and tranquillity of the American republic, but differed over the reasons for such success. In 1803 C. F. Volney repeated one of the most common explanations. After apologizing in the preface of his *Tableau du climat et du sol des Etats-Unis* for the work's limited scope, he recalled his original intention to present a more general analysis of the American nation, which would have proven "by incontestable facts . . . that the United States have owed their public prosperity, their civil and individual ease, much more to their isolated position, to their distance from any powerful neighbor, from any theater of war, finally to the general facility of their circumstances, than to the essential goodness of their laws or to the wisdom of their administration."[1]

Much to his own regret, Volney fell far short of the broad study he had once envisioned. His text failed even to address the puzzle of America's success, much less to provide the "faits incontestables" necessary to prove the author's contention. But his idea did not languish; apparently it was standard furniture for the European mind, for so many later commentators offered the same opinion to their readers that in 1833, two years before the first part of Tocqueville's *Democracy* appeared, the *North American Review* denounced the prevailing attitude:

> When we venture to assign [as one of the causes of our prosperity], the character of our Government, the sages of Europe smile in conscious superiority at our simplicity, and assure us that we have become what we

> are in spite of our institutions, and not in consequence of them. When we hint at the fixed religious principles, the stern morality, the persevering industry of the pilgrim fathers of New England, who have formed the kernel of the whole population of the Union, we are scornfully told that the mass of the original settlers were, after all, the refuse of the British jails. The only principle of our success, which is readily admitted by our friends abroad as real, (it being one which confers no credit upon us) is the immense extent of our territory.

The *Review* urged the sages of Europe to reconsider their choice: "If this circumstance alone could make a people prosperous, it is not easy to see why civilization should not be as active on the vast central *plateaux* of Tartary and Mexico, as it is in the valley of the Mississippi."[2]

Tocqueville, like his predecessors, would not escape the hard choices involved in this controversy. Eight days after he and Beaumont arrived in the New World, he wrote to Ernest de Chabrol and requested a lengthy description of his friend's ideas about America. Hoping to lighten the imposed task, he also suggested several possible topics for reflection, among them: "To what cause do you attribute the prosperity of this nation?"[3] The old riddle was clearly on his mind.

In October 1829, Tocqueville had explained to his new friend, Gustave de Beaumont: "There is a science that I have long disdained and that I now recognize not as useful, but as absolutely essential: it is geography. Not the knowledge of the exact meridian of some city, but . . . for example, to get very clearly in one's head the configuration of our globe in so far as it influences the political divisions of peoples and their resources; there is such and such a country which, by its solitary geographic position (*position géographique*) is called almost inevitably to enter into such and such an aggregation, to exercise such and such an influence, to have such and such a destiny. I admit that this is not the geography which one learns at college, but I imagine that it is the only one which we are capable of understanding and retaining."[4]

So it was not only the challenge of a time-honored puzzle, but also his own expectations about the influence of *géographie* that led Tocqueville to devote much of his attention during his American visit to the *ressources* and the *position géographique* of the United States.

Like most travelers, Tocqueville found his first glimpse of land after a long ocean voyage "a delightful spectacle."[5] But on 10 May, a more prolonged view of the American coastline between Newport and New York gave him quite a different impression. From Long Island Sound the country seemed "not very attractive." "All this coast of America," he wrote, "is low and not very picturesque,"[6] and another letter described the coast as low and sterile.[7]

So strong was this first reaction to the North American continent that in 1835 the author of the *Democracy* would observe: "On the eastern slopes of the Alleghenies, between the mountains and the Atlantic, there is a long strip of rock and sand which seems to have been left behind by the retreating ocean. . . . It was on that inhospitable shore that the first efforts of human industry were concentrated. That tongue of arid land was the cradle of those English colonies which were one day to become the United States of America."[8]

Yet the trip from Rhode Island also had a more pleasant result. The steamboat rumbling under his feet, the immense distances, and especially a very peculiar American attitude caught hold of Tocqueville's imagination. "In this country people have an incredible disdain for distances. Immense rivers . . . and the canals that have been created to connect them allow traveling while doing four leagues [ten miles] an hour night and day, all in a superb structure which proceeds all by itself without jostling you in the least. . . . Thus people do not say that we are a hundred leagues from a country, but 25 hours."[9] Here was a people who thought not in terms of distance, but of time, and who made all possible efforts to whittle time into insignificance.

On 11 May, the travelers took rooms at a boardinghouse on Broadway. New York struck Tocqueville as "odd for a Frenchman and not very agreeable," but the city's surroundings elicited cries of admiration. "Imagine shores indented most fortunately, slopes covered with lawns and flowering trees and descending to the sea . . .—add to that if you can—a sea covered with sails."[10]

Soon more thoughtful consideration—no doubt inspired to some degree by talk with his many new friends in the city[11]—replaced these initial emotional reactions to America's *géographie*. And on 18 May, Tocqueville recorded some additional observations. In a diary note he first announced his recognition of several basic facts about the American continent: its immensity, its abundance, and the still (relatively) untouched condition of its interior. Here he also hinted about several broader effects of "accidental circumstance": these republicans were an incredibly busy people who made the most of a physical situation that encouraged the full and free use of human energies.[12]

Tocqueville soon learned that the available opportunities even remedied some problems which had long tormented Europe. Schooling, for example, ceased to be a threat. "There is less to fear here than anywhere else from the malaise caused to a State by a great number of people whose education lifts them above their standing and whose restlessness could disturb society. Here nature provides resources which are still so far beyond all human efforts to exhaust them, that there is no moral energy and no intellectual activity but finds ready fuel for its flames."[13]

Two weeks later he returned to these and other themes in a long letter to his father:

"Up to now I am full of two ideas: the first, that this people is one of the happiest in the world; the second, that it owes its immense prosperity much less to its peculiar virtues, less to a form of government of itself superior to other forms, than to the particular circumstances in which it finds itself, which are peculiar to it and which make its political constitution to be perfectly in accord with its needs and its social condition. [How closely the first part of this statement resembled Volney's thesis of 1803.]

". . . To sum up: the more I see this country the more I admit myself penetrated with this truth: that there is nothing absolute in the theoretical value of political institutions, and that their efficiency depends almost always on the original circumstances and the social condition of the people to whom they are applied. I see institutions succeed here which would infallibly turn France upside down; others which suit us would obviously do harm in America; and yet, either I am much mistaken, or a man is neither other nor better here than with us. Only he is otherwise placed."[14]

Who or what might have suggested this relativistic hypothesis to Tocqueville? In one of his drafts for the 1835 *Democracy*, he would write: "Ideas for the preface. Irresistible movement of Democracy. Great fact of the modern world. . . . Aim of the work: to give some fair and accurate notions about this fact; beyond that I do not judge this fact. I do not even believe that there is anything in institutions of an absolute good. Montesquieu."[15]

So possibly by a combination of observation and remembered reading, the young inquirer had deepened his analysis of the environment's influence on the character of both the Americans themselves and their institutions. But even more important, he had judged the various reasons for the Union's success and awarded primary importance to "particular" or "original circumstances," a loosely defined term that apparently included both America's physical and historical settings.

Scarcely a week later, Tocqueville composed yet another preliminary synthesis of his early impressions about the effects of America's *circonstances.*

"Picture . . . a society formed of all the nations of the earth . . . in a word a society without roots, without memories, without prejudices, without habits, without common ideas, without national character; . . . What serves as a tie to those diverse elements? What makes of them a people? *L'intérêt.* That's the secret. Individual *intérêt* which sticks through at each instant, *l'intérêt*, which, moreover, comes out in the open and calls itself a social theory.[16]

"We are a long way from the ancient republics, it must be admitted, and yet this people is republican and I don't doubt it will long remain so. And the Republic is for it the best of governments.

"I can only explain this phenomenon in thinking that America finds itself, for the present, in a physical situation so happy that the interest of the individual is never opposed to the interest of the whole, which is certainly not the case in Europe.

"What is it that in general leads men to trouble the state? On one side, the desire to attain to power; on the other, the difficulty of creating for himself a happy existence by ordinary means.

"Here there is no public power and, to tell the truth, there is no need of it. The territorial boundaries are very limited; the states have no enemies, consequently no armies, no tax, no central government; the power of the executive is nothing, it gives neither money nor power. So long as things stay thus, who will torment his life to attain it?[17]

"Now, on examining the other half of the proposition, you reach the same result. For if a career in politics is almost closed, a thousand, ten thousand others are open to human activity. *The whole world here seems a malleable substance that man turns and fashions to his pleasure*; an immense field whose smallest part only has yet been traversed, is here open to industry. . . .[18]

"Thus, in this happy country nothing draws the restless human spirit toward political passions; everything, on the contrary, draws it toward an activity that has nothing dangerous for the state. . . .

"This last reason I have just given you, in my estimation fundamental, explains equally the only salient characteristics which distinguish this people here: the industrial turn of mind, and the instability of character. [So the physical environment decisively, if indirectly, shaped the American physiognomy.]

"Nothing is easier than to enrich oneself in America. Naturally the human spirit, which needs a dominating passion, ends by turning all its thoughts toward gain. It results from this that at first appearance this people seems to be a company of merchants gathered together for trade; and as one digs further into the national character of Americans, one sees that they have sought the value of all things in this world only in the answer to this one question: how much money will it bring in?[19] [Obviously here was one result of the republic's physical situation which Tocqueville did not find attractive.]

"As for the instability of character, that crops up in a thousand places. An American takes up, leaves, goes back to ten occupations in this life; he is constantly changing his domicile and is continually forming new enterprises. Less than any other man in the world does he fear to compromise an acquired fortune, because he knows with what facility he can gain a new one.

"Besides, change seems to him the natural state of man; and how would it be otherwise? Everything about him is in constant movement: laws, opinions, public officials, fortunes, *the very land here changes in appearance from day to day.* In the midst of this universal movement which surrounds him, the American couldn't keep still."[20]

Here, while again pursuing his consideration of the social, political, and psychological implications of the Union's environment, Tocqueville had also introduced another significant physical feature: America's isolation from Europe. His travel diaries would record few conversations directly connecting the republic's distance from Europe and the possible advantages of that separation.[21] But such links were apparently obvious, for he clearly understood that the absence of an active, centralized government, a powerful executive,[22] a large army or high taxes, the freedom from constant fears of war, and the ability to prosper despite the inefficiency and vacillation of democratic government, were all due in some degree to the lack of close and hostile rivals.[23] [Cf. ". . . there is such and such a country which, by its solitary geographic position is called almost inevitably . . . to have such and such a destiny."]

He also recognized that isolation from Europe and the strong attraction of America's natural wealth had some serious disadvantages, the foremost of which concerned the republic's political life. As he had written: "We are told that it is hard to get men to take public offices that would take them out of private business. . . . The art of government seems to me to be in its infancy here."[24]

And in a letter of 10 October 1831, Tocqueville would cite some additional dark areas in the American scene: "In the United States, people have neither wars, nor plagues, nor literature, nor eloquence, nor fine arts, few great crimes, nothing of what rouses Europe's attention; here people enjoy the most pallid happiness that one can imagine."[25] The *ressources* and the *position géographique* of the continent unfortunately turned Americans from higher pursuits of mind and spirit toward the goals of private success and a pleasant but colorless comfort.

"The whole world here seems a malleable substance . . . the very land . . . changes in appearance from day to day."[26] With these words, Tocqueville returned to a theme which he had first announced on 7 June. The American people were so rapidly reshaping their continent that the transformation itself seemed an essential part of the environment.

"[Here] through a singular inversion of the usual order of things, it's nature that appears to change, while man stays immobile." In America, Tocqueville wrote, the same man has witnessed a wilderness penetrated, then tamed, has seen a thick woods turned into a farm, a small village, and finally a great city. Rivers have been harnessed. To the American, even the climate seemed different from what it used to be.

The effects on the American mind and imagination were immense. "There is not a country in the world where man more confidently seizes the future, where he so proudly feels his intelligence makes him master of the universe, that he can fashion it to his liking. It's an intellectual movement which can only be compared to that which led to the discovery of the new world three centuries ago. . . .

"Born often under another sky, placed in the middle of an always moving scene, himself driven by the irresistible torrent which draws all about him, the American has no time to tie himself to anything, he grows accustomed to change, and ends by regarding it as the natural state of man. He feels the need of it, more, he loves it; for the instability, instead of meaning disaster to him, seems to give birth only to miracles all about him. (The idea of perfection, of a continuous and endless amelioration of social conditions, this idea is presented to him unceasingly, in all its aspects.)"[27]

Tocqueville knew that the westward movement constituted a crucial part of the continent's subjugation, so he began to accumulate information about the settlers who actually tamed the wilderness. New York, his investigation revealed, was the gateway to the interior. "Each year thousands of foreigners who are going to populate the wilderness in the West, arrive through here."[28] Like most visitors, he still assumed that the players in the great drama were Europeans newly arrived in North America.

Before leaving Manhattan, the Frenchman also indicated his awareness of the possibly far-reaching effects of another physical feature: climate. "In general the seasons in America are much more marked than in Europe. At New York, for example, people have a summer like Italy and a winter like Holland." Lest *maman* worry about his always delicate health, Alexis hastened to add: "The human body apparently finds these transitions marvelous; at least, doctors attribute the longevity of the inhabitants largely to this cause."[29] More profound reflection about the influence of climate would follow later.

On the last day of June, Tocqueville and Beaumont boarded the steamboat *North American*, literally raced another ship to Albany, and then proceeded by stagecoach to Auburn and Buffalo. "This voyage which seems immense on the map is made with an unmatched rapidity; it's the fashionable way to travel in this country."[30]

The arrival at Albany came even more quickly than the two friends desired,[31] but travel westward by stage—over "roads as detestable as the roads of lower Brittany"[32]—jolted them back to reality. Their ride assuaged one early disappointment, however: the two shaken commissioners finally beheld the American forest. Or at least, until reaching Michigan, they thought they had. "I believe," Tocqueville confessed on 17 July, "that in one of my letters I complained that one hardly ever found any forests in America; here I must make due apology. Not only does one find woods and trees in America; but the entire country is still only one vast forest, in the middle of which people have cut some clearings."[33]

Two days later, the companions left Buffalo on the steamboat *Ohio* bound for Detroit—and beyond. They couldn't resist the opportunity to see the American wilderness for themselves.

On the frontier, Tocqueville, still persuaded of the importance of "particular circumstances," expected to see a conclusive demonstration of the environment's influence on American society. But by the end of his "Fortnight in the Wilderness,"[34] he drastically revised his thinking.

"The nineteenth of July, at ten in the morning, we go on board the steamboat *Ohio*, heading for Detroit. . . . we hugged the southern shores of the lake, often within shouting distance. These shores were perfectly flat. . . . Immense forests shadowed them and made about the lake a thick and rarely broken belt. From time to time, however, the aspect of the country suddenly changes. On turning a wood one sights the elegant spire of a steeple, some houses shining white and neat, some shops. Two paces further on, the forest, primitive and impenetrable, resumes its sway and once more reflects its foliage in the waters of the lake.[35]

"'Those who have travelled through the United States will find in this tableau a striking emblem of American society. . . . Everywhere extreme civilization and nature abandoned to herself find themselves together and as it were face to face. . . . As for me, with my traveller's illusions, . . . I anticipated something quite different. I had noticed that in Europe the situation more or less remote in which a province or a city lay, its wealth or poverty, its smallness or extent, exercised an immense influence on the ideas, the customs, the entire civilization of its inhabitants, and placed often the difference of several centuries between the diverse parts of the same territory.

"I imagined it was thus, and with all the more reason, in the new world, and that a country like America, peopled in an incomplete and partial way, ought to offer all the conditions of culture and present the image of society in all its ages. . . .[36]

"Nothing in this tableau is true. . . .[In America] those who inhabit these isolated places have arrived there since yesterday; they have come with the customs, the ideas, the needs of civilization. They only yield to savagery that which the imperious necessity of things exacts from them; thence the most bizarre contrasts."[37]

Frontier towns unexpectedly failed to reflect either the primitive conditions of their wilderness surroundings or their distance from eastern centers of civilization. Instead, each town, even each cabin was an "ark of civilization lost in the midst of an ocean of leaves."[38] The institutions, ideas, customs, and efforts of the settlers appeared to overcome the effects of the environment.

Tocqueville had indeed anticipated something different, so having temporarily championed an environmental or frontier theory of America, he herewith abandoned it. After the wilderness experience he would never again claim predominant importance for physiographic causes.

But he remained, nonetheless, sensitive to the profound effects of *situation physique* on the United States. And the 1835 *Democracy*, with insights remarkably similar to those of Frederick Jackson Turner and other advocates of the frontier hypothesis, would brilliantly pinpoint some of the specific links between natural circumstances and American society.

"At the end of the last century a few bold adventurers began to penetrate into the Mississippi valley. It was like a new discovery of America; . . . previously unheard of communities suddenly sprang up in the wilderness. . . . It is in the West that one can see democracy in its most extreme form. [frontier democracy] . . . [In these states the inhabitants] hardly know one another, and each man is ignorant of his nearest neighbor's history. [frontier individualism and self-reliance] So in that part of the American continent the population escapes the influence not only of great names and great wealth but also of the natural aristocracy of education and probity. [frontier equality] . . . There are inhabitants already in the new states of the West, but not as yet a society. [the frontier's repeated reconstruction of social institutions]"[39]

A letter written in December 1831 had expressed the last idea more forcefully. The Americans were "A people . . . cutting their institutions like their roads in the midst of the forests where they have just settled."[40]

The fortnight in the wilderness also drew several familiar themes back into Tocqueville's writings. "We are assured," he had declared in May, "that the wildernesses of the Mississippi are being populated still more rapidly. Every one tells us that the most fertile soil in America is to be found there, and that it stretches almost indefinitely." This glimpse of the possibilities waiting in the great interior valley would eventually become one of Tocqueville's favorite symbols of America's future. But for now, after his exciting trek with Beaumont to the farthest fringe of European civilization, he concentrated his attention on the incredible potential wealth of the lands surrounding Lake Huron. "These places which form only an immense wilderness will become one of the richest and most powerful countries in the world. One can assert it without being a prophet. Nature has done everything here. A fertile land, possibilities like no others in the world. Nothing is lacking except civilized man and he is at the door."[41]

This spectacle of America's subjugation of the West struck Tocqueville as at once magnificent and terrible to behold. Yet the American, "a daily witness of all these marvels, . . . sees nothing astonishing in them."[42] "Add that . . . he only esteems the works of man. He will willingly send you to visit a road, a bridge, a fine village; but that one has a high regard for great trees and a beautiful solitude, that's entirely incomprehensible to him."[43]

"It's this idea of destruction," Tocqueville reflected, "this conception of near and inevitable change which gives . . . so original a character and so touching a beauty to the solitudes of America. One sees them with melancholy pleasure. One hastens in a way to admire them. The idea of this natural and wild grandeur which is to end mingles with the superb images to which the march of civilization gives rise. One feels proud to be a man, and at the same time one experiences I know not what bitter regret at the power God has given us over nature."[44]

But who actually undertook this struggle with the wilderness? Something unexpected was troubling the travelers.

" 'One last question,' " Tocqueville promised his host at Pontiac. " 'It is generally believed in Europe that the wilds of America are being peopled with the help of emigration from Europe. How then does it happen that since we have been in the forest we have not met a single European?'

"A smile of condescension and satisfied pride spread over our host's face as he heard this question. [He had just completed a long description of the capital, skills, and good fortune required to carve a farm out of the wilderness.] 'It is only Americans,' he answered emphatically, 'who could have the courage to submit to such trials and who know how to purchase comfort at such a price. The emigrant from Europe stops at the great cities of the coast or in their neighborhood. There he becomes a craftsman, a farm labourer or a valet. He leads an easier life than in Europe and feels satisfied to leave the same heritage to his children. The American, on the other hand, gets hold of some land and seeks by that means to carve himself a fortune.' "[45]

This news was worthy of repetition. Another long letter to Chabrol, dated 17 August 1831, revealed that during May and June over five thousand new settlers had come to Michigan. "As you can imagine, the size of this number surprised me; even more so because it is the common opinion among us, I believed, that all these *new settlers* were Europeans. The land agent informed me that out of 5000 persons there were not 200 emigrants from Europe. Yet the proportion is greater than usual."[46] So the Americans were themselves the agents of civilization. One more preconception fell before Tocqueville's journey experiences.

Later this discovery would be placed in a broader framework of Tocqueville's own making and would appear in the pages of the *Democracy*.[47]

In the same letter of August to Chabrol, Tocqueville also returned briefly to the political implications of the abundance and activity which he had just witnessed: "How can anyone imagine a Revolution in a country where such a career is open to the needs and passions of man . . . ?"[48] Social and political stability—at least on certain levels—was another of nature's gifts.

So by July 1831, Tocqueville had already discovered many of the nation's physical characteristics and had begun a perceptive analysis of how those features influenced the Union and its inhabitants. Most important, his experiences in the wilderness had by then persuaded him to abandon his early thesis that *géographie* in its broader sense was the primary force in the shaping of American society.

CHAPTER 4

Further Considerations of Environment

After their frontier adventures, the two friends briefly visited Canada and then headed toward Boston. Experiences in that city during September and October 1831 gave special prominence to (some familiar and some new) nonphysical features of the United States, especially the moral and religious attitudes, the education, the practical political experience, and the origins and history of the Americans.[1] Yet there Tocqueville also learned several important lessons about the physical environment.

He had once mentioned the presumably invigorating effect of America's climate, but since that early letter the topic had been totally neglected. All suddenly changed, however, when a Mr. Clay, a planter from Georgia who was also visiting Boston, implied to the inquisitive foreigner that a major reason for the extensive use of slaves in much of the South was that "white people cannot get acclimatised."[2]

The possible import of this remark left Tocqueville troubled—and skeptical. So on 1 October, he asked John Quincy Adams for his opinion. "[Q.] Do you think that actually it is impossible to do without Negroes in the South? [A.] I am convinced to the contrary, Europeans cultivate the land in Greece and Sicily; why should they not do so in Virginia or the Carolinas? It is not hotter there."[3] Yet the ex-President's prompt and firm denial did not end the debate that had started in the visitor's mind, and the issue would be repeatedly raised in later interviews.

Something else of interest concerning the natural environment also came out of his talk with Adams. The honorable gentleman "appeared to think that one of the greatest guarantees of order and internal security in the United States was found in the movement of the population toward the West. 'Many more generations yet will pass,' he added, 'before we feel that we are overcrowded.' "[4]

So not only did the almost inevitable material rewards for private effort deflect men from political careers and dangerous ambitions,—Tocqueville had long ago realized that—but also the very existence of open areas, of available land in the West, scattered the population and aided the Americans in avoiding the concentrated powers and agonies of great cities.[5] In the New World, space served as a safety valve for republican institutions.[6]

In November, the aged Charles Carroll would add a special twist to this idea: "A mere Democracy is but a mob. . . . if we tolerate [our form of government], that is because every year we can push our innovators out West."[7]

Combining these and previous comments, Tocqueville would declare in a section of the 1835 *Democracy* entitled "Accidental or Providential Causes Helping to Maintain a Democratic Republic in the United States": "In Europe we habitually regard a restless spirit, immoderate desire for wealth, and an extreme love of independence as great social dangers. But precisely those things assure a long and peaceful future for the American republics. Without such restless passions the populations would be concentrated around a few places and would soon experience, as we do, needs which are hard to satisfy. What a happy land the New World is, where man's vices are almost as useful to society as his virtues!"[8]

Several Bostonians also urged the crucial importance of history on their guests. Alexander Everett stressed the American "point of departure," and Jared Sparks reminded Tocqueville that the root cause of American government and manners was "our origins." The United States was unique. "Those who would like to imitate us should remember that there are no precedents for our history."[9]

On 20 September, in the course of some additional remarks about history, Josiah Quincy, President of Harvard, reminded Tocqueville of a use of the term *circumstance* which would later prove to be immensely valuable. Previously, the observer had not been especially precise about the ingredients which went into his "particular," "accidental," or "original circumstances." Sometimes when he had employed these terms, he had been thinking mainly of America's physical situation. But often he had also at least hinted at the inclusion of certain social and economic conditions (such as relative equality) or even some moral or intellectual attitudes (such as respect for religion, education, and law).[10] Thus *circonstances* had served as a cumbersome catchall.

Quincy attempted a less ambiguous usage. After urging Tocqueville to consider history, he remarked: "I think our present happy state is even more due to circumstances beyond our control than to our constitution. Here all a man's material needs are satisfied and furthermore we are born in freedom, knowing no other state."[11] If the listener chose to follow the Brahmin's lead, he would henceforth include under the concept *circumstances* both the physical and the historical situations, or preconditions, of the United States—neither more nor less. But Tocqueville would proceed only slowly along the path that Quincy had indicated.

The Boston experience had so broadened his thinking that Tocqueville decided, probably in early October, to list the most important of the many possible explanations that he had noted for the happy condition of the United States. After heading his summary "Reasons for the social state and present government in America," he itemized:

1st. *Their origin*: excellent point of departure. Intimate mixture of the spirit of religion and liberty. Cold and rational race.

2nd. *Their geographical position*: no neighbors.

3rd. *Their commercial and industrial activity*: Everything, even their vices, is now favourable to them.

4th. *The material prosperity* which they enjoy.

5th. *The spirit of religion that prevails*: Republican and democratic religion.

6th. The diffusion of useful knowledge.

7th. Morals very chaste.

8th. Their division into little states. They prove nothing for a large one.

9th. The absence of a great capital where everything is concentrated. Care to avoid it.

10th. Commercial and provincial activity which means that everyone has something to do at home.[12]

As yet Tocqueville seemed reluctant to weigh the relative significance of these various physical and nonphysical causes. But the nation's *ressources* (fourth) and its *position géographique* (second) were specifically mentioned among these ten points, and he also cited several other reasons known to be closely related to the republic's physical situation (third, ninth, tenth). So although the astute visitor had already abandoned the theory that America was shaped primarily by its environment, he saw quite clearly that *géographie*, in its broadest sense, nonetheless enormously influenced the United States. More difficult judgments would have to wait.

After Massachusetts the commissioners headed back to New York via Connecticut and then continued on to Philadelphia and Baltimore. In Baltimore, Tocqueville once again faced the puzzle of a possible link between climate and slavery.

"Do you think you could do without slaves in Maryland?" he asked Mr. Latrobe on 30 October.[13]

"Yes, I am convinced of it. Slavery is in general an expensive way of farming, and it is more so with certain crops. Thus wheat-farming requires many labourers, but only twice in the year, at sowing time and at harvest. Slaves are useful at those two seasons. For the rest of the year they must be fed and kept without, one may say, employing them. . . . So generally speaking slavery is worth nothing in wheat growing country. And that applies to the greater part of Maryland."

Not satisfied, Tocqueville persisted: "But if sugar and coffee are more profitable crops than [wheat], and if slave labour for agriculture is more expensive than free, it surely follows that the Southerners *can* keep their slaves, but it also follows that they would get a better return from their lands if they cultivated them themselves or employed free labour?"

"No doubt," Latrobe responded, "but in the South the white man cannot, without getting ill or dying, do what the black does easily. Besides there are certain crops that are raised much more economically by slaves than by free workers. Tobacco for example. Tobacco needs continual attention; one can employ women and children in cultivating it. . . . it is a crop admirably suited for slave labour."

So for most of the South, the type of agriculture gave the crucial impetus to slavery. Apparently climate's influence on the peculiar institution, through the encouragement of certain crops, was primarily indirect. Tocqueville was almost convinced.

After a thorough study of the prisons of Philadelphia, Tocqueville and Beaumont turned westward once again, crossed Pennsylvania to Pittsburgh, and there bought passage on another of America's dangerous steamers. The two investigators intended to follow the Ohio and Mississippi rivers to New Orleans where they could begin an intensive examination of the South (a project never realized).[14]

While going down the Ohio, Tocqueville resolved to inquire once more about the identity of the American pioneer. As if to make certain that the settling of Michigan was not a special case, he asked "a great landowner from the State of Illinois": "Do many Europeans go there?" "No," the westerner answered, "the greatest number of immigrants come from Ohio."[15]

Here was another strange feature of the westward movement. Not only were settlers almost always Americans, but they were frequently men or the sons of men who had moved before. In 1835 Tocqueville would not forget this astonishing lesson. After presenting his notion of the double migration, from Europe across the Atlantic and from the coastal areas toward the Mississippi,[16] he would continue: "I have spoken about emigration from the older states, but what should one say about that from the new? Ohio was only founded fifty years ago, most of its inhabitants were not born there, its capital is not thirty years old, and an immense stretch of unclaimed wilderness still covers its territory; nevertheless, the population of Ohio has already started to move west; most of those who come down to the fertile prairies of Illinois were inhabitants of Ohio. These men had left their first fatherland to better themselves; they leave the second to do better still."[17]

At the beginning of December, the two Frenchmen arrived at Cincinnati, where the city's rapid, practically visible growth amazed them. Yet even more surprising than the enthusiastic activity in Ohio was the striking contrast between that state and its neighbor, Kentucky. Compared to the pace immediately north of the river, growth to the south seemed to occur slowly or not at all. Tocqueville was again perplexed.

"The State of Ohio is separated from Kentucky just by one river; on either side of it the soil is equally fertile, and the situation equally favourable, and yet everything is different."[18] But what made the two states different if their physical setting was the same? Tocqueville heard and saw for himself that the contrast resulted from a peculiar institution. "These differences cannot be attributed to any other cause but slavery . . . . So nothing shows more clearly than the comparison I have just made, that human prosperity depends much more on the institutions and the will of man than on the external circumstances that surround him."[19]

The distinction between Ohio and Kentucky strongly reaffirmed Tocqueville's earlier decision about the physical environment: it was important, but not, in itself, decisive.

One citizen of Cincinnati, Timothy Walker, convinced of a glorious future for the entire region, repeated a now familiar incantation. "There are already 5,000,000 inhabitants in the Mississippi valley. I do not doubt that in twenty years time the majority of the population of the United States will be to the west of the Ohio; the greatest wealth and the greatest power will be found in the basin of the Mississippi and Missouri."[20]

By New Year's Day, 1832, the companions reached New Orleans, and here too they heard the myth of the interior valley. Mr. Guillemin, the French Counsel in that city, had grand visions. "New Orleans has a very great future. If we succeed in conquering, or only in greatly diminishing, the scourge of yellow fever, New Orleans is certainly destined to become the largest city in the New World. In fifty years the Mississippi Valley will hold the mass of the American population, and here we hold the gate to the river."[21]

Even later in Paris Tocqueville would not escape the legend, for his printed sources would offer no contradictions. Justice Joseph Story, while discussing the acquisition of western territories in his *Commentaries*, had turned expectation into fact: "And it scarcely requires the spirit of prophecy to foretell, that in a few years the predominance of numbers, of population, and of power, will be unequivocally transferred from the old to the new states."[22]

If Tocqueville still harbored any trace of doubt, William Darby's *View of the United States* would surely dispel it. After analyzing the sparse distribution and the scarcely believable growth rate of the American population, Darby had announced "the certain change of the seat of power . . . from the Atlantic slope into the central basin."[23]

"The general population," Tocqueville would summarize in an

early draft, "doubles in twenty-two years. That of the Mississippi Valley in ten years. Three and one-quarter percent for the whole. Five percent for the Valley. Darby p. 446 calculates that by 1865 the preponderance will be in the Mississippi Valley."[24]

Such an apparently universal message would not escape retelling in the *Democracy* and would eventually find its way into several parts of the work. The opening chapter, entitled "Physical Configurations of North America," would rhapsodize: "All things considered, the valley of the Mississippi is the most magnificent habitation ever prepared by God for man." Beyond the Appalachian Mountains "are assembling, almost in secret, the real elements of the great people to whom the future of the continent doubtless belongs."[25]

And in another section, while weighing the probable chances for the survival of the Union, Tocqueville would once again tell of the Mississippi Basin's destiny. "The western states . . . offer an unlimited free field to enterprise. . . . the Mississippi basin is infinitely more fertile than the Atlantic coast. This reason, added to all the others, is a powerful incentive driving the Europeans toward the West. Statistics emphatically prove this. . . . If the Union lasts, the extent and fertility of the Mississippi basin make it inevitable that it will become the permanent center of federal power. Within thirty or forty years [Darby: by 1865], the Mississippi basin will have assumed its natural rank. . . . So in a few years' time . . . the population of the Mississippi valley will dominate federal councils."[26]

In addition to the repetition of a legend, New Orleans also offered the opportunity once again to resume the long inquiry concerning the relationship of climate to slavery. Tocqueville returned to the problem on 1 January 1832.

"Do you think that in Louisiana the whites could cultivate the land without slaves?" "I do not think so," replied Mr. Mazureau. "But I was born in Europe and arrived here with the ideas you seem to have on that point. But experience has seemed to me to contradict the theory. I do not think that Europeans can work the land, exposed to this tropical sun. Our sun is always unhealthy, often deadly." Mazureau ended by offering the example of whites from various districts of Louisiana who, unable to labor diligently in the local climate, eked out only marginal existences. "But might not their poverty be attributed to their laziness rather than to the climate?" Tocqueville countered. The southerner's response was blunt: "In my view the climate is the chief reason."[27]

Within two weeks, as Tocqueville and Beaumont rode toward Washington, another chance to probe the issue presented itself in the person of Joel Poinsett. "What are the reasons for [the differences between the social state of the South and that of the North?]" "The first," Poinsett said, "is slavery; the second, the climate."[28]

But how were these two reasons linked? An essential part of the debate was still unresolved. The accumulated weight of Tocqueville's conversations made it clear that climate wielded an important if indirect power. Any lingering doubts of that fact were dissolved by the acute differences which he detected between the French of New Orleans and the French of Canada.

On 16 January 1832, he wrote to Chabrol: "When you see men who tell you that the climate has no influence on the constitution of peoples, assure them that they are mistaken." Fifteen degrees of latitude separated the French Canadians from the French of Louisiana. "Truly it is the best reason that I can give for the difference."[29]

Largely because of his talk with Latrobe, Tocqueville had earlier inclined toward the view that the climate's most significant influence on slavery was indirect: it encouraged certain crops which in turn invited the use of slave labor. Despite the assertions of Mazureau, the direct effects of climate, through sun, heat, and humidity, remained highly suspect in Tocqueville's mind. The 1835 *Democracy* would therefore reflect Latrobe's viewpoint.[30] But in his text Tocqueville would also pointedly echo several of his other conversations on the topic:

> The farther south one goes, the [more difficult] it becomes to abolish slavery. There are several physical reasons for this which need to be explained.
>
> The first is the climate: certainly the closer they get to the tropics, the harder Europeans find it to work; many Americans maintain that below a certain latitude it is fatal for them, whereas Negroes can work there without danger [Clay and others]; but I do not think that this idea, with its welcome support for the southerner's laziness, is based on experience. [A long delayed rejoinder to Mazureau] The south of the Union is not hotter than the south of Spain or of Italy. Why cannot the European do the same work there? [Adams][31]

In January 1832, only a few weeks before his departure from America, Tocqueville finally attempted to judge the relative weight of the ten reasons which he had set forth in October:

"There are a thousand reasons which concur to support republican liberty in the United States, but a few are enough to explain the problem.

"In the United States, it is said, society has been built from a clean slate. . . .

"But the whole of South America is in this position, and a republic only succeeds in the United States.

"The territory of the Union offers an immense field to human activity. . . .

"But in what part of the world could one find more fertile lands, . . . more inexhaustible or more untouched riches than in South America? But yet South America cannot maintain a republic.

"The division of the Union into little States reconciles internal prosperity and national strength; . . . but Mexico forms a federal republic; it has adopted the constitution of the United States almost without alteration, and yet Mexico is still far from prospering. Lower Canada is surrounded, as is New England, by fertile and limitless lands. Yet, up to our day, the French population of Canada, unstirred by enlightenment, remains cupped in a space much too narrow for it. . . .

"There is one great reason which dominates all the others and which, when one has weighed every consideration, by itself sways the balance: the American people, taken in mass, is not only the most enlightened in the world, but, what I rank as much more important than that advantage, *it is the people whose practical political education is the most advanced*."[32]

Tocqueville had finally singled out a few major causes of American success and had even selected the most significant from among his choices. But his statement, merely reaffirming what he had decided months before, said nothing significantly new about the role of the environment. Further developments in the traveler's thinking about the importance of physical setting had to wait until his return to France.

During his nine months in the New World, Tocqueville had recognized many significant features of America's environment, particularly its beauty, variety, size, fertility, (relative) virginity, and isolation. Another less obvious characteristic—the continent's transformation at the hands of an energetic and civilized people—had also struck his imagination, and one misconception about the Union's physical situation had been discovered and discarded when he had learned to his surprise that the Americans themselves settled the West.

But, while in the United States, the visitor had gone beyond the mere recognition of physical features and had also undertaken a careful consideration of the various social, political, intellectual, and even psychological effects of the republic's natural setting. More important, after at first adopting an environmental hypothesis, he had rejected such a doctrine in favor of a pluralistic explanation.

Finally, despite his notice of several important disadvantages or regrettable results of the country's physiography, Tocqueville had concluded that, by and large, America's environment contributed enormously to the nation's success.[33] In 1835 and 1840, the *Democracy* would faithfully reflect that basic outlook.

Cloistered in his attic room on the rue de Verneuil, Tocqueville continued to consider the haunting riddle of causes. "It is not due to idle curiosity that I seek the predominance of the causes which allow peoples to be free."[34]

While compiling the index to his own papers, the author included the heading "Causes which maintain the present form of government in America" and several other closely related entries.[35] So he clearly recognized that such influences were many and that any monistic interpretation of American success was inadequate.

An early effort to clarify his thinking ended when he drew up the following list of major influences: "(1) The geographic position, the nature of the country, (2) the laws, (3) the *moeurs*."[36] Apparently America's origins and history were subsumed under *moeurs*.

But soon, as drafts of the *Democracy* proceeded, Tocqueville began to use and even elaborate upon Josiah Quincy's concept of *circumstances*. "Circumstances, without number. Theory to make: *Point of departure*. The most important of all in my eyes. . . . Equality, Democracy introduced in germ. [Had Alexander Everett, Sparks, Quincy, and others persuaded the Frenchman that origins and history were the key circumstances?] *Ease*. result of the small population and the immense resources of the country. emigration, new resources equal to new needs. *The absence of neighbors*, no wars, no permanent army. *New country*, no large cities, no manufacturing districts. *Men are not pressed* one against the other. . . . It is a land which presents itself with all the strength and the fertility of youth."[37]

Here again, in what seemed in part a recapitulation of the major lessons learned in America about the republic's physical situation, a multiple rather than a single explanation was advanced. The term *circonstances* still remained too inclusive and cumbersome, but at least Tocqueville had restricted its use to historical and environmental features and their effects.

Yet despite his best efforts, his theory remained somewhat unsettled. Was the historical or the physical setting more important? Tocqueville was never able finally to decide. In the draft quoted above, in a deleted comment found in the working manuscript,[38] and once in the 1835 *Democracy* itself, he indicated that *le point de départ* or *l'origine* was the crucial circumstance. "I have said before that I regarded the origin of the Americans, what I have called their point of departure, as the first and most effective of all the [accidental or providential] elements leading to their present prosperity."[39]

But elsewhere in his published text he would more than once label *le choix du pays*, *la position géographique*, or *les causes physiques* the most significant single circumstance. "Among the lucky circumstances that favored the establishment and assured the maintenance of a democratic republic in the United States, the most important was the choice of the land itself in which the Americans live."[40]

In any case, the somewhat unwieldy concept did allow the writer to reach the classification of fundamental causes (both physical and nonphysical) which would appear in the 1835 *Democracy*:

"I thought that the maintenance of political institutions among all peoples depends on three great causes. The first, entirely accidental, results from the circumstances in which Providence has placed different men. The second comes from laws. The third is derived from their habits and their *moeurs*."[41]

The "thousand causes" of January 1832 were finally reduced to three. The first, *les circonstances*, included both America's origin and its environment, both its historical and its physical situations. In the 1835 *Democracy,* Tocqueville would occasionally use the phrase "la nature du pays et les faits antécédents" rather than *circonstances*.

Les lois invoked for Tocqueville the republic's legal, political, and institutional framework. The phrase called to mind everything from the balance of powers written into the Constitution by the Founding Fathers to American press laws and voting rights. In particular, the phrase reminded Tocqueville of America's federal structure, local institutions, and independent judiciary.[42]

The third major cause, *les moeurs*, embraced even more than the other two. *Les moeurs* signified the morality, intelligence, political experience, and ceaseless activity of the Americans, as well as a long list of other characteristics. The phrase meant nothing less than the sum of American values, ideas, attitudes, and customs.[43]

From among these three major causes, Tocqueville had also now chosen the most important. Throughout the drafts of the 1835 volumes, as in the published text, his position was clear and unchanging: *les moeurs* constituted the most important single explanation for the stunning success of the American republic.[44]

But what part did *circonstances* play? Was the influence exerted by history and the physical environment greater than that of laws? In an unpublished draft of the chapter entitled "The Main Causes Tending to Maintain a Democratic Republic in the United States,"[45] Tocqueville sketched a tentative conclusion: "Of the three causes the least influential is that of laws."[46]

Pursuing this thought to its logical conclusion, he wrote: "Of these three causes the first [circumstances] is the most permanent.[47] The circumstances in which a people find themselves change less easily, in general, than its laws and its *moeurs*. . . .

"Of the three causes the least influential is that of laws and it is, so to speak, the only one which depends on man. . . . people cannot change their position and the original conditions of their existence. A nation can, in the long run, modify its habits and its *moeurs,* but one generation cannot succeed in doing it. It [a single generation] can only change the laws. But, of the three causes about which we are talking, the least influential is precisely that which results from the laws. Not only[48] does man exercise no[49] power over his surroundings, but he possesses, so to speak,[50] none over himself and remains almost completely a stranger to his own fate."[51]

In the margin of this passage, he added: "Of these three causes there is, so to speak, only one that depends on man to bring forth."[52]

Something in this argument disturbed Tocqueville, however. Upon rereading he realized that his thesis seriously undermined the dignity of man. If *laws* were the only major influence subject to human will and, at the same time, the least important of fundamental causes, what control did man have over his own destiny? If man believed that he was essentially impotent, what would become of his sense of moral responsibility and his efforts? "One must not disdain man," Alexis would later warn Gustave, "if one wants to obtain great efforts from others and from oneself."[53] Tocqueville the moralist could not accept his own argument; so he denied his original reasoning and struck out the offending section.

Soon, with similar words, but a strikingly different conclusion, he tried again to settle the dilemma. "So of the three causes which work together to maintain institutions the least essential is the only one that man can not create at will [i.e. circumstances], and God, by making their happiness depend particularly on laws and *moeurs,* has in a way placed it in their hands."[54]

In an added parenthesis, Tocqueville summed up his position. "So physical causes contribute less to the maintenance of institutions than laws; laws, less than *moeurs*."[55] Finally, after many false starts and hesitations, he had reached the conclusion which would appear in the published text of the 1835 *Democracy.* Much of the durability of Tocqueville's reputation for genius and originality may be attributed to his brilliant recognition that *moeurs* weighed most in the destinies of human societies.

But in resolving this moral dilemma, Tocqueville had shrunk the meaning of *circonstances* to include only physical causes. History's momentary disappearance had undoubtedly made it easier to downgrade the significance of circumstances. Thus he had in part satisfied himself by shifting definitions, by taking advantage of the indefinite meaning of one of his fundamental concepts. *Circonstances,* as we shall see, would not be the only word in the *Democracy* with such a valuable and convenient plastic nature.

CHAPTER 5

Was Race a Sufficient Explanation of the American Character?

Tocqueville's fortnight in the wilderness, while transforming his ideas about the effects of the natural environment, had also alerted him to another possible physical explanation of American society: Americans were what they were because of their biological inheritance.

"The village of Saginaw," Tocqueville wrote in August, "is the last point inhabited by the Europeans, toward the northwest of the vast peninsula of Michigan. It can be considered an advance post, a sort of refuge that the whites have come to place among the Indian nations. . . .

". . . Thirty persons, men, women, old men, and children, at the time of our passage composed the whole of this little society, scarce formed, germ confided to the wilderness that the wilderness is to make fruitful.

"Chance, interest, or passions had gathered these thirty persons in this narrow space. Between them were no ties; they differed profoundly from each other. One noted among them Canadians, Americans, Indians, and half-breeds."[1] Even the Canadians and the Americans, both Europeans by heritage, were basically dissimilar. The first remained essentially French; the second, thoroughly English.

Such profound contrasts among the few inhabitants of one isolated village baffled Tocqueville and pushed him toward some rather radical reflections.

"Philosophers have believed that human nature, everywhere the same, varied only following the institutions and laws of the different societies. That's one of those opinions that seems to be disproved at every page of the history of the world. Nations like individuals all show themselves with a face that is their own. The characteristic features of their visage are reproduced through all the transformations they undergo. Laws, customs, religions change, empire and wealth come and go, external appearance varies, clothes differ, prejudices replace each other. Under all these changes you recognize always the same people. It's always the same people which is growing up. Something inflexible appears in human flexibility." But what was this indelible "something" which, more than other causes, determined the features of a society?

". . .Thus, in this unknown corner of the world, the hand of God had already thrown the seeds of diverse nations. Already several different races . . . found themselves face to face.

"A few exiled members of the great human family have met in the immensity of the woods. Their needs are common; . . . and they throw at each other only looks of hatred and suspicion. The colour of their skin, poverty or wealth, ignorance or knowledge, have already established indestructible classifications among them: national prejudices, the prejudices of education and birth divide and isolate them.

". . . The profound lines which birth and opinion have traced between the destinies of these men do not end with life but stretch beyond the tomb. Six religions or sects share the faith of this embryo society."

In this long passage, Tocqueville returned to an idea which he had already briefly introduced several times in his travel diaries and letters: the concept of national character (which he sometimes loosely called "race").[2] As early as April 1831, while still on shipboard, he and Mr. Peter Schermerhorn had discussed the "National Character of the Americans."[3] And among first impressions at Newport, Rhode Island, in May, had been the following description: "The inhabitants differ but little superficially from the French. They wear the same clothes, and their physiognomies are so varied that it would be hard to say from what races they have derived their features. I think it must be thus in all the United States."[4]

Additional observations, more developed but otherwise similar to those elicited by Schermerhorn and Newport, had appeared in one of Tocqueville's alphabetic notebooks on 29 May: "When one reflects on the nature of the society here, one sees [that] . . . American society is composed of a thousand different elements recently assembled. The men who live under its laws are still English, French, German, and Dutch. They have neither religion, morals nor ideas in common; up to the present one cannot say that there is an American character, at least unless it is the very fact of not having any. There is no common memory, no national attachments here. What then can be the only bond that unites the different parts of this huge body? *Interest.*"[5]

So, though surprised and puzzled by certain peculiarities, Tocqueville clearly assumed from the very first that some identifiable American character existed. His initial task was to isolate the essential qualities. But how profoundly did national traits from Europe influence society in the New World? And what forces (of blood or inheritance, of education or social custom) shaped and fostered the dominant American characteristics?

In his account of the Saginaw experience he first attempted some preliminary answers to these questions. From the viewpoint of Michigan, the peculiar physiognomy displayed by each nation—fashioned primarily by "birth," "opinion" and religion—seemed more durable an influence on society than even "laws, customs, religions [which] change; empire and wealth [which] come and go; external appearance [which] varies; . . . [and] prejudices [which] replace each other. Under all these changes you recognize always the same people. . . . Something inflexible appears in human flexibility."[6]

When, a month later, the traveling companions visited Montreal and Quebec, the lessons of Saginaw were repeated and reinforced. "We have seen in Canada," Tocqueville later recalled, "Frenchmen who have been living for seventy years under English rule, and remain exactly like their compatriots in France. In the midst of them lives an English population which has lost nothing of its national character."[7]

The amazing durability of recognizable French and English traits led Tocqueville, on 7 September, immediately after returning to the United States from Canada, to ask his friend and teacher, the Abbé Lesueur: "Wouldn't one be truly tempted to believe that the national character of a people depends more on the blood from which it came than on the political institutions or the nature of the country?"[8] Clearly, he was close to advancing a biological explanation of national differences.

Yet Tocqueville never made the necessary last step toward an hypothesis based solely on biological inheritance. Instead he continued to advance a pluralistic viewpoint and to explore a variety of possible causes. "American morals are, I think," he ventured in a diary note of

21 September 1831, "the most chaste that exist in any nation, a fact which can, it seems to me, be attributed to five chief causes." His first choice was: "Physical constitution. They belong to a Northern race." But he also emphasized religion, preoccupation with business, special attitudes toward marriage, and the education and character of American women.[9] No single answer would do.

The October list of "Reasons for the social state and present government in America" also included under point one, their origin; "Cold and rationalist race." But again, Tocqueville carefully acknowledged many additional factors as well.[10]

In November 1831, after learning about the tenacious habits of the Pennsylvania Germans, he continued his speculations:

> If nature has not given each people an indelible national character one must at least admit that physical or political causes have made a people's spirit adopt habits which are very difficult to eradicate, even though it is no longer subject to the influence of any of those causes. . . .
>
> Not less than fifty years ago, colonies of Germans came to settle in Pennsylvania. They have kept intact the spirit and ways of their fatherland. . . . Immobile in the midst of [illegible] general movement, the German limits his desire to bettering his position and that of his family little by little. He works unendingly, but leaves nothing to chance. He gets rich slowly; he sticks to his domestic hearth, encloses his happiness within his horizon and shows no curiosity to know what there is beyond his last furrow.[11]

This statement was more cautious than either his account of Saginaw or his query to the old priest had been. Tocqueville here seemed inclined to substitute durable but slowly changing habits or *moeurs* for the concept of a constant and ineradicable national character. And he hedged on whether physical or political causes most affected these national habits.

About the same time, Joel Poinsett forewarned Tocqueville about the contrast which he would find between Ohio and Kentucky as he continued westward and suggested that the differences could be explained by the *moeurs* of the settlers: Ohio had been peopled largely by New Englanders, and Kentucky, largely by Virginians.[12]

By December, however, when the commissioners found themselves in the Ohio Valley, Tocqueville, with the help of comments by John Quincy Adams and Timothy Walker, had pushed beyond Poinsett's overly facile explanation to ask what had produced the dissimilar sectional characters in the first place. Just as the people of Ohio and Kentucky shared the same favorable environment, they also—except for the Negroes—sprang from the same race. So biology did not supply an answer to account for the sharp contrast any more than physiography had.[13] As we have seen, Tocqueville was now forced to look toward social causes, rather than natural or physical causes. Specifically, he decided that slavery best explained the differences he observed, and he theorized that the South's "peculiar institution" wrought its effects by the gradual transformation of *moeurs*.[14]

Henceforth Tocqueville would never again consider bloodlines as the primary or even a possible primary explanation, but would instead devote ever greater attention to national traits or *moeurs* and the human forces which shaped them.[15] A few weeks later he was writing: "I imagine that often what one calls the character of a people is nothing but the character inherent in its social state. So the English character might well be nothing but the aristocratic character. What tends to make me think that is the immense difference between the English and their descendants in America."[16]

When on 14 January the Frenchman undertook a further analysis of "What maintains the Republic in the United States," he significantly made no specific mention of race and clearly implied that *moeurs* were the "one great reason which dominates all the others."[17] So Tocqueville left the United States having briefly considered and then rejected a predominantly biological explanation of national differences.

In the years after, Tocqueville never totally discarded the idea that race played some role in the shaping of human societies. Race, for example, became one element of *l'origine*.[18] But what precisely did he mean by race? By the end of his American journey, he thought usually in terms of tenacious but slowly evolving national characteristics or *moeurs* rather than inherited biological traits. Yet what was the exact nature of the connection between bloodlines and national character or *moeurs*? Unfortunately he failed to pinpoint the meanings of these words.[19] Once again vaguely defined terms permitted Tocqueville to avoid the painful task of mastering some troubling complexities.

Between 1832 and 1835, while drafting the first part of the *Democracy*, Tocqueville thought and wrote little about either doctrines of race in the abstract or the cloudy relationships between race, national character, and *moeurs*. Apparently Beaumont, more forcibly struck while in America by the plight of the Negro and the Indian, claimed these topics as his portion. His *Marie, or Slavery in the United States* was presented not only as a discussion of race in the United States, but also as a broad picture of American *moeurs*.[20]

Insofar as Tocqueville concerned himself with these issues in his first two volumes, he concentrated primarily on the contrasting futures of the three races in America.[21] (Distinguishing between Indians, Negroes, and Anglo-Americans did not present quite the same possibilities for confusion as had his earlier comparisons between "French" and "English" inhabitants of Saginaw or the Americans of Ohio and Kentucky.) Even here, however, he refused to explain the divergent destinies of these two minorities and the white majority by referring solely to innate biological differences. "The men scattered over it [the territory occupied or claimed by the United States] are not, as in Europe, shoots of the same stock. It is obvious that there are three naturally distinct, one might almost say hostile, races. Education, law, origin, and external features too have raised almost insurmountable barriers between them; chance has brought them together on the same soil, but they have mixed without combining, and each follows a separate destiny."[22] His lengthy discussion expanded upon this introductory paragraph and repeatedly emphasized the radically dissimilar social, legal, and historical circumstances of the three races. Nowhere would he defend biological determinism.[23]

After 1835, Tocqueville, increasingly aware of the growing interest in deterministic theories,[24] began once again to ponder the significance of biological inheritance for national destinies. During a visit to Switzerland in 1836, for example, he informed Claude-François de Corcelle of his reservations about the Swiss constitution and republic and made the following revealing judgment on racial hypotheses: "I am also already struck with how little political life prevails among the population. The kingdom of England is one hundred times more republican than this republic. Others would say that this is due to the difference of race. But it is an argument that I will never admit except in the last extremity and when absolutely nothing else remains for me to say."[25]

In addition, while composing his last two volumes, he penned at least three fragments on racial theories that would unfortunately largely disappear from the 1840 text. His sentiments on race, therefore, have not usually been connected with the writing of his masterpiece on America.

In a draft of the chapter entitled "How Democracy Leads to Ease and Simplicity in the Ordinary Relations between Americans,"[26] he described the basic attraction of biological explanations:

"Nowadays people talk constantly of the influence exercised by race on the conduct of men. . . . Race explains all in a word. It seems to me that I can easily discover why we so often have recourse to this argument that our predecessors did not employ. It is incontestable that the race to which men belong exercises some power or other over their acts, but then again it is absolutely impossible to pinpoint what this power is. So we can at will either infinitely restrict its action or extend it to all things according to the needs of the discourse; valuable advantage in a time when we require reasoning with little cost, just as we want to grow rich without trouble."[27]

Upon rereading, however, he realized: "All this is decidedly out of place. To put somewhere else. . . . But take the idea for the transition from there. People believe that this reserve of the English comes from the blood. The example of America proves the contrary."[28] So he deleted his digression and relegated it to the "Rubish." Tocqueville had not yet concluded his musings about race, however.

"To say in the preface if not in the book. Idea of races. I do not believe that there are races destined to freedom and others to servitude; the ones to happiness and enlightenment, the others to misfortunes and ignorance.[29] These are cowardly doctrines. Doctrines however. Why? That results, during democratic times, from a natural vice of the human mind and heart which causes these people to tend toward materialism. This idea of the invisible influence of race is an essentially materialistic idea. The *idée-mère* of this book is directly the contrary, since I start invincibly from this point: whatever the tendencies of the social condition (*état social*), men can always modify them and avert the bad while adapting to the good."[30]

Yet another fragment, dated 12 March 1838, expressed similar thoughts: "Beware, during democratic centuries, of all soft and cowardly opinions which lull men and paralyze their efforts, such as the system of the physical and moral inferiorities of races."[31]

So familiar demands for human freedom, responsibility, and dignity formed the background for these remarks, and Tocqueville's own moral convictions once again significantly shaped his *grande affaire*. The text of 1840 would read: "I am aware that many of my contemporaries think that nations on earth are never their own masters and that they are bound to obey some insuperable and unthinking power, the product of pre-existing facts, of race, or soil, or climate. These are false and cowardly doctrines which can only produce feeble men and pusillanimous nations. Providence did not make mankind entirely free or completely enslaved. Providence has, in truth, drawn a predestined circle around each man beyond which he cannot pass; but within those vast limits man is strong and free, and so are peoples."[32]

But gone was Tocqueville's earlier explicit and personal disavowal: "I do not believe that there are races destined to freedom and others to servitude; the ones to happiness and enlightenment, the others to misfortunes and ignorance."

Some fifteen years later, in October 1853, Tocqueville would receive copies of the first two volumes of Arthur de Gobineau's *Essai sur l'inégalité des races humaines*.[33] And his initial reactions to his protégé's doctrines, expressed in three magnificent letters of 11 October, 17 November, and 20 December 1853, have justly become famous.

In the first epistle, he warned the younger man: "If I am a reader very much led, by the lively friendship that I bear toward you, to see your book through rose-colored spectacles, I am, on the other hand, drawn by my pre-existent ideas on the subject to pick a quarrel with you. So I am in no sense an impartial judge, that is to say a good judge. But still, I will do my best."[34]

Tocqueville proceeded to offer his basic criticism of the work: "I have never hidden from you . . . that I had a great prejudice against what appears to me to be your *idée-mère*, which seems to me, I confess, to belong to the family of materialistic theories and to be one of its most dangerous members." [Cf. "This idea of the invisible influence of race is an essentially materialistic idea."]

By November, after receiving an initial reply from Gobineau, he boldly announced: "I will confess to you frankly that you have not convinced me. All my objections remain.[35] Nevertheless, you are quite right to deny being a materialist. Your doctrine is, in effect, rather a sort of fatalism, of predestination if you wish; . . . [Your system ends] in a very great restriction if not in a complete abolition of human freedom. But I confess to you [that] . . . I remain placed at the opposing extreme of these doctrines.[36] I believe them very likely false and very surely pernicious."[37] [Cf. "I am aware that many of my contemporaries think that nations on earth are never their own masters and that they are bound to obey some insuperable and unthinking power, the product of pre-existing facts, of race, or soil, or climate."; also "The *idée-mère* of this book is directly the contrary. . . ."]

He continued: "One can believe that there are, among each of the different families which compose the human race, certain tendencies, certain peculiar aptitudes born from a thousand different causes. But that these tendencies, that these aptitudes are unconquerable, not only is this what has never been proved, but it cannot, in itself, be proved, for it would be necessary to have at one's disposition not only the past but even the future. [Cf. "It is incontestable that the race to which men belong exercises some power or other over their acts, but then again it is absolutely impossible to pinpoint what this power is."]

"Still, if your doctrine . . . were more useful to humanity! But it is obviously the contrary. What interest can there be in persuading some faint-hearted people who live in barbarism, in indolence, or in servitude, that, since they are so by the nature of their race, nothing can be done to ameliorate their condition, to change their *moeurs* or modify their government?"

Tocqueville concluded his second letter on a pessimistic note: "We are separated by too wide a distance for the discussion to be fruitful. There is an intellectual world between your doctrine and mine."

The third letter elaborated on the charge that Gobineau's theory, since it discouraged effort, was even worse than useless. "You have taken precisely the thesis that has always appeared to me the most dangerous that one could uphold in our time. . . . The last century had an exaggerated and a bit childish confidence in the power which man exercises over himself and which people exercise over their destiny. . . . After having believed ourselves capable of self-transformation, we believe ourselves incapable even of self-reformation; after having had an excessive pride, we have fallen into a humility which is not less excessive; we believed ourselves able to do everything, today we believe ourselves able to do nothing; and we like to believe that struggle and effort are henceforth useless, and that our blood, our muscles, and our nerves will always be stronger than our will and our virtue. It is properly the great sickness of our time; sickness completely opposite to that of our fathers. Your book, no matter how you would put it, favors rather than combats it: despite you, it pushes the soul of your contemporaries, already too soft, toward weakness."[38] [Cf. "Beware, during democratic centuries, of all soft and cowardly opinions which lull men and paralyze their efforts, such as the system of the physical and moral inferiorities of races."; also "These are false and cowardly doctrines which can only produce feeble men and pusillanimous nations."]

In short, Tocqueville's initial response to Gobineau's thesis in 1853 would strikingly parallel, in both argument and word, previous manuscript reflections hidden in the drafts of the second part of the *Democracy* or the 1840 text itself. So it is a mistake to think that Tocqueville's fully developed condemnation of racial doctrines first emerged in the 1850s during his epistolary debate with his protégé. An explicit and deeply personal repudiation of such ideas had its roots in his American experience and dated from the late 1830s, when he wrote the last two volumes of his great work.[39]

Tocqueville's thoughts about physical causes thus underwent some fascinating developments. He came to America with a special interest in *géographie*, and during the early weeks of his journey, he, like many others, became persuaded that national destiny depended primarily on the natural environment. His first months in the New World also tempted him toward a racial explanation of national characteristics. In both instances, however, despite a tendency to seize upon a single answer which had momentarily captured his attention, Tocqueville ultimately rejected any monistic thesis.

Moreover, a permanent conversion to pluralistic explanations was greatly speeded by his penchant for what might be called the comparative method. Again and again, Tocqueville's ideas evolved in response to parallel but sharply contrasting American experiences: the differences between the two "races" of Saginaw, and then between the English and the French Canadians; the juxtaposition of Ohio and Kentucky; the distinctions between the North and South, and even between the two American continents; the comparison of the men of New Orleans with those of Montreal. The cumulative lessons of these succeeding pairs of experiences amply demonstrated the wisdom of one of Tocqueville's basic methodological principles: "It is only by comparison that one can judge things."[40]

Personal convictions also helped to drive him toward certain of his conclusions. Whether deciding the final significance of *circonstances* or the ultimate influence of race, he often fell back on firmly held beliefs about man's dignity, freedom, and responsibility. In addition, his strong and persistent distaste for any materialistic doctrine repeatedly led him to stress nonphysical causes, ones which were at least somewhat under human control. So his own moral judgments and leanings joined with his experiences, conversations, and readings in shaping the *Democracy*.

Finally, key terms involved in his discussions of physical causes, like *circonstances* or race, remained annoyingly ambiguous. At various times in the development of his thinking, Tocqueville found this vagueness a convenient way to avoid difficult decisions. But, on the other hand, the depth and variety of his insights were often well served by the rich if somewhat imprecise connotations which he sometimes gave a word. Such untamed but valuable complexities were part of what Tocqueville meant when, in 1836, he exclaimed: "I would never have imagined that a subject that I had already revolved in so many ways could present itself to me under so many new faces."[41]

CHAPTER 6

The Transformation of a Continent

Commentators have often remarked that Tocqueville failed to detect what Michel Chevalier and other foreign observers noticed.[1] Somehow the author of the *Democracy* overlooked the astonishing developments in transportation and communication that signaled an American technological revolution. He had traveled on steamboats, talked of railroads, and inspected canals, but had inexplicably missed the transformation being wrought on both the shape of the continent and the nature of the republic by America's fascination with machines.

Restudy of his manuscripts shows that Tocqueville did indeed neglect many of these developments. His enthusiasm in the presence of the railroads, for example, was restrained at best, and his interest in manufacturing was not great enough to push him from the salons of Boston to the factories of Lowell.[2] Yet his travel diaries and letters reveal a greater interest in technology and its impact than some critics have implied.

Although technology never became one of Tocqueville's primary concerns, his sense of wonder and pride at the spectacle of the continent's subjugation did stimulate his interest in the specific instruments of the American assault, and he sought from his hosts in almost every corner of the United States facts and opinions about the "improvements" being imposed upon the land.

During the early 1830s, the steamboat and the railroad ranked as the two most striking and significant advancements in American transportation; the application of steam had revolutionized travel in the New World. "Floating palaces" had already appeared on rivers and lakes everywhere in the nation, but the railroad, by contrast, was in its infancy when the investigators arrived in the United States.[3] Even so, Tocqueville's failure to recognize the full importance of the railroad was certainly one of his most serious oversights. His enthusiasm focused instead on that older use of steam, and although on more than one occasion during the journey the steamboat nearly cost the two friends their lives,[4] Tocqueville never recovered from an early fascination with the *superbe maison* which had carried him from Newport to New York.[5]

A more general subject, the republic's expanding network of internal improvements, also demanded probing, and in Baltimore he had a profitable discussion about American canal projects with William Howard, "a very distinguished engineer of this country."[6] While talking with Salmon P. Chase of Cincinnati, Tocqueville also learned that as of 1831 the state of Ohio had already spent the enormous sum of six million dollars on canal construction.[7]

The commissioners were often annoyed by the deplorable condition of American roads, but even so, the size and thoroughness of the web seemed impressive. So before leaving Boston at the beginning of October, they left a long series of questions with Jared Sparks. Although designed primarily to uncover the mysteries of the New England town, these queries concerned several other significant matters as well, including the "System of Roads." "1. In Massachusetts what is the system of roads? Are certain roads, bridges, or canals made by the state? 2. If roads are made by the towns, are they good? What is the means of maintaining them so? . . . Is there an inspection done by the state? 3. Can the state form a general plan of a road or a canal?"[8]

Beaumont presented similar questions to B. W. Richards of Philadelphia, who answered: "Our turnpike roads throughout the state have for the most part been made by private individuals and corporate companies." The Pennsylvanian noted, however, that "the state in many cases subscribes to the stock."[9]

In January 1832, Tocqueville interrogated Joel Poinsett: "How are the roads in America made and repaired?" Poinsett remarked that this involved "a great constitutional question," but attempted nonetheless to answer, and his questioner later summarized the diplomat's comments. "Doubt whether central government has the right.[10] Sometimes by the state. More often by the counties. Badly kept up. Substantial loans in the localities. *Turnpikes* better system. Difficulty of getting a people used to them. Ineffectiveness of the law which allows help to counties."[11]

Evidently no single agent shouldered the responsibility for American internal improvements, and no single method of financing, building, or maintaining these works existed. Despite Poinsett's warnings, the danger of such confusion about powers and responsibilities did not preoccupy Tocqueville until later. For the moment he was more fascinated than troubled by the various forms of American transportation activity. The private corporation, in particular, became a frequent subject of conversation.

The perceptive Frenchman studied American private associations for many reasons, but one undoubtedly involved the role which the corporation played in the creation of American internal improvements. Whenever he committed his early thoughts about associations to paper, he connected the private groups with America's ambitious projects. "The spirit of association . . . is one of the distinctive characteristics of America; it is by this means that a country where capital is scarce and where absolutely democratic laws and habits hinder the accumulation of wealth in the hands of a few individuals, has already succeeded in carrying out undertakings and accomplishing works which the most absolute kings and the most opulent aristocracies would certainly not have been able to undertake and finish in the same time."[12] Tocqueville had stumbled on one of the most significant economic developments of Jacksonian America: the rise of corporations.

When, in December 1831, he began studying James Kent's four volumes of *Commentaries*, he carefully noted the jurist's statements about corporate institutions, especially any comments about the new ease in obtaining charters and the expanded privileges and numbers of corporations. He also discerned the worry behind Kent's words. "The number of charters of incorporation increases in the United States with a rapidity that appears to alarm Kent. I do not know why."[13]

During his journeys into the interior, Tocqueville also discovered several implications of American transportation and communication beyond the constitutional and the institutional. His frontier experiences, in particular, demonstrated additional advantages of the republic's road system. In Michigan, for example, he first realized that in the United States paths and roads *preceded* settlement and were an essential step in the movement westward.

While in Kentucky and Tennessee, during December 1831, he and Beaumont also "traveled with the mail." "There is an astonishing circulation of letters and newspapers among these savage woods. . . . I do not think that in the most enlightened rural districts of France, there is intellectual movement either so rapid or on such a scale as in this wilderness."[14] Later, thinking back to Michigan, Tocqueville asserted that "in America one of the first things done in a new state is to make the post go there; in the forests of Michigan there is no cabin so isolated, no valley so wild but that letters and newspapers arrive at least once a week; we have seen that."[15] The significance of such rapid transit of information and ideas did not long elude the companions.

By January 1832, Tocqueville had gathered a considerable amount of information about America's projects and felt ready to speculate about their importance for the future of the American republic.

"I only know of one means of increasing the prosperity of a people, whose application is infallible and on which I think one can count in all countries and in all places.

"That means is none other than increasing the facility of communication between men.

"On this point what can be seen in America is both strange and instructive.

"The roads, the canals, and the post play a prodigious part in the prosperity of the Union. It is good to examine their effects, the value attached to them, and the way they are obtained.

". . . America has undertaken and finished the construction of some immense canals. It already has more railways than France; no one fails to see that the discovery of steam has incredibly increased the power and prosperity of the Union; and that is because it facilitates speedy communications between the different parts of that immense land. . . .

"Of all the countries in the world America is that in which the spread of ideas and of human industry is most continual and most rapid.

". . . As to the means employed to open up communications in America, this is what I have noticed about the matter.

"It is generally believed in Europe that the great maxim of government in America is that of laisser-faire, of standing by as a simple spectator of the progress of society, of which individual interest is the prime mover; that is a mistake.

"The American government does not interfere in everything, it is true, as ours does. It makes no claim to foresee everything and carry everything out; it gives no subsidies, does not encourage trade, and does not patronize literature or the arts. But where great works of public utility are concerned, it but seldom leaves them to the care of private persons; it is the State itself that carries them out; . . .

"But it is important to observe that there is no rule about the matter. The activity of companies, of [towns], and of private people is in a thousand ways in competition with that of the State. All undertakings of moderate extent or limited interest are the work of [towns] or companies. Turnpikes or toll-roads often run parallel to those of the State. In some parts of the country, railways built by companies fulfill the functions of the canals as main thoroughfares. The local roads are maintained by the districts through which they pass. So then no exclusive system is followed; in nothing does America exemplify a system of that uniformity that delights the superficial and metaphysical minds of our age."[16]

So even before he began to draft the 1835 *Democracy*, Tocqueville had recognized several general results of the American technological revolution. What he had seen demonstrated the benefits of a flexible approach to public improvements, in general, and of a reliance on private action, in particular. (Somewhat paradoxically, the task of transformation also threatened a dangerous debate over the proper division of powers and responsibilities.) Improvements and the application of steam unfortunately stimulated the materialism and commercialism that were the blights of the republic, but America's instruments of progress also made possible a rapid exchange of ideas, encouraged the creation of a well-informed and self-aware citizenry, and helped to unite a huge and diverse nation.[17] In sum, the changes in technology and transportation seemed to promise a prosperous and powerful future for the American republic.

While drafting the first part of his book, Tocqueville pursued his quest for information about America's internal improvements. At various times, he had collected six major works on the republic's *situation physique*: Malte-Brun's *Annales de voyages*; C. F. Volney's *Tableau du climat et du sol des Etats-Unis*; accounts of two of Major Stephen H. Long's expeditions, *Account of an Expedition from Pittsburgh to the Rocky Mountains* and *Narrative of an Expedition to the Source of St. Peter's River*; Timothy Pitkin's *Statistical View of the Commerce of the United States*; D. B. Warden's *Description . . . des Etats-Unis*; and William Darby's *View of the United States*.

The works by Malte-Brun, Volney, and Long, because of age or intention, provided no information whatsoever on American technology. Tocqueville used them primarily for facts about natural features, flora and fauna, and Indians. Pitkin's *Statistical View of Commerce*, almost twenty years old when Tocqueville read it, was only marginally useful.[18] Only Warden, almost fifteen years old, and Darby, published in 1828, included discussions of developments in American transportation and communication. Warden's small chapter on canals, railroads, and manufacturing in the United States appeared in the last of his five volumes. And, since Tocqueville cited Warden only when describing America's physical features, it is possible that he had failed to study Warden's final volume.[19] If so, then his major single printed source on American internal improvements was William Darby's *View of the United States*.

For anyone interested during the early 1830s in American transportation and communication, Darby's volume was among the best available sources. Additional and more recent information could be gleaned from official documents, newspapers, and almanacs—all of which Tocqueville also used[20]—but Darby's work was one of few single-volume treatments.

Only the works of Mathew Carey and Guillaume-Tell Poussin's *Les Travaux d'améliorations intérieures* . . . , published in Paris in 1834,[21] ranked in importance with Darby's *View*. Unfortunately, the author of the *Democracy* apparently did not know of Carey's writings on American economics and technology.[22] Poussin's analysis of 1834 was neglected for quite another reason, however. As is well known, Tocqueville insisted on insulating his own ideas and reactions from the influence of other recent European, and especially French, travelers to the United States. Poussin's status as a fellow foreign visitor necessarily condemned the work to inattention.

So Tocqueville, though fully aware of the weaknesses of Darby's book, made do. In his own list of statistical and general sources, he noted that "this work is highly regarded but already old; it dates from 1828,"[23] and in 1834 he even wrote to James Gore King to request as a substitute, or at least as an addition, "some work of general statistics like Darby."[24] Either the American did not suggest a replacement or Tocqueville failed to pursue his recommendation.

In this matter, he committed another serious oversight, for in 1833 a new work had been published by Darby and Theodore Dwight, Jr., entitled *A New Gazetteer of the United States*, which offered valuable information about American manufacturing and even devoted a few paragraphs to Lowell, Massachusetts, which the authors called "the American Manchester . . . destined to be a manufacturing city."[25]

Despite its age, Darby's *View* provided Tocqueville with a treasure trove of information about American improvements. Throughout the volume Darby urged the improvement of rivers, bays, and lakes, and the construction of canals or any other project that would benefit American commerce. In short, the work introduced Tocqueville to a vigorous nationalistic outlook typical of what he would have discovered in the works of Mathew Carey. Darby, like Mathew Carey, Hezekiah Niles, or Henry Clay, was one of those Americans of the 1820s and 1830s eager for any undertaking that would increase American wealth and link Americans with one another. Darby, like the others, envisioned a continent crisscrossed by improvements and a nation united by commerce and prosperity. He almost certainly encouraged Tocqueville's personal inclination to concentrate on commercial developments and to foresee a mercantile, rather than an industrial, future for the United States.[26]

Possibly in response to Darby's enthusiasm, Tocqueville sent off requests for additional materials. While thinking of the American road and postal systems, for example, he wondered how French and American efforts compared, and reminded himself to ask "d'Aunay"[27] and "N. (?) Roger of the Académie française"[28] for information about the number of letters carried, distances covered, and revenues raised by the French system.

Poinsett's "great constitutional question" also still disturbed him, so he badgered Edward Livingston and finally received the following note in March 1834: "Mr. Livingston agreeably to his promise sends to M. de Tocqueville the volume containing the President's message in relation to the bill for internal improvements and will add to it some other documents on the same subject."[29]

Still pursuing his curiosity about corporations and canals, Tocqueville wrote again to James Gore King for one report on New York City corporations, another on state corporations, and a third by the commissioners of the canal fund. Reports, statistics, and other information about America's technological revolution continued to accumulate among the Frenchman's papers.[30]

Despite his documentary searches, the drafts of the 1835 *Democracy* broke little new ground. They merely restated earlier insights about possible future influences of the startling transformation taking place in the United States. Of greatest importance, perhaps, was Tocqueville's refusal to collect, organize, and devote to his ideas on this subject a separate chapter in his advancing work. Here was a possible significant addition to the *Democracy* that never materialized.

One striking and related idea did, however, appear for the first time in the early drafts of Tocqueville's initial volumes: his fears about the influence of manufacturing on democratic liberty. Among some fragments labeled "Various and important notes. . . . Two or three new chapters which I do not know where to place," Tocqueville listed ". . . [31] on the influence of manufacturing on democratic liberty."[32] And after discussing various kinds of *égalité* in another draft, he concluded: "Thus greater equality not only among all the peoples of European races, but also among all peoples, in all times." Just one more statement underlining the march of equality? It would seem so, until he added a cautionary note: "however *manufacturing*."[33] In other words, equality moves irresistibly forward; however, manufacturing may affect it.

The idea survived even into the working manuscript of the 1835 *Democracy*, where in the margin of one page of the chapter entitled "Social State of the Anglo-Americans" the author wrote: "Here, I believe, put the inequality born out of the accumulation of personal wealth from *industry*."[34] Then, for some unknown reason, Tocqueville decided against developing and including this concept in the first part of his work; and only these tantalyzing hints of what-might-have-been can be found in his drafts and his working manuscript. Not until 1840 would he finally complete his phrase "however manufacturing . . ." by theorizing that manufacturing would accumulate wealth in the hands of a few and might, therefore, result in a new inequality more terrible in some ways than the former one.[35]

Tocqueville's travel diaries noted no comment or experience from his American journey which hinted at such a danger. The only recorded conversation in the United States concerning the perils of manufacturing occurred on 27 October 1831, when Tocqueville spoke with Roberts Vaux of Philadelphia. The American voiced the familiar fear that industrialization might undermine democratic institutions by debasing the populace and warned of the poverty and public disorder which might result from the rise of manufacturing. But he did not suggest that manufacturing would result in a new and dangerous aristocracy of wealth.[36] Nor did any of Tocqueville's major sources on American internal improvements warn of a new manufacturing elite.

Those who recognize the brilliance of Tocqueville's insight on manufacturing usually assume that the young Frenchman's voyages to England in 1833 and 1835 provided the germs of this thought. In 1833, however, he had stayed in England only a few weeks and had visited no industrial centers, and the 1835 visit occurred *after* his forebodings were written into the early drafts of the 1835 *Democracy*.

Perhaps the key source, for Tocqueville, was a three-volume work of political economy, published in Paris in 1834, written by Alban de Villeneuve-Bargemont, and read by Tocqueville when, in 1834, he prepared a memoir on pauperism.[37] In the first volume of the study, Villeneuve-Bargemont included a chapter entitled "Concerning a New Feudalism" and wrote "a new feudalism formed, a thousand times harder than the feudalism of the Middle Ages. This feudalism was the aristocracy of money and of industry."[38] The economist was not offering a new idea. The concept of a possible new industrial aristocracy was fairly common in works of political economy written during the late 1820s and early 1830s.[39] But a reading of Villeneuve-Bargemont's treatise may have first sparked Tocqueville's thoughts and engendered his hints about a manufacturing aristocracy.

The drafts of the *Democracy* offer a second surprise of a somewhat different sort. The part played by private associations in the American effort to transform the continent had long intrigued Tocqueville, but he refrained from devoting much space in his first two volumes to either civil associations or corporations. Instead, he dealt with political associations and promised to treat civil ones in the second part of his work.[40] The 1840 text would make good his pledge, but the complex relationship between private associations and government would still receive very little attention.

Tocqueville did explore this relationship, however, in the drafts of the 1840 *Democracy* where a small as yet unpublished chapter entitled "On the Manner in Which the American Governments Act toward Associations" is to be found.[41] In this chapter he compared the ways in which the English and American governments reacted to private groups wanting to undertake public works, and he suggested what he considered to be the most effective way to encourage private activity within a nation.

Even while writing this brief section, Tocqueville debated whether or not to include it. The title page recorded his doubts: "This chapter contains some good ideas and some good sentences. All the same I believe that it is useful to delete it." Several reasons were given for his decision to delete. He feared it would be repetitious, "because it gets back into the order of ideas of the large political chapters at the end"; he noted that "it is obvious in any case that this chapter is too thin to stand alone. It must be either deleted or joined to another"; and he reminded himself to consult "L. et B." So perhaps his two friends vetoed the chapter.

But the most intriguing reason was the one listed first. He thought he should eliminate the short essay "because it very briefly and very incompletely treats a very interesting[42] subject which has been treated at length by others, among them Chevalier."[43]

Tocqueville valued—perhaps wrongly—his lack of exposure to other recent writings on the United States and insisted that this isolation enabled him to know his own mind and to maintain his intellectual integrity and originality. But if the author made it a rule to avoid the reports of other travelers, how did he know what the writings of Michel Chevalier, Guillaume-Tell Poussin, and others contained?

On 3 December 1836 he wrote to Beaumont. "Blosseville[44] sent me word the other day that Chevalier's book had appeared. . . . You know that I am always on the alert where America is concerned. However I do not want to read Chevalier's work; you know that that is a principle with me. Have you cast your eyes over it, and, in that case, what is your opinion of it? What is the spirit of it; where does it go? Finally what impact does it make in the world and how could it be prejudicial to the *ouvrage philosophico-politique* that I am preparing? If, without *sidetracking yourself*, you can answer these questions, I will be pleased."[45]

Unfortunately, Beaumont's response is lost. Possibly he told his former traveling companion about the content and purpose of Chevalier's *Lettres d'Amérique*.[46] But, in any case, as evidenced by the manuscript comments, the works of Chevalier and others apparently at least helped to discourage Tocqueville from including, in the 1840 *Democracy*, this short chapter on the relationship of governments to private associations.

Tocqueville's letters, notebooks, and drafts thus demonstrate a surprising awareness of most facets of America's technological metamorphosis. He failed to foresee the industrial future of the United States and projected instead a commercial destiny for the young nation. Yet he did devote considerable time and thought to the changes in communication and transportation which were taking place in the United States. Why, then, his failure adequately to discuss these transformations in the *Democracy*?

One possibility is that the appearance of works by Chevalier, Poussin, and others dissuaded him from developing and publishing certain of his ideas: since the republic's technological revolution had been examined so competently by others, perhaps he decided that he had better turn his mental energies toward other problems.

The more basic explanation, however, almost certainly concerns Tocqueville's intention to write an "ouvrage philosophico-politique." For him certain issues seemed more intriguing and more important than any technical or economic ones. But Tocqueville had searched out and digested much of the available information on the American effort to transform the continent. One can dispute his choices, but not his knowledge.

From these studies of Tocqueville's thinking about physical causes and changes in America, we see that the majority of his ideas on these topics developed in uncomplicated ways from the accumulated lessons of his journey experiences or from his readings. Many of his most perceptive insights about the effects of the republic's *situation physique*, for instance, even occurred during the very first weeks in the New World.

Some ideas, however, had more tangled histories. A few, the concept of *géographie*'s role in determining a nation's destiny, for example, seemed at first destined to key places in Tocqueville's thought, but ultimately filled more humble positions. The surprising revelation that the Americans themselves were the pioneers of civilization in the New World exemplified those ideas that were late but necessary corrections of erroneous European presuppositions. A few, like the de-emphasis of *circonstances* or the rejection of racial doctrines, arose in part out of Tocqueville's own moral convictions. Some, the theory of a manufacturing aristocracy for instance, were at first buried in discarded early drafts, only to reappear mysteriously in 1840. Still others, because of the author's personal preferences and his apparent concern to avoid twice-told tales, were cast permanently into oblivion. Tocqueville's ideas on American technology, in particular, were more extensive and profound than has been recognized. But they, like the others, suffered strange fates.

Part III

Tocqueville and the Union: the Nature and Future of American Federalism

CHAPTER 7

The Bond between the States and the Central Government

During his first six months in the New World, Tocqueville had had little chance to understand the workings of American federalism.[1] He had heard frequently about state and local government in the United States, but few of his hosts had spoken about the complex relationship between the federal government in Washington and the governments of the twenty-four states. An early impression that "in this lucky country, there truly is no government" had seemed particularly true of the republic's central authority.[2]

Only twice had he learned anything specific about the nature of the federal bond in America. In a conversation of October 1831 Tocqueville had asserted to a Mr. Clay that "your country is composed of little almost entirely separate nations," and Clay had reacted with hearty but misleading agreement. Two months later more profound remarks had come from Timothy Walker of Cincinnati, who had stressed the inherent rivalry between the state and federal governments by describing various "points of collision" between the states and the Union and noting that "in all the States there is a fund of jealousy of the central government."[3] In early December 1831, these two comments constituted Tocqueville's meager stock of recorded ideas about the connection between the American federal and state governments. But somewhere along his route he had purchased a copy of the *Federalist*,[4] and on 27 December he began to repair the gap in his knowledge.

Since previous scholars have consistently either overlooked or neglected to pursue various clues contained in his travel diaries, drafts, and original working manuscript, the edition of the *Federalist* which

Tocqueville used has until now been unknown. Several English passages copied from the famous essays into Tocqueville's papers indicate that he relied upon an American edition of "Publius's" work.[5] (Occasionally rough French translations accompany these excerpts, but these versions duplicate no French edition of the *Federalist* and are presumably Tocqueville's own.)[6]

Other hints consist of the many references in drafts and working manuscript to specific pages of his copy. By securing samples of all American editions published before 1835[7] and comparing each to these citations, it has been possible to identify the matching edition and to conclude a search which has always promised to provide new insights about the Frenchman's reliance on "Publius."

Tocqueville's *Federalist* was the one published as a single volume in the year 1831 by Thompson and Homans of Washington, D.C., and labeled as "A New Edition with a Table of Contents and a Copious Alphabetical Index. The Numbers Written by Mr. Madison Corrected by Himself." The recent date, the full index, and the imprimatur of Madison had all probably appealed to the curious visitor.

From 27 to 29 December 1831, Tocqueville read and took notes on his acquisition, filling several pages of travel notebook E with observations and excerpts collected under the titles "Union: Central Government" and "Sovereignty of the People." He specifically cited numbers 12, 15, 21, 23, and 18, referred to "others" (probably numbers 19 and 20, which continued the discussion of topics introduced in 18) and presumably had at least glanced at several additional papers as well.[8] It is noteworthy that his initiation came largely from the pen of Alexander Hamilton, who had written or collaborated on all of the essays which Tocqueville read first and who most vehemently argued for a strong and energetic central government.[9]

In papers 15 through 22, in order to demonstrate the unique advantages of the proposed American Constitution, the authors of the *Federalist* surveyed the histories of previous confederations and recounted the misfortunes of the American republic under the Articles of Confederation.[10] The Constitution, they observed, would remedy the chronic weakness which had plagued the nation during the period of the Articles by adopting a novel principle: the new national government would act directly upon individuals.

Tocqueville quickly grasped the significance of "Publius's" point. "The old Union," he wrote in his notebook, "governed *the States,* not the individuals. . . . The new federal government is in very truth the government of the Union in all things within its competence; it addresses, not the *States*, but *individuals*; its orders are addressed to each of the American citizens, whether he is born in Massachusetts or in Georgia, and not to Massachusetts or to Georgia."[11]

At the same time, the *Federalist* also taught him that in theory each government in America had its own area of interest, but that in fact these spheres were not always clearly delimited. "If the circumstances of our country," wrote Hamilton, "are such as to demand a compound instead of a simple, a confederate instead of a sole, government, the essential point which will remain to be adjusted will be to discriminate *the objects*, as far as it can be done, which shall appertain to the different provinces or departments of power."[12] So Tocqueville was quickly aware that the problem of separating the responsibilities of the state and national governments was a chronically troublesome characteristic of American federalism.

Readings from the *Federalist* and recollections of earlier lessons also led him to observe in a note dated 29 December 1831:

"This much can be stated, that it is only a very enlightened people that could invent the federal constitution of the United States and that only a very enlightened people and one accustomed to the representative system, could make such complicated machinery work, and know how to maintain the different powers within their own spheres. . . . The constitution of the United States is an admirable work, nevertheless one may believe that its founders would not have succeeded, had not the previous 150 years given the different States of the Union the *taste for, and practice of, provincial governments*, and if a high civilization had not at the same time put them in a *position to maintain a strong, though limited, central government.*"[13]

Several already familiar ideas hid just beneath the surface of these comments. Tocqueville here implied, first of all, that the political precepts involved in the workings of American federalism appeared on all political levels in the United States. Concerning, for example, the hard task of assigning state and federal responsibilities, he had noted only the day before that "it is an axiom of American public law that every power must be given full authority in its own sphere which must be defined in a way that prevents it stepping beyond it: that is a great principle and one worth thinking about."[14]

Secondly, he once again acknowledged that such basic principles were deeply embedded in the national experience. As he would later declare in the 1835 *Democracy*: "The federal government was the last to take shape in the United States; the political principles on which it was based were spread throughout society before its time, existed independently of it, and only had to be modified to form the republic. . . . The great political principles which now rule American society were born and grew up in the *state*; there is no room for doubt about that."[15]

Finally it seemed to him that the Americans, as a whole, were the most broadly educated and politically experienced of all peoples. This conviction, first announced in Boston three months earlier,[16] would soon find an additional proponent in Joel Poinsett, who would remark to Tocqueville in January 1832: "The Mexicans have ended by adopting, bar some unimportant exceptions, the United States Constitution. But they are not yet advanced enough to use it as we do. It is a complicated and difficult instrument."[17]

Later, in the 1835 *Democracy*, Tocqueville would combine his own observations based on the *Federalist* with the evidence supplied by Poinsett and others and describe at length the fragile intricacy of the American Constitution.

> The government of the Union rests almost entirely on legal fictions. The Union is an ideal nation which exists, so to say, only in men's minds and whose extent and limits can only be discerned by the understanding.
>
> When the general theory is well understood, there remain difficulties of application; these are innumerable, for the sovereignty of the Union is so involved with that of the states that it is impossible at first glance to see their limits. Everything in such a government depends on artificially contrived conventions, and it is only suited to a people long accustomed to manage its affairs . . .
>
> . . . The Constitution of the United States is like one of those beautiful creations of human diligence which gives their inventors glory and riches but remains sterile in other hands.[18]

A second important printed source of information about American federalism which Tocqueville first used during December came from Chancellor James Kent, who had met the two French visitors in

New York and had later thoughtfully forwarded the four thick volumes of his *Commentaries on American Law*.[19] While assimilating parts of the *Federalist*, Tocqueville also perused the first two volumes of Kent's massive work, which he would later describe as "highly respected; it presents a tableau of all the principles contained in the political and civil laws of the United States."[20]

During the early months of his American voyage, he had learned from Albert Gallatin, John Canfield Spencer, and others that in the United States judges possessed the right to declare laws unconstitutional and were, therefore, a considerable force in the political affairs of the nation, serving as a barrier to democratic excesses and to legislative aggression against the other branches of government.[21] So many Americans had concurred in these ideas that on 16 October Tocqueville had remarked in his notebook on "Civil and Criminal Law in America" that "the provisions concerning the powers of the judges are among the most interesting features of American constitutions."[22]

But not until he read the Chancellor's tomes in December did he realize that the American judiciary also played a necessary role in the relationship between the states and federal government. "I see clearly," he concluded after reading Kent's discussion of the problem of conflicting jurisdictions, "that the Court of the United States should have the effect of forcing each State to submit to the laws of the Union, but only when it is seized of a case. But when there is a violation of the laws of the Union and no one complains, what happens then?"[23]

So by New Year's Day 1832, after dipping into the writings of both "Publius" and Kent, Tocqueville had not only learned to appreciate the astounding subtlety of American federalism and discerned the principle which distinguished the Union from all other confederations—the central government acted directly upon individuals—but he had also perceived the major weak point in the system: the definition and maintenance of proper bounds for the state and national governments. Discovery had also been made by then of the admittedly inadequate device, the power of judges to declare laws unconstitutional, which the Americans had invented to remedy this dangerous flaw. Already the essential points of a penetrating analysis of American federalism were firmly in Tocqueville's mind.

After the return to France, he and his two American aides, Francis

J. Lippitt and Theodore Sedgwick, began, in the early months of 1833, to digest an already formidable collection of materials on the legal and political structures of the United States. Tocqueville now added several other works to his list of major authorities, including two volumes of Thomas Jefferson's papers, selected by L. P. Conseil and entitled *Mélanges politiques et philosophiques extraits des mémoires et de la correspondance de Thomas Jefferson*,[24] and Joseph Story's one-volume abridgement of his larger work, *Commentaries on the Constitution of the United States*.[25] "The book of M. Conseil," Tocqueville would later write, "is assuredly the most valuable document that has been published in France on the history and the legislation of the United States."[26]

From his study of these and other sources, a more complete picture of America's federal system began to emerge. As early as 3 December 1831, Timothy Walker had voiced deep concern over the internal rivalries which strained the federal bonds, and now, during a rereading of the *Federalist*, Tocqueville noticed that the authors manifested an anxiety not unlike Walker's about the antagonism between the states and the Union. Normally, Hamilton observed, "Power controlled or abridged is almost always the rival or enemy of that power, by which it is controlled or abridged."[27] Applied to the American federation, this principle exposed the states as "a complete counterpoise, and, not infrequently, dangerous rivals to the power of the Union."[28] Moreover, Hamilton assured his reader in Paper Number 17, the advantage in any clash between these natural competitors rested unquestionably with the states. "It will always be far more easy for the State governments to encroach upon the national authorities than for the national government to encroach upon the State authorities."[29]

Here was an idea far beyond Walker's comment about conflict. According to Hamilton, one of the architects of the Union, the states rather than the national government dominated the American federation. As Tocqueville developed a late revision of his large chapter entitled "The Federal Constitution,"[30] he recalled the statesman's words: "It is even easy to go farther and it is necessary to say with the celebrated Hamilton in the *Federalist* that of the two sovereignties the strongest is certainly the sovereignty of the state. In fact the more one examines the constitutions of the United States the more one begins to think that if the power of the law-maker has gone as far as lessening the probability of a struggle between the two rival sovereignties, it has not been able to assure that, in case of struggle, the strength of the Union will be preponderant or even equal to that of the states."[31]

In 1835 Tocqueville would offer a similar version of this passage, but with two significant changes. First, in the published *Democracy* Tocqueville would refrain from flatly declaring that "of the two sovereignties the strongest is certainly the sovereignty of the state." Secondly and more interestingly, all mention of Hamilton or the *Federalist* would be deleted, and he would therefore neglect to indicate a major source of his ideas about the power and the aggressiveness of the states.[32]

In Number 17, Hamilton had also summarized the reasons for the alleged predominance of the state governments:

"It is a known fact in human nature," the American explained, "that its affections are commonly weak in proportion to the distance or diffusiveness of the object: Upon the same principle that a man is more attached to his family than to his neighborhood, to his neighborhood than to the community at large, the people of each state would be apt to feel a stronger bias towards their local governments than towards the government of the Union. . . . This strong propensity of the human heart would find powerful auxiliaries in the objects of State regulation.

"The variety of more minute interests, which will necessarily fall under the superintendence of the local administrations . . . will form so many rivulets of influence, running through every part of the society. . . . The operations of the national government, on the other hand, [fall] less immediately under the observation of the mass of the citizens. . . . Relating to more general interests, they will be less apt to come home to the feelings of the people."[33]

Similar arguments appeared elsewhere in the *Federalist*. "Many considerations . . . seem to place it beyond doubt that the first and most natural attachment of the people will be to the government of their respective States," James Madison remarked in Number 46. "By the superintending care of these, all the more domestic and personal interests of the people will be regulated and provided for. With the affairs of these, the people will be more familiarly and minutely conversant. And with the members of these will a greater proportion of the people have the ties of personal acquaintance and friendship, and of family and party attachments; on the side of these, therefore, the popular bias may well be expected more strongly to incline."[34]

Although nowhere in Tocqueville's papers is there any hint that he noted these particular paragraphs by Hamilton and Madison, his explanation in the 1835 *Democracy* of why the states kept "the love and the prejudices of the people" would strongly echo their words. If the similarity between his arguments and those in the *Federalist* was not merely coincidental, then Tocqueville once again neglected to give credit to "Publius."[35]

One author of the *Federalist* also attempted a general description of the American Union. "The government of the United States," Tocqueville wrote in his manuscript, "is not truly speaking a *federal* government. It is a national government of which the powers are limited. *Important.* Blend of *national* and *federal* in the Constitution." A citation followed: "See Federal. [*Federalist*] p. 166."[36]

In Paper Number 39, Madison presented a detailed analysis of the nature of the Union and, on page 166, concluded: "The proposed Constitution, therefore, is, in strictness, neither a national nor a federal Constitution, but a composition of both."[37]

"Neither, nor, but a mixture" was hardly enough to satisfy Tocqueville, who proceeded to create a label of his own for the American federation. In the margin of the working manuscript, after cataloguing four general types of government, "temporary alliance—league; durable alliance—confederation; incomplete national government; complete national government," he declared that "the Union is not a confederation,[38] but an incomplete national government."[39]

This original classification, based in part upon the thirty-ninth paper of the *Federalist*, would appear in the 1835 *Democracy*:

"A form of society is . . . discovered in which several peoples really fused into one in respect of certain common interests, but remained separate and no more than confederate in all else.

"Here the central power acts without intermediary on the governed, administering and judging them itself, as do national governments, but it only acts thus within a restricted circle. Clearly here we have not a federal government but an incomplete national government. Hence a form of government has been found which is neither precisely national nor federal; but things have halted there, and the new word to express this new thing does not yet exist.[40]

Justice Story's *Commentaries* amply reinforced the impressions which Tocqueville had received from Chancellor Kent about the special role of the American judiciary,[41] but it was primarily directly from the *Federalist* that he gathered additional information about how the courts operated to resolve conflicts between Washington and the states and how the federal judiciary also influenced the balance between the rival powers.

In a draft entitled "Federal Courts," he wrote: "Utility and necessity for a federal court. Disadvantages resulting from the contrary. Fed. [*Federalist*] p. 93."[42]

There Hamilton, special champion of a strong and independent judiciary, discussed "A circumstance which crowns the defects of the Confederation . . . —the want of a judicial power." "Laws are a dead letter without courts to expound and define their true meaning and operation. . . . To produce uniformity in these determinations, they ought to be submitted, in the last resort, to one SUPREME TRIBUNAL. . . . If there is in each state a court of final jurisdiction, there may be as many different final determinations on the same point as there are courts. . . . To avoid the confusion which would unavoidably result from the contradictory decisions of a number of independent judicatories, all nations have found it necessary to establish one court paramount to the rest. . . .

"This is the more necessary where the frame of the government is so compounded that the laws of the whole are in danger of being contravened by the laws of the parts. In this case, if the particular tribunals are invested with a right of ultimate jurisdiction, besides the contradiction to be expected from difference of opinion there will be much to fear from the bias of local views and prejudices and from the interference of local regulations. As often as such an interference was to happen, there would be reason to apprehend that the provisions of the particular laws might be preferred to those of the general laws."[43]

Tocqueville continued in his draft: "It is quite true that the sovereignty of the *Union* is circumscribed; but when it is in competition with the sovereignty of the *States*, it is a *federal* court which decides. p. 165."[44]

"It is true," Madison explained, again in Number 39, "that in controversies relating to the boundary between the two jurisdictions, the tribunal which is ultimately to decide is to be established under the general government. . . . Some such tribunal is clearly essential to prevent an appeal to the sword and a dissolution of the compact; and it ought to be established under the general rather than under the local governments, or to speak more properly, that it could be safely established under the first alone, is a proposition not likely to be combated."[45]

The lesson was obvious. Only the federal judiciary promised to check the aggressive power of the states without, at the same time, inflaming the dangerous rivalry which was built into the Union. The 1835 *Democracy* would read:

"To entrust the execution of the Union's laws to courts established by [the states] would be handing over the nation to foreign judges.

"Furthermore, each state is not only foreign to the Union at large but is its perpetual adversary, since whatever authority the Union loses turns to the advantage of the states.

"Thus, to make the state courts enforce the laws of the Union would be handing the nation over to judges who are prejudiced as well as foreign.

"Besides this, it was not only their character which made the state courts incapable of serving the national end, but even more their number.

". . . How could [a government] carry on if its fundamental laws could be interpreted and applied in twenty-four different ways at the same time? Such a system would be equally contrary to reason and to the lessons of experience. . . .[46]

"The intention in creating a federal tribunal was to deprive the state courts of the right to decide, each in its own way, questions of national interest. . . . That aim would not have been achieved if the courts of the particular states, while abstaining from judging cases as federal, had been able to judge them by pretending that they were not federal.

"The Supreme Court of the United States was therefore entrusted with the right to decide all questions of competence.

"That was the most dangerous blow dealt against the sovereignty of the states. It was now restricted not only by the laws but also by the interpretation of the laws. . . . It is true that the Constitution had fixed precise limits to federal sovereignty, but each time that that sovereignty is in competition with that of the states, it is a federal tribunal that must decide.[47] Here once again was a silent reflection of the views of Hamilton and Madison.

Tocqueville's analysis of America's federal machinery had its weak points. Despite an apparently sound understanding of the complexities involved in the state-federal connection,[48] he would occasionally exhibit a lingering confusion in his published work, sometimes speaking of the Union as forming a single people, and at other times describing it as merely "an assemblage of confederated republics."[49]

Perhaps this persistent contradiction arose from Clay's overly enthusiastic acceptance of his earlier statement about twenty-four "little, almost entirely separate nations." But a more likely reason was Tocqueville's tendency to focus so intensely from time to time on one facet of a problem that he momentarily excluded other perspectives from his mind. The American federation was, after all, as the *Democracy* would repeatedly assert, both a single nation (or an incomplete nation) and a collection of small political societies (or a federation or a confederation).

Also, in at least one instance, the *Democracy* would push the arguments from the *Federalist* and other sources beyond what the authors had originally intended.

One of Madison's attempts to separate the legitimate interests of the states from those of the Union impressed Tocqueville so much that he would quote it in his text: "The powers delegated by the proposed Constitution to the federal government are few and defined. Those which are to remain in the State governments are numerous and indefinite. The former will be exercised principally on external objects, as war, peace, negotiation, and foreign commerce. . . . The powers reserved to the several States will extend to all the objects which, in the ordinary course of affairs, concern the lives, liberties, and properties of the people, and the internal order, improvement, and prosperity of the State."[50]

Possibly he also stumbled upon the concurring opinions of Joseph Story and Thomas Jefferson. "The powers of the general government," the Justice announced in his *Commentaries,* "will be, and indeed must be, principally employed upon external objects. . . . In its internal operations it can touch but few objects. . . . The powers of the states, on the other hand, extend to all objects, which, in the ordinary course of affairs, concern the lives, the liberties, and property of the people."[51]

And in a letter appearing in Conseil's volumes, Jefferson advanced a similar thesis: "To the State governments are reserved all legislation and administration, in affairs which concern their own citizens only, and to the federal government is given whatever concerns foreigners, or the citizens of other States; these functions alone being made federal. The one is the domestic, the other the foreign branch of the same government."[52]

In apparent agreement with these voices, Tocqueville would twice conclude in his work of 1835: "The federal government is something of an exception, whereas the government of each state is the normal authority (*règle commune*),"[53] and would also declare, in what he probably assumed to be obvious harmony with unimpeachable authorities, "The federal government is hardly concerned with anything except foreign affairs; it is the state governments which really control American society."[54]

Such conclusions, if not erroneous, were at least controversial and later drew criticism from some readers of the *Democracy.*[55]

By repeatedly mining the treasure contained in the *Federalist,* Tocqueville gathered so many arguments and ideas that he could not always separate "Publius's" thinking from his own. In 1835 he would warmly praise and often acknowledge obligations to the American essays, but the uncovering of additional undeclared debts[56] makes his reliance seem even more substantial than perhaps he himself realized.

What then of Justice Story's severe accusation of 1840 that the *Democracy* contained information and theories largely pirated from the *Federalist* and his *Commentaries*? Certainly, more than once, Tocqueville would obscure links between his ideas and their origins by failing to include in the *Democracy* specific citations which appeared in drafts or the working manuscript. But repeated references to Story and the *Federalist* and several quotations from each would make it clear that there was no intention in his published volumes to hide his heavy use of the two works. Also, when Tocqueville and Beaumont visited the United States, the viewpoints espoused by "Publius" and the Justice were part of the knowledge common to practically every educated American whom the two visitors met, so the travelers could hardly avoid absorbing them.[57]

Moreover, Story evidently overlooked one significant departure made by the author of the *Democracy* from the *Federalist* or "orthodox" school of thought. The apparently acceptable opinion that the states held the balance of power within the Union led Tocqueville to conclude, more heretically, that the duration of the American republic depended upon the will of the states. On this matter he adopted an idea repugnant to the Justice and to most of the other authors whom he read.

His working manuscript observed that the Union, like other confederations, rested "on a contract obligatory for all parties."[58] But contracts broken by one party could be terminated by the other, and in 1835 Tocqueville would write that the Union rested on the freely given consent of the states. The states, he would boldly declare, were parties to the contract, and, if one or more decided to withdraw, the federal government could not constitutionally prevent them from doing so. "The confederation was formed by the free will of the states; these, by uniting, did not lose their nationality or become fused in one single nation. If today one of those same states wished to withdraw its name from the contract, it would be hard to prove that it could not do so. In resisting it the federal government would have no obvious source of support *either in strength or in right*."[59]

Neither Story nor the *Federalist* granted the states the right to secede, so where might Tocqueville have encountered such doctrine?

In 1825, William Rawle, a lesser-known commentator, had published a volume of analysis entitled *A View of the Constitution of the United States*,[60] and although Tocqueville's papers give no indication that he read Rawle's exposition while drafting the *Democracy*, he was, nevertheless, exposed to Rawle's somewhat eccentric explanation of the nature of the American Union. Conseil's *Mélanges* contained a short treatise and annotations on the Constitution of the United States "taken, for the most part, from the work published on this Constitution by

William Rawle, L.L.D.,"[61] and in a footnote, Rawle, through Conseil, perhaps sowed the seeds of confusion: "It is necessary to note that the United States, in their present form, constitute a society composed not only of a people divided into other secondary societies, but also, in certain respects, of these secondary societies themselves. The State, as well as the people who inhabit it, is a member and integral part of the Union; however, it does not take part as a confederated power."[62]

Presumably Rawle entered Tocqueville's thinking even more substantially through the person of Francis J. Lippitt. Sixty years after his service to Tocqueville, Lippitt would recollect "certain particulars not wholly mal-à-propos." "In my senior year in college we had Rawle on the Constitution for six months." The young American possibly analyzed and summarized Rawle into many of Tocqueville's materials, and if he and his employer ever discussed the states and the Union, Rawle almost certainly appeared repeatedly as a third participant in their conversations.[63]

The treatise which Conseil used and which Lippitt studied at Brown reproduced, for the most part, the standard account of the Constitution and of the nature of the Union as told by Story, Kent, Hamilton, or Madison, but it differed substantially on one vital issue. While professing the usual affection for the Union, Rawle insisted that "the states . . . may wholly withdraw from the Union."[64]

A minor scandal erupted among the followers of the Chancellor and the Justice when they discovered this strange opinion at the end of Rawle's book,[65] but evidently Tocqueville—at least at times—approved of the unusual doctrine; echoes of it would occasionally sound in the 1835 *Democracy*.

Tocqueville's view of the relationship between the American federal and state governments, as presented in the *Democracy*, was a profound and largely accurate one, particularly when compared to the explanations of most other French travelers who committed their impressions to paper.[66] Even the traces of confusion and possible error in Tocqueville's work pale into insignificance with the realization that in 1835 the Americans themselves remained unsure of what their Union was or how it was supposed to function.[67]

His heavy reliance on the dominant nationalist interpretation as expounded by "Publius," Kent, Story, and others exposed Tocqueville to some of the best of American constitutional thought and was, therefore, primarily advantageous to his understanding. But in 1835, his *affaire américaine* would reflect the *Federalist* probably more than he realized and certainly more than the *Democracy* would disclose.

In his use of those famous essays, Tocqueville also apparently failed to detect any noteworthy differences between Hamilton's and Madison's accounts of the Constitution or of the nature of the American Union. In Hamilton he found reinforcement for beliefs about the threat of the states, the necessity for a strong central government, and the desirability of a powerful and independent federal judiciary. From Madison he learned that the Union, though clearly not an historically familiar confederation, was also not quite a unified nation, but rather a new and unique political form. It was also Madison who helped to convince him that the central authority was, after all, a government of severely restricted jurisdiction and decidedly the exception rather than the rule. Tocqueville evidently did not notice that these two embodiments of "Publius" frequently offered views with significantly different points of emphasis.

Finally, even in 1835, he would entertain two unreconciled ideas about the states' supposed right to secede. On the one hand, faithful to his eminent teachers, he would summarize, then denounce as essentially destructive, the theories of John C. Calhoun and the *nullificateurs*. Yet elsewhere he would grant the states the full constitutional right to withdraw from the Union whenever they might choose to do so. Either unaware of his self-contradiction, or unable finally to decide, he would strangely present both of these conflicting opinions in the pages of his *grand ouvrage*.

CHAPTER 8

A Prophet in Error

In March 1831, when Tocqueville and Beaumont climbed aboard the *Havre* and prepared to leave France, they carried with them an elementary history of the United States, perhaps Arnold Scheffer's short *Histoire des Etats-Unis de l'Amérique septentrionale* which had appeared in Paris in 1825.[1] Scheffer, in fewer than three hundred pages, ambitiously surveyed events in America from the voyages of discovery to 1824 and even found room for occasional interpretive comments. Near the end of his work, after citing census statistics and noting the rapid admission and growing influence of new states, he speculated about the future of the American republic. "One day the immense extent of territory contained in the United States . . . will have reached the full limit of its population; it is probable that North America will then number two or several republics."[2] Was his prediction correct? Would the American Union ultimately dissolve into several smaller nations?[3]

While still on shipboard, Tocqueville asked Peter Schermerhorn, wealthy New Yorker and fellow passenger, what he thought. "When I spoke to Mr. Schermerhorn of the possible division which might take place between the united provinces [states], he did not seem to believe that it was the least in the world to be feared in the near future." But the merchant did think that "it would come someday, *by and by*."[4]

Other Americans, including a man recently President of the United States, also supported Scheffer's contention. "I then spoke to [John Quincy Adams] about the more immediate dangers to the Union and the causes which might lead to its dissolution. [He] did not answer at all, but it was easy to see that in this matter he felt no more confidence than I did in the future."[5]

Another citizen more willingly gave words to his fears. According to Timothy Walker, controversies over the tariff, the public lands, and other matters, the rapidly shifting balance between the North and South, and state suspicion and resentment of the central government dangerously weakened the federal bonds.[6]

Joel Poinsett, in partial dissent, later denied that the "nullificators," spawned by the tariff affair, threatened the Union, but he too worried aloud about the relative decline of the South and the increasing bitterness of sectional disputes. The South Carolinian readily agreed with Tocqueville's observation that "It is impossible that this state of affairs should not create a state of *jealousy* and *suspicion* in the South. The weak do not generally believe in the fairness of the strong."[7]

Yet curiously, the Americans often mixed a vigorous distrust of the central government with their uncertainty about the duration of the Union. Mr. Clay, for example, evinced a common fear by warning Tocqueville about one great flaw in the French democracy, the preponderance of Paris.[8] "The Americans," Tocqueville observed not long afterwards, "have . . . a fear of centralization and of the power of capitals."[9]

Later, while drafting his work and reflecting upon his experiences in America, he would recall: "More than once in the United States I had the occasion to notice . . . a strange preoccupation: . . . the idea of the consolidation of sovereignty in the hands of the central government constantly torments the imagination of statesmen as well as that of the people."[10]

Which future was the more likely, disunion or consolidation? His hosts appeared mired in indecision, but by the end of his visit to America, a prediction of disintegration began to take shape in Tocqueville's mind. On 31 January 1832, under the heading "Future of the Union," he observed:

> One of the greatest dangers that the Union runs, which seems to result from its very prosperity: the speed with which the new nations are arising in the West and the South-West certainly subjects it to a severe test.
>
> The first result of this disproportionate growth is violently to change the balance of forces and of political influence. Powerful States become weak; nameless territories become powerful States. Wealth as well as population changes place. These changes cannot take place without bruising interests, or

without arousing violent passions. The speed with which they come about renders them a hundred times more dangerous yet.[11]

Walker and Poinsett had left their marks on his thinking.

While leading his monk's existence in Paris and at Baugy and working on the early chapters of the *Democracy*, Tocqueville can hardly have failed to notice a thesis in the *Federalist* which seemed almost designed to confirm his doubts about the durability of the United States. Turning away from statistical or political considerations, Hamilton had offered an argument based upon the very structure of the American Union. Federations, he had declared, verged naturally toward disintegration. "In every political association which is formed upon the principle of uniting in a common interest a number of lesser sovereignties, there will be found a kind of eccentric tendency in the subordinate or inferior orbs by the operation of which there will be a perpetual effort in each to fly off from the common center."[12]

A later paper had elaborated the same point. "Several important considerations . . . ," Madison had argued in Number 45, "discountenance the supposition that the operation of the federal government will by degrees prove fatal to the State governments. The more I revolve the subject, the more fully I am persuaded that the balance is much more likely to be disturbed by the preponderancy of the last than of the first scale. We have seen, in all the examples of ancient and modern confederacies, the strongest tendency continually betraying itself in the members to despoil the general government of its authorities, with a very ineffectual capacity in the latter to defend itself against the encroachments." He had even admitted that the Constitution did not grant the American republic total immunity to this historical disease. "Although, in most of these examples, the system has been so dissimilar from that under consideration as greatly to weaken any inference concerning the latter from the fate of the former, yet, as the States will retain under the proposed Constitution a very extensive portion of active sovereignty, the inference ought not to be wholly disregarded."[13]

As the 1835 *Democracy* took form, Tocqueville made "Publius's" premise his own, and, in a draft entitled "What must be understood by the word *sovereignty* and the words 'rights of sovereignty,' " theorized that sovereign nations could be formed by the union either of individuals or of small independent societies. "When the sovereign is composed of *individuals* [there is] a tendency to gather the exercise of all principal acts into the same hands. . . . When [the sovereign is] composed of nations, [there is] a contrary tendency.[14]

"So the way in which the sovereign is formed," he continued, "exercises a great influence over the division that it makes of its authority. That is a *point de départ* about which one hardly thinks. . . .[15]

". . . The natural tendency of a people . . . is indefinitely to concentrate social forces until one reaches pure administrative despotism. The natural tendency of confederations is indefinitely to divide these forces until one reaches dismemberment."[16]

So the very nature of the American federation apparently condemned it to a brief existence. Lacking the strength needed to check this natural centrifugal impulse, the Union would continue to exist only on the pleasure of the states,[17] and, although material and certain nonmaterial interests urged the states to adhere to the federation,[18] various other forces weakened their attachment to the national government.[19]

In remarks reminiscent of the anxiety expressed in the travel notes of December 1831 and January 1832, Tocqueville wrote in his working manuscript: "What most compromises the fate of the Union is its very prosperity, is the rapid increase of some of its parts."[20] The Americans, he declared, were "an entire people who travel."[21] They prided themselves on their headlong rush westward, but Tocqueville noted with misgivings that "there is something revolutionary in such progress."[22]

Both faults of structure and uncontrolled growth thus made the conclusion inescapable, and, in a margin of the manuscript, Tocqueville summarized his argument. "So the existence of the Union, a risk. Its dismemberment, something always possible. Something *certain* in time."[23]

In 1835, various passages would hint at the misfortune ahead, but nowhere in the published text would the author quite so boldly proclaim the inevitable dissolution of the American nation.[24]

A prediction of disunion did not end the inquiry, however, for Tocqueville realized that the Union's demise could result from a gradual decrease in national vigor as well as from the sudden withdrawal of jealous and unruly states. "Among the causes which can hasten the dismemberment of the Union is found, in the first rank, the condition of weakness and inertia into which the federal government might fall. If, in this way, the central power arrived at such a degree of feebleness that it could no longer serve as arbiter among the different provincial interests and could not effectively defend the confederation against foreigners, its usefulness would become doubtful and the Union would no longer exist except on paper."[25]

"Publius" had theorized that the states would constantly sap the strength of the Union, but, to discover whether the national government was, in fact, becoming impotent, Tocqueville turned once again to Kent, Story, and Conseil, to a variety of official and unofficial papers, and to three additional volumes: Joseph Blunt's *A Historical Sketch of the Formation of the Confederacy*,[26] William Alexander Duer's *Outlines of the Constitutional Jurisprudence of the United States*,[27] and Thomas Sergeant's *Constitutional Law: Being a View of Practice and Jurisdiction of the Courts of the United States and of the Constitutional Points Decided*.[28]

Sergeant's work, which Tocqueville described as "an excellent commentary on the Constitution of the United States,"[29] was the first to use court decisions[30] to advance the thesis that many of the federal government's legitimate and once-acknowledged prerogatives had been lost through timidity. Citing cases on every page, Sergeant asserted that under the powers to establish post offices and post roads, to regulate commerce, and to provide for the general welfare the national government had clear authority to undertake internal improvements, and that until Monroe's veto of 1817, it had freely done so.[31] He declared, in addition, that the "necessary and proper" clause granted the federal government the right to establish a national bank.[32] Only executive vetoes and national inaction had allowed the states to question these long established federal responsibilities.

Joseph Blunt's volume preached a similar message, but directed it toward two other problems; the full title read: *A Historical Sketch of the Formation of the Confederacy Particularly with Reference to the Provincial Limits and the Jurisdiction of the General Government over the Indian Tribes and the Public Territory*. Like many of his fellow citizens in 1825, Blunt was alarmed by the frequent charges of usurpation made against the national government because of its Indian and land policies, and, in the hope of answering these accusations, he undertook a detailed study of both issues. "In this imperfect volume," his introductory dedication stated, "I venture to present to the public the result of my examination. . . . If it be correct, it not only vindicates the federal government from all charges of undue attention, but shows that in its desire to conciliate the good will of the state authorities, it has conceded more than they could have reasonably demanded."[33]

Tocqueville received a copy of the *Outlines* from the author[34] and discovered that Duer also presented a strongly nationalist viewpoint, based, according to his preface, upon the *Federalist*, the writings of Kent, Story, and Rawle,[35] the speeches of Daniel Webster, and the opinions of Chief Justice John Marshall.[36]

These three volumes addressed themselves to most of the principal issues of the Jacksonian period, but for the details of the tariff and nullification controversy, Tocqueville was forced to undertake his own research; a list of some of the papers which he consulted appeared in a draft:

1. Legislative documents. 22nd Congress. 2nd session. no. 30.
2. Report made to the convention of South Carolina. . . .
3. Ordinance of Nullification of November 24, 1832.
4. Proclamation of Governor Hamilton [*sic*] of November 27, 1832.
5. December 13, 1832. Proclamation of Gov. Ham. [*sic*].
6. . . . [37]Laws of December 20, 1832.[38]

From these and other sources, he concluded that in several of the key areas of conflict between the states and the Union—"Nullification, Indians, Internal Improvements, Lands, Bank"[39]—the federal government had ignominiously retreated. It seemed, moreover, that the government in Washington actually possessed fewer recognized prerogatives in the 1830s than it had in 1789. Still somewhat incredulous about such a loss of authority, Tocqueville advised himself to see "in *Story* all the matters which have concerned the federal government and those which still concern it in order to know if its power[?][40] increases or decreases."[41]

Evidently the Justice stilled any doubts, for, in another draft, Tocqueville summarized his findings: "*Weakness of the Union* proved by the progress of events. . . . All the *amendments* to the Constitution have been made to restrict the federal power. The federal government has abandoned in practice certain of its prerogatives and has not acquired a single new one. Every time that a State has resolutely stood up to the Union, [the State] has more or less obtained what it desired."[42]

"The real force," he concluded briefly, "has remained with the States. This proved by events. . . . For forty years the central bond has constantly loosened. The Union loses constantly and does not recover."[43] In 1835, the *Democracy* would contend that "a careful study of the history of the United States over the last forty-five years readily convinces one that federal power is decreasing."[44]

Certain that the Union would break apart in one way or another, Tocqueville dealt harshly in his drafts with Americans haunted by what he termed the "absurd" specter of consolidation.[45] Perhaps Story's *Commentaries*, written largely in reaction to John C. Calhoun's doctrine of nullification,[46] reinforced his skepticism. In the firm belief that the power of the states was the real threat to the Union, the Justice scoffed at those who worried about federal ambitions. "Hitherto our experience has demonstrated the entire safety of the states, under the benign operation of the constitution. No man will venture to affirm, that their power, relative to that of the Union, has been diminished."[47] "As for me," Tocqueville avowed in agreement, ". . . I search in vain for what is real and perceptible in such a terror." The 1835 *Democracy* would offer a somewhat more diplomatic version of the same sentiment.[48]

Only one of Tocqueville's major authorities, Thomas Jefferson, clearly disagreed with this view. In several letters contained in Conseil's two volumes the Virginian claimed that the central government gained rather than lost power, and that the independence of the states diminished steadily.[49] In 1825, for example, he had lamented to William B. Giles:

> I see, as you do, and with the deepest affliction, the rapid strides with which the federal branch of our government is advancing towards the usurpation of all the rights reserved to the States, and the consolidation in itself of all powers, foreign and domestic; and that too, by constructions which, if legitimate, leave no limits to their power. Take together the decisions of the federal court, the doctrines of the President, and the misconstruction of the constitutional compact acted on by the legislature of the federal branch, and it is

but too evident, that the three ruling branches of that department are in combination to strip their colleagues, the State authorities, of the powers reserved by them, and to exercise themselves all functions foreign and domestic.[50]

Jefferson had proceeded to explain in some detail how the national government used the power to regulate commerce, the general welfare clause, and other tools to subjugate the states. Unfortunately for Tocqueville's reputation as a prophet, he failed to heed the great democrat's dissent.

The 1835 *Democracy* would only vaguely date the beginning of the Union's decline as when "America again took her due place among the nations, peace returned to her frontiers, and confidence in public credit was restored; a settled state of affairs followed the confusion, and each man's industry could find its natural outlet and develop in freedom."[51]

The drafts and manuscript, however, indicated a much more precise time for the onset of the nation's infirmity, and even assigned responsibility to one particular American statesman. "Reveal how the various Presidents since Jefferson have successively despoiled the federal government of its attributes," Tocqueville resolved in one early outline.[52]

In a margin of the working manuscript, he ventured a more straightforward opinion: "I believe, but it is to be verified, that the entry of the Republicans to federal power was the first step, a step indirect but real, on this path."[53]

"The federal government," he explained, "was from then on in a very critical situation; its enemies had popular favor, and it was by promising to weaken the federal government that they obtained the right to direct it. Since that period, it is easy to trace, in events, the successive symptoms of this weakening of the central power. The reaction against the central power began around 1800. It continues today."[54]

But before he sent his manuscript to the printer, the author cautiously deleted both the marginal comment and the specific reference to 1800; the published text of the *Democracy* would blame no man for the Union's advancing weakness.[55]

So once again during the writing process, Tocqueville decided to moderate one of his views concerning the fate of the Union. The text of

1835 would refrain from any assertion of inevitable dissolution, any scornful rejection of American fears of consolidation, or any condemnation of Jefferson. Several possible explanations for this retreat come to mind. The author of the *Democracy* undoubtedly labored to avoid unnecessarily offending the Americans, and so probably thought better of his transparent contempt for a common American torment and of his attack on the Republican hero. He was also extremely suspicious of men who claimed to see into the future, and, after the excitement of composition had passed, probably decided to back away from some of his bolder projections. Writing of events which might stop, slow, or hasten the Union's weakness, he ultimately concluded: "That is hidden in the future, and I cannot pretend to be able to lift the veil."[56]

That he might have been persuaded toward moderation by one or more of his American friends is another possible explanation. Perhaps prodding by Sedgwick, Lippitt, Edward Livingston, or others caused him to reassess his estimation of Jefferson's role. As early as the summer of 1833, for example, long before the first part of the *Democracy* appeared, Tocqueville had received strong indications from America that his ideas about "l'affaiblissement de l'Union" were mistaken.

On 30 August 1833, Jared Sparks had devoted part of a letter to a description of recent events.

> Since you were in America, there has been a ferment in our political affairs. The nullification madness of South Carolina caused an alarm. It is now subdued, and all is tranquil. The voice of the nation was so strong against the doctrines of the nullifiers, that they could make no progress; and although these will probably appear again in some form, yet there is no fear, that the republic will suffer a serious injury. Any attempts to disunion, from whatever quarter will be met with an overwhelming opposition. What will be effected by time, it is difficult to foresee; but, for many years to come, the union of the States will remain firmly established.[57]

Less than a month later a similar letter from H. D. Gilpin had indicated that Sparks's view was not merely idiosyncratic. "The difficulties in the South are we trust at an end, and if so it is a matter of no small congratulation that what threatened us so seriously should have passed off with results calculated rather to strengthen than to weaken the union."[58]

Although in 1835 Tocqueville would not give much credit to these optimistic assessments of the Union's durability, we have already noted that in 1838 he would finally recognize and decide to admit his error about the decline of the American federation. "It will be necessary to show how recent events justify the greater part of the things that I said," he would write at that time; but he would cryptically add: "The weakening of the federal bond . . . admit my error."[59] A belated recognition was better than none at all, but in 1833, by ignoring these letters from America, Tocqueville had missed a second opportunity to enhance his standing as a seer.

Tocqueville thus superseded his readings and conversations to invent an original name for the new creation which he understood the American Union to be: *un gouvernement national incomplet.* His view of this strange government, perceptive and largely accurate, was also, however, profoundly pessimistic in many significant ways, for he saw it as powerful only within a severely limited sphere of authority, as totally dependent on the consent of aggressive and preponderant states, as suffering from a progressive and shameful senility, and as certainly doomed to ultimate dissolution. "So the existence of the Union, a risk. Its dismemberment, something always possible. Something *certain* in time."

Paradoxically, this bleak aspect of his description of the nature and destiny of the American Union,[60] except for his anomalous contention about secession, largely reflected the writings of "Publius," Story, and other ardent nationalists. Tocqueville never fully considered the implications of the fact that these men wrote with a dread of anarchy and a desire to calm the anxieties of fellow citizens always fearful of a strong central government. Consequently, he never awoke to the strong possibility that his experts, in order to meet a pervasive distrust of central authority, might have underplayed the vigor, the powers, and the activities of the federal government and exaggerated the strength, the rights, and the ambitions of the states. Here, if anywhere, was the basic error of Tocqueville's exposition of the nature and future of the American federation.

CHAPTER 9

How Large Might a Republic Be?

Despite "Publius's" assurances that America was unique among federal republics, Tocqueville concluded that growth in numbers (of both citizens and states) and the centrifugal forces natural to federations endangered the Union's future. Equally disturbing to him was the threat posed by the immense area of the republic. Timothy Walker's boasts, in December 1831, about the Union's rapid increase in both territory and population first drew Tocqueville's anxiety into the open. "Have you no fear," he asked the Ohioan, "that it may be impossible to hold together this huge body?" Walker's frank admission of uneasiness probably only increased Tocqueville's own concern.[1] A month later, Mr. Etienne Mazureau of New Orleans also addressed himself to this matter and voiced a time-honored opinion: "A small State . . . is always able to govern itself. Hardly any of the troublesome consequences of the sovereignty of the people are to be feared in small societies."[2] Was a republic as large as the United States inherently unstable?

Later, while drafting a short essay on the problem of size,[3] Tocqueville would write in the margin: "Perhaps this chapter should be transferred to the place where I will speak of the future of the Union."[4] Evidently he had decided that the Union's future depended in part on the answer to an old query: could a vast republic long endure?

Several of Tocqueville's American acquaintances shared his and Walker's doubts about the durability of large republics, but they also insisted that the Union's federal structure would surely overcome any risks involved in size.[5] "What I find most favourable with us to the establishment and maintenance of republican institutions," Mr. MacLean declared, "is our division into States. I do not think that with our democracy we could govern the whole Union for long, if it formed but one single people. . . . I hold too that the federal system is peculiarly favourable to the happiness of peoples. . . . By our federal organization we have the happiness of a small people and the strength of a great nation."[6]

After reading the *Federalist* in December, Tocqueville reflected that "the federal constitution of the United States seems to me the best, perhaps the only arrangement that could allow the establishment of a vast republic,"[7] and in January he found that Joel Poinsett agreed. "I do not believe," Poinsett affirmed, "that a great republic can endure, at least unless it is a federation."[8]

The idea that a *federated* republic could be extensive was not new. Charles-Louis de Secondat, Baron de Montesquieu, had reached the same conclusion nearly a century before his compatriot's journey to America. "It is in the nature of a republic," Montesquieu had written in his *De l'esprit des lois*, "that it have only a small territory; without that it can scarcely continue to exist." He had added, however, that one constitutional form existed which combined the internal advantages of a republic with the strength of a monarchy. "I am speaking of the federated republic. . . . This kind of republic . . . can sustain its greatness without becoming corrupt on the inside: the form of this society avoids all the disadvantages."[9]

Having fiercely debated the optimum size of a republic during the struggle over ratification of the Federal Constitution, the American republicans were well aware of Montesquieu's ideas. Opponents of the Constitution had often cited his writings to support their belief that the proposed Union would be too large, asserting that such an immense republic would either divide or become a consolidated monarchy. In vain had Alexander Hamilton revealed that his antagonists sadly misunderstood the famous Frenchman. "The opponents of the Plan proposed," Hamilton had written, "have, with great assiduity, cited and circulated the observations of Montesquieu on the necessity of a contracted territory for a republican government. But they seem not to have been apprised of the sentiments of that great man expressed in another part of his work." Quoting at length from *De l'esprit des lois*, he had noted triumphantly that Montesquieu "explicitly treats of a Confederate Republic as the expedient for extending the sphere of popular government and reconciling the advantages of monarchy with those of republicanism."[10]

James Madison had also grappled with the problem of size in his contributions to the *Federalist*, but unlike Hamilton he had done more than merely quote Montesquieu's opinion. Turning the Frenchman's assumptions on end, the American had contended that size benefited rather than threatened a republic.[11]

In a republic dedicated to the rule of the majority, the despotism of an unjust minority could be effectively circumvented. But what if the majority itself attempted oppression?[12] Sheer size, Madison had theorized, was the best safeguard against that calamity. In a vast republic, no particular or local interest could bend the entire nation to its purposes; rival interests would check each other and only permit the formation of a majority clearly dedicated to justice and the common good. The difficulty of forming a despotic majority would increase in direct proportion to the size and the diversity of the nation. Thus, any republic huge enough to enclose a great variety of interests would be relatively secure, and if, by unhappy chance, a despotic majority did coalesce in an extensive republic, the very size of the nation would continue to hinder the execution of any oppressive schemes.

A federal republic, Madison had noted in addition, possessed an extra safeguard. Since each subordinate government would jealously guard its own prerogatives, the division into states automatically multiplied the number of interests enclosed within the nation. So a large republic was inherently superior to a small one, but a great federation was the best possible republican form.

During Tocqueville's travels in the New World, no American had explained Madison's argument to him, nor is there any evidence that in December he had read the particular *Federalist* papers which contained the statesman's ideas.[13] Apparently his first encounter with the perceptive thesis took place only after his return to France.

Nonetheless, while writing his book, he cited Madison's Number 51 four times in his drafts and even copied a passage from the essay into one of them.[14] In another, he reminded himself to see page 225 of his edition of the *Federalist* where a concise statement of Madison's theory could be found.[15] Declared Madison: "In a free government the security for civil rights must be the same as that for religious rights.

It consists in the one case in the multiplicity of interests, and in the other in the multiplicity of sects. The degree of security in both cases will depend on the number of interests and sects; and this may be presumed to depend on the extent of the country and number of people comprehended under the same government." The paper concluded: "The larger the society, provided it lie within a practicable sphere, the more duly capable it will be of self-government. And happily for the *republican cause*, the practicable sphere may be carried to a very great extent by a judicious modification and mixture of the *federal principle*."[16]

Tocqueville recognized the same argument in one of Thomas Jefferson's letters and copied an excerpt into still another of his drafts.[17] The letter read: "I suspect that the doctrine, that small States alone are fitted to be republics, will be exploded by experience, with some other brilliant fallacies accredited by Montesquieu and other political writers. Perhaps it will be found, that to obtain a just republic . . . it must be so extensive that local egoisms may never reach its greater part; that on every particular question, a majority may be found in its councils free from particular interests, and giving, therefore, an uniform prevalence to the principles of justice. The smaller the societies, the more violent and more convulsive their schisms."[18]

In both the working manuscript and the text of the 1835 *Democracy*, Tocqueville would assert that federalism made large republics feasible, thus adopting a thesis developed by Montesquieu, advocated by Hamilton, and repeated by MacLean and Poinsett.[19] Occasionally, his discussion of the superiority of federalism would even echo the words of Madison and Jefferson. An elaboration of the idea that the federal system helped to preserve the American republic would note that the states acted as barriers to unhealthy partisan emotions. "The confederation of all the American states presents none of the ordinary inconveniences resulting from large associations of men . . . and political passions, instead of spreading over the land like a fire on the prairies, spends its strength against the interests and the individual passions of every state."[20] And the towns and counties had a similar function. "Municipal bodies and county administrations are like so many hidden reefs retarding or dividing the flood of the popular will."[21]

So Tocqueville would admit that federalism theoretically saved large republics from some of their most obvious perils. But even here there was a limit beyond which he would not go; he would credit federalism only up to a certain size. "I think that before that time has run out [the next hundred years], the land now occupied or claimed by the United States will have a population of over one hundred million and be divided into forty states. . . . but I do say that the very fact of their being one hundred millions divided into forty distinct and not equally powerful nations would make the maintenance of the federal government no more than a happy accident. . . . I shall refuse to believe in the duration of a government which is called upon to hold together forty different nations covering an area half that of Europe."[22]

A large republic, if federal, was possible; but an excessively large republic, federal or not, was inconceivable. Perhaps Tocqueville simply could not imagine a self-governing nation of one hundred million people spread over hundreds of thousands of square miles.

Yet despite his qualified praise for federal republics, the author of the *Democracy* would either overlook or decline to accept Madison's novel thesis about size and would continue to lament "the ordinary inconveniences resulting from large associations of men" and to warn against largeness. "What can be said with certainty is that the existence of a great republic will always be more exposed than that of a small one. All passions fatal to a republic grow with the increase of its territory, but the virtues which should support it do not grow at the same rate."[23]

The perils which threatened a large republic—including personal ambition, partisan emotions, a disturbing contrast between the wealth of the few and the poverty of the many, large metropolitan areas, the decline of morality, and the "complication of interests"—could only be counteracted by the firm support of the majority. Unfortunately, however, "the more numerous a people is and the more varied its attitudes and interests, the harder it becomes to form a compact majority."[24]

Tocqueville would thus persist in condemning the very feature which Madison had acclaimed. He had either missed or rejected the American's brilliant observation that size itself was beneficial.

Madison's argument had implications not only about the success of large republics, but also about a second problem of special interest to Tocqueville: the tyranny of the majority. Madison had indicated that in extended republics—with their greater varieties of interests and viewpoints—opposition to the majority's opinions was more likely to be effective. So his exposition of the advantages of size was equally a demonstration of a very significant safeguard against despotic majorities. As we shall see, Tocqueville, normally so alert to possible checks on the power of the majority, curiously failed to respond to Madison's idea. He saw how the states, counties, and towns, sanctioned by American federalism and decentralization, served to check potentially dangerous tides of opinion,[25] but he overlooked the powerful additional barrier to majoritarian tyranny which Madison had suggested: size (and variety) itself.

Tocqueville's final evaluation of American federalism was curiously ambivalent. The American federation was a brilliant new form in the gallery of political theory (*un gouvernement national incomplet*); it overcame some of the weaknesses of previous federations, made a moderately large republic possible, and even served as a possible barrier to majoritarian despotism. But the Union also suffered from inherent faults of structure and practical problems of growth and size which made its future dark.

The major culprits in the story were the states which, in their jealousy and ambition, effectively drained the central government of its power and authority. Yet, even here, Tocqueville's attitude was somewhat contradictory, for if, on the one hand, the states threatened the durability of the Union, on the other, they actually benefited the maintenance of a just republic by helping to check "political passions" and "the popular will."

On the topic of federalism, Tocqueville undertook a truly impressive and eminently successful effort to cure his initial lack of knowledge. His list of sources, especially his readings, was extensive and of the highest quality. In this endeavor was one of the best demonstrations of Tocqueville's scholarship. Yet we have also seen that he depended heavily, and probably more than he realized, on a limited number of favorite authors and acquaintances. In the course of his research, the names of Sparks, Walker, and Poinsett and the volumes by "Publius" and Story recurred constantly. For much of what eventually became his completed analysis, the starting points were the words and works of these few men.

Finally, for a variety of reasons which we will examine later,[26] it is significant that Tocqueville could not bring himself to embrace James Madison's fascinating and original idea and thus to abandon the teachings of Montesquieu and the traditional European distrust of size. Here was one conviction that even "Publius" could not shake.

Part IV

Democracy, Centralization, and Democratic Despotisms

CHAPTER 10

Centralization and Local Liberties

For the great majority of readers, Tocqueville is at his most original and provocative when he struggles with the fundamental concepts of centralization, despotism, liberty, individualism, and democracy itself. These are ideas crucial not only to the American experiment, but also to the broader "democratic" experiment of the nineteenth and twentieth centuries; here questions raised in the New World merge with those raised in the Old.

In recent decades, few issues have been more troublesome and important than the connection between centralization and freedom. Political, economic, educational, social, and other opportunities have been seen as prerequisites for meaningful freedom in the United States, and the federal government has been cast as the guarantor of those opportunities. Yet the enormous increase in the power and size of the federal government has raised doubts about the reality of citizen participation, the responsiveness of the centers of authority, and the ultimate effect of such pervasive (and always expanding) influence on the lives of individuals. Very different segments of the political spectrum have raised slogans about a New Federalism, about dismantling the Washington bureaucracy, about returning authority and responsibility to the states and localities, about reviving neighborhood control, about empowering the people.

Are centralization and freedom compatible? This uncomfortable dilemma is one which Tocqueville faced, and his insights, warnings, and suggestions continue to have value in the latter part of the twentieth century. He came early to see that *démocratie* fostered a major threat to liberty: the concentration of power. By the late 1830s, the closely intertwined themes of centralization and despotism became two of the major organizational threads of his book.

During the years of Tocqueville's American journey and the making of his book, criticisms of excessive centralization and proposals for greater local or provincial freedom of action were a familiar part of French political life. In fact throughout the entire period of the parliamentary monarchy—the Restoration and the July regime (1814–48)—thoughtful Frenchmen turned repeatedly to consideration of the possible dangers and benefits of decentralization.[1] In 1831, for example, Le Peletier d'Aunay, a prominent political figure and cousin to Tocqueville, on hearing belatedly of Alexis's and Gustave's actual departure for America, wrote a long letter of advice about what particularly to notice in the United States. He singled out centralization for attention.

> Above all examine—as much in regard to the [national] government as in regard to the local administration—the effects of the small degree of centralization. Either in how it can be favorable by speeding the expedition of private affairs and by generating interest in the townhalls of all the cities and villages; or in how it can be unfavorable by a lack of harmony in affairs which concern security and by the opening that it gives to passions in each locality. Be assured that such discussions will most occupy France during the coming years and set about to show yourself [in those discussions] with the advantage given by examining the question from two points of comparison.[2]

It should be no surprise therefore that Tocqueville in America was very quick to notice signs of the relative authority of general and local governments and began almost immediately to examine the causes and results of the apparent lack of centralized power.

Several of Tocqueville's and Beaumont's earliest letters home reflected their amazement at the seeming absence of government in America. This appearance of nongovernment, they realized, arose from extreme decentralization, and Tocqueville's epistles of June and July often indicated frustration and irritation at the inefficient results. "In general," he told his father on 3 June 1831, "this country, as for administration, seems to me to have gone to precisely the opposite extreme as France. With us the government is involved in everything. [Here] there is no, or at least there doesn't appear to be any government at all. All that is good in centralization seems to be as unknown as what is bad. No central idea whatsoever seems to regulate the movement of the machine."[3]

Additional complaints surfaced while the companions visited the prison at Auburn. Temporarily exasperated by the lack of any uniform penal administration, Tocqueville remarked in a letter to Chabrol that only special circumstances permitted the thorough decentralization which prevailed in the United States. He implied that nations like France which found themselves surrounded by powerful potential enemies and beset by complex external pressures needed more centralized authority, if they hoped to survive, than the American republic required.[4] And even then, American local government exhibited certain distinct disadvantages when specific projects like prisons or other reform proposals were involved.

By September, however, conversations with prominent Bostonians, such as Josiah Quincy and Francis Lieber, began to divert Tocqueville's attention from the inconveniences to the benefits of decentralization.

"One of the happiest consequences of the absence of government (when a people is happy enough to be able to do without it, a rare event) is the ripening of individual strength which never fails to follow therefrom. Each man learns to think and to act for himself without counting on the support of any outside power which, however watchful it be, can never answer all the needs of man in society. The man thus used to seeking his well-being by his own efforts alone stands the higher in his own esteem as well as in that of others; he grows both stronger and greater of soul. Mr. Quincy gave an example of that state of things when he spoke of the man who sued the town that had let the public road fall into disrepair; the same goes for all the rest. If a man gets the idea of any social improvement whatsoever, a school, a hospital, a road, he does not think of turning to the authorities. He announces his plan, offers to carry it out, calls for the strength of other individuals to aid his efforts, and fights hand to hand against each obstacle. I admit that in fact he often is less successful than the authorities would have been in his place, but, in the total, the general result of all these individual strivings amounts to much more than any administration could undertake; and moreover the influence of such a state of affairs on the moral and political character of a people, would more than make up for all the inadequacies if there were any. But one must say it again, there are but few people who can manage like that without government. . . . The most important care of a good government should be to get people used little by little to managing without it."[5]

The locality, as an arena for individual and group efforts, was thus a superb place for political education and for development among the people of a sense of responsibility and capacity in public affairs. This focus on the moral, social, and political rather than the administrative effects of decentralization would remain fundamental in all of Tocqueville's future discussions of centralization.

The very next day he asked State Senator Francis Gray more about local government in Massachusetts and learned another basic feature of American administration. "The general principle is that the whole people by its representatives has the right to look after all local affairs, but it should refrain from exercising that right in everything that relates to the internal management of the localities. . . . The rule agreed is that as long as the local authority is acting only on its own account and does not injure anybody's rights, it is all-powerful in its sphere."[6]

Gray also warned about the difficulty of maintaining this local independence and alerted Tocqueville to a certain "spirit" which helped to support self-government in the United States. "I think it is even harder to establish municipal institutions among a people than great political assemblies. When I say municipal institutions I speak not of the forms but of the very spirit that animates them. The habit of dealing with all matters by discussion, and deciding them all, even the smallest, by means of majorities, that is the hardest habit of all to acquire. But it is only that habit that shapes governments that are truly free."[7]

The value and uniqueness of this attitude was particularly praised by Jared Sparks, who informed the visitors that, in Massachusetts at least, local government predated any central authority. "Almost all societies, even in America, have begun with one place where the government was concentrated, and have then spread out around that central point. Our forefathers on the contrary founded *the locality before the State.* Plymouth, Salem, Charlestown existed before one could speak of a government of Massachusetts; they only became united later and by an act of deliberate will. You can see what strength such a point of departure must have given to the *spirit of locality* which so eminently distinguishes us even among other Americans."[8]

Tocqueville's travel diaries quickly disclosed his enthusiastic reaction to these ideas. "Every individual, private person, society, community, or nation, is the only lawful judge of its own interest, and, provided it does not harm the interests of others, nobody has the right to interfere. I think that one must never lose sight of this point."[9]

"Another principle of American society of which one must never lose sight," he continued the day after talking with Sparks: "every individual being the most competent judge of his own interest, society must not carry its solicitude on his behalf too far, for fear that in the end he might come to count on society, and so a duty might be laid on society which it is incapable of performing. . . . But the useful mean between these theories is hard to grasp. In America free morals (*moeurs*) have made free political institutions; in France it is for free political institutions to mould morals. That is the end towards which we must strive but without forgetting the point of departure."[10]

So Quincy's and Lieber's descriptions of town activities (both official and private), and Gray's rule about local responsibility for local matters, and Sparks's concept of the "spirit of locality" combined to carry Tocqueville to two ideas that would become permanent parts of his views on decentralization. During the next nine years and beyond, he would consistently attribute the success of decentralization in the United States primarily to American *moeurs* and repeatedly prescribe vigorous local institutions for France as an essential way to develop habits favorable to liberty.[11]

These provocative conversations had also encouraged Tocqueville to pursue further the whole troublesome question of centralization. Several persons were now requested to furnish additional details and commentary. On 1 October, Jared Sparks was left with a long list of questions about New England's towns, one of which touched on the relative merits of centralization and local control. Joseph Tuckerman, while discussing the supervision of schools, had reminded Tocqueville only three days before that the lack of any central authority entailed certain inevitable defects.[12] The Frenchman now asked Sparks: "In town affairs have you sometimes felt the need or the utility of a central administration, of what we call centralization? Have you not noticed that this independence of the *parts* injured the cohesion of the nation, hindered the uniformity of the state, and prevented national enterprises? In a word, what is the bad side of your system, for the best systems have one?"[13]

Sparks's journal revealed the specific motives of the visitors.

"[Beaumont and Tocqueville] have been very desirous to get some ideas of the municipal or town governments in New England. . . . The principles are important in regard to any changes that may be contemplated in the municipal establishments of France."[14]

Even more significantly, within two weeks of leaving Boston Tocqueville dispatched letters to his father, to Chabrol, and to Ernest de Blosseville asking each for information and his views on the French system of administration. Tocqueville's objective was to repair gaps in his own knowledge, to compare France and America, and to gain a better understanding of what now became a primary concern: "*ce mot de centralisation*."[15]

It has sometimes been assumed that Tocqueville's intense interest in American administration and its implications concerning centralization arose largely in response to the Boston experience of September and October.[16] His introduction by Quincy, Gray, Sparks, and others to the wonders of town government had clearly stimulated his inquiries to his father, Chabrol, and Blosseville and helped to start him on the road that led by 1835 to an original and fully developed rationale for local liberties. But this interpretation can be overstated. Thoughtful Frenchmen of the times were almost inevitably attracted to the subject. And as early as the beginning of June, some of Tocqueville's letters from America had touched briefly on centralization and disclosed his interest in the topic. An even more complete and surprising demonstration of his pre-Boston commitment to municipal freedom had appeared in a long missive to Louis de Kergolay dated "Yonkers, 29 June 1831." In that letter-essay he had unveiled some early impressions about America and discussed the pervasive trend toward *démocratie*. He had also quite pointedly applied some of his observations to France.

"We are going toward a *démocratie* without limits. I am not saying that this is a good thing, what I see in this country convinces me on the contrary that France will adapt itself poorly; but we are going there [toward *démocratie*] pushed by an irresistible force. . . .

"To refuse to embrace these consequences seems to me a weakness and I am led inevitably to think that the Bourbons, instead of seeking to reinforce openly an aristocratic principle which is dying among us, should have worked with all their power to give interests of order and of stability to the *démocratie*.

"In my opinion the communal and departmental system should

have drawn all their attention from the outset. Instead of living from day to day with the communal institutions of Bonaparte, they should have hastened to modify them, to initiate the inhabitants little by little into their affairs, to interest them there with time; to create local interests and above all to lay the foundation, if possible, of those habits and those legal ideas which are in my opinion the only possible counterweight to *démocratie*."[17]

This passage strongly foreshadows the themes and even the language of the 1835 and 1840 *Democracy*. It demonstrates that at a very early stage in his American journey Tocqueville had already come to see local liberties as an invaluable countermeasure to the dangers of *démocratie*. This program and this hope predated the visit to Massachusetts by three months and apparently arose more out of current French concerns than out of Tocqueville's American experience.

In the autumn of 1831, Tocqueville continued to ruminate upon the lessons of Boston and to weigh the value of local liberties. On 25 October, for example, he observed in his diaries: "When the detractors of popular governments claim that in many points of internal administration, the government of one man is better than the government of all, they are, in my view, incontestably right. It is in fact rare for a strong government not to show more consistency in its undertakings, more perseverance, more sense of the whole, more accuracy in detail, and more discretion even in the choice of men, than the multitude. So a republic is less well administered than an enlightened monarchy; republicans who deny that, miss the point; but if they said that it was there that one must look for the advantages of democracy, they would win back the initiative. The wonderful effect of republican governments (where they can subsist) is not in presenting a picture of *regularity* and *methodical order* in a people's administration, but in the *way of life*. Liberty does not carry out each of its undertakings with the same perfection as an intelligent despotism, but in the long run it produces more than the latter. It does not always and in all circumstances give the peoples a more skillful and faultless government; but it infuses throughout the body social an activity, a force, and an energy which never exist without it, and which bring forth wonders. . . . It is there that one must look for its advantages."[18]

He still could not forget his frustrations as a prison investigator or the warnings of men like Tuckerman; but these administrative defects, though undeniable, had clearly become secondary to the larger benefits of local control, especially the broader social and moral advantages.

These reflections of 25 October also revealed Tocqueville's increasing awareness of the possible economic fruits of decentralization; the lack of central administration apparently helped to stimulate prosperity (at least in America). And on New Year's Day, 1832, he asked Mr. Guillemin, French consul at New Orleans, whether that city owed its prosperity to free institutions. His countryman's response was ambiguous. Guillemin began by insisting "that prosperity is not due to political institutions, but is independent of them," but ended by declaring that: "This government . . . has the merit of being very weak, and of not hampering any freedom. But here and now there is nothing to fear from freedom. That does not apply only to Louisiana but to the whole of the United States."[19]

Three days later Tocqueville wrote: "The greatest merit of the government of the United States is that it is *powerless* and *passive*. In the actual state of things, in order to prosper America has no need of skillful direction, profound designs, or great efforts. But need of liberty and still more liberty. It is to nobody's *interest to abuse it*. What point of comparison is there between such a state of affairs and our own?"[20] And soon he composed the essay entitled "Means of Increasing Public Prosperity" in which he not only highlighted the transportation and communication revolution then taking place in America, but also described the role played in that transformation by decentralization: "The activity of companies, of [towns], and of private people is in a thousand ways in competition with that of the State. . . . Everything adapts itself to the nature of men and places, without any pretension to bend them to the strictness of an inflexible rule. From this variety springs a universal prosperity spread throughout the whole nation and over each of its parts."[21]

Most Americans cherished local control as the bedrock of liberty, and Tocqueville quickly accepted this view. Local self-government seemed an unsurpassed school for politics and for developing an understanding of private and public responsibilities. It helped not only to secure freedom but also to stimulate social energy and to promote prosperity. Tocqueville was now persuaded that such a "spirit of locality" was something for France to emulate. "In America free morals (*moeurs*) have made free political institutions; in France it is for free political institutions to mould morals."[22]

In January 1832, the first lengthy response to Tocqueville's questions of October about the administration in France came into his hands. "I want to thank you my dear father. Your work has been of great use to me for grasping the nuances which can make the administration of this country understandable. The mind, as you know, becomes clear only by comparison. Your memoir has already been for me the basis for a crowd of highly useful questions."[23] But opportunities for fully digesting his father's answer and those from Chabrol and Blosseville would not present themselves until the return to France.

Of the three papers, by far the longest, most thoughtful, and stimulating was that of Alexis's father, the Count Hervé de Tocqueville, who had been a singularly able prefect during the Restoration. His essay, entitled "A Glance at the French Administration," began grandly (and apparently in a tradition common to father and son) by announcing the underlying rule. "The principle in France is that the King is the head of the administration and directs it. . . . The Royalty exercises a general tutelage over all the branches of the administration. It appoints, it directs, it approves, it prevents."[24]

From there, M. le Comte proceeded to survey the various parts of the French administrative machine and then to present his personal evaluations under the telling phrase: "Centralization. Abuses to reform." "We see by what precedes that the various branches of the administration form a chain which ends at a principal link which is the Government, and one cannot fail to recognize the regularity and order which result from this whole. In a Monarchy surrounded by powerful and jealous States, a center of unity is necessary. For centuries our Kings have worked to establish this unity."

The need (recognized by both father and son) for some degree of centralization given the particular geographical situation of France made the Count critical of extreme proposals, such as those made by the legitimist press, for the reestablishment of the old provinces and the creation of provincial assemblies. "It is probable that these assemblies would tend continually to increase their own power and that

France would soon be nothing more than a vast federation, the weakest of governments, in the midst of the compact monarchies which surround her."

So a too thoroughgoing decentralization was dangerous and unacceptable. But the question remained whether the French administration was not perhaps overly centralized, whether "the protective and tutelary power of the Crown has not in certain respects gone beyond the limit of attributions which it must retain for the maintenance of good order and the prosperity of the whole."

The former prefect felt that it had. A primary fault seemed to be that officials appointed by the King were frequently unacquainted with the regions under their jurisdiction and thus all too often misunderstood local interests and problems. Moreover, even the smallest affairs were wastefully, but inexorably, shunted upward to the Ministry of the Interior for decision. "[Centralization] becomes particularly painful to endure when it is exerted on the portion of private interests which are debated and regulated administratively."

Clearly some modification or limited dismantling of the system was needed, but the nobleman remained pessimistic about the possibility of reform. "There exist too many persons for whom centralization is profitable, or who hold a position [in the centralized bureaucracy] that they would seek in vain elsewhere, for these abuses to be uprooted for a long time. These people have established as an article of faith that nothing is done well except by the government itself, and they will defend this dogma with obstinacy."

On several crucial points this essay matched the positions which Tocqueville would later take. First, the Count implied a key distinction between government and administration. And father and son would share, as well, both the view that history had long driven France toward centralization and the conviction that no federal system, however admirable, was suitable for France. The feature of American decentralization which captivated Tocqueville would always be more the vigor of the localities than the prerogatives of the states; he apparently believed that American federalism, despite its originality, was too bound to the peculiar historical and physical situation of the United States to be of much use to France. Father and son would also insist, nonetheless, that France was now overly centralized and that some moderate reform—

probably involving more local responsibility—was essential for the greater good and prosperity of all. Finally, Alexis would agree with his father's pessimistic assessment that, despite arguments for change, government bureaucrats would strive doggedly to preserve their swollen prerogatives.

The papers by Chabrol and Blosseville contained fewer generalizations and judgments. (Blosseville, in particular, offered little more than an unorganized catalogue of details.) But both friends criticized the degree of centralization which existed and voiced support for reform. Chabrol called more specifically for the simplification of bureaucratic procedures and recommended the good example of England. He also illustrated his complaint that red tape often damaged local interests by including an amusing hypothetical example.

"A *commune* wants to make some repairs to its church or its town hall. It cannot do it *de plano*. The request must be made to the sub-prefect, then transmitted by him to the prefect, and then to the Ministry of the Interior with a long report which perhaps required the work of two or three clerks; at the Ministry of the Interior the report is examined, discussed, then finally passed along to a special council called *Conseil des bâtiments civils*. This council deliberates further, gives its opinion, and at last the Ministry orders the repairs, returns [the order] to the prefect who transmits to the sub-prefect who forwards to the Mayor. And during all these delays which are, it would seem, immense, the buildings have delapidated further, the repairs have become more considerable, and finally the funds allowed no longer suffice. Imagine that for everything it is the same thing. Add that the employees of the Interior and of all the Ministries only arrive at their offices at 11 o'clock and leave at 4, that chats and newspaper reading take yet another part of their time; add again that a letter is first written by a *rédacteur*, then copied by an *expéditionnaire*, then submitted to the office manager who corrects it, then to the assistant manager of the division, and finally to the manager of the division who also make their corrections. Imagine all this and the number of clerks in this Ministry will cease to astonish you. You will then understand the long delays that this process causes."[25]

The contrast between this portrait of how town buildings were repaired in France and the descriptions given by Quincy and Lieber of how local projects were undertaken in America could not have been more complete. After reading Chabrol's letter Tocqueville must have marveled even more at the advantages of American local independence and private initiative.

In 1833 a chapter from *Du système pénitentiaire aux Etats-Unis et de son application en France* surveyed some of the difficulties which the authors feared would hinder any effort to apply the American prison system to France. Among hindrances cited was "the too great extent to which the principle of centralization has been carried [among us], forming the basis of our political society." Beaumont, presumably reflecting ideas common to the two companions, argued further:

"There are, no doubt, general interests, for the conservation of which the central power ought to retain all its strength and unity of action.

"Every time that a question arises concerning the defense of the country, its dignity abroad, and its tranquillity within, government ought to give a uniform impulse to all parts of the social body. This is a right which could not be dispensed with, without compromising public safety and national independence.

"But however necessary this central direction respecting all subjects of general interest may be to the strength of a country like ours, it is as contrary, it seems to us, to the development of internal prosperity, if this same centralization is applied to objects of local interest. . . .

"Our departments possess no political individuality; their circumscription has been to this day of a purely administrative character. Accustomed to the yoke of centralization, they have no local life. . . . but it is to be hoped that 'political life' will enter more into the habits of the departments, and that the cares of government will have, more and more, a tendency to become local."[26]

This attempt by Beaumont to draw some logical limit to centralization, this call for greater local responsibility and initiative amounted to another faithful preview of Tocqueville's 1835 *Democracy.*

After helping to complete the *Penitentiary System* but before beginning the composition of his other American book, Tocqueville visited

England for the first time. There he saw for himself the English system of decentralization. On 24 August 1833, John Bowring offered a long explanation of the English approach and possibly also helped to lead Tocqueville toward a distinction which would become crucial in the 1835 *Democracy.*

"Dr. Bowring said to me today . . . 'England is the country of decentralization. *We have got a government, but we have not got a central administration.* Each county, each town, each parish looks after its own interests. . . . I consider that nothing is more difficult than to accustom men to govern themselves. There however is the great problem of your future. Your centralization is a magnificent idea, but it cannot be carried out. It is not in the nature of things that a central government should be able to watch over all the needs of a great nation. Decentralization is the chief cause of the substantial progress we have made in civilization. You will never be able to decentralize. Centralization is too good a bait for the greed of the rulers; even those who once preached decentralization, always abandon their doctrine on coming into power. You can be sure of that.' "[27]

The gentleman thus deepened earlier impressions about both the link between decentralization and prosperity and the unlikelihood that centralization, once done, could ever be undone. He also criticized the failure of France to realize that a system good in the abstract did not necessarily fit the reality of a large and varied country. Finally, Bowring distinguished between government and administration and so probably helped to keep Tocqueville thinking in those terms.

After the discussion, Tocqueville mused: "England illustrates a truth I had often noticed before; that the uniformity of petty legislation instead of being an advantage is almost always a great evil, for there are few countries all of whose parts can put up with legislation which is the same right down to its details. Beneath this apparent diversity which strikes the view of the superficial observer and shocks him so strongly, is to be found real political harmony derived from government appropriate to the needs of each locality.

"But in France this is not appreciated in the least. The French genius demands uniformity even in the smallest details. . . . We should thank heaven for being free, for we have all the passions needed to smooth the path to tyranny."[28]

This was not the first or the last time that Tocqueville speculated about the connection between excessive administrative centralization and despotism.

At home in Paris, Tocqueville plunged into further study of American administrative and governmental structures, taking additional notes from various collections of state laws, Goodwin's *Town Officer*, Sparks's essay on towns, the *Federalist Papers*, and other works.[29] As already noted, he soon resolved to begin with an examination of the New England town, then to turn to the states, and finally to consider the American federal system. A perusal and comparison of the histories, laws, and constitutions of many of the states eventually led to a decision to take five as models or types: Massachusetts, New York, Pennsylvania, Virginia, and Ohio.[30] From a thorough examination of these five, and especially of Massachusetts, Tocqueville attempted to grasp the fundamentals of American administration.

> [1] Put somewhere, either in front or in back, how the administration functions in the United States. This will fit into the great theme of the advantages and the inconveniences of decentralization.
>
> [2] We saw in the United States that no administrative centralization existed. . . . You can even say that decentralization has been brought to a level that no European nation could endure without uneasiness and that produces harmful results even in America.[31]
>
> [3] No hierarchy and no centralization, characteristic of the American administration. So in the town, more powers and more officials than in the *communes* of France, but all independent.
>
> [4] Rights and duties in the town are multiplied in order to attach men by benefits, the way religions do by observances. Town life makes itself felt at every moment. Duty flexible and easy to fulfill; social importance which that *spreads about* (*éparpille*).[32]
>
> [5] Europeans believe that to achieve liberty, power in the hands of those who hold it must be reduced and they end up in disorder. The Americans do not *decrease* power but *divide* it (*important*). Division of administrative power; concentration of legislative power. *American principle* (important).[33]

So in the United States, local governments and officials enjoyed great authority and independence, and everywhere in America administrative authority was distributed among as many hands as possible. The result was not chaos, but a social and political wonder. That such a fragmentation of power worked (without undue costs) testified not only to the unique position of the United States, but also to something in the American spirit. "It is obvious that the political and *administrative* laws of the towns [in America] assume other *moeurs* than our own."[34]

After distilling these and other essential principles, Tocqueville penned a brief three-point outline to guide his thoughts and composition.

1. Difference between centralization of the government and administrative centralization.
2. Difficulty of decentralizing the administration once it is [centralized]. Europe.
3. Advantages of decentralization when it exists.[35]

Expanding on his first point he wrote: "When we speak of centralization we are always fighting in the shadows because of a failure to make the distinction between governmental and administrative centralization."[36]

In another draft, he elaborated: "Governmental centralization and administrative centralization attract one another. But one can consider them as separate however. Indeed they often have been (under Louis XIV for example). What I call governmental centralization is the concentration of great social powers in a single hand or in a single place. The *power* to make the laws and the *force* to compel obedience to them. What I call administrative centralization is the concentration in the same hand or in the same place of a power to regulate the ordinary affairs of the society, to dictate and to direct the everyday details of its existence. . . . The first however is far more necessary to the society than the other. And I can not believe that they are inseparable. That seems to me [to be] the problem of a *strong* government reigning over a *free* people. . . . In the United States, there is a *government*; there is not any administration as we understand it."[37]

How had Tocqueville arrived at this notion of the two centralizations? Both Hervé de Tocqueville and Bowring had distinguished between administration and government. But the peculiarities of American centralization and decentralization also clearly had a part in Tocqueville's musings. It was not that the United States had no government (as he had too hastily declared in some early letters), or that there was simply less centralization in the New World republic than in France. The concentration of powers which existed in America tended to be legislative in nature. The authority which was so relentlessly divided tended to be executive. "Division of administrative power; concentration of legislative power. *American principle* (important)." So Tocqueville was at times inclined to explain the crucial difference not as governmental versus administrative, but as legislative versus executive (or administrative).

When Tocqueville defined administrative and governmental in his 1835 book, he would emphasize not who or what branch held power, but which powers were exercised. If an assembly passed statutes dealing with the everyday details of local affairs, that was administrative centralization, even though legislative in origin. And if an executive (like Louis XIV) determined all issues of general importance but was unable to rule in detail, a high degree of governmental centralization prevailed with relatively little administrative centralization. Apparently, however, his perception of certain unusual American attitudes toward executive and legislative functions had helped to stimulate his theoretical insight about the two different sorts of centralization.

The draft definitions of the two centralizations quoted above also echoed Tocqueville's simultaneous efforts, while considering the future of the Union, to distinguish two types of sovereignty. "Sovereignty is nothing other than the right of free will applied to a society instead of being applied to an individual. A people, like a man, can do *all* to itself. Every time that a people acts, it thus undertakes an act of sovereignty. . . . What one can do is to designate among the habitual actions of the sovereign the most important and the least. The most important acts of the sovereign will are those that directly touch the interests of all the members of the society, such as peace, war, treaties, taxes, civil and political rights, justice. The lesser acts are those that directly touch only a part of the members of the group, such as the direction of provincial and local affairs or finally, in the last instance, individual affairs."[38]

The major acts of sovereignty cited here were apparently nothing more than the powers exercised under governmental centralization, called in his drafts "great social powers" and mentioned in the 1835 text as "Certain interests, such as the enactment of general laws and the nation's relations with foreigners, . . . common to all parts of the nation." And a centralized *administration* might be identified, in turn, by its control over even the lesser acts of sovereignty: "interests of special concern to certain parts of the nation, such, for instance, as local enterprises."[39] So possibly this brief examination of the old puzzle of sovereignty had also helped to lead the author toward his distinction between governmental and administrative centralization.[40]

Some commentators have chided Tocqueville for the ultimately unsatisfactory nature of his concept of two centralizations.[41] But it is instructive to recognize that distinctions between legislative and executive functions and between lesser and greater acts of sovereignty also went into the final definitions of the 1835 text. Tocqueville had wrestled not only with centralization, but also with the equally profound issues of sovereignty and the separation of powers. Any lack of precision in the *Democracy*'s descriptions may thus presumably be laid, in part, to an intellectual boldness which shaded into foolhardiness.

Both the second point in Tocqueville's brief outline and his draft discussion of the two types of centralization repeated an observation made by the Count de Tocqueville and by John Bowring and demonstrated by the history of France as Tocqueville understood it: "prove for Europe that it is always easy to centralize the administration and almost impossible to decentralize it, even though that seems easy."[42]

In a passage stricken from the original working manuscript and therefore unpublished until now, he elaborated:

"Moreover, like nearly all the harmful things of this world, administrative centralization is easily established and once constituted can hardly thereafter be destroyed except with the social body itself.

"When all the governmental strength of a nation is collected at one point, it is always easy enough for an enterprising genius to create administrative centralization. We ourselves saw this phenomenon produced under our very eyes. The Convention had centralized the government to the highest degree. Bonaparte had only to will it in order to centralize the administration. It is true that for centuries in France our habits, our *moeurs*, and our laws have always united simultaneously to favor the establishment of an intelligent and enlightened despotism.

"Once administrative centralization has lasted for a while, the same power that founded it, were it later to want to destroy it, is always incapable of bringing about its ruin.

"As a matter of fact administrative centralization assumes a skillful organization of authority; it forms a complicated machine of which all the gears engage each other and lend each other mutual support.

"When the legislator undertakes to scatter this administrative force that he had concentrated at one point, he does not know where to start or begin because he can not remove a piece of the work without putting the whole thing into disorder. At every moment he notices that it is necessary to change either all or nothing. But what hand, bold enough, would dare to break with a single blow the administrative machine of a great people? To attempt it would be to want to introduce disorder and confusion in the state."[43]

In the margin, Tocqueville debated: "Perhaps delete all that as not related." For whatever reason, the piece would be cut in the later stages of revision.

Tocqueville's designation between 1833 and 1835 of two varieties of centralization helped immensely to clarify his thoughts about the future. He now came to the third point in his outline: "Advantages of [administrative] decentralization when it exists." By 1835 the *Democracy* would propose a bold program of local liberties as part of Tocqueville's hopes for France.[44]

In the small section entitled "The American System of Townships" Tocqueville would rhapsodize "The strength of free peoples resides in the local community. Local institutions are to liberty what primary schools are to science; they put it within the people's reach; they teach people to appreciate its peaceful enjoyment and accustom them to make use of it. Without local institutions a nation may give itself a free government, but it has not got the spirit of liberty. Passing passions, momentary interest, or chance circumstances may give it the external shape of independence, but the despotic tendencies which have been driven into the interior of the body social will sooner or later break out on the surface.[45] . . .

"It often happens in Europe that governments themselves regret the absence of municipal spirit, for everyone agrees that municipal spirit is an important element in order and public tranquillity, but they do not know how to produce it. In making municipalities strong and independent, they fear sharing their social power and exposing the state to risks of anarchy. However, if you take power and independence from a municipality, you may have docile subjects but you will not have citizens."[46]

He would summarize: "For my part, I cannot conceive that a nation can live, much less prosper, without a high degree of centralization of government. But I think that administrative centralization only serves to enervate the peoples that submit to it, because it constantly tends to diminish their civic spirit (*esprit de cité*)."[47]

Administrative centralization, Tocqueville insisted, was pernicious; it opened the doors to tyranny and eventually destroyed both individual and national strength. But local liberties, in contrast, nurtured both "a taste for freedom and the art of being free."[48] It was there that Tocqueville placed his hopes for France.

Still facing Tocqueville as he shaped the first volumes of his book was the difficult problem of the relationship between centralization and *démocratie*. In America he had seen full democracy side by side with extreme administrative decentralization, and one draft fragment seemed to indicate that he would portray centralization and *démocratie* as mutually antagonistic. As he considered the nature of the Union and the forces which bound or splintered federations he stated that two basic principles undergirded American political society: "The first, *Sovereignty of the people*, Democracy, the principle of which divides and dissolves; the second, *Federation*, the principle of which unites and conserves."[49]

This view of *démocratie* as a force for social disintegration and, by implication, for decentralization apparently arose from Tocqueville's understanding of the corrosive rivalry between the American states and the federal government. The pressures and jealousies which had weakened and threatened eventually to destroy the Union were especially potent in the western and southwestern states where excessive democracy flourished.

But such an analysis was short-lived. In another draft Tocqueville declared: "One must not be deceived on this. It is democratic governments which arrive the fastest at administrative centralization while losing their political liberty."[50]

One probable source of this conviction was once again the *Federalist Papers*. While reading Paper Number 51, Tocqueville had apparently been captivated by Madison's exposition of the connection between democracy, centralization, and despotism. "How *démocratie* leads to tyranny and will happen to destroy liberty in America. See the beautiful theory on this point exposed in the *Federalist*. [p.] 225. It is not because powers are not concentrated; it is because they are too much so that the American republics will perish."[51]

The 1835 *Democracy* would read: "I am convinced that no nations are more liable to fall under the yoke of administrative centralization than those with a democratic social condition. . . .

"It is a permanent tendency in such nations to concentrate all governmental power in the hands of the only power which directly represents the people. . . .

"Now, when one sole authority is already armed with all the attributes of government, it is very difficult for it not to try and penetrate into all the details of administration, and in the long run it hardly ever fails to find occasion to do so."[52]

So the drafts and text of the 1835 *Democracy* would clearly argue that democracy and centralization went forward together. Even early versions of the 1835 *Democracy* expressed the conviction that democracy encouraged centralization—both governmental and administrative—and this thesis would run throughout both halves of Tocqueville's masterpiece.[53]

As Frenchmen, Tocqueville and Beaumont came to the New World already concerned about the issue of centralization and therefore strongly predisposed to examine the details of the governmental and administrative structures in the United States. Unlike some other ideas which arose primarily from the stimulus of the American experience, the question of centralization seems to have occupied Tocqueville's thoughts primarily because of preexistent French concerns. France both stimulated his awareness of the disadvantages of excessive centralization and persuaded him of the wisdom of limited reforms which, though utopian to some, seemed moderate enough to Tocqueville. Given the French context, it should also be noted that his praise for local liberties was not in itself remarkable; what made his views new and refreshing to Frenchmen in the 1830s was his bold theory that such decentralization could serve, not as the final refuge of aristocratic privilege, but as a primary means of furthering popular participation and of reconciling advancing equality with social and political stability.[54]

But Tocqueville's fascination with decentralization, his original effort to distinguish two fundamental types of centralized authority, and his continuing examination of the links between *démocratie* and centralization also resulted from the inherently interesting nature of the American experiment. (How strange for a European to behold a large nation apparently running itself.) It was the American journey, and particularly his stay in Boston, that so irrevocably fixed Tocqueville's attention on the benefits—especially political, social, and moral—of local liberty and taught him about the subtle, fragile, and crucial nature of the "spirit of locality." The New World republic introduced him to a novel approach to political authority: "The Americans do not *decrease* power but *divide* it (important). Division of administrative power, concentration of legislative power. *American principle* (important)." And Madison's "beautiful theory" apparently helped him to see the way in which democracy, by encouraging centralization, might lead to despotism. By 1833 or 1834, as he composed the first half of his work, Tocqueville had already captured a sense of one of the most significant tensions of *démocratie*: the very local liberties which could help to avoid democratic flaws were discouraged by democracy's affinity for concentrated power.

CHAPTER 11

Where Would Power Accumulate?

Tocqueville's knowledge of events in France since 1789 made him acutely aware of the variety of tyrannies which men were able to fashion. In January 1832, after observing the well-ordered American republic, he would recall: "What we [in France] have called the republic has never been anything but a monstrosity that one does not know how to classify . . . and what does it matter to me whether tyranny is clothed in a royal mantle or in a Tribune's toga? If I feel its hand heavy on me? When Danton had wretched men, whose only crime was not to think as he did, slaughtered in the prisons, was that liberty? . . . When the majority of the Convention proscribed the minority, . . . when an opinion was a crime, . . . was that liberty? But some one might say, I am looking into the blood-stained annals of the Terror. Let us pass over the time of *necessary* severities, shall I see liberty reign in the time when the Directory destroyed the newspapers . . . ? When Bonaparte as Consul substituted the power, the tyranny of one man for the tyranny of factions? Again was that liberty, was that a republic? No, in France we have seen anarchy and despotism in all its forms, but nothing that looked like a republic."[1]

His catalogue of abuses might easily have included more recent personal observations of the reactionary and oppressive policies of Charles X during the last years of the Restoration and the troubling transformation undergone by the "men of 1830" who had apparently abandoned their liberal principles upon coming to power. His experiences with the mob during the July Revolution had also made a strong impression. In a letter of 1837 to Henry Reeve, he would react with skepticism to accounts of the enthusiasm shown in England for the new Queen, Victoria, and would soberly remind his friend of the totally contrasting emotions of the crowds towards Charles X in 1825 and 1830. "I confess to you that that has given me a natural and lasting coldness for popular demonstrations."[2]

During the early nineteenth century, political theorists like Benjamin Constant, Pierre-Paul Royer-Collard, François Guizot, and others also repeatedly attempted to alert their countrymen to the dangers of arbitrary government whether under the guise of royal prerogative, popular sovereignty, or whatever. One of the common themes of liberals and *doctrinaires* alike was the limitation and balancing of powers so as to avoid any absolute authority.[3]

So Tocqueville arrived in America already mindful of the dangers of consolidated authority and of the oppressive potential of capricious governments of any sort, whether of assemblies, factions, individuals, or the mob. Looking back over forty years, he wondered whether France was destined to endless episodes of social and political upheaval. When and where would the cycle of revolution end? In a letter written from Cincinnati in December 1831, he speculated about this question and for the first time posed a dilemma that would lie at the heart of the making of the *Democracy*. "The clearest fact is that we live in an epoch of transition; but are we going toward liberty? are we heading for despotism? God alone knows exactly what to believe on this point."[4]

One of the curiosities that first struck Tocqueville and Beaumont in the United States—and a feature also related to the theme of centralization—was the peculiar status of American public officials, especially of the chief executives of states and nation. By the first of June, he observed: "They [public officials] are absolutely on the same footing as the rest of the citizens. They are dressed the same, stay at the same inn when away from home, are accessible at every moment, and shake everybody by the hand. They exercise a certain power defined by the law; beyond that they are not at all above the rest."[5]

At first this official humility only reinforced the impression of general social equality which so captivated the two aristocrats. Familiarity between citizen and government officer seemed merely one of the most telling features of America's unique social condition. But during the autumn and winter, Tocqueville began to see another meaning in this low executive profile. American executives often were, in fact, relatively powerless and had little political stature. The governor of New York spent half of each year supervising his farm. The governor of Massachusetts, Jared Sparks told him, "has but little power." And the governor of Ohio apparently also counted "for absolutely nothing."[6]

The only substantial qualification of this opinion came in October when Tocqueville read Isaac Goodwin's *Town Officer* and noticed with surprise the extensive authority of certain local magistrates within their allotted areas of competence. "When the social state allows a people to choose its magistrates, the magistrates so elected can without disadvantage be clothed in a power which no despotic authority would dare to confer on them. So it is that the selectmen in New England have . . . a power of censorship [that] would be found revolting under the most absolute monarchy. People submit to it easily here. When once things are organized on that basis, the lower the qualification to vote and the shorter the time for which a magistrate holds office, by so much greater is the magistrate's power."[7]

But local leaders apparently benefited from this republican trait far more than did the chief officers of states and nation. Even the President apparently shared the weakness characteristic of major executives. Joel Poinsett told Tocqueville in January that "The President in fact has . . . little influence on [the people's] happiness. It is in very truth Congress that rules." The Chief Executive, Tocqueville summarized, was "without power."[8]

As Tocqueville traveled to the West and South he began to learn why major executives had so little authority. In these sections, his acquaintances began more frequently and passionately to mention the various dangers of democratic rule. Talk of "democratic excesses" became increasingly common. Several leading citizens of Ohio complained, for instance, that "we have granted too much to democracy here," or that "our [state] Constitution tends toward too unlimited a democracy."[9] And two gentlemen from Cincinnati were particularly distressed by the legislature's new power to appoint judges.[10] On 3 December 1831, Timothy Walker expanded upon these feelings:

> Our [state] Constitution was drafted at a time when the democratic party represented by Jefferson was triumphing throughout the Union. One cannot fail to recognize the political feelings under the power of which it was drafted.

It is democratic. The government is a very great deal weaker beyond bounds than any other. The Governor counts for absolutely nothing and is paid only 1,200 dollars. The people appoint the Justices of the Peace and control(?) the ordinary judges. The Legislature and the Senate change every year. . . .

At the moment we are making the experiment of a democracy without limits; everything tends that way; but can we make it work? No one can yet assert that.[11]

In January, the lawyer from Montgomery, Alabama, agreed. "The erroneous opinion is spreading daily more and more among us that the people can do anything and is capable of ruling almost directly. From that springs an unbelievable weakening of anything that could look like executive power; it is the outstanding characteristic and the capital defect of our [state] Constitution, and of those of all the new States in the South-West of the Union."[12]

The tendency was apparently to strip the executive of all real power, to undermine the independence of the judiciary by introducing election (either directly by the electorate or indirectly by the legislature), and to submit the legislature to the immediate control of the people through "universal" suffrage, frequent election, and mandates.[13] The result was more and more direct rule by "the people." And the legislature, as the instrument of the will of the majority, increasingly overshadowed the other two branches of government. One of the hallmarks of the American system appeared to be an almost mandatory combination of executive weakness and legislative supremacy. The only exception to this rule seemed to be the troubling arbitrariness of certain local officers.

Tocqueville believed that despotism would result from extreme centralization. But which hands would wield this consolidated authority? Who or what would the probable tyrant be? The drafts of the *Democracy* offered several answers. Tocqueville's knowledge of the Convention, his observations in America, and his readings of the *Federalist Papers* combined to suggest an initial type of democratic despotism: legislative omnipotence.

"*Tyrannie de la démocratie.* Confusion of all powers in the hands of the *assemblies.* Weakness of the executive power for reacting against these assemblies to which it is only an instrument. See the very curious article of the *Federalist* on this subject. p. 213. id. *215*. id. 224. Moreover that is a necessary result of the reign of democracy. There is force only in the people; there can be force only in the constitutional power which represents them.

"In America the executive and judiciary powers depend absolutely on the legislative power. It fixes their salaries in general, modifies their organization, and nothing is provided so that they might resist its encroachments. *Feder*. p. 205 [*sic*: 215?]."[14]

In Number 48 of the *Federalist*, Madison discussed the best means for rendering the three branches of government mutually independent. In his argument he criticized the makers of previous American state constitutions for overlooking the threat of legislative preponderance.

"I shall undertake . . . to show that unless [the legislative, executive, and judiciary] departments be so far connected and blended as to give to each a constitutional control over the others, the degree of separation which the maxim requires, as essential to a free government, can never in practice be duly maintained. . . .

"Will it be sufficient to mark, with precision, the boundaries of these departments in the constitution of the government, and to trust to these parchment barriers against the encroaching spirit of power? This is the security which appears to have been principally relied on by the compilers of most of the American constitutions. But experience assures us that the efficacy of the provision has been greatly overrated; . . . The legislative department is everywhere extending the sphere of its activity and drawing all power into its impetuous vortex.

"The founders of our republics have so much merit for the wisdom which they have displayed that no task can be less pleasing than that of pointing out the errors into which they have fallen. A respect for truth, however, obliges us to remark that they seem never for a moment to have turned their eyes from the danger, to liberty, from the overgrown and all-grasping prerogative of an hereditary magistrate. . . . They seem never to have recollected the danger from legislative usurpations, which, by assembling all power in the same hands, must lead to the same tyranny as is threatened by executive usurpations."[15]

American constitution-makers had apparently been so concerned since the 1770s about avoiding repetitions of what they saw as the executive oppression and corruption of George III and his various agents that they had failed to grant their own executives power enough to withstand the equally dangerous pretensions of assemblies.

To seal his argument, Madison offered the examples of Virginia and Pennsylvania and, for the former, quoted at length from Jefferson's *Notes On the State of Virginia.* While criticizing the constitution of his state Jefferson had observed: "All the powers of government, legislative, executive, and judiciary, result to the legislative body. The concentrating of these in the same hands is precisely the definition of despotic government. It will be no alleviation that these powers will be exercised by a plurality of hands, and not by a single one. One hundred and seventy three despots would surely be as oppressive as one."[16]

In Number 51, Madison returned to the same point and once again joined a statement of the principle of departmental balance with a critique of state constitutions for failing in most cases to provide the necessary safeguards. "But it is not possible to give each department an equal power of self-defense. In republican government, the legislative authority necessarily predominates." (The essay then offered several remedies for this "inconveniency," including bicameralism, the qualified veto, and some specific connection between the executive and the upper house of the legislature.) "If the principles on which these observations are founded be just, . . . and they be applied as a criterion to the several State constitutions, and to the federal Constitution, it will be found that if the latter does not perfectly correspond with them, the former are infinitely less able to bear such a test."[17]

In accord with Madison, Tocqueville's drafts also assumed that power in democratic societies concentrated naturally in the assembly (as the body representing the people) and, recalling the states of the West and Southwest, maintained that the American states had artificially heightened this and other tendencies.[18] His manuscripts also agreed, therefore, that in democracies (and particularly in the individual American states) legislative despotism was a primary threat to liberty. In 1835 all of these ideas would emerge.

"Democracies are naturally inclined to concentrate all the power of society in the hands of the legislative power. That being the authority which springs most directly from the people, it is also that which shares its all-embracing power most.

"Hence one notes its habitual tendency to gather every kind of authority in its hands. . . .

"Two main dangers threaten the existence of democracies:

"Complete subjection of the legislative power to the will of the electoral body.

"Concentration of all the other powers of government in the hands of the legislative power.

"The lawgivers of the states favored the growth of these dangers. The lawgivers of the Union did what they could to render them less formidable."[19]

Elsewhere in the 1835 *Democracy* Tocqueville would observe:

"In America the legislature of each state is faced by no power capable of resisting it. Nothing can check its progress, neither privileges, nor local immunities, nor personal influence, nor even the authority of reason, for it represents the majority, which claims to be the unique organ of reason. So its own will sets the sole limits of its action. . . .

"The republics of the New World are not going to perish, as is often asserted, for lack of centralization; so far from being inadequately centralized, one can assert that the American governments carry it much too far [Cf. the "beautiful theory" of Madison]; . . . The legislative assemblies are constantly absorbing various remnants of governmental powers; they tend to appropriate them all to themselves, as the French Convention did."[20]

Once again Tocqueville's drafts, as we have observed, credited an idea to a specific source which would not be cited in the printed text. Even in the margin of his working manuscript, next to this last sentence about legislative usurpations and the Convention, Tocqueville observed: "Moreover this is a defect inherent in a government of democratic form. See the *Federalist.* page 213."[21] Only the published work would fail to indicate Madison's considerable contribution.

As a final witness to the truth of this analysis, Tocqueville—like Madison—would call upon Jefferson: "The executive, in our government is not the sole, it is scarcely the principal, object of my jealousy. The tyranny of the legislature is the most formidable dread at present and will be for many years. That of the executive will come in its turn, but it will be at a remote period."[22]

As these excerpts indicate, the unlimited power of the "people" underlay any possible legislative tyranny in a democracy. So between

1832 and 1835, as the first two volumes of the *Democracy* took shape, a vision of a second type of democratic despotism emerged: Tocqueville's famous notion of the tyranny of the majority, which we will later take up separately.[23]

A third possible democratic despot in 1835 would be the state. Administrative (or bureaucratic), rather than legislative or popular, consolidation of power would be the means; but tyranny would still be the end.[24] We have seen how, in both America and England, Tocqueville frequently speculated on the possible links between an overly centralized administration and tyranny. Vigorous local institutions, he repeatedly observed, seemed essential to a truly free society. But the concept of local liberties went beyond the mere power of municipalities to manage their own affairs. As the New England town demonstrated, local initiative, by fostering citizen interest in public affairs, also encouraged the birth of all sorts of private associations, organizations highly desirable in democratic nations. An undated draft observed: "Aristocracies are *natural* associations which need neither enlightenment, nor planning to resist the great national association that we call the government. Because of that they are more favorable to liberty than democracy is. Associations can also form in a democracy, but only by means of enlightenment and talents and they are never lasting. In general when an oppressive government has been able to form in a democracy, it encounters only isolated men, not any collective forces. Thus its irresistible strength."[25]

Precisely this stimulus to the individual's public participation and sense of responsibility was the most valuable function of local liberties. "Administrative centralization works toward despotism and destroys *civic virtue*. People get used to living as strangers, as settlers (*colons*) in their own country, to saying: 'That does not concern me. Let the government look after that.' "[26] In these brief remarks, probably dating from 1833, Tocqueville for the first time explicitly wove together three themes that would later become fundamental: centralization, despotism, and *individualisme*.[27]

These remarks also indicated more broadly that what left democratic societies so vulnerable to the usurpations of the state was, in part, the lack of intermediate social and political groupings—such as local governments, associations, families, or classes—which might serve as buffers between the individual and the nation as a whole.[28] Another analysis warned more pointedly that consolidated nations, like France, tended naturally "to concentrate social forces indefinitely until pure administrative despotism is reached."[29]

The 1835 *Democracy* would offer at least one portrait of this centralized and bureaucratic tyranny:

"What good is it to me, after all, if there is an authority always busy to see to the tranquil enjoyment of my pleasures and going ahead to brush all dangers away from my path without giving me even the trouble to think about it, if that authority, which protects me from the smallest thorn on my journey, is also the absolute master of my liberty and of my life? . . .

"There are countries in Europe where the inhabitant feels like some sort of farm laborer (*colon*) indifferent to the fate of the place where he dwells. The greatest changes may take place in his country without his concurrence; he does not even know precisely what has happened; he is in doubt; he has heard tell by chance of what goes on. Worse still, the condition of his village, the policing of his road, and the repair of his church and parsonage do not concern him; he thinks that all those things have nothing to do with him at all, but belong to a powerful stranger called the government."[30]

Elsewhere Tocqueville would add: "One appreciates that centralization of government acquires immense strength when it is combined with administrative centralization. In that way it accustoms men to set aside their own wills constantly and completely, to obey not just once and in one respect, but always in everything. Then they are not only tamed by force, but their habits too are trained; they are isolated and then dropped one by one into the common mass."[31]

These passages would announce the ultimate danger in the democratic tendency toward administrative centralization and would strikingly foreshadow the final section of the 1840 *Democracy*.[32] Democratic nations would slide inexorably toward the concentration of power in the hands of the state. Under centralization, individuals would grow accustomed to obedience. Each person would begin to feel isolated and weak and become lost in the crowd. All authority would accumulate at some center. And liberty would finally succumb to despotism. Yet relatively little other than these few passages in the first two volumes of Tocqueville's book would point to the possibility of administrative or bureaucratic tyranny. This third vision of democratic despotism would not become primary until five more years of reflection had passed.

Still another, a fourth possible embodiment of democratic tyranny was of a more traditional sort: the gathering of all power into the hands of a single despot (*le despotisme d'un seul*). Given increasing equality of conditions, men could either strive to combine equality and liberty or they could accept equality alone and fall under "the yoke of a single man."[33] "How can we believe that the lower classes of society, nearly equal to the others in knowledge, more energetic than they, will put up with remaining excluded from the government? Can that possibly be imagined? Perhaps this will lead to the establishment of tyranny. Why democracy endures a tyrant rather than superiority of ranks and a hierarchy. Equality, dominant passion of democracies. Finish by this piece, men have only one way to be free, but they have two to be equal."[34]

And in 1835 he would declare: "Now, I know of only two ways of making equality prevail in the political sphere; rights must be given either to every citizen or to nobody. So, for a people who have reached the Anglo-Americans' social state, it is hard to see any middle course between the sovereignty of all and the absolute power of one man."[35]

To Tocqueville this danger seemed particularly acute if the potential tyrant was a military hero (*le despotisme d'un seul militaire*). The principal inspiration for this fear was almost certainly Napoleon, but America had clearly reinforced Tocqueville's view. During the American journey, he had heard about Andrew Jackson's incompetence and corruption and read about his demagogic attitudes.[36] But Jared Sparks had told him that, although most informed persons opposed Jackson, "the majority is still at the General's disposal."[37] The riddle of Jackson's attraction had not been solved by a January 1832 meeting in the White House; Tocqueville and Beaumont had left Old Hickory's presence singularly unimpressed. [38]

How then did a man so seemingly undistinguished in character or ability maintain such a hold on the emotions of the American people? Reflecting upon his knowledge of history (especially of Bonaparte's career) Tocqueville thought he saw an answer. "How can one be in doubt about the pernicious influence of military glory in a republic? What determines the people's choice in favor of General Jackson who, as it would seem, is a very mediocre man? What still guarantees him the votes of the people in spite of the opposition of the enlightened classes? The battle of New Orleans."[39]

Here essentially was the glib and one-sided answer which he would confidently offer his readers in 1835. After declaring that military glory was the most terrible scourge for republics, he would observe:

"How can one deny the incredible influence military glory has over a nation's spirit? General Jackson, whom the Americans have for the second time chosen to be at their head, is a man of violent character and middling capacities; nothing in the whole of his career indicated him to have the qualities needed for governing a free people; moreover, a majority of the enlightened classes in the Union have always been against him. Who, then, put him on the President's chair and keeps him there still? It is all due to the memory of a victory he won twenty years ago under the walls of New Orleans. But that New Orleans victory was a very commonplace feat of arms which could attract prolonged attention only in a country where there are no battles; and the nation who thus let itself be carried away by the prestige of glory is, most assuredly, the coldest, most calculating, the least militaristic, and if one may put it so, the most prosaic in all the world."[40]

As if to drive his point home, Tocqueville would add an illustration later deleted from his working manuscript. "During our stay in America a medal was struck in honor of General Jackson which had for its inscription: 'What Caesar did Jackson surpassed.' "[41] This sensitivity to the danger of new Caesars (or Napoleons) would remain with Tocqueville throughout his life, influencing the shape of the *Democracy* and becoming especially acute after the painful experiences of 1848-51.[42]

In 1835 the *Democracy* would especially emphasize this threat of the despotism of a single man.

"If it is true that there will soon be nothing intermediate between the sway of democracy and the yoke of a single man, should we not rather steer toward the former than voluntarily submit to the latter? And if we must finally reach a state of complete equality, is it not better to let ourselves be leveled down by freedom rather than by a despot? . . .

". . . I do think that if we do not succeed in gradually introducing democratic institutions among us, and if we despair of imparting to all citizens those ideas and sentiments which first prepare them for freedom and then allow them to enjoy it, there will be no independence left for anybody, neither for the middle classes nor for the nobility, neither for the poor nor for the rich, but only an equal tyranny for all; and I foresee that if the peaceful dominion of the majority is not established among us in good time, we shall sooner or later fall under the *unlimited* authority of a single man."[43]

Shortly after the publication of the first part of the *Democracy*, Tocqueville, in an effort to clarify his views to Kergolay, would more precisely if less eloquently restate his opinions. Louis had apparently been deeply troubled by what he had understood to be certain implications of Alexis's book. So Tocqueville would explain:

"Conditions once equal, I admit that I no longer see any intermediary between a democratic government . . . and the government of an individual (*d'un seul*) operating without control. I do not doubt for an instant that we will arrive with time at the one or at the other. But, I do not want the second; if an absolute government ever managed to establish itself in a country democratic in its social condition and demoralized like France, we can not imagine what the limits of tyranny would be; we have already seen some fine examples of this regime under Bonaparte and if Louis Phillippe were free, he would make us see many even more perfect ones. There remains then the first. I hardly like that one any better, but I prefer it to the other, moreover if I fail to reach the former, I am certain that I will never escape the other. So between two evils, I choose the lesser. But it is very difficult to establish a democratic government among us? Agreed. Also, I would not attempt it if I had a choice. Is it impossible to succeed at it? I doubt very much that it is impossible, for apart from political reasons which I have not the time to develop, I can not believe that for several centuries God has pushed two or three hundred million men toward equality of conditions in order to bring them in the end to the despotism of Tiberius or Claudius."[44]

So something (someone) like the worst of the Roman emperors, *le despotisme d'un seul*, was the fourth and most frequently mentioned despotism that Tocqueville would foresee in 1835. In these passages, the options were: a democratic government in harmony with the developing equality of conditions (either a monarchy or a republic) or a tyrant. Tocqueville's moral presuppositions encouraged him to hope for the first. For him it was morally inconceivable that the mighty labors of God in the world were directed toward a long night of tyranny.

One basis for Tocqueville's continuing reputation is his perceptive recognition of new developments and his conscientious call for new names and understandings. In his drafts, he now demonstrated these talents while musing about democratic despotism. "Here a portrait of the *new tyranny*, without counterbalance in the institutions, in the *moeurs*."[45] His published text would repeat: "If absolute power were to be established again among the democratic nations of Europe, I have no doubt that it would take a *new form* and display features unknown to our fathers."[46] But, as we have just noticed, when he attempted in 1835 to describe this new despotism, he would search for analogies in ancient history and end by writing of *despotisme d'un seul* and by specifically portraying a military tyrant modeled on the Roman emperors.

"To find anything analogous to what might happen now with us, it is not in our history that we must seek. Perhaps it is better to delve into the memorials of antiquity and carry our minds back to the terrible centuries of Roman tyranny, when mores (*moeurs*) had been corrupted, memories obliterated, customs destroyed; when opinions became changeable and freedom, driven out from the laws, was uncertain where it could find asylum. . . .

"I find those very blind who think to rediscover the monarchy of Henry IV or Louis XIV. For my part, when I consider the state already reached by several European nations and that toward which all are tending, I am led to believe that there will soon be no room except for either democratic freedom or the tyranny of the Caesars."[47]

So, despite Tocqueville's recognition that something very different was possibly at hand, no truly original image of the "new tyranny," of the supposedly novel democratic despotism, would emerge in 1835. Although Tocqueville would present a theory and even a brief portrait of administrative tyranny, he would not identify it in 1835 as the new despotism. Instead, his efforts to describe the possible coming oppression would draw upon examples from the distant past and emphasize the tyrant rather than the all-powerful bureaucracy. The centralized bureaucratic state would have to await its prominent place until the publication of the 1840 *Democracy*.

So at least four major despotisms appeared in Tocqueville's notes, drafts, and manuscripts between 1831 and 1835: legislative omnipotence, tyranny of the majority, administrative (or bureaucratic) despotism, and the rule of a tyrant (especially a military hero). Ambiguities persisted, however. Although in America legislatures by far overshadowed the other two branches, democratic executives (especially on the local level) had amazingly arbitrary authority. And was not legislative power itself merely the shadow of popular rule? Futhermore, how were "direct rule by the people" and "tyranny of the majority" to be distinguished? Did "administrative" and "bureaucratic" mean the same thing? Might not a tyrant (military or civilian) exert his will through the administration (or bureaucracy) rather than through direct, personal rule? And finally, was not a democratic tyrant possible? Despite these issues, Tocqueville had begun to analyze the many possible meanings of "democratic despotism."

Of Tocqueville's several 1835 visions of despotism, legislative tyranny may be said to have turned out to be the least real (for America). Tocqueville understood the presidency well enough to predict accurately the growing stature of the Chief Executive once the United States became entangled in major wars or momentous foreign affairs.[48] But his awareness of the potential power of the president was not enough to overcome his belief reinforced by "Publius"—in the inherent tendency of legislatures to usurp authority. One reason for this was probably his conviction that, in a democracy, it was the legislator who truly represented the people and who therefore wielded the power and spoke with the moral authority of the people. Here his failure to notice one of the major symbolic changes of Jackson's presidency cost him dearly; a recognition of how the President might be seen as the *only* representative of *all* of the people would perhaps have dramatically altered his sense of where the greater danger resided in America. Here again his reliance on the *Federalist Papers*, with their effort to downplay the prerogatives of the President to a populace wary of executive power, probably helped to lead him astray. It also seems likely, in this case, that his knowledge of the French Revolution and especially his sensitivity to the excesses of the Convention influenced his perceptions of the American situation far too much.[49] Moreover, despite his astute analysis of the functions of the American judiciary and of the extraordinary roles in American politics and society played by lawyers, judges, juries, and courts, he apparently could not imagine a judicial branch so independent and powerful that it might, in itself, ever become an effective instrument of oppression. So in his 1835 *Democracy*, Tocqueville ended by projecting an image of a possible legislative despotism in the United States that turned out to be largely illusory.

CHAPTER 12

Administrative Centralization and Some Remedies

We have observed that Tocqueville's 1835 volumes advocated the political, moral, social, and economic benefits of local liberties; lamented democracy's encouragement of centralization; distinguished between two types of centralization, governmental and administrative; and warned that the administrative variety undermined freedom. Between 1835 and 1840 Tocqueville continued to be haunted by "*ce mot de centralisation,*" and the longer he revolved the idea, the more meanings he discovered.

Shortly after the first part of the *Democracy* appeared, Tocqueville journeyed for a second time to England where centralization again became one of the major themes of his travel notes.[1] On 11 May 1835, Henry Reeve confirmed Tocqueville's impression that "a strong tendency to centralization" existed in England. The exchange led Tocqueville to a brief but key summation of ideas. In a few brief sentences he sketched much of the last part of his famous work.

"Centralization, a democratic instinct; instinct of a society which has succeeded in escaping from the individualistic system of the Middle Ages. Preparation for despotism. Why is centralization dear to the habits of democracy? Great question to *delve into* in the third volume of my work, if I can fit it in. A *fundamental* question."[2]

Two weeks later Tocqueville asked another English friend, John Stuart Mill, whether he also believed that England was moving toward centralization, and, if so, whether he was worried by the tendency. Mill admitted the movement, but denied any great concern. "Up to now centralization has been the thing most foreign to the English temperament.

"(1) Our habits or the nature of our temperament do not in the least draw us towards general ideas; . . . So we have divided administrative functions up infinitely and have made them independent of one another. We have not done this deliberately, but from our sheer inability to comprehend general ideas on the subject of government or anything else.

"(2) . . . The taste for making others submit to a way of life which one thinks more useful to them than they do themselves, is not a common taste in England. We are attacking the present parochial and provincial institutions because they serve as tools of the aristocracy. Taking power from our adversaries we naturally hope to vest it in the government, because nothing is prepared within the present institutions for inheriting some of this power. But if democracy was *organized* in our parishes and our counties so that it could take over the tasks of government, I am sure that we would leave them quite independent of the central government. Perhaps we will try to do it too late, and by a compromise the government will be enriched with the chief spoils from the aristocracy."

But Tocqueville did not find Mill's explanation entirely convincing, and he suggested another idea to the Englishman. "Could it not be that what you call the English temperament, is the aristocratic temperament? Would it not be part of the aristocratic temperament to isolate oneself and, as each enjoys a fine estate, to be *more* afraid of being disturbed in one's own domain, *than* wishful to extend it over others? Is not the instinct of democracy exactly the opposite, and may it not be that the present tendency which you consider as an accident, is an almost necessary consequence of the basic cause?"[3]

Both men agreed that there was a trend toward greater centralized supervision of individual and local affairs, but what Mill understood as an historical circumstance, Tocqueville perceived as characteristic of the advance of *démocratie*. Beyond this, their conversation also reminded Tocqueville of a basic structural principle that he had noticed in America nearly four years earlier: the division or fragmentation of administrative power. Mill's remarks reemphasized as well a lesson of special importance for France: the need to *prepare* localities for eventual responsibility.

On three later occasions, Tocqueville filled several pages of his English travel diaries with long and significant reflections on centralization, each of which anticipated sections of the last part of his book.

"*Ideas concerning centralization.* . . . How one should conceive of society's obligations to its members.

"Is society obliged, as we think in France, to guarantee the individual and to create his well-being? Or is not its only duty rather to give the individual easy and sure means to guarantee it for himself and to create his own well-being?

"The first notion; simpler, more general, more *uniform*, more easily grasped by half-enlightened and superficial minds.

"The second; more complicated, not uniform in its application, harder to grasp; but the only one that is true, the only one compatible with the existence of political liberty, the only one that can make citizens or even men.

"Application of this idea to public administration. Centralization, division within the administrative power. That is an aspect of the matter that I do not want to deal with at the moment, but on which what I see in England and have seen in America casts a flood of light and allows one to form general ideas. The English themselves do not realize the excellence of their system. There is a mania for centralization which has got hold of the democratic party. Why? Passions analogous to those of France in '89 and from much the same motives. Ridiculousness of medieval institutions. Hate for the aristocracy which has superstitiously preserved them, and uses them to its profit. Spirit of innovation, revolutionary tendency to see abuses only of the present state; general tendency of democracies.

"Lucky difficulties which obstruct centralization in England; laws, habits, manners, English spirit rebellious against general or uniform ideas, but fond of peculiarities. Stay-at-home tastes introduced into political life. . . .

"Principles of the English[4] in questions of public administration. . . . Division of the local administrative authorities. No hierarchy among them. Continual intervention of the judicial power to make them obey. . . .

"Why the English government is strong although the localities are independent. Special and often hierarchic administration for matters of importance to the whole Empire. . . .

"Application of these ideas to France. That the future of political liberty depends on the solution of the problem. . . . We are working towards the independence of the provinces, or to their complete subordination and the destruction of municipal life. . . .

"Practical discussion on this subject. Gradual introduction of the English and American principle which, in truth, is only the *general principle of free peoples*. Precautions that must be taken to preserve a strong central power. Perhaps that is the only way by which it can continue to be."[5]

Tocqueville touched briefly in these paragraphs on a theme that would become a separate chapter in his work: the fortuitous causes that hinder or hasten centralization in various nations.[6] He also explicitly returned here to his search for first principles of public administration. Throughout the passage—sometimes directly, sometimes only by implication—he compared the English and American systems of decentralization and contrasted the structures of both of these "free peoples" with that of France. "The future of political liberty" at home, he was vividly aware, depended greatly on what the French were willing to learn from the English-speaking nations. This type of three-cornered analysis would be frequently applied to a wide variety of issues in the 1840 *Democracy* and would be another major reason for the "less American" nature of his last two volumes.

Within a week, his thoughts returned to the topic at hand, and his jottings revealed that once again he was wondering where power would accumulate and was connecting the two types of centralization with particular branches of government. "There is a great deal of centralization in England; but of what sort? Legislative and not administrative; governmental rather than administrative; but as with us it sometimes extends down to very small, puerile details. The mania for *regimentation*, which is not a French mania, but one of *men* and of *power*, is found here as elsewhere. But it can only have a single, passing effect, and can only imperfectly achieve its object.

"That is because the *centralizing* power is in the hands of the *legislature*, not of the *executive*.

"*Annoying consequences*: Delays, expenses, impossibility of certain measures, impossibility of inspection.

"*Lucky consequences*: Publicity, respect for rights, obligation to refer to local authorities for the execution of the law; natural tendency to divide administrative authority so as not to create too strong a rival power. Centralization very incomplete since it is carried out by a legislative body; *principles* rather than *facts*; *general* in spite of a wish to be *detailed*.

"*Greatness and strength* of England, which is explained by the power of centralization in certain matters.

"*Prosperity, wealth, liberty* of England, which is explained by its *weakness* in a thousand others.

"Principle of *centralization* and principle of *election of local authorities*: principles in direct opposition . . . the one is essential to the power and existence of the State, the second to its prosperity and liberty. England has found no other secret. The whole future of free institutions in France depends on the application of these same ideas to the genius of our laws."[7]

Though exceedingly compressed, these reflections of 3 July 1835 were fundamental. He repeated his conviction that the "mania for regimentation" was pervasive and returned explicitly once again to the crucial distinction between governmental and administrative centralization (which he significantly linked to the difference between legislative and executive authority). A summary of the benefits and disadvantages of decentralization then followed. And prominent among advantages were the economic ones. Finally, while maintaining that decentralization was essential for "prosperity and liberty," Tocqueville recognized that nations like France and England needed some degree of centralization to preserve "the power and existence of the State." A proper combination of these two principles was the basic problem. France needed to move toward some balance between effective national government and independent local authorities.

In still another passage, Tocqueville mulled over at length the possible influence of free institutions on prosperity. "I think it is above all the spirit and habits of liberty which inspire the spirit and habits of trade. . . .

"To be free one must have the capacity to plan and persevere in a difficult undertaking, and be accustomed to act on one's own; to live in freedom one must grow used to a life full of agitation, change and danger; to keep alert the whole time with a restless eye on everything around; that is the price of freedom. All those qualities are equally needed for success in commerce. . . .

"Looking at the turn given to the human spirit in England by political life; seeing the Englishman, certain of the support of his laws, relying on himself and unaware of any obstacle except the limit of his own powers, acting without constraint; seeing him, inspired by the sense that he can do anything, look restlessly at what now is, always in search of the best, seeing him like that, I am in no hurry to inquire whether nature has scooped out ports for him, and given him coal and iron. The reason for his commercial prosperity is not there at all: it is in himself.

"Do you want to test whether a people is given to industry and commerce? Do not sound its ports, or examine the wood from its forests or the produce of its soil. The spirit of trade will get all those things and, without it, they are useless. Examine whether a people's laws give men the courage to seek prosperity, freedom to follow it up, the sense and habits to find it, and the assurance of reaping the benefit."[8]

The essence of this discussion would eventually be transferred directly to the pages of the 1840 *Democracy*.[9] But we should note two striking portions. In the passage above, Tocqueville eloquently enumerated the requirements of freedom: foresight, perseverance, self-reliance, adaptability, courage, vigilance, and a touch of discontent. He also could not prevent the old question of environment from poking through once again. He asserted yet another time that the moral dimension, the "human spirit," was a more powerful force than physical setting in shaping a society.

The voyage to England in 1835 was an important addition to what Tocqueville had seen and learned in America during 1831 and 1832. On the topic of centralization, much was simply a covering of old ground; but significant details were added by English stimulations to further thought and particularly by a new point of comparison. England served especially as confirmation of certain earlier judgments about the benefits of vigorous localities, the varieties of centralization, the dangers of administrative consolidation of power, and, above all, democracy's "mania for centralization."

The theme of centralization would reappear in many parts of Tocqueville's 1840 volumes. In the second section, "The Influence of Democracy on the Sentiments of the Americans," for example, he would argue at length that local liberties were essential to citizen participation in public affairs and that freedom of association and liberty of the press were important safeguards against administrative centralization.[10]

But Tocqueville's major treatment of centralization in 1840 would come in the final segment of his work: "On the Influence of Democratic Ideas and Feelings on Political Society." According to the author, this last part of his book, which ultimately proved so difficult to write, would be its culmination: both the most eloquent statement of his "doctrine" and the best possible presentation of his recommendations for the future of France.[11] His brother Edouard received an outline of the section in July 1838, just as four months of intensive work got under way.

"I will tell you first of all, to speak to you immediately of my *grande affaire*, that I am back at work and that for the past eight days I am finally busy again; I am resolved not to let go again until these last chapters are finished. I have already sketched the plan; here it is; you will understand me even though I say only a few words because you are abreast of all of my ideas. The *idée-mère* of the first of the two chapters which remain for me to do (for I have felt the necessity to do two) is on "The General Influence of the Democratic Ideas and Sentiments Which the Book Has Just Exposed on the Form of Government." I begin by showing how, *theoretically*, these ideas and sentiments must facilitate the concentration[12] of powers. Then I indicate what special and accidental circumstances can hasten or retard this tendency; which leads me to show that the greater part of these circumstances do not exist in America and exist in Europe. So I get to speaking about Europe and showing by *facts* how all European governments centralize constantly; how the power of the State always grows and that of individuals always diminishes. That leads me to define the type of democratic despotism which could arrive in Europe, and finally to examine in a general way what the tendencies of legislation must be to struggle against this tendency of the social condition. There is the next-to-last chapter, in the middle of which I find myself at this moment. I hope that, like me, you will find something of richness and grandeur there.

"The last chapter which, in my plan, must be very short, will be a *résumé oratoire* of the diverse tendencies of equality, of the necessity of not wanting to compete with this very equality, but of making use of it. This will be something which will tie the end of the book to its introduction. All of that has loftiness; and I get excited looking at it. But the difficulty is immense, and days slip by in a way that makes me despair."[13]

So Tocqueville now planned two chapters: one, a long discussion of centralization and despotism; the other, a brief summation of the entire book.[14] His letter also stated explicitly what his 1840 text would only imply: this final section of his work—perhaps more than any other portion—would speak primarily of Europe, rather than America. The United States, he reiterated, was singularly free from many of the special forces which in Europe tended to hasten the concentration of power and the possible decline into democratic despotism.

A short outline of the proposed major chapter was scribbled into a draft.

General Influence of Democratic Ideas and *Moeurs* on Government

1. How democratic ideas favor the establishment of a centralized government.

2. How [democratic] *moeurs* do [the same].

3. Particular causes, but related to the great cause of democracy, which can lead [to a centralized government].

4. Type of despotism to fear. Here show administrative despotism and the manner in which it could successively take hold of private life. Dangers of this state.

5. Remedies. Here all that I can say about association, aristocratic persons, liberty, great passions.[15]

And a sketch of plans and ideas for the proposed *résumé oratoire* again highlighted his (relative) abandonment of America and revealed the elevated tone which he hoped to achieve as he concluded his work.

"Ideas to see again. . . . Last chapter. General survey of the subject. General estimate of the effects of equality. I can only tackle this summary in an open and noble manner, otherwise it would seem out of place and incomplete. I must appear [as] wanting to compress into a narrow frame the whole picture that I have just painted, [as] brushing aside details by closing my eyes to them, [as] no longer being interested in America which opened the way for me. . . . Begin by recalling the course of the four volumes. . . .

"Finish the book by a grand chapter which attempts to summarize the whole democratic theme and to draw out oratorically the consequences for the world and in particular for Europe and France. Maxims of *conciliation*, of resignation, of union with the course of Providence, of complete impartiality. A movement simple and solemn like the subject. Essential idea. I must attempt to get away from particular points of view in order to take a position, if possible, among the general points of view which depend neither on time nor place. See as much as possible through the thought of God and judge from there."[16]

So Tocqueville's professed strategy, from the "Introduction" of 1835 to the final summary of 1840, was always to remain ostensibly neutral, to avoid becoming a spokesman for any party, and to assume a posture of dignified detachment. He hoped to place himself on the side of what he perceived as providential necessity and to persuade readers of all political descriptions that they too should use their God-given freedom to shape the best possible democratic future.[17]

Another letter, written to Royer-Collard about a month after the one to Edouard, again underscored the importance which Tocqueville attached to this final effort and disclosed some of the problems which he was then encountering. "It is true that I am now at the most difficult and delicate place in the whole work. After having examined throughout the course of the book how the fact of equality influences the opinions and sentiments of men, which is an idea more philosophical than political, I am finally at the point of inquiring how these opinions and sentiments, thus modified, influence the working of society and of government. This chapter [the entire last section of the 1840 *Democracy*] which must terminate the work gives me all sorts of difficulties. One of the greatest is to be concise. I have more things to say than space. I am perpetually stuck between the fear of being too long and that of being too general because of wanting to limit myself. That is the form. The substance gives me plenty of other concerns: I sense that I am treating there the most important idea of our time; its grandeur raises me up, but my own inadequacy weights me down. I catch sight of all that could be said concerning such a subject, and I know that it is not I who will say it."[18]

These remarks to Royer-Collard revealed yet another facet of Tocqueville's own conception of his book. This last segment was meant, in part, to bring both author and reader back to the problems of political reality. While, on the one hand, this section was designed to be lofty and impartial, it was, on the other, equally intended to counteract the unrelentingly philosophical level of the previous parts of the

1840 volumes. Tocqueville wanted finally to put his feet firmly on the ground and to recommend some specific proposals for the reform of French government and society. The letter also exposed an acute anxiety that he might not measure up to his vision of the task at hand. As time passed, as his ideas expanded, and as his hopes for the second half of his book grew, Tocqueville's doubts about his own capacities also multiplied.

As he worked there were some false starts. Tocqueville's penchant for making distinctions, for example, led him to declare in a fragment found in the "Rubish" entitled "That Centralization Is the Greatest Peril Facing the Democratic Nations of Europe": "And I, I say to you: the world is turning toward tyranny. Two tendencies to distinguish: 1. one which tends to concentrate all powers in the state. 2. the other which tends to concentrate the exercise of all powers in the executive."[19] He was presumably attempting here a fuller analysis of administrative centralization. But the distinction between "state" and "executive" concentrations of power apparently struck him as unsatisfactory, for he never elaborated more fully.

The comment remained an important mark of distance traveled, however, for it contrasted sharply with a statement written nearly five years before. "Two main dangers threaten the existence of democracies: Complete subjection of the legislative power to the will of the electoral body. Concentration of all the other powers of government in the hands of the legislative power."[20] Although while writing the 1835 *Democracy* he had at times been especially concerned about popular and legislative concentrations of power, he now worried not about legislative (or even primarily about executive) power, but about the increasing accumulation of authority in the hands of the State (and its bureaucracy).[21] A noteworthy feature of the 1840 volumes would be the near disappearance of any expressed concern about legislative usurpation. The identity of the dreaded center of power had changed drastically.

In the last part of his work Tocqueville would also attempt to identify several significant "particular causes" which hastened centralization in democratic time. One of these would be industrialization.[22] In both America and England Tocqueville had witnessed the beneficial effects of decentralization on the economic life of nations, and in 1840 he would discuss this connection briefly.[23] But in 1837 and 1838, other relationships began to capture his attention. In a passage from one draft, for example, he tentatively explored the complex connection between industry and *démocratie*. Note the changes in emphasis from his earlier discussion, written in England, of the links between liberty and trade.

"I demonstrated in this chapter how democracy was useful to the development of industry. I would have been able to show as well how industry, in turn, hastened the development of democracy. For these two things work together and react upon one another. Democracy gives birth to the taste for material pleasures which push men toward industry and industry creates a multitude of mediocre fortunes and forms in the very heart of aristocratic nations a class apart where ranks are poorly defined and poorly preserved, where people constantly rise and fall, where they do not enjoy leisure, and where instincts are all democratic. (This class long forms in the heart of aristocratic nations a sort of small democracy which has its separate instincts, opinions, and laws.) As a people expands its commerce and its industry, this democratic class becomes more numerous and more influential; little by little its opinions pass into the *moeurs* and its ideas into the laws, until finally having become preponderant and, so to speak, unique, it takes hold of power, directs everything as it likes, and establishes democracy."[24]

In the margin of this paragraph he wondered: "I do not know if I should include this fragment or where I should put it." Ultimately he decided to delete it.

Events in France during 1837 and 1838 also helped to suggest to Tocqueville that industrial development, stimulated by democracy, in turn greatly encouraged not only democracy, but also the rise of the centralized bureaucracy. During these years Frenchmen debated government proposals concerning the regulation of mines and the construction of a railroad system. The drafts of the *Democracy* contained repeated mention of these issues and indicated that the general direction of developments troubled Tocqueville. "M. Thiers told me today (27 May 1837) concerning the commission for the railroad from Lyon to Marseilles that he had finished by persuading *all* the members of this commission that great public works must always be done in France at the expense of the State and by its agents. Do not forget that when I speak of the ultra-centralizing tendency in our time."[25]

The following year Tocqueville stated in another fragment that the discussions concerning mines had suggested several ideas to him, especially that the State would inevitably become the great industrial proprietor, in control of all important enterprises, and so would also eventually become the master and director of the entire society.[26]

On 6 April 1838, he observed to Royer-Collard, again with current government proposals in mind: "In the present century, to deliver to the government the direction of industry is to surrender to it the very heart of the next generations. . . . It is one more great link added to the long chain that already envelops and presses the existence of the individual on all sides."[27]

In the "Rubish" of the chapter concerning centralization as the greatest peril, Tocqueville put his apprehensions even more strongly. "*Equality* is the great fact of our time. Industrial development [is] the second. Both augment the power of the government or rather the two are only one."[28]

And in his working manuscript, at the end of his discussion of the influence of industry on centralization, he wrote: "Perhaps readers will find that I have dwelt too much on this last part. Its importance will be my excuse: the progress of equality and the development of industry are the two great facts of our time. I wanted to show how the one and the other contribute to enlarge the sphere of the central power and each day to restrict individual independence within narrower limits."[29]

So in his drafts and working manuscript Tocqueville for a time boldly ranked the industrial revolution with the advance of *démocratie* (in these places defined as equality) as the two great social developments of modern Western culture. But his 1840 text would back away from that assertion and declare instead: "In the modern nations of Europe there is one great [particular] cause, apart from those already indicated, which constantly aids the growth of government activity and extends its prerogatives, and it is one which has not attracted sufficient attention. I refer to the development of industry, which is favored by the progress of equality. . . . Governments . . . appropriate to themselves and put to their own use the greater part of the new force which industry has created in the world of our time. Industry leads us along, and they lead industry."[30]

Tocqueville's penultimate chapter would also attempt to present his political program for maximizing the benefits of *démocratie* and minimizing its dangers,[31] but not without causing some misgivings about his presumption. The proposed title of this important chapter was simply "Continuation of the Preceding Chapters," and Tocqueville admitted on the title page in his working manuscript: "This title means nothing at all, but all those that I want to put in its place imply too much. The only [illegible word] title would be: 'What must be done to avoid the evils that are indicated in the preceding chapters.' But such a title would announce much more than the chapter can bear. . . . In such cases, it is better to be meaningless than ambitious."[32] Always modest and still afraid that his elephantine labors might produce only a mouse, he hesitated to affirm that he had the needed answers. He consoled himself by observing elsewhere: "Remedies to the perils which I have just indicated. That it is necessary to direct all efforts against centralization. Even if I could not point out remedies, it would be something just to indicate the perils."[33] But one of Tocqueville's major purposes for writing was to relate his reflections and warnings to the future of France. So obviously he could not now refrain from offering some recommendations to his readers.

"Decentralize. Develop this idea practically, demonstrate clearly that I do not want to decentralize beyond a certain limit. . . . that I understand that one proceeds in that direction *slowly*, *prudently*, but *sincerely* and *firmly*. I know of a strong, speedy, agile government in a decentralized country and I understand that it will show these characteristics even more as its wheels become more free of the minute details of administrative centralization.

"Give common interests to men, join them in common affairs, facilitate their association, give a practical and simple character to this development, constantly draw them closer together, elevate their spirits and their hearts as much as possible. Govern them *honestly* and *prudently*. I can imagine making ourselves guardians to the *communes* if we want to emancipate them. That the government, if it wishes, may treat the local powers like *children,* I allow; but not like *fools*. Only fools are kept under supervision throughout their lives."[34]

A sketch on an extra sheet enclosed in the working manuscript put his argument more succinctly:

Begin by a sentence indicating that what is going to follow will be a sort of summary; the moral of what precedes.

Danger of democratic peoples without liberty.

Necessity for liberty greater for these peoples than for all others. Those who desire liberty in democratic times must not be enemies of equality but only seek to make the most of it.

One must resign oneself to having a more centralized government in these times than in others.

Means of preventing excessive centralization. Secondary bodies. Aristocratic persons.

If these means should prove worthless, let us find others, but let us find them in order to save human dignity. Seek such means; direct attention to this aspect. The most general idea of the whole book.[35]

These summaries and outlines reasserted several familiar themes. In 1840 as in 1833, Tocqueville recognized the folly of too radical a reform of the French administrative machine. Nothing that would weaken France in the face of unified and potentially hostile neighbors gained his support. Instead he aimed for limited changes, prudently and gradually achieved. What he proposed specifically was the distribution of more independence and wider responsibilities to the localities and the introduction of greater ease and freedom of association for individuals. Above all he sought to check the tendency toward administrative centralization. If his recommendations smacked of paternalism, of the privileged aristocrat helping out his inferiors, and seemed overly moderate and resigned, Tocqueville was nonetheless still intent on his one fundamental purpose: the preservation of human freedom and dignity.

Tocqueville realized early that the United States benefited from two major levels of political decentralization, the local liberties so lauded by Sparks and others and the unique American system of federalism. But he also recognized from a very early date in his journey that only the first of these types of decentralization could be safely imitated in France. Federalism too closely reflected the American *situation physique* to be a viable remedy for democratic flaws at home. So although one of the unchanging messages of his entire book was a call for administrative decentralization, what he preached more specifically was the need for more vigorous local government.

From another point of view, however, Tocqueville's recommendation for decentralization went far beyond support for active municipal government. "Give common interests to men, join them in common affairs, facilitate their association, . . . constantly draw them closer."[36] In the broadest sense what he urged when he praised decentralization was a pluralistic society. Local liberties were to be supplemented by groups of all sorts. "An association, be it political, industrial, commercial, or even literary or scientific, is an educated and powerful body of citizens which cannot be twisted to any man's will or quietly trodden down, and by defending its private interests against the encroachments of power, it saves the common liberties."[37]

Tocqueville supported any institutions that might become centers for bringing together otherwise isolated individuals and encouraging them to participate in public life. He desired the re-creation of whatever *corps secondaires* and *personnes aristocratiques* might serve as "artificial" substitutes for the "natural" groupings that had once served as buffers between the solitary person and the whole nation. To decentralize, in these terms, meant to disperse power in the society. And Tocqueville was quick to offer more ways to achieve this scattering of authority than merely the empowerment of the localities.

As illustrated by the maturation of his ideas on centralization, much more went into the making of the *Democracy* than the American experiences of 1831 to 1832. French interests, needs, and possibilities helped significantly to shape Tocqueville's attitudes. Long before the journey to the New World, debate over the governmental proposals of 1828 had already alerted him to the value of local initiative.[38] And the observations of his father and others knowledgeable about the administrative situation at home also greatly influenced his evaluation of the prospects for reform and especially his rejection of any plans for extreme decentralization. It was also primarily because of developments in France that he gradually came to recognize that democracy had helped to spawn another fundamental force in the modern world, industrialization, and that the rise of industry, in turn, encouraged some of the harmful effects of democracy. Indeed his insight that democracy (defined as equality) and industrialization were the two major forces at work in the world is another intriguing example of an idea which grew long enough to work its way into Tocqueville's drafts and even his working manuscript, but then (because it would have blurred the focus of his book?) was uprooted and discarded.

The two voyages to England also contributed to the enrichment of his thought by providing important examples and new points of comparison. England in 1833 apparently helped to lead him to the notion of the two centralizations, and in 1835 it almost certainly sharpened his awareness of industry. Across the channel he also found reinforcement for his key idea that democracy bred centralization.

Very early, Tocqueville focused on the twin issues of the advantages of decentralization and the severe disadvantages of administrative centralization, and throughout both parts of his book he continued to explore these two themes. Most important, during the entire period of the writing of the *Democracy*—with only one or two brief hesitations—Tocqueville never swerved from his conviction that one of the greatest dangers of *démocratie* was the trend toward the concentration of power.

CHAPTER 13

Tocqueville's Changing Visions of Democratic Despotism

While shaping the last part of his book, Tocqueville also continued to weigh the chances for despotism and to examine its various forms. Sometime after 1835, he decided to consult some earlier definitions of despotism, and he turned to the famous *Encyclopédie ou dictionnaire raisonné* by Diderot, D'Alembert, and others. He copied the definition which he found there into his drafts, but not without a significant amendment.

" 'Despotism. Tyrannical, arbitrary, and absolute government of a single man.* The principle of despotic states is that a single person . . . governs everything there according to his wishes, having absolutely no other laws than those of his caprices.' *Encyclopédie.*" To this Tocqueville added: "This was written before we saw the despotism of an assembly under the Republic. *It is necessary to add 'of a single power.' "[1]

The excesses of the Convention during the Revolution still so vividly reminded Tocqueville of possible legislative usurpations that he felt obliged to add his qualification to the definition of the *Encyclopédie*. Curiously, however, such an apprehension would rarely appear in the 1840 *Democracy*. His general distrust of assemblies would surface at least once,[2] and on one occasion in his working manuscript, when returning to a specific description of America, he would mention the omnipotence of legislatures there.[3]

But the final text would delete even this reference to legislative power, and the warnings of incipient legislative despotism which had been so strong in 1835 would almost disappear in 1840. Perhaps in

Tocqueville's mind that tyranny was primarily associated with the democratic excesses of the American states.[4] Its relative disappearance may be still another measure of Tocqueville's shift between 1835 and 1840 from America in particular to *démocratie* in general.

The second part of the *Democracy* would discuss the tyranny of the majority, though with an emphasis somewhat different from that of 1835.[5] And Tocqueville's last two volumes would also not neglect the risk of the "tyrannical, arbitrary, and absolute government of a single man." The 1840 text would revive the idea that there were two ways to be equal, in liberty or in servitude; and one possible master would be identified as the despot. "There can even be a sort of equality in the world of politics without any political freedom. A man may be the equal of all his fellows save one, who is the master of all without distinction."[6]

For a time between 1835 and 1838, a particular version of this despot, the military tyrant modeled after Caesar and Napoleon, apparently captured Tocqueville's imagination. He recognized that, in general, war played a significant role in undermining the liberty of nations.

"The first tyrant is about to come; what will he be called? I do not know, but he approaches. What is still lacking for this false image [?] of public order to disappear and for a profound, frightful, and incurable disorder to come into sight? What more is needed for this sublime authority, this visible providence that we have established among us, to trample under foot the most sacred laws, to violate at will our hearts, and to march over our heads? War. Peace has prepared despotism, war will establish it. Not only as a consequence of victory, but war simply by the need for power and concentration that it creates."[7]

He added elsewhere: "In order to make war it is necessary to create a very energetic and almost tyrannical central power; it is necessary to permit it many acts of violence and arbitrariness. The result of war can deliver over to this power the liberty of the nation [which is] always poorly guaranteed in democracies, especially newly born democracies."[8]

But Tocqueville's heightened interest in the possibility of the general turned dictator went beyond these reflections on the wider influence of war. As he wrote, he began to develop a particular image of military despotism. Again, Louis de Kergolay probably served as a source of inspiration.

During the last months of 1836 and the first months of 1837, Louis was in Germany for travel, study, and observation. Alexis, who had advised him about topics worthy of investigation and methods of information gathering, was kept well informed of his progress and reflections.[9] On one occasion Louis wrote:

"I see democracy in the process of advancing not only in France, but also in many other countries. In America you witnessed the spectacle of democracy managing its own affairs or at least having at its head intriguers so dispersed that none were dangerous. But what will we say of democracy if, in Europe, we see it grounding itself in the government of a single person (*d'un seul*) . . . ; but we will then find that men have strangely forgotten all the ideas of personal independence about which they have made so much noise. I tremble to see all of Europe in the near future governed in the name of equality by armies and their leaders (hereditary or not), with this duty to maintain order (*détail de police*) which exists in a regiment, in a classroom, in a prison. After each man, even the least, wanted to be somebody, I picture to myself all turned into small boys that one spanks. Have you noticed how there are demagogues who are very little frightened by this outlook? Many of them are sharp fellows capable of leading their band of disciples to complete equality, of then putting their followers into the hands of whatever government to do with them as it pleases, of getting good positions for themselves, and of saying afterwards to this band: 'My friends, you should be content because you are now all equal; now get yourselves out of this by yourselves; good-by.'

"It makes little difference to me whether I live in a country more or less democratic; but I feel myself a decided enemy, an enemy by nature, taste, and conscience, of a situation such as I have just depicted to you."[10]

Kergolay here described a somewhat different sort of democratic despotism: rule of a nation by the military as though the entire society were a regiment.

In drafts of Part III of the 1840 *Democracy*, almost certainly written after receiving this letter, Tocqueville mused: "To reflect—if instead of the disordered despotism of the *soldatesque*, idea already known, it would not be better to introduce here the portrait of a methodical despotism where everything happens with as much order, detail, and tyranny as in a barracks." And he prophesied reluctantly: "If I were permitted to raise the veil which hides the future from us, I would not dare to do it. I would be afraid to see all of society in the hands of soldiers. A *bureaucratic*, *military* organization, the soldier and the clerk. Symbol of the future society."[11]

He also observed on one occasion: "The new aristocracy of soldiers is the only one which still seems practicable to me."[12] Even as late as July 1838, a brief outline of the last portion of the 1840 work would include the idea of the "Aristocracy of the men of war."[13]

But eventually these visions would be largely shunted into footnotes. Only his general remarks about war opening the door to despotism would survive in the main body of the text.[14] His deepest apprehensions would focus elsewhere. By 1840 a renewed dread of administrative despotism (and the rule of clerks) would largely displace his fear of military tyranny (and the aristocracy of soldiers). Nevertheless, Louis's portrait of military dictatorship would contribute important elements to Tocqueville's developing image of the Leviathan State.

The final part of the *Democracy*[15] would contain the major portion of Tocqueville's 1840 observations on despotism. He apparently accomplished most of the work on this important section between July and October 1838, while living at the château in Normandy.

One somewhat puzzling outline of this last segment, dated 28 July 1838, suggested a focus for the entire section quite different from the emphasis of 1840.

Order of ideas for this chapter[16]

1. Summary of the book.
   That equality of conditions is an irresistible, accomplished fact which will break all those who would like to struggle against it.
   Equality of conditions suggests equally to men the taste of *liberty* and the taste of *equality*. But the one is a *superficial* and *temporary* taste. The other is a *tenacious* and *ardent* passion.
2. That despotism can hope to succeed in becoming established only by respecting equality and by flattering democratic inclinations.

3. What a government which aspires to despotism must set out to do, and the facilities which the ideas, habits, and instincts of Democracy furnish.
   Why democratic peoples are naturally carried to the centralization of power. Theory of centralization presents itself naturally to the mind of men when equality exists. Difficulty of knowing to whom to hand over intermediate powers. Jealousy against neighbors . . . All this augmented by revolutions.
   Democratic taste for material well-being which inclines men to become engrossed in its pursuit or its enjoyment.
   Individualisme which makes each person want to be busied only with himself.
4. Once the government is master of all, only war is needed for it to destroy even the shadow of liberty.
   Facility that [the government] still finds in a democratic social state for that.
   This process, which will establish despotism, will successively overthrow despots; portrait analogous to that of the end of the Roman Empire. Aristocracy of the men of war.
   Having reached this point, we can hope to see the end of a tyrant but not the end of tyranny.[17]

This outline, though incomplete, combined themes from several of Tocqueville's last chapters, but departed substantially from the order in which these ideas would finally appear and concluded by emphasizing a pessimistic vision of social chaos and military despotism. What is most striking about this résumé, however, is the explicit use of despotism as the organizing thread. In 1840 the stated focus of the last section would be the concentration of power; despotism would be the inevitable but (almost) silent companion to the centralized state.

Since at least 1831, Tocqueville had worried that the trend toward equality might end in despotism. But between 1835 and 1840, just as he changed his mind about the center of the consolidated power which democracy entailed, so he now envisioned a different sort of despotism. What he had then briefly described, he now thoroughly developed. "I noticed during my stay in the United States that a democratic state of society similar to that found there could lay itself peculiarly open to the establishment of a despotism. And on my return to Europe I saw how far most of our princes had made use of the ideas, feelings, and needs engendered by such a state of society to enlarge the sphere of their power. I was thus led to think that the nations of Christendom might perhaps in the end fall victims to the same sort of oppression as formerly lay heavy on several of the peoples of antiquity." In 1835 he had specifically cited the tyranny of the Caesars and had prophesied a future of *despotisme d'un seul.* But now he would declare: "More detailed study of the subject and the new ideas which came into my mind during five years of meditation have not lessened my fears but have changed their object."[18]

After describing how democratic ideas and sentiments naturally favored the concentration of power and the establishment of a unified, ubiquitous, and omnipotent government[19] and how various accidental causes exaggerated this tendency in Europe,[20] Tocqueville would observe that this multiplication of governmental prerogatives threatened a totally new type of tyranny. "I think that the type of oppression which threatens democracies is different from anything there has ever been in the world before. Our contemporaries will find no prototype of it in their memories. I have myself vainly searched for a word which will exactly express the whole of the conception I have formed. Such old words as 'despotism' and 'tyranny' do not fit. The thing is new."[21]

What he now foresaw more clearly was the possibility of the dictatorship of the centralized and bureaucratic state. "The social power is constantly increasing its prerogatives; it is becoming more centralized, more enterprising, more absolute, and more widespread. The citizens are perpetually falling under the control of the public administration. They are led insensibly, and perhaps against their will, daily to give up fresh portions of their individual independence to the government, and those same men who from time to time have upset a throne and trampled kings beneath their feet bend without resistance to the slightest wishes of some clerk."[22]

His readers would be offered several elaborate descriptions of this New Despotism, including the following chilling portrait:

"I see an innumerable multitude of men, alike and equal, constantly circling around in pursuit of the petty and banal pleasures with which they glut their souls. Each of them, withdrawn into himself, is almost unaware of the fate of the rest. Mankind, for him, consists in his children and his personal friends. As for the rest of his fellow citizens, they are near enough, but he does not notice them. He touches them but feels nothing. He exists in and for himself, and though he still may have a family, one can at least say that he has not got a fatherland.

"Over this kind of man stands an immense, protective power which is alone responsible for securing their enjoyment and watching over their fate. That power is absolute, thoughtful of detail, orderly, provident, and gentle. It would resemble parental authority if, father-like, it tried to prepare its charges for a man's life, but on the contrary, it only tries to keep them in perpetual childhood. It likes to see the citizens enjoy themselves, provided that they think of nothing but enjoyment. It gladly works for their happiness but wants to be sole agent and judge of it. It provides for their security, foresees and supplies their necessities, facilitates their pleasures, manages their principal concerns, directs their industry, makes rules for their testaments, and divides their inheritances. Why should it not entirely relieve them from the trouble of thinking and all the cares of living?

"Thus it daily makes the exercise of free choice less useful and rarer, restricts the activity of free will within a narrower compass, and little by little robs each citizen of the proper use of his own faculties. Equality has prepared men for all this, predisposing them to endure it and often even regard it as beneficial.

"Having thus taken each citizen in turn in its powerful grasp and shaped men to its will, government then extends its embrace to include the whole of society. It covers the whole of social life with a network of petty, complicated rules that are both minute and uniform, through which even men of the greatest originality and the most vigorous temperament cannot force their heads above the crowd. It does not break men's will, but softens, bends, and guides it; it seldom enjoins, but often inhibits, action; it does not destroy anything, but prevents much being born; it is not at all tyrannical, but it hinders, restrains, enervates, stifles, and stultifies so much that in the end each nation is no more than a flock of timid and hardworking animals with the government as its shepherd."[23]

The omnipresence and apparent gentleness of this new tyranny were two of its most significant features. Unlike despotisms of old, it avoided violence and obvious brutality. But even though mild and benign, it, too, labored incessantly to render entire populations docile; it, too, enervated first individuals and then the entire nation.

Tocqueville described another important characteristic of the possible new despotism on an extra sheet in his working manuscript dated May 1838. "Show clearly that the administrative despotism which I am talking about is independent of representative, liberal, or revolutionary institutions, in a word of political power; whether the political world is led by an absolute king, by one or several assemblies, whether it is contested in the name of liberty or of order, whether it even falls into anarchy, whether it grows weaker and splits apart, the action of the administrative power will be neither less restrained, nor less strong, nor less overwhelming. It is a true distinction. . . . The man or the power [?] which puts the administrative machine in motion can change without the machine changing."[24]

So the dictatorship of the state was different from and immune to most political changes, even seemingly fundamental ones. In the face of political upheavals the public bureaucracy would quietly continue to gather power and subjugate the nation.

By demonstrating that administrative tyranny did not necessarily mean an end to political confusion, Tocqueville hoped to disabuse many of his compatriots of a popular misconception about despotism. "Idea to introduce somewhere in this chapter, because my contemporaries fear disorder much more than servitude and because to get through to them it is necessary to use that fear. I know that the world in our time is full of people who lightly value human dignity and who would willingly buy, with all the liberty of the human species, the right to sell their harvest in peace."[25]

People who would not respond to appeals for freedom had to be persuaded that their bargain for peace would be a bad one; the oppression which they initiated would be no guarantee of the social or political order they desired.

This insight about the peculiarly insulated nature of administrative tyranny also led Tocqueville to chastise his countrymen for their short-sighted concerns. "When, from the point where the natural development of my subject has led me, I notice all that happens in the world, I cannot keep myself from thinking that men are strangely preoccupied there by secondary interests and that they forget the principal need of the times in which they live. As a matter of fact, it is much less the business of our contemporaries to regulate the exterior forms of the society, to found or destroy dynasties, to establish republics or maintain monarchies, than it is to know if each one among them will retain the most precious privileges of their race and if they will fall below the level of humanity."[26]

How far Tocqueville himself had come from his earlier concerns about legislative usurpations or new Caesars! He now saw that the greatest danger in democratic ages came from a much more fundamental trend toward the suffocation of individual liberties by the state, whatever its structural characteristics or its philosophical attachments. "We can quarrel over who will hold the instrument of tyranny, but the instrument remains the same."[27]

This subtle ability of administrative despotism to flourish under many different political structures troubled Tocqueville for still another reason. He saw the grim possibility that such an adaptable tyranny could also clothe itself in the outward forms of liberty and rule in the name of the people.[28] Of particular concern was the attempt by some of his contemporaries to legitimize centralization by appealing to the sovereignty of the people; they risked falling even more quickly into despotism.

"I listen to those among my contemporaries who are the greatest enemies of popular forces and I see that, according to them, the public administration must get involved in almost everything and that it must impose the same rules on all. . . . To direct, to restrain citizens constantly in principal as well as in minor affairs, such is for them its role. I go [?] from there to those who think that all authority must emanate directly from the people and I hear them maintain the same discourse. And I finally return doubting myself whether the exclusive friends of liberty are not more favorable to the centralization of power than its most violent adversaries."[29]

Some men apparently believed that popular control, especially through elections, would sanitize the growing power of the state. So they mistakenly encouraged administrative centralization as democratic forms advanced. Tocqueville realized, however, that such procedures would only legitimize the despotism which he most feared.[30] Even in 1835, remembering the increasing "democratic excesses" of certain American states, he had observed: "There is nothing as irresistible as a tyrannical power commanding in the name of the people, for while being clothed in the moral strength derived from the will of the greatest number, it also acts with the decision, speed, and tenacity of a single man."[31]

On an extra sheet from the working manuscript of the chapter on "What Sort of Despotism Democratic Nations Have to Fear," Tocqueville finally summarized his forebodings about what later came to be called plebiscite democracy. "We tend toward liberty and servitude at the same time. We want to combine them even though they can not be joined. Not being able to be free, we at least want to be oppressed in the name of the people. Perhaps begin all this part of the chapter in this manner, in a harsh and abrupt manner, instead of letting myself run as I do. We rebel at having a class or a man for a guardian, but we are willing for the state to be one. Provided that one has the right to choose his master, that is sufficient."[32]

Tocqueville had also once written in his working manuscript for the 1835 volumes that "one of the greatest miseries of despotism is that it creates in the souls of men who are subjected to it a type of depraved taste for tranquillity and obedience and a sort of contempt of themselves which end by rendering them indifferent to their interests and enemies to their own rights."[33] But now he wondered whether an elective tyranny might not be less degrading, at least in the short run. There the citizenry could at least embrace the myth that it submitted only to itself. In a gloomy moment, he even suggested in a margin of his 1840 working manuscript that such hollow freedom was all that people in democratic times could expect. "I do not know if, considering everything, this isn't still the best . . . that one can reasonably hope from equality and the only type of liberty it is capable of leaving to men."[34] But such deep pessimism would not last.

During times of *démocratie* the road to tyranny seemed alarmingly broad and easy. "As for me," Tocqueville declared, "I see clearly what must be done to subject the world to tyranny in the name of democracy."[35] And the 1840 text would observe: "The chief and, in a sense, the only condition necessary in order to succeed in centralizing the supreme power in a democratic society is to love equality or to make believe that you do so. Thus the art of despotism, one so complicated, has been simplified; one may almost say that it has been reduced to a single principle."[36]

To Tocqueville the successful strategy for any would-be despot or despotism seemed simple: offer equality in return for liberty. As early as January 1837, he wrote: "What it is necessary to do in order to take hold of despotic power among democratic peoples and during the centuries of democratic transitions. Ease of turning democratic passions against their object, of sacrificing liberty to the blind love of equality and to the revolutionary passions that it brings forth."[37] Elsewhere he queried: "What is the danger? To flatter the feelings of hate and democratic envy, and in this way to obtain power. To ladle out equality by the handful; to take liberty in return."[38]

As a countermeasure, Tocqueville recommended an ardent attachment to political liberties. Here was the best hope for escaping the New Despotism. "Political liberty is the greatest remedy for nearly all the evils with which equality menaces man."[39] In various draft fragments he explained his position more fully.

"Equality of conditions, the absence of classes . . . are evils you say. It makes human nature smaller, establishes mediocrity in all things. Perhaps you are right.

"Do you know a way to cure the evil by its opposite, that is by the establishment or even the maintenance of inequality, the permanent classification of men? No, at the very bottom of your heart you do not believe in the possibility of all these things.

"But admitting that equality of conditions is an invincible fact, you contest its consequences in the political world; and you blame liberty and you call despotism to your aid; and you seek to assure present security at the expense of future races. And it is here that you are certainly wrong. For there is only Democracy (by this word I understand self-government)[40] which can lessen and make bearable the inevitable evils of a democratic social state. 5 September 1837. . . .

"How will we be able to understand each other? I seek to live with dignity and honor and you, you seek only to live. What you fear the most from the democratic social condition are the political troubles that it brings forth, and I, that is what I fear the least from it. You dread democratic liberty and I, democratic despotism.

"Many people consider democratic civil laws as an evil and democratic political laws as another and greater evil; as for me, I say that the one is the only remedy that one can apply to the other.

"The whole idea of my politics is here.[41] . . .

"I want to make it understood to all that a democratic social state is an invincible necessity of our times.

"Then, dividing my readers into enemies and friends of democracy, I want to make it understood to the first that in order for a democratic social state to be tolerable, in order for it to produce order, progress, in a word, in order to avoid all, [or] at least the greatest of the evils that they foresee, it is necessary with all one's might to hasten to give *enlightenment* and *liberty* to people who already have such a social state.

"To the second, I want to make it understood that Democracy can not give the happy fruits that they await except by combining it with morality, spirituality, beliefs. . . .

"Thus I try to gather together all honest and generous minds under a small number of common ideas.

"As for the question of knowing if a similar social state is or is not the best that humanity can have, leave that to God. Only God is able to say.[42]

Tocqueville summarized his position in yet another fragment: "Use Democracy to moderate Democracy. It is the only path to salvation that is open to us. To discern the feelings, the ideas, the laws which, without being hostile to the principle of Democracy, without having a natural incompatibility with Democracy, can nonetheless correct its troublesome tendencies and will blend with it while modifying it. Beyond that all is foolish and imprudent."[43]

Thus centralization and despotism were both possible, or as Tocqueville believed at times, even probable results of *démocratie*. And whatever the possible democratic tyranny, Tocqueville saw centralization as the fundamental cause. Accumulated and unchecked power anywhere carried the seeds of oppression.[44]

Different probabilities about the establishment of one or the other of the various types of despotism resulted primarily from the question of who or what would gather power. If the legislature, then legislative despotism; if the people, then tyranny of the majority; if a leader (especially a military one), then *despotisme d'un seul* (*militaire*); if the administration or bureaucracy, then the Leviathan State.

But the chances for each of these despotisms also depended on two other major issues: Did the oppression result from the excesses of popular government, or from an effort, despite advancing equality, to resist political democracy? And probably more important, did the example concern Europe or America?

Tocqueville's notions of despotism, especially in 1835, seemed essentially to be of two sorts. He began by assuming advancing equality of conditions and reasoned that two basic responses were possible. Social equality might be met with political democracy, that is, with some degree of popular participation, or, more broadly still, political liberty. In that case, the primary danger was excessive power delivered in the name of the whole people to the legislature, majority, or administration. And of these possible democratic despotisms, the most fundamental and threatening, because it usually served as the foundation for either legislative or bureaucratic authority, was the tyranny of the majority.

But the second response, instead of self-government, was a retreat to the authority of some leader who would offer himself as a refuge from the confusion of social democracy. Here the danger was the coming of a tyrant in the name of order. Some of the democratic despotisms described by Tocqueville arose from the coupling of political and social democracy, and some from a frantic effort to escape the political consequences of advancing equality.

The other important question about possible tyrannies involved the setting; was the Old or the New World meant? America had a peculiar but strong bias against powerful executives. And, as Tocqueville repeatedly made clear in 1840, the United States was also largely immune to several factors which hastened the coming of the Leviathan. In the New World, therefore, despotisms other than administrative or individual seemed more likely, at least for the near future. Tocqueville believed that the immediate danger in America was rather majoritarian tyranny, particularly as exercised through the state legislatures.

In Europe, however, a different fate threatened. Especially in France, the traditions of administrative centralization and Bonapartism enhanced the probability of other democratic despotisms. So what most frightened Tocqueville when he considered the future of his own country in 1835 was *despotisme d'un seul*, and by 1840 the centralized and bureaucratic state.

The basic trend of Tocqueville's thinking between the early 1830s and 1840 was toward an ever greater focus on administrative despotism. The 1835 text offered a theory and even the beginnings of a portrait of such a tyranny, but the 1840 volumes presented a fully developed vision of the New Despotism of the state. By 1840 Tocqueville's image of the Leviathan, especially for Europe, had eclipsed most of his other notions of democratic despotisms. Just as his attention turned increasingly from the more "American" despotism—majoritarian—to the more "European"—bureaucratic—so too his entire book shifted, between 1835 and 1840, from what was more concretely American to what was more theoretically "democratic."

Two other special changes in emphasis also occurred between 1835 and 1840. The first half of the *Democracy* stressed the despotisms of the society as a whole (the people or the majority) and the more traditional governmental or political despotisms of the assembly or the tyrant. The second part emphasized instead a novel vision of the democratic tyranny of the state. The concept of the Leviathan was not new with Tocqueville, but his idea that *démocratie* especially fostered this particular kind of oppression was much more original.

Moreover, Tocqueville in his 1835 volumes was still seeking to identify the potential agents of despotism in democratic societies. But by 1840 his thinking had pushed far beyond these earlier anxieties. He had now come to believe that the relentless concentration of power in the hands of the public administration was a far more fundamental threat to liberty than any potential usurpation of democratic authority by legislatures, factions, military heroes, or other individuals. By 1840, the threat of the New Despotism had, in some senses, made his concern about most other possible democratic tyrannies somewhat beside the point.

Still another measure of the link in Tocqueville's mind between centralization and despotism in democratic times was the almost identical list of remedies which he offered for both. Although the 1840 volumes presented a somewhat more detailed political program, both halves of the *Democracy* made essentially the same recommendations for combating these twin dangers of democracy. Among the many possible antidotes prescribed in his book, Tocqueville especially urged local liberties, freedom of association, liberty of the press, an independent judiciary, and individual civil and political rights.[45] The ultimate check on any threatened democratic despotism, he still insisted, rested with the opinions and *moeurs* of a people.[46] Once again the crucial nature of *moeurs* in Tocqueville's thinking was underscored.

At times during the making of the *Democracy*, as Tocqueville reflected on the threat of the various democratic despotisms, he was driven almost to the point of despair. Sometimes he "trembled" for liberty;[47] sometimes he gave himself over to the idea that a sort of hollow, symbolic freedom was the best that democratic nations could expect. He reluctantly recognized that in many ways *démocratie* was more compatible with tyranny than with liberty.

But ultimately he backed away from such pessimism. He could not bring himself to believe that the prognosis, even for France, could be so bleak as to make despotism an almost inevitable result of advancing equality. Once again, personal moral presuppositions about human freedom and the benevolence of God led Tocqueville to the side of hope.[48]

One of the abiding attractions of Tocqueville's work is the gallery of despotisms which he presented as the possible results of *démocratie*. Particularly for his contemporaries, one of the more intriguing of his ideas was the assertion that what men had to fear from democracy was not anarchy—the collapse of authority and social and political disintegration—but despotism—the gathering of all power into the hands of some symbol of democracy, whether the majority, the legislature, a leader, or the state itself. For the twentieth century, his fears about bureaucratic regimentation and militarism and his visions of plebiscitarian "democracy" and the Leviathan state have proved only too prophetic. As a draft of his 1840 volumes put the dilemma facing modern man: "Two questions to resolve. Despotism with equality. Liberty with equality. The whole question of the future rests there."[49]

Part V

Democracy, the Individual, and the Masses

CHAPTER 14

The Tyranny of the Majority

As his ongoing analysis of centralization and despotism demonstrates, Tocqueville focused, at times, largely on the saving of political liberty in democratic times. Later his emphasis shifted somewhat, and he concentrated instead on intellectual liberty. These two freedoms are not unrelated; both are connected to what was always central to Tocqueville's understanding of liberty: the dignity and responsibility of the individual. But freedom for the development and expression of new and/or uncommon ideas was increasingly important to Tocqueville. He sought more and more, in the face of democracy's advance, to preserve the individual who dared to think differently. He wanted neither sheep for the bureaucratic shepherd nor identical pieces of a democratic mass.

Between 1831 and 1840 Tocqueville considered at least four major democratic despotisms. One, legislative omnipotence, had a prominent place in 1835, but declined rapidly in importance after that. Another, tyranny *d'un seul*, also had a key part in 1835, enjoyed a second flurry of interest in 1836 and 1837 in the guise of the military dictator, and then went, as well, into eclipse. A third, administrative despotism, made a brief, relatively unheralded appearance in 1835; this modest beginning was followed by a steady increase in importance until, by 1840, Tocqueville's image of the oppressive bureaucratic state dominated the last section of the *Democracy*. The fourth variety played a major role in 1835 and then, in more subtle form, entered almost as significantly into the 1840 volumes. This final vision remains perhaps the best known of Tocqueville's concepts of democratic despotism: the tyranny of the majority.

Among the first entries in Tocqueville's American diaries was a conversation with Albert Gallatin. While discussing the legal profession Gallatin made several points about the political roles of American judges and the influence of public opinion. "The judges . . . are held in very high esteem. Being entirely dependent on public opinion, they need to make continual efforts to keep this esteem. . . . I look on the judges . . . as the regulators of the irregular movements of our democracy, and as those who maintain the equilibrium of the system."[1]

After talking of reasons for bicameralism, John Canfield Spencer of Canandaigua, New York, also focused on the connection between public opinion and American judges, but his comments were somewhat more critical. "They are a little too fond of flattering the people, and . . . they will not fight courageously against a view that they believe is shared by the masses. We have seen some examples of that in cases with a political side to them."[2]

In September, Jared Sparks put the whole matter into a broader context. "The political dogma of the country is that the majority is always right. By and large we are very well satisfied to have adopted it, but one can not deny that experience often gives the lie to the principle. (He quoted several examples of this.) *Sometimes the majority has wished to oppress the minority*."[3] This was the first mention of an idea that would become one of the fundamental themes of the *Democracy.*

The next day, in response to these remarks, Tocqueville fixed a new intellectual guidepost in one of his pocket notebooks. One of "two great social principles which seem to me to rule American society and to which one must always return to find the reason for all the laws and habits which govern it" was that "the majority may be mistaken on some points, but finally it is always right and *there is no moral power above it*. . . . A completely democratic government," he continued, recalling Gallatin, Spencer, Sparks, and others, "is so dangerous an instrument that, *even in America*, men have been obliged to take a host of precautions against the errors and passions of Democracy. The establishment of two chambers, the governor's veto, and above all the establishment of the judges."[4]

Soon, as though to test Sparks's observation, Tocqueville began to record specific instances of the dangers of democracy and of the majority's occasional desire "to oppress the minority."

" 'The people is always right,' that is the dogma of the republic just as, 'the king can do no wrong,' is the religion of monarchic states. It is a great question to decide whether the one is more false than the other: but what is very sure is that neither the one nor the other is true.

"Mr. Washington Smith told me yesterday that almost all the crimes in America were due to the abuse of alcoholic drinks. 'But,' said I, 'why do you not put a duty on brandy?'

" 'Our legislators have often thought about it,' he answered. 'But are afraid of a revolt, and besides the members who voted a law like that would be very sure of not being re-elected, the drinkers being in a majority and temperance unpopular.'

"Yesterday also another Mr. Smith, a very respected Quaker, told me: 'The Negroes have the right to vote at elections, but they cannot go to the Poll without being ill treated.'

" 'And why,' said I, 'is the law not carried out on their behalf?'

"He answered me: 'The laws have no force with us when public opinion does not support them. Now the people is imbued with very strong prejudices against the Negroes, and the magistrates feel that they have not the strength to enforce laws which are favorable to the latter.' "[5]

The Pennsylvanians' examples demonstrated that the majority could oppress not only by pressuring judges or other officials or by legislating unjust measures, but also by refusing either to enact or to enforce laws which countered popular prejudices. Particularly when racial minorities were involved, sovereignty of the people or majority rule sometimes led directly to great injustice.

In 1835 Tocqueville would combine this information with two other examples and conclude: "The people, surrounded by flatterers, find it hard to master themselves. Whenever anyone tries to persuade them to accept a privation or a discomfort, even for an aim that their reason approves, they always begin by refusing. The Americans rightly boast of their obedience to the laws. But one must add that in America legislation is made by the people and for the people. Therefore law in the United States patently favors those who everywhere else have the greatest interest in violating it. It is therefore fair to suppose that an irksome law of which the majority did not see the immediate utility either would not be passed or would not be obeyed."[6]

On 1 November 1831, Tocqueville spoke with Mr. Stewart, "a distinguished Baltimore doctor," and heard that public opinion had even more subtle influences. The physician described the immense power of religion in America and the pressures on men like himself to be known as "believers."

"Does not such a state of affairs," Tocqueville interjected, "make for many hypocrites?"

"Yes, but especially it keeps them from speaking. *Public opinion does with us what the Inquisition could never do.* . . . I have known a lot of young people who . . . thought they had discovered that the Christian religion was not true; carried away by the ardor of youth they have started loudly proclaiming this opinion. . . . What then! Some have been forced to leave the country or to vegetate miserably there. Others, feeling the struggle unequal, have been constrained to an external religious conformity, or have at least kept quiet. The number who have thus been suppressed by public opinion is very considerable. Anti-Christian books are never published here, or at least that is very rare."[7]

Tocqueville realized that what Mr. Stewart described was a different sort of democratic despotism: an almost irresistible pressure on individuals to conform to the ideas of the many. By 1835 this awesome power of public opinion would become the most disturbing and original feature of his portrait of the tyranny of the majority.

Still another episode related to Tocqueville in Baltimore demonstrated how the majority sometimes enforced conformity by violent actions which were, in turn, sanctioned or even encouraged by other popular institutions, such as the militia and jury.

"Mr. Cruse, a very talented man and editor of one of the principal newspapers in Baltimore, told me today: With us there is no power external to the people; whatever it wants, one must submit. The militia itself is the people, and is of no avail when it shares or excuses the passions of the majority. We saw a terrible instance of this twenty years ago. It was the time of the war against England, a war which was very popular in the South. A journalist ventured violently to attack war feeling. The people assembled, broke his presses, and attacked the houses where he and his friends (belonging to the first families of the town) had shut themselves up. An attempt was made to call out the militia; they refused to march against the rioters, and did not answer the call. The municipal authorities could only save the journalist and his friends by sending them to prison. The people did not feel itself satisfied. That night it assembled and marched against the prison. Again one tried to assemble the militia, but without being able to do so. The prison was taken by storm; one of the prisoners was killed on the spot and the rest left for dead; one wanted to make prosecutions, but the juries acquitted the offenders."[8]

This story was a particularly troubling example of the power of the people. How apt some earlier jottings on the jury now seemed. "The jury is the most powerful and the most direct application of the sovereignty of the people. Because the jury is nothing but the people made judge of what is allowed and of what it is forbidden to do against society."[9]

Leading citizens of Ohio repeatedly told Tocqueville in December about alarming democratic excesses in their state. There democracy seemed at flood level, and still rising. "At the moment we are making the experiment of a democracy without limits."[10] The result was mediocre leadership, impulsive legislation, poor administration, and, most alarming, growing judicial dependency.[11]

When Tocqueville asked if it were not dangerous to entrust to the legislature the powers to appoint and to limit the tenure of judges, Salmon P. Chase agreed that it was. "The judges in America are there to hold the balance between all parties, and their function is particularly to oppose the impetuosity and mistakes of democracy. [How closely he echoed Gallatin.] Sprung from it, depending on it for the future, they cannot have that independence."[12]

A first reading of James Kent's *Commentaries* at the end of the month underscored these concerns. The Chancellor particularly stressed the desirability of judicial independence. "It is . . . salutary in protecting the constitution and laws from the encroachments and tyranny of factions."[13]

The legislators, he implied, also needed a certain insulation from the immediate desires of the people. It especially disturbed Tocqueville to learn from Kent that "in several constitutions in the United States, the right of the electors to force their representatives to vote in a certain way has been recognized. The principle is contested by the best minds. If it was generally adopted, it would deal a deadly blow at the representative system, that great discovery of modern times, which seems destined to exercise so great an influence over the fate of humanity. It would then be the people itself that acted, the deputies becoming its mere passive agents."[14] So, in some states, the mandate was a significant additional means to enforce the will of the majority.

Not long afterward, another American reviewed some basic flaws in the government of Alabama and "all the new States in the South-West." "The erroneous opinion," he summarized, "is spreading daily more and more among us . . . that the people can do everything and is capable of ruling almost directly."[15]

Tocqueville's journey in the New World had enabled him to compile a formidable list of ways in which the many in America wielded their extraordinary and apparently growing power. The majority exercised more and more direct control over legislatures, which in turn increasingly dominated the executive and judicial branches. It spoke through juries and acted (or failed to act) through the militia. Sometimes it even coerced minorities by violence or threats of violence.[16] Perhaps most noteworthy was the overwhelming authority which public opinion in America had not only over judges, legislators, and other public officials, but also over minorities and private nonconforming individuals. It was this subtle but irresistible moral pressure which the majority could bring to bear, rather than any political, legal, or even physical coercion, which most troubled the visiting Frenchmen.

By the time Tocqueville finally gathered his materials in Paris and began to write, he had apparently already decided that an analysis of this worrisome trend toward popular omnipotence would be a significant part of his book. In his compilation of sources he used as one organizing theme: "*Sovereignty of the people.* Tyranny of the majority. Democracy, irresistible march of Democracy.— . . . Tyrannical power over speech. Power without counterweight.—Generating principles of American constitutions."[17] Here apparently was Tocqueville's first written use of the phrase which would become so familiar, tyranny of the majority.

As the task of composition proceeded, Tocqueville also continued to develop a catalogue of possible checks on the power of the majority in the United States; "On What Tends to Moderate the Omnipotence of the Majority in America": "In America there are a thousand natural causes which, so to speak, by themselves work together to moderate the omnipotence of the majority. The absence of ranks,[18] the extreme harmony of interests which reigns among all in the United States, the material prosperity of the country, the diffusion of enlightenment (*lumières*), and the mildness of *moeurs,* which is the result of the progress of civilization, greatly favor the mildness of the government. I have already indicated the different causes; the time has come to examine what barriers the institutions themselves have taken care to raise against the power from which they come."[19]

During the journey, Tocqueville had received a strongly negative impression of the authority of American state and national executives. In his drafts he now declared: "In America the executive power is nothing and can do nothing. All of the force of the government is confided to the society itself organized under the most democratic form that has ever existed. In America all danger comes from the people; it is never born outside of them."[20] After further reading and reflection he finally concluded that, as a result of this general executive debility, "The veto of the governor is not a barrier to the democracy; the governor proceeds entirely from it."[21] On this point, at least, Tocqueville had changed his mind, and Jared Sparks had been judged wrong.

The significance which Sparks, the Ohioans, Kent, Story, the writers of the *Federalist*, and others placed on the maintenance of judicial independence and the high opinion that they all had of the American judiciary made it unlikely that Tocqueville would ever similarly deemphasize the "establishment of the judges" as a check on the majority's power.[22] The drafts of the 1835 *Democracy* continued to declare that "the judicial power in the United States is a barrier raised by design against the omnipotence of the majority. We can consider it as the only powerful or real obstacle that American laws have placed before the steps of the people."[23]

In a fragment, Tocqueville presented a thumbnail sketch of the independent judge who, armed with the power to declare laws unconstitutional, worked to maintain the balance of the system and to preserve liberty.

"Influence Exercised by the Judicial Power on the Power of the Majority.

"When political society in the United States is examined, at first glance one notices only a single principle which seems to bind all the parts strongly together: the people appear as the only power. Nothing seems able to oppose their will nor to thwart their plans.

"But there is a man who presents himself as, in some sense, above the people; he does not hold his mandate from them; he has nothing to fear, so to speak, from their anger, nor anything to hope from their favor. However, he is clothed with more power than any of the representatives of the people; for by a single blow, he can strike with sterility the work which issued from the common will."[24]

But would judges in America remain truly independent? From Alexander Hamilton, Tocqueville learned that the judicial branch was by its very nature feeble. "Importance of the judicial power as barrier to Democracy; its weakness. See *Federalist*, p. 332."[25]

In Paper Number 78, Hamilton argued: "The judiciary is beyond comparison the weakest of the three departments of power. . . . from the natural feebleness of the judiciary, it is in continual jeopardy of being overpowered, awed, or influenced by its co-ordinate branches; . . . as nothing can contribute so much to its firmness and independence as permanency in office, this quality may therefore be justly regarded as an indispensable ingredient in its constitution, and, in a great measure, as the citadel of the public justice and the public security."[26]

Yet the Frenchman knew from conversations and other readings that judicial independence was at that very time under attack in America. Justice Story's book, for example, warned him once again of the growing trend to submit judges to popular election.[27] Pushed on the one hand to argue how necessary and potent a barrier the judiciary was to popular passions, and on the other to recognize the inherent weakness of the courts and the growing tendency toward judicial dependence, Tocqueville was caught between contrary lessons. He finally resolved the dilemma by concluding in a draft: "So the high prerogatives granted to American magistrates never place them out of the reach of the majority, and their independence is not such that a single dominating power always exists at the heart of the society to which all must definitively submit. *The judicial power retards the people, it can not stop them.*"[28]

In the New World Tocqueville had also heard repeatedly that

the states were the primary arena for popular excesses. Works by Kent and Story, read or reread in Paris, now repeated this message. He also discovered in the *Federalist Papers* that Madison, on more than one occasion, severely criticized the states for serious flaws in their governments. According to Madison, the proposed Constitution would be a superior frame of government precisely because it guarded against many of the weaknesses inherent in most of the state constitutions: submissive executives, dependent judges, and unchecked legislatures.[29]

When Tocqueville came to consider the threat of tyranny of the majority, he argued in a draft: "So in the democratic republics [of America] the majority forms a genuine power. . . . Yet this power of the majority can be moderated in its exercise by the efforts of the law-maker. The authors of the federal Constitution worked in this sense. They sought to hobble the march of the majority. In the individual states, on the contrary, men strove to render it more rapid and more irresistible."[30]

He wrote even more strongly elsewhere: "*The Union can not present a tyrannical majority*. Each state would be able to do so. . . . Two causes: 1. The division of sovereignty [federalism]; 2. The splitting up of administration [administrative decentralization]." So like other democratic despotisms, tyranny of the majority might be checked, in part, by decentralization. "Since the national majority is thus thwarted in its designs by the majority of the inhabitants of a city or locality, the tyranny which can be very great at several points cannot become general. . . . And since these two majorities may find themselves opposed in their designs, liberty always finds some sanctuary and the despotism which can be exerted irresistibly at several points of the territory, cannot however become general."[31]

The words of the 1835 *Democracy* would not be so absolute, but Tocqueville would remark that "however far the national majority may be carried away by its passions in its ardor for its projects, it cannot make all the citizens everywhere bow to its will in the same way and at the same time."[32]

He would also mention in a footnote: "There is no need to remind the reader that here, and throughout this chapter ["The Omnipotence of the Majority in the United States and Its Effects"], I am speaking not of the federal government but of the governments of each state, where a despotic majority is in control."[33]

On the basis of observations and readings Tocqueville was therefore at times inclined to accept the efficacy of American federalism and administrative decentralization as barriers to the tyranny of the majority on the national level.[34] Apparently the people could not abuse the power of the central government as easily as they sometimes did that of the states. (Decentralization even tended to blunt the possibility of majoritarian despotism on the state level.) So at times, for Tocqueville, the tyranny of the majority—at least in its more concrete political and legal manifestations—was largely a danger within the states.

But by 1835 Tocqueville would make an important distinction which significantly qualified this positive evaluation of decentralization and the federal Constitution as barriers to popular oppression. There were dangers beyond those which threatened in the states. In America the majority actually wielded two different powers: legal and political control ("une immense puissance de fait") and authority over opinion and thought ("une puissance d'opinion presque aussi grande").[35]

The first was exercised largely through the branches of government (particularly through the legislature, the special instrument of majority), the jury system, the *force publique* (militia and police), and other institutions. It was this power which state constitutions had artificially enhanced and which could so easily degenerate into tyranny.

The second and more original portion of Tocqueville's vision of majoritarian despotism resulted from the more subtle influences suggested by the narrative of Mr. Stewart. In 1835 he would observe: "It is when one comes to look into the use made of thought in America that one most clearly sees how far the power of the majority goes beyond all powers known to us in Europe.

"Thought is an invisible power and one almost impossible to lay hands on, which makes sport of all tyrannies. In our day the most absolute sovereigns in Europe cannot prevent certain thoughts hostile to their power from silently circulating in their states and even in their own courts. It is not like that in America; while the majority is in doubt, one talks; but when it has irrevocably pronounced, everyone is silent, and friends and enemies alike seem to make for its bandwagon. . . .

"I know no country in which, generally speaking, there is less independence of mind and true freedom of discussion than in America.[36] . . .

"In America the majority has enclosed thought within a formidable fence. A writer is free inside that area, but woe to the man who goes beyond it. Not that he stands in fear of an *auto-da-fé*, but he must face all kinds of unpleasantness and everyday persecution. . . .

"Formerly tyranny used the clumsy weapons of chains and hangmen; nowadays even despotism, though it seemed to have nothing more to learn, has been perfected by civilization.

"Princes made violence a physical thing, but our contemporary democratic republics have turned it into something as intellectual as the human will it is intended to constrain. . . .

"Absolute monarchies brought despotism into dishonor; we must beware lest democratic republics rehabilitate it, and while they make it more oppressive toward some, they do not rid it of its detestable and degrading character in the eyes of the greatest number."[37]

In his drafts, Tocqueville attempted to explain his conclusions. "That tyranny in America acts directly on the soul and does not torment the body results from two causes: 1. that it [tyranny] is exercised by a *majority* and not by a *man*. A man, never being able to obtain the voluntary support of the mass, can not inflict on his enemy this moral punishment which arises from isolation and public contempt. He is obliged to act directly in order to get at him. 2. that, in effect, *moeurs* have become milder and people have perfected and *intellectualized* despotism."[38]

In some unpublished paragraphs from the working manuscript of his chapter on the press in America, Tocqueville also pointedly declared that, on certain issues, the power of the majority over thought had effectively destroyed freedom of the press and imposed a unique and highly effective type of censorship.

"When liberty of the press, as often happens, combines with the sovereignty of the people, one sometimes sees the majority pronounce clearly in favor of one opinion; then the opposing opinion no longer finds a means of being heard. . . . Certain thoughts seem to disappear all of a sudden from the memory of men. Liberty of the press then exists in name, but in fact censorship reigns and a censorship a thousand times more powerful than that exercised by any power. *Note*:

I do not know a country where on certain questions liberty of the press exists less than in America. There are few despotic countries where the censor does not lean more on the form than on the content of thought. But in America, there are subjects that cannot be touched upon in any way whatsoever."[39]

The majority's almost unlimited power over ideas and opinions thus opened the door to a frightening tyranny of a new and deceptively mild sort. Despite Tocqueville's repeated assurances that majoritarian despotism was primarily something to fear in the states, the implications of his discussion of this other power of the majority made intellectual tyranny a national and present danger. "There is no freedom of the mind (*liberté d'esprit*) in America."[40]

Nearly a half-century later, in *The American Commonwealth* (1888), James Bryce criticized Tocqueville's "tyranny of the majority" on the grounds that the Frenchman's theory exaggerated the dangers of active oppression of a minority by the majority and slighted the real threat: a pressure so subtle that it would paralyze the will of most dissenters and, almost without their being aware, convert them to the majority's opinion. The very desire to be different would be undermined and what Bryce called the "fatalism of the multitude" would result.[41]

But Bryce, it seems, missed the richness of Tocqueville's concept. Tocqueville did indeed worry about specific acts of oppression which a majority might commit against minorities or dissenting individuals. He also recognized, however, the quiet pressure, the benign but inescapable influence, of the moral authority of the many. In 1835 and increasingly afterward, this passive and deceptively mild side of the tyranny of the majority, this weakening of the individual's will to stand apart from the crowd, this extremely subtle restriction on the freedom of thought and opinion were what disturbed Tocqueville most.

Tocqueville believed that in addition to barriers erected by circumstance, national character, or governmental structure, there were also limitations of an ideal or moral nature on majoritarian power. Most of the time, the republicans of the New World seemed to recognize this.

In a draft he wrote: "What one calls the Republic in the United States is the tranquil reign of the majority. The majority, after it has had the time to get to know itself and to verify its existence, is the source of all powers. But the majority itself is not all-powerful; above it in the moral realm is humanity and reason. . . . The majority in its omnipotence recognizes these two barriers and if it has sometimes overturned them, [it is because,] like the men who compose it, the majority has yielded to passions and felt itself carried by them beyond its rights."[42]

The 1835 *Democracy* would declare that the highest limitation on the rule of the majority was justice. "There is one law which has been made, or at least adopted, not by the majority of this or that people, but by the majority of all men. That law is justice.

"Justice therefore forms the boundary to each people's right.

"A nation is like a jury entrusted to represent universal society and to apply the justice which is its law. Should the jury representing society have greater power than that very society whose laws it applies?

"Consequently, when I refuse to obey an unjust law, I by no means deny the majority's right to give orders; I only appeal from the sovereignty of the people to the sovereignty of the human race."[43]

Even if these ideals did not effectively check the pretensions of the many, they at least provided a rationale for questioning the presumed moral authority of any majority—especially an oppressive one. Humanity, reason, and justice were thus for Tocqueville significant moral safeguards for any minority or individual.

Tocqueville now summarized the major obstacles to the tyranny of the majority in America. A brief outline from his working manuscript mentioned:

> Omnipotence of the majority.
> Its tyrannical effects. . . .
> Its counterweight in the *laws*—Judicial power. Lack of administrative centralization.
> In the *moeurs*.
> And in the *local circumstances*.
> *Jury*.[44]

But his 1835 text would finally narrow this list and stress instead the three major *institutional* barriers to the despotism of the many: administrative decentralization, the legal corps (with its *esprit légiste*), and the jury. Most other items on his list would be transferred to the more general discussion of what helped to maintain the democratic republic in America.[45]

In 1835 Tocqueville would begin his textual discussion of the power of the majority with the axiom that democratic government meant rule by the majority. "The very essence of democratic government consists in the absolute sovereignty of the majority (*l'empire de la majorité*)."[46] In America, however, attachment to the idea of the sovereignty of the people had led to the artificial heightening of majority rule in the states; only the framers of the federal Constitution had possessed the wisdom to erect barriers to the majority's will.

According to the first part of the *Democracy* the key to the power of the majority was its moral authority ("l'empire moral de la majorité"),[47] an authority especially strengthened in the United States by the wide acceptance of the doctrine of equality and the prevailing harmony of interests. Americans assumed that the combined intellects and judgments of the many were superior to those of the few and that the interests of the greater number were naturally to be preferred to the interests of the minority. In addition, the New World republic was not divided into great irreconcilable interest groups. So the privileges and rights of the present majority were recognized without serious quarrel.

Tocqueville would describe several familiar but important results that followed from this overwhelming power. The legislature, as the voice of the majority, became the dominant branch of government and, at the same time, closely mirrored the changing desires of the many. Projects were launched with zeal and energy when the people were stirred, but languished when popular interest waned, as often quickly happened. There was, in short, a chronic instability in the laws and administration wherever the majority reigned so unhampered. Furthermore, since American officials were armed with the moral authority of the majority which had placed them in office, they often enjoyed shockingly arbitrary powers within their own restricted spheres of responsibility.

The omnipotence of the majority, Tocqueville would observe, even more profoundly influenced the American national character. The many had constantly to be flattered and reinforced in its assumption of superiority. The demagogue, the man of little principle, the crowdpraiser, was the more politically viable figure in America; consequently, a low standard of leadership prevailed. Since the majority resisted criticism of its attitudes and actions from either its own leaders or the members of minorities, a currying of favor pervaded the society. Few were willing to speak out; a smug conformity reigned.

So unlimited was the power of the majority in the United States that tyranny threatened; the 1835 text would argue that the strength of the many became "not only predominant but irresistible."[48] "Omnipotence in itself seems a bad and dangerous thing. . . . So when I see the right and capacity to do all given to any authority whatsoever, whether it be called people or king, democracy or aristocracy, and whether the scene of action is a monarchy or a republic, I say: the germ of tyranny is there, and I will go look for other laws under which to live."[49]

The American states, Tocqueville would insist, provided almost no real guarantees against the abuse by the many of its authority and the oppression of an individual or a minority. "When a man or a party suffers an injustice in the United States, to whom can he turn? To public opinion? That is what forms the majority. To the legislative body? It represents the majority and obeys it blindly. To the executive power? It is appointed by the majority and serves as its passive instrument. To the police (*la force publique*)? They are nothing but the majority under arms. A jury? The jury is the majority vested with the right to pronounce judgment; even the judges in certain states are elected by the majority. So, however iniquitous or unreasonable the measure which hurts you, you must submit."[50]

He would carefully add, however, that the majority in America did not yet habitually abuse its strength. "I am not asserting that at the present time in America there are frequent acts of tyranny. I do say that one can find no guarantee against it."[51] The omnipotence of the majority did not necessarily mean the tyranny of the majority. The common and despotic misuse of power was still primarily a potentiality and something to fear in America's future. Tocqueville left unresolved the contradiction between this conclusion and his insistence that intellectual liberty did not exist in America.

Between 1835 and 1840, as work on the final volumes of his book went forward, Tocqueville worried increasingly about the fragility of intellectual freedom in democratic times. His attention began to focus more and more on what he had called in the first half of his book the *puissance d'opinion* or the power which the majority in America had over thought, rather than on the majority's legal and political control (*puissance de fait*). The last part of the *Democracy* would therefore reflect a growing sensitivity to the overwhelming intellectual authority of the crowd, and other facets of his theory of the omnipotence and possible tyranny of the majority would largely recede from view.

By 1840 the dangerous power of the majority over ideas and opinions would also be closely linked with the larger relationship between the individual and the mass in democratic societies. What he had previously almost always described as the omnipotence (*l'omnipotence*) or authority of the majority (*l'empire de la majorité*) or of the greatest number (*le plus grand nombre*), or the power of public opinion (*opinion publique*), he would now frequently call the influence of the crowd, the mass, or the public (*la foule, la masse, le public*).[52] Among the many significant consequences of the isolation and weakness of the individual which Tocqueville would emphasize in 1840, for example, would be the tendency of the solitary person to defer *intellectually* to the views of his fellows. "As equality spreads and men individually become less strong, they ever increasingly let themselves glide with the stream of the crowd and find it hard to maintain alone an opinion abandoned by the rest."[53]

In the chapter entitled "Concerning the Principal Source of Beliefs among Democratic Peoples," he would identify the influence of the many as a major cause "which must in the long run hold the independence of individual thought within fixed, indeed sometimes narrow, bounds."[54]

"The nearer men are to a common level of uniformity, the less are they inclined to believe blindly in any man or any class. But they are readier to trust the mass, and public opinion becomes more and more mistress of the world.

"Not only is public opinion the only guide left to aid private judgment, but its power is infinitely greater in democracies than elsewhere. . . .

"The citizen of a democracy comparing himself with the others feels proud of his equality with each. But when he compares himself with all his fellows and measures himself against this vast entity, he is overwhelmed by a sense of his insignificance and weakness. . . .

"So in democracies public opinion has a strange power of which aristocratic nations can form no conception. It uses no persuasion to forward its beliefs, but by some mighty pressure of the mind of all upon the intelligence of each it imposes its ideas and makes them penetrate men's very souls."[55]

Tocqueville would then proceed to revive the distinction which he had originally made in 1835. He would distinguish between the *omnipotence politique de la majorité* (augmented by various laws) and the *empire . . . sur l'intelligence* and then argue that, although in the United States the former enhanced the strength and danger of the latter, the intellectual authority of the majority did not necessarily need the support of excessively democratic institutions. Basic democratic social conditions, rather than particular political forms, were the most fundamental causes of the dominance which the mass exercised over thought and opinion.[56]

Tocqueville would conclude his chapter with a description of the possible tyranny of the majority which would almost exclusively stress the intellectual, rather than any legal or political, consequences of such despotism. "Thus it might happen that, having broken down all the bonds which classes or men formerly imposed on it, the human mind (*esprit*) might bind itself in tight fetters to the general will of the greatest number.

"If democratic peoples substituted the absolute power of a majority for all the various powers that used excessively to impede or hold back the upsurge of individual thought, the evil itself would only have changed its form. Men would by no means have found the way to live in independence; they would only have succeeded in the difficult task of giving slavery a new face. There is matter for deep reflection there. I cannot say this too often for all those who see freedom of the mind as something sacred and who hate not only despots but also despotism. For myself, if I feel the hand of power heavy on my brow, I am little concerned to know who it is that oppresses me; I am no better inclined to pass my head under the yoke because a million men hold it for me."[57]

These and other ideas also appeared in an earlier draft of the second chapter of the 1840 *Democracy*.[58] Previously unpublished, the manuscript, entitled "Concerning the Particular Causes Which Might

Be Harmful in America to the Free Development and to the Generalization of Thought," was a substantially different version that more emphatically stressed the ominous power of the majority over thought. It also revealed more of Tocqueville's personal reactions to and remedies for this democratic threat to intellectual freedom.

He began in the margin with an outline of the particular causes which worked against theoretical and innovative thinking in America.

"Religion (I have already discussed it).

"Examine the equality of conditions. Maintained by the material condition of the country.

"Despotism of the majority.

"Exclusively commercial and industrial character of the country. People direct their efforts only toward certain things.

"No memory of another social and political state.

"Origin of the middle classes.

"I demonstrated in the preceding chapter how dogmatic and traditional opinions maintained in religious matters restricted the innovating mind of the Americans on several sides, so to speak. There is another cause, less powerful, but more general, which threatens to stop and which already slows the free development of thought in the United States. This cause, which I have already indicated in another part of this work, is nothing other than the . . .[59] power exercised by the majority in America.

"A religion is also a power; but its movements are set in advance and move in a known sphere; and many persons believe that in this sphere its effects are beneficial, and that a dogmatic religion goes further toward obtaining the desired results than one which is rational.

"The majority is a . . . [60] power which, in a way, goes at random and can successively extend to all things.

"Religion is the law; the omnipotence of the majority is arbitrary.

"Religion inclines the human mind to stop by itself and to offer obedience, the free choice of a moral and independent being.

"The majority compels the human mind to stop, despite what it may want, and by constantly forcing it to obey, ends by taking away even the desire to be free, to act for itself.

"In the United States, the pernicious influence exercised on thought by the omnipotence of the majority is noticeable above all in political life. It is principally in governmental matters, on political questions that the majority's opinion has been formed up to now; but American laws are such that, whatever direction it decides to take, the majority will make its omnipotence equally felt.

"So its limits are in its own will and not in the constitution of the country. One cannot conceal the fact that the Americans have let themselves be carried in the direction common to democratic peoples. In democracies, whatever one thinks, the majority and the power that represents it are always provided with a rough strength. And even if the laws in the smallest degree favor rather than combat this tendency, it is nearly impossible to say where the limits of tyranny will be.

"It could happen that in democracies people would escape from the domination of class, family, or national attitudes in order to submit to those of the majority. One cannot hide the fact that this is the natural tendency in democracies. It must be combated, not only by those who do not want political tyranny, but also by those who desire the general freedom of the human mind.[61] . . .

"Among aristocratic peoples the interests of class forbid men to see anything other than what exists under their eyes and prevent them from noticing new roads which could lead to truth. It is probable that, once submitted to the omnipotence of the majority, men would not even seek to discover these new paths or would not follow them after they were found.[62]

"The prejudices of all types which are born and maintained in the heart of an aristocracy limit the human mind in certain ways and prevent it from developing along these lines; but it does not attack intellectual freedom in principle and in an absolute manner. In democracies constituted in the way that I mentioned above, the majority in a way oversees the human mind; it compresses its whole scope in a permanent and general manner; and to bend men to its will, it ends by taking away from each of them the habit and the taste of thinking for himself. . . .

. . . I expect people to serve the cause of democracy, but I want them to do so as moral and independent beings who, while pledging their support, retain the use of their liberty; that people see in the majority the most tolerable of all powers, I understand; but I would like them to be its counselors and not its courtiers. . . .

"I say that among democratic peoples, I clearly notice two contrary tendencies. One carries men toward new and general thoughts. The other could reduce them, so to speak, to not thinking at all.[63]

"So if I found myself suddenly charged with giving laws to a democratic people, I would seek clearly to distinguish these two tendencies and to make it so that they did not cancel one another out, or at least that the second did not become preponderant. In this design, I would try not to destroy the authority (*l'empire*) of the majority, but to moderate its use. And I would do my utmost to assure that after it had overthrown all rival powers, it would limit itself.

"This is why—to furnish not a complete picture, but an example—if I lived among a democratic people, I would prefer to see them adopt a monarchical constitution rather than a republican form. I would like it better if they instituted two legislative assemblies rather than one, an immovable judiciary rather than elected judges, provincial powers rather than a centralized administration. For all of these institutions can be combined with democracy without altering its essence.[64]

"As the social state became more democratic, I would put more of a price on obtaining all or some of these things. And while proceeding thus, I would have in view not only saving political liberty, as I have said in another part of this work, but also protecting the general progress of the human mind. If you should say that such maxims are not popular, I will try to console myself with the hope that they are true."[65]

This draft chapter explained how natural groupings in aristocratic society tended to restrain freedom of thought and how *démocratie* both liberated men from these older limitations and carried the potential for new and more fearful restrictions. It also briefly contrasted the different ways in which religion and a democratic majority encircled intellectual exploration and development; and it implied that Tocqueville could much more easily concede some benefit to religious limitations on free inquiry.

What was newer about this earlier deleted variation, however, was his statement that, so far, American conformity of opinion was greatest in basic governmental and political attitudes. This explicit observation occurred solely in this draft. Also noteworthy was the program of remedies that concluded the chapter. Once again, as he did in other drafts and would in both 1835 and 1840, Tocqueville stressed decentralization and an independent judiciary. But here he also declared his preference for a democratic monarchy rather than a democratic republic. This idea too would never appear in the text of his *Democracy*.

Finally and most important, this variant clearly demonstrated that Tocqueville feared not only the silencing of individual and minority ideas and the resulting conformity of opinion; he also dreaded the further possibility that in democratic times new ideas might be denied a hearing and that the advance of civilization might therefore come to a halt. By 1840, these intellectual dangers had apparently become, for Tocqueville, the primary meaning of tyranny of the majority and a major focus of personal anxiety.[66]

CHAPTER 15

The Tyranny of the Majority: Some Paradoxes

From James Madison, among others, Tocqueville had learned about the nature and inherent structural weaknesses of the Union, the tendency of legislatures to accumulate power, and the danger to liberty which came from excessive centralization. Madison had also helped to teach the Frenchman how the states (because of federalism) and the counties and municipalities (because of the division of administrative authority) served both to help maintain a large republic and to lessen the potentially despotic pressure of public opinion. But, as we have seen, the republican statesman had not been able to persuade Tocqueville that size itself was an advantage to free societies. The *Democracy* persisted in praising small rather than large nations as the natural sanctuaries of liberty. And in his analysis of the causes and cures of the tyranny of the majority Tocqueville continued to place great hopes in independent and responsible localities as essential centers of freedom during democratic times.

These beliefs led him into a few strange paradoxes, not the least of which was his ranking of the jury as one of the great barriers to majoritarian despotism.[1] In 1835 he praised the jury for teaching respect for law, awareness of rights, and a sense of civic responsibility, and for forming the judgment and augmenting the practical knowledge of the people.[2] Yet on more than one occasion he had been told that the jury sometimes served as a legal stamp of approval for local excesses and prejudices rather than as a check upon them. "The jury," he had once declared, "is nothing but the people made judge of what is allowed and of what it is forbidden to do against society."[3]

Mr. Cruse had recounted for him the story of a jury during the War of 1812 which had acquitted members of a mob which had pursued and beaten an antiwar journalist and his friends. The crowd had even murdered one opponent of the war.[4] In January 1832, Tocqueville had heard another example as well from the lawyer who had discussed Alabama's reputation for violence and the frequent resorts to knife or gun to settle quarrels there. "But," Tocqueville had asked, "when a man is killed like that, is his assassin not punished?" "He is always brought to trial, and *always acquitted by the jury,* unless there are greatly aggravating circumstances. . . . The violence has become accepted. Each juror feels that he might, on leaving the court, find himself in the same position as the accused, and he acquits. . . . So it is the people that judges itself, and its prejudices in this matter stand in the way of its good sense." After hearing this surprising commentary, Tocqueville could not refrain from asking his acquaintance what he thought of the jury system in general. "One of the disadvantages of our juries," the American replied, "is that they are drawn from too small areas (the counties). The jurors know about the matter before it is argued. It is judged before it is heard and judged in a tavern."[5]

So both Mr. Cruse and the lawyer from Alabama had hinted that juries had a critical failing: they would not convict a man for actions —however heinous—which a local majority applauded. The lawyer claimed, moreover, that too often jurors merely reflected regional prejudices and legitimized verdicts previously reached in neighborhood taphouses.

A third incident, fictional but perhaps suggested by something which Gustave and Alexis had witnessed while attending a trial in America,[6] was dramatically described in *Marie; Or, Slavery in the United States*, Beaumont's companion piece to the 1835 *Democracy.*

"One day in New York," Gustave's hero, Ludovic, related, "I attended a session in court. Among those awaiting trial sat a young mulatto accused by an American of acts of violence. 'A white man beaten by a colored man! What an outrage! What viciousness!' voices cried out everywhere. The public, the jurors themselves were indignant at the accused man, without knowing whether he was guilty. I do not know how to tell you how distressing was my impression as he came to trial—each time the poor mulatto wished to speak, his voice was drowned out, either by the judge or by the noise of the crowd. All the witnesses damned him. . . . The friends of the plaintiff had good memories; those to whom the defendant appealed remembered nothing. He was found guilty without any deliberation on the part of the jury. A quiver of joy went through the crowd: a murmur a thousand times more cruel to the heart of the unhappy man than the judge's sentence; for the judge was paid for his task, while the hate of the people was gratuitous. Perhaps he was guilty; but, innocent, would he not have suffered the same fate?"[7]

Beaumont's tale echoed the remarks of the two American critics and again exposed a basic flaw in the jury system. That institution could be no more dispassionate, no more just, no more impartial than the public which supplied the jurors. For better or for worse, it was simply a mirror of public opinion and, as such, a potential instrument of tyranny.

So Tocqueville's extremely positive attitude toward the jury was somewhat puzzling. Although he once observed that the jury was merely "the majority vested with the right to pronounce judgment,"[8] he largely failed in his book to recognize or to warn his readers that the jury could also be one of the more fearful tools of an oppressive majority. The 1835 *Democracy* presented instead an essentially one-sided view of the jury as a major check on majoritarian despotism.

But Tocqueville's evaluation of the jury—an eminently local institution—was only part of a greater paradox: his stress on the value of the "spirit of locality." On the one hand, a major antidote that Tocqueville recommended for majoritarian tyranny was administrative decentralization. On the other hand, he seemed to recognize on several occasions that tyranny of the majority was more likely and, if it occurred, more virulent within localities. On one occasion, for instance, he wrote in a draft that the ardor of local passions once kindled could only be compared to intense fraternal hatreds.[9] And all of his specific examples of tyranny of the majority took place in the towns and cities of America. It was there that dissenting individuals or minorities found themselves most at the mercy of popular institutions such as the police or the jury, most vulnerable to mob violence, and most exposed to the other more subtle pressures and intimidations of local majorities.

Several times the 1835 *Democracy* seemed to indicate Tocqueville's awareness of this melancholy truth. At the beginning of his book he described with some amazement the moral and religious regulations of the Puritans of Massachusetts and Connecticut and could only partially excuse their "bizarre or tyrannical laws" by noting that in those early New England communities of the "like-minded" such measures were voted by the people themselves.[10]

While comparing large and small nations, he again carefully exposed the potential dangers of the city-state. "In small nations the watchfulness of society penetrates everywhere. . . . When tyranny is established in a small nation, it is more galling than elsewhere because, operating within a comparatively restricted sphere, it affects everything within that sphere. Unable to engage in any great design, it turns to a multitude of little ones; it is both violent and petty. From the political world which is properly its domain, it penetrates into private life. After actions, it aspires to regiment tastes; after the state, it wants to rule families."[11] What better possible portrait of the public interest in private attitudes and behavior, of the pettiness, and of the pressurized conformity which often prevailed in the small town or locality?

Finally, Tocqueville's concern about the arbitrary power of public officials in America also reflected, in part, his recognition of the possibility of local oppression.[12] After studying the *Town Officer* he had written to Jared Sparks in December 1831, asking incredulously if the selectmen still had the right to denounce immoral persons publicly and if the constables and tythingmen also still possessed the power to search out and act against blasphemers and others who failed to respect the Sabbath. Tocqueville could not quite believe that local elected officials might actually have such authority to meddle and to censor. In reply Sparks tried to assuage the Frenchman's sense of shock by assuring him that specific actions were taken only rarely and in particularly flagrant cases. But he did reiterate and reaffirm the basic proposition which had apparently so troubled Tocqueville: local officials did indeed still have the duty to "watch over the morals . . . of the inhabitants."[13]

Thus the very local control which he applauded as an alternative to administrative centralization and as a major barrier to the tyranny of the majority also facilitated the oppression of individuals and minorities by local majorities. Tocqueville had now come upon a fundamental democratic paradox. Vigorous local government, he insisted, was a necessary counterweight to the democratic trend toward centralization. But it was the local majority that was potentially most oppressive. The locality was, after all, the very heart of the majority's physical, moral, and psychological power. The normal homogeneity and lack of privacy which marked the town made being different there much more difficult and dangerous. And the more independent the locality, the fewer were the possible restraints on the will of the local majority. A flourishing "spirit of locality" meant that one path to democratic despotism—via administrative centralization—was blocked, but another—via tyranny of the local majority—was opened wide. Yet Tocqueville never saw this basic dilemma about local freedom which he himself had posed.[14]

We can suggest a few possible reasons for Tocqueville's effusive praise for local self-government and his failure adequately to acknowledge the enhanced likelihood, given decentralization, for tyranny on the local level. Probably one of the most important explanations was that, while in America, he had obviously been more impressed by the benefits of town government than by its disadvantages. Theoretically, a town of enlightened and politically experienced citizens, such as those in New England, significantly diminished the probability of abuses by a local majority.

But Tocqueville might also have deliberately refrained from any serious critique of local control because of his larger commitment to a program of administrative decentralization in France. He was almost certainly aware that the ignorance and deeply rooted prejudices of the inhabitants of the *communes* were major arguments cited by the proponents of centralization in response to reformers like Tocqueville who suggested a partial dismantling of the French administrative machine. Why needlessly strengthen the position of your opponents?

It is also possible that his high opinion of local self-government reflected his own good experiences in the department of La Manche. In his first campaign in the region he had been greeted by cries of "No more nobles!" The spirit of 1789 had seemed very much alive. But within little over one year, Tocqueville had been heard, accepted, and elected; and until Louis Napoleon's *coup d'état* the citizens of La Manche would continue to send him to Paris as their representative. So the people in localities could apparently be "educated," "elevated," and "molded." Perhaps the standards of the New England town were not so impossible after all.[15]

Another peculiar feature of Tocqueville's discussion of majoritarian tyranny was the way in which he thought of the majority. Tocqueville apparently understood *majorité* primarily as an abstract, singular, and essentially fixed entity. In his mind, the majority usually involved not tangible and temporary interests, but basic attitudes of social consensus or public opinion. For Tocqueville, the majority in its most essential guise was a commanding moral authority.[16]

Such a view was in sharp contrast to the concept—first explored by Madison—of majorities as shifting coalitions of interests temporarily formed over particular public issues. In Madison's scheme, majorities were fluid and pluralistic. Since a member of a majority on one day might easily find himself in the minority on the next, no one's long-term interests and security would be furthered by the majority's abuse of power. Enduring (and potentially despotic) majorities would not form except on principles general or innocuous enough to threaten no minority group.[17]

During 1841, in letters written in criticism of the *Democracy*, Jared Sparks twice isolated the distinctive features of Tocqueville's analysis and raised what became common objections. A first epistle declared that "in what he says of the tyranny of the majority, I think he is entirely mistaken. . . . M. de Tocqueville's theory can only be true where the majority is an unchangeable body, and where it acts exclusively on the minority, as distinct from itself." A few months later a second letter added: "I think too much confidence is placed in M. de Tocqueville's ideas of the 'tyranny of the majority.' On this subject his imagination leads him far astray. In practice we perceive no such consequence as he supposes. If the majority were large and always consisted of the same individuals, such a thing might be possible; but with us, as in all free governments, . . . a man who is in the majority at one time is likely to find himself in the minority a few months afterwards. What inducement has a majority thus constituted to be oppressive? Moreover, M. de Tocqueville often confounds the majority with public opinion."[18]

If Tocqueville's theory of the tyranny of the majority is one of his most famous ideas, it is also one of his most disputed. Others since Sparks have also insisted that Tocqueville's concept of the majority was too abstract and too rigid, and that his theory was therefore inappropriate to the American political system of compromise, shifting coalitions, and countervailing powers. Some have also objected that his "majority" is really "public opinion" which rules all societies, democratic or otherwise. One commentator has even argued that Tocqueville's "majority" simply does not exist and that his fear of majoritarian despotism is pure fantasy.[19]

But in at least one critical instance, Tocqueville's analysis brilliantly described American reality. In various states of the Union, Tocqueville had noticed the second-class status of free Negroes. Particularly in states where slavery had been abolished, prejudice and injustice severely burdened the Negro population.[20] In Massachusetts, for example, "the prejudice is so strong against them that their children cannot be received in the schools."[21] And the white majority in Maryland, Tocqueville had learned, sharply restricted the political rights of free Negroes and created special codes of law to supervise their behavior. Mr. Latrobe of Baltimore had even confessed that he was "very much afraid that the incoming Legislature may pass unjust and oppressive laws against the Blacks. People want to make it intolerable for them to remain in Maryland."[22]

In Ohio, too, Mr. Walker had admitted, "We try and discourage [free Negroes] in every possible way. Not only have we made laws allowing them to be expelled at will, but we hamper them in a thousand ways. A Negro has no political rights; he cannot be a juror; he cannot give evidence against a white. That last law sometimes leads to revolting injustices."[23] Apparently the white majority in many states exercised (and therefore abused) its power in order to give legitimacy to its prejudices.

The 1835 *Democracy* summarized these injustices and concluded:

"Race prejudice seems stronger in those states that have abolished slavery than in those where it still exists, and nowhere is it more intolerant than in those states where slavery was never known.

"It is true that in the North of the Union the law allows legal marriage between Negroes and whites, but public opinion would regard a white man married to a Negro woman as disgraced, and it would be very difficult to quote an example of such an event.

"In almost all the states where slavery has been abolished the Negroes have been given electoral rights, but they would come forward to vote at the risk of their lives. When oppressed, they can bring an action at law, but they will find only white men among their judges.

It is true that the laws make them eligible as jurors, but prejudice wards them off. The Negro's son is excluded from the school to which the European's child goes. In the theaters he cannot for good money buy the right to sit by his former master's side; in the hospitals he lies apart. He is allowed to worship the same God as the white man but must not pray at the same altars. He has his own clergy and churches. The gates of heaven are not closed against him, but his inequality stops only just short of the boundaries of the other world. When the Negro is no more, his bones are cast aside, and some difference in condition is found even in the equality of death.

"So the Negro is free, but he cannot share the rights, pleasures, labors, griefs, or even the tomb of him whose equal he has been declared; there is nowhere where he can meet him, neither in life nor in death."[24]

Even more instructive about the abuses which the permanent nature of the white majority in America invited was a passage from *Marie*.

"In a society where everyone suffers equal misery, a general feeling grows up which leads to revolt, and sometimes liberty emerges from excessive oppression.

"But in a country where only a fraction of society is oppressed, while the rest is quite comfortable, the majority manages to live at ease at the expense of the smaller number; everything is in order and well-regulated: well-being on the one hand, abject suffering on the other. The unfortunate may complain, but they are not feared, and the disease, however revolting it may be, is not cured because it only grows deeper without spreading.

"The misery of the black people oppressed in American society cannot be compared with that of any of the unfortunate classes among other peoples. Everywhere there exists hostility between the rich and the proletariat; however, the two classes are not separated by any insurmountable barrier: the poor become rich, the rich, poor; that is enough to temper the oppression of the one by the other. But when the American crushes the black population with such contempt, he knows that he need never fear to experience the fate reserved for the Negro."[25]

In a society where all instruments of power—public opinion, legislature, executive, police and militia, jury, even judges in some states

—responded to the pressures of an absolute majority, what recourse remained for the oppressed minority? Tocqueville rejected the common opinion that democracies would perish through weakness and disorder, and with Madison argued instead that the real danger was the misuse of concentrated power. While musing on the issue of the omnipotence of the majority, he wrote in a draft:

"Like all other authorities (*empires*), the moral sway (*l'empire moral*) of the majority is lost by abuse. Tyranny of the majority brings appeals by the minorities to physical force. From there, confusion, anarchy, and the despotism of an individual (*d'un seul*). The American republics, far from raising the fear of anarchy at the present time, raise only the fear of despotism of the majority; anarchy will come only as a consequence of this tyranny. . . .

"In America the sway (*empire*) of the majority will not be overthrown because it lacks force, but wisdom. The government is centralized in such a way that the majority which governs is all-powerful. It will lack not physical force, but moral force."[26]

His 1835 work prophesied: "I do not think a lack of strength or resources is part of the nature of democratic authority; on the contrary, I believe that it is almost always the abuse of that strength and the ill use of those resources which bring it down. . . . If ever freedom is lost in America, that will be due to the omnipotence of the majority driving the minorities to desperation and forcing them to appeal to physical force. We may then see anarchy, but it will come as the result of despotism."[27]

Five years later, Tocqueville's message was even clearer and more specific. "If ever America undergoes great revolutions, they will be brought about by the presence of the black race on the soil of the United States; that is to say, they will owe their origin, not to the equality, but to the inequality of condition."[28]

Yet in his chapters on the power of the majority Tocqueville did not draw special attention to racial divisions in America. He did not even seem to recognize the Negro/White situation as a particularly pertinent example of the tyranny of the majority. Instead, he repeatedly insisted that the United States was uniquely fortunate in not having severe conflicts of interests, or bitter, unyielding divisions within the society.[29] Why?

He may once again have shied away from an elaborate application of his ideas to the racial issue in America because of an unwillingness to tread upon Beaumont's territory. Considering both the focus of Gustave's work and Alexis's obvious awareness of the plight of the Negro minority in America that explanation is at least a possibility.

But, as some readers have suggested, a more likely reason was that Tocqueville's thoughts during the making of most of the *Democracy* were primarily focused on white Americans and even more narrowly on what he frequently called the Anglo-Americans. Was he thinking mostly about white majorities and white minorities while he pondered the danger of majoritarian despotism? If so, the restricted scope of his reflections cost him one of the best possible illustrations of his concept. The racial situation in America might easily have been a model for the type of majority/minority relationship which Tocqueville envisioned when he discussed the omnipotence and possible tyranny of the majority.

In any case, Tocqueville had here put his finger on yet another of the dilemmas of democracy. Given a government that truly reflected the will of the people, how were individuals or minorities to be protected from measures or institutions that made popular errors and prejudices legitimate? When the people ruled what would prevent them from enacting their own worst impulses? Were not the new laws against free Negroes in Jacksonian America a superb example of this danger?

We should also recall that while Tocqueville mused about the "majority" and the possible consequences of its power in America, his attention was drawn increasingly to what he saw as the most disturbing feature of any despotism of the many: the deceptively mild, but highly effective repression of uncommon or original ideas. One of the consistent concerns of the *Democracy* was the freedom, in times of equality, for the individual or small group to hold and to express views which were new and/or not shared by the larger community.[30]

But most important, his definition of majority primarily emphasized the basic moral authority of the majority; he focused on the fundamental consensus necessary for any society. Tocqueville's majority was, therefore, unitary and (relatively) permanent, and what he feared more than any specific legal, political, or administrative oppression (which one of Madison's temporary coalitions might perpetrate) was the most subtle and profound tyranny over ideas, values, and opinions which the many might establish. Here perhaps was the most significant reason for both Tocqueville's failure to present racial oppression in terms of majoritarian tyranny and his inability either to hear or to accept Madison's argument that size—through diversity—lessened the chances for oppression by a majority.

Two general lessons of American history are that the majority does sometimes abuse its power, especially to oppress racial and ethnic minorities and to still dissenting opinions, and that majoritarian tyranny has occurred more often and more easily on the local, state, or regional levels than on the federal level. Especially in the twentieth century, it has, by and large, been the branches of the federal government which —in opposition to local, state, or regional inertia—have taken the initiative in enacting measures to help assure social justice, minority rights, and civil liberties.[31] So the serious misuse of power by the many, especially in the localities and states, was not a figment of Tocqueville's imagination. He was perceptive enough both to recognize the danger of the tyranny of the majority and to realize that this potential oppression was more threatening in the states.

What he failed either to see or to admit was the possibility that administrative decentralization, by freeing especially the localities from most restrictions by federal (or state) government, would not only stimulate practical political experience and a sense of civic responsibility, but would also deliver the towns and counties over to the local majorities. The more independent the locality, the more unrestrained the majority to impose its own values and opinions by means of the agencies of government, or public pressure, or the jury, or even violence.

So Tocqueville's recommendations for local self-government involved one of those difficult choices, one of those ambiguous issues of delicate balance which he was usually so quick to notice about democratic society. His remedy would paradoxically hinder the rise of administrative despotism, but at the same time open the door even wider to tyranny of the majority precisely where it was most absolute—in the locality. In this case he apparently did not see the dilemma which he had posed for himself.

Also Tocqueville felt a strange ambivalence toward the states. If they were essential elements in American federalism and administrative decentralization (and therefore involved in all of the benefits conjured up in Tocqueville's mind by those structural traits), they were also the major villains in his reflections about the Union's destiny. (Their relentless jealousy and aggression toward the central government was a major reason for Tocqueville's inclination to predict the ultimate dissolution of the Union.) But, as we have now seen, his contradictory attitude went even further. Although he sometimes praised the states as valuable barriers to any possible national sweep by destructive political passions, he more frequently condemned them for the inadequacies of their constitutions and for the openings which they gave to democratic excesses of all sorts. The existence of the states helped to insulate the nation from many democratic despotisms, but it was precisely on the state level, the 1835 *Democracy* insisted paradoxically, that such tyrannies were most likely to flourish.

Finally, as various critics have observed, Tocqueville erred as he developed his notion of the despotism of the majority by largely overlooking the chance of oppression by some minority.[32] Once again his intense temporary focus on a single concept made him lose sight of (or in this case entirely overlook) another equally significant idea. His belief that "in America tyranny can only come from the majority"[33] failed to allow for the possibility of domination by some small group with political, social, intellectual, or economic privilege. In twentieth century America, at least, the machinations of the few have often seemed more of a threat to democratic liberty than any abuses of power by the majority.

CHAPTER 16

Would *Démocratie* Usher in a New Dark Ages?

Particularly after 1835, Tocqueville's concern about the tyranny of the majority reflected a growing interest in intellectual liberty. He worried that one probable result of advancing equality would be massive pressure on individuals to conform in matters of thought and opinion to the views of the many. A related, but even more serious possible consequence, he feared, would be the suppression of innovative thinking altogether. Without new ideas or the freedom to express them, what would then become of cultural progress? For Tocqueville, even the possibility of such a disastrous development evoked some troubling questions for the future.

When describing the results of the New Despotism, of equality without liberty, Tocqueville usually wrote of men falling "below the level of humanity" (*au-dessous du niveau de l'humanité*) or of "barbarism" (*la barbarie*).[1] But from a very early period in the making of the *Democracy,* he also worried about another sort of "barbarism." In November 1831, after reflecting for several months on the many effects of America's pervasive equality, he asked in one of his travel notebooks: "Why, as civilisation spreads, do outstanding men become fewer? Why, when attainments are the lot of all, do great intellectual talents become rarer? Why, when there are no longer lower classes, are there no more upper classes? . . . America clearly poses these questions. But who can answer them?"[2]

Such doubts were not unusual. Tocqueville probably knew even before going to the New World that, in the opinion of many of his contemporaries, democracy was incompatible with civilization.[3] The queries of November 1831 reveal that, even then, he too suspected that democracy might usher in an era of intellectual and cultural stagnation.

Between 1832 and 1835, Tocqueville's fears about democracy's threat to civilization resurfaced in several of his drafts. He titled one page, for example, "Influence of *Démocratie* on *moeurs* and ideas," and wrote beneath: "Influence of the progress of equality on human intelligence. Disappearance of intellectual classes, of theoretical talents; possible return toward barbarism by this path."[4]

His concern even led him to compare the irresistible march of democracy to the barbarian invasions of Rome. "What new order will come out of the debris of that which is falling? Who can say? The men of the fourth century, witnesses of the invasions of the Barbarians, gave themselves over, like us, to a thousand conjectures; but no one had the idea to foresee the universal erection of the feudal system which, in all of Europe, was the result of this invasion."[5] Pursuing his analogy, he explained: "I spoke above of the men who were present at the ruin of the Roman empire. Let us fear that a similar fate awaits[6] us. But this time the Barbarians will not come out of the frozen lands of the North; they will rise up in the hearts of our fields and in the very midst of our cities."[7] Although the potential barbarians of the nineteenth century differed from their predecessors of the fourth, they too threatened to plunge the West into a Dark Age. In an unusually emotional peroration, Tocqueville begged his compatriots: "Let us save ourselves from a new invasion of Barbarians. The Barbarians are already at our gates and we amuse ourselves with discoursing. They are all around us . . . There is that to fear."[8]

In 1835, however, none of these fragments would appear, and the first half of the *Democracy* would consequently largely fail to disclose Tocqueville's grave doubts about the survival of Western culture in the face of democracy's advance. He would candidly concede that America possessed neither individuals dedicated to higher intellectual pursuits nor classes interested in supporting such endeavors.[9] He would note that the enormous power exercised in America by majority opinion inhibited freedom of thought and particularly literary genius,[10] and he would even admit that *démocratie* retarded the development of certain branches of knowledge. "So democracy . . . harms the progress of the art of government . . . Moreover, this does not apply only to the science of administration. Democratic government . . . always assumes the existence of a very civilized and knowledgeable society."[11]

But the work would contain no indication that these flaws had serious implications for the future of Western civilization as a whole. One ironic comment in the working manuscript would even argue that Europeans should be relieved to find no commanding intellects in America: "So in America we come upon none of those great intellectual centers which shoot forth heat and light at the same time. I do not know if perhaps we should not thank Heaven; America already carries an immense weight in the destinies of the world; and perhaps only great writers are lacking for her to overthrow violently all the old societies of Europe."[12]

By stressing the singularity of the American nation, Tocqueville would also find a way in 1835 partially to excuse the cultural deficiencies of the United States. The first colonists had come not as ignorant savages, he would remind his readers, but as intelligent men firmly grounded in European learning, and, if necessary, the men of the New World could always borrow ideas and techniques from the Old. Furthermore, and most important, although the American republic lacked outstanding men of the arts and sciences, the citizenry as a whole exhibited an uncommonly high level of education, experience, and intelligence.[13]

So in 1835, by scrupulously maintaining his focus on the United States and its unique situation,[14] Tocqueville would largely avoid the difficult task of generalizing about the effects of *démocratie* on cultural progress. Unable to soothe his own anxiety and unwilling once again to offer unnecessary support to the enemies of democracy, he apparently chose temporarily to conceal his doubts.

There was yet another possible reason for his silence. Beaumont had already decided to include a lengthy discussion of "Literature and Fine Arts" in his novel, *Marie*.[15] Perhaps Tocqueville, though willing to offer some isolated observations about intellectual and cultural life in America, felt reluctant in 1835 to compete with Gustave's work by presenting a fully developed analysis of his own. Once again Beaumont's book may have inhibited Tocqueville as he established the dimensions of the 1835 *Democracy*.

Between 1835 and 1840, while drafting the second half of the *Democracy*, Tocqueville continued his musings about the probable effects of *démocratie* on civilization. One possible way out of his quandary would have been to unearth and present to his readers a flourishing American cultural life; the threat to civilization would have been considerably less cogent if even the world's most democratic society stimulated artistic and literary activities.

In fact, such a demonstration would not have been especially difficult. Even before the late 1830s some European commentators had made a reasonable case for American cultural vigor, based largely on the works of Washington Irving and especially James Fenimore Cooper,[16] writers whose names and achievements were familiar to both Tocqueville and Beaumont.[17] Developments in New England as Tocqueville drafted the last two volumes of his work would have strengthened the argument considerably if he had been adequately aware of them.[18]

But evidently he, like Beaumont, felt that mention of Cooper, or Irving, or Channing, or any other literary figure would not really satisfy his doubts.[19] Such men were too much the exceptions in American society. Instead, he chose once again to couple an admission of American poverty in arts and letters with a denial that the United States proved anything in general about the effects of democracy on culture. "Thus the Americans are in [a wholly] exceptional situation."[20]

Having dismissed America as unique, he finally turned to a broader examination of the cultural influence of democracy. In an unenlightened society, he declared, the rise of *démocratie* would indeed be a condemnation to continued darkness. An unpublished essay drafted during the writing of the 1840 *Democracy* explained the reasons for his conclusion:

"Equality does not suit barbaric peoples; it prevents them from enlightening and civilizing themselves. Idea to introduce perhaps in the chapters on literature or the sciences. . . .[21]

". . . I have never thought that equality of conditions suited the infancy of societies. When men are uncivilized as well as equal, each among them feels himself too weak and too limited to seek knowledge (*la lumière*) separately; and it is almost impossible that, by a common accord, all will exert themselves at the same time to discover it.

"Nothing is so difficult to take as the first step out of barbarism.[22] I do not doubt that it requires more effort[23] for a savage to discover the art of writing than for a civilized man to penetrate the general laws which regulate the world. But it is unbelievable that men can ever imagine the necessity of a similar effort without its being clearly shown to them, or that they will subject themselves to doing it without grasping the result in advance.

"In a society of barbarians equal among themselves, the attention of each man is equally absorbed by the first needs and the grossest interests[24] of life, so the idea of intellectual progress can only with difficulty occur to the mind of any of them; and if by chance it came to the point of appearing, it would soon be sort of suffocated in the midst of the nearly instinctive thoughts that the poorly satisfied needs of the body[25] always bring forth. The savage lacks all at the same time: the idea of study and the possibility of giving himself over to it.

"I do not believe that history presents a single example of a democratic people who raised themselves, by themselves and gradually, toward knowledge (*la lumière*); and that is easily understood. We have seen that among nations where equality[26] and barbarism reign at the same time it was difficult for an individual to develop his intelligence[27] in isolation. But if it happens by extraordinary circumstances that he does, the superiority of his knowledge[28] suddenly gives him so great a preponderance over all who surround him[29] that he is not slow to desire to benefit from his new advantages by ending equality to his profit.

"If peoples[30] remain democratic, civilization can not then be born in their midst; and if it happens by chance to penetrate there, they cease to be democratic. I am persuaded that humanity owes its enlightenment (*lumières*) to such chances and[31] that it is under an aristocracy or under a prince that men still half-savage gathered the diverse notions which later must have permitted them to live enlightened, equal, and free."[32]

So among the semicivilized *démocratie* and culture were incompatible; a society composed of barbarians would be either democratic and perpetually ignorant or aristocratic and progressively civilized. But what about nations already enlightened? "It is very necessary," Tocqueville cautioned, "to guard against confusing a democratic people, enlightened and free, with another which would be ignorant and enslaved."[33] "I take the European peoples such as they appear to my eyes with their ancient traditions, their acquired enlightenment, their liberties," he wrote in the manuscript of the 1840 *Democracy*, "and I wonder if by becoming democratic they run the risk of falling back into a sort of barbarism."[34] He had returned to the fundamental question.

A tentative "Ordre des idées" appeared in an early outline of the chapter on the aptitude of democratic nations for arts and sciences.[35] "Prove first that there will always be some men in our democracies who will love the sciences, letters, and the arts. This proven, it will be easy for me to establish that a democracy will furnish to those men all that they need. In order to know what to say here it is necessary to amalgamate the reproaches that people make to *Démocratie* when they accuse it of extinguishing enlightenment."[36]

As a first step, Tocqueville theorized that some inherent human quality drove men everywhere toward the affairs of the mind. "There is in the very nature of man a natural and permanent disposition which pushes his soul despite habits, laws, usages . . . toward the contemplation of elevated and intellectual things. This natural disposition is found in democracies as elsewhere."[37] He even argued in one draft that *démocratie* supplied more than the usual stimulation to those who pursued activities of the mind and spirit. In democracies the inborn tendency toward higher things was strengthened "by a sort of reaction to the *material* and the *ordinary* which abounds in these societies."[38]

But would such intellectual impulses be given a chance to bear fruit? The key once again was free institutions. In the "Rubish," discarded drafts of the 1840 volumes, he wrote: "The great object of the lawmaker in democracies thus must be to create common *affairs* which *force* men to enter into contact one with another.

"The laws which have this result are useful to all peoples; to democratic peoples they are necessary. Here they augment the well-being of the society; there they allow society to survive. For what is society, for thinking beings, if not the communication and the intercourse of minds and hearts? . . .

"I have treated free institutions as diminishing *égoïsme*;[39] what is involved here is showing them as necessary to *civilization* among democratic peoples. . . .

". . . [40][equality of conditions] leads men not to communicate with each other. Each one, being obliged to oversee his own affairs by himself, has not the leisure nor the taste to seek out, without necessity, the company of his fellows and to share his ideas and theirs. . . .

"If the men of democracies were abandoned to their instincts they would then end by becoming almost entirely strangers to one another, and the circulation of ideas and of sentiments would be stopped. . . .

"The circulation of ideas is to civilization what the circulation of blood is to the human body.

"Here a striking portrait, if possible."[41]

So the hope for democratic nations rested with whichever free institutions (such as local liberties and associations) brought men together in the pursuit of public business.[42] Only then would issues be discussed, ideas stimulated, and intellectual life preserved. Moreover, the energies excited among democratic peoples by such civic and political activities would inevitably spill over into intellectual ventures. "Give a democratic people enlightenment and liberty," Tocqueville declared in his working manuscript, "and I do not doubt that you will see them carry over into the study of the sciences, letters, and the arts the same feverish activity that they show in all the rest."[43]

Another draft revealed that this idea grew particularly out of Tocqueville's knowledge of French history during the years following the French Revolution. Describing the effects of the revolution, he wrote: "Minds strongly stirred and put into motion by politics, afterwards throw themselves impetuously into all other channels. Free institutions, always in action, produce something analogous in a sustained way. They excite a certain chronic agitation in the human mind which sets it going for all things."[44]

So in democratic times and among cultured peoples, there would be men endowed with the essential intellectual interests and capacities and activated by the necessary drives and energies. After some hesitation and a brief but interesting theoretical investigation, Tocqueville, with the enlightened nations of Europe specifically in mind, was thus finally able to conclude that, *assuming free institutions*, "Equality of conditions seems to me very appropriate for precipitating the march of the human mind."[45]

But most of these more optimistic reflections occurred in various drafts or "Rubish" of the 1840 volumes. The published text would be considerably more ambivalent. Especially in the chapter entitled "Why Great Revolutions Will Become Rarer," which once again considered the probable effects of equality on intellectual innovation, Tocqueville's conclusions would be much gloomier. Equality of conditions and similar viewpoints, a busy preoccupation with mundane matters, a belief in intellectual equality, the isolation of individuals, the power of public opinion, and the authority of the mass, he would then argue, all joined to discourage new insights and ideas.[46]

"The more closely I consider the effects of equality upon the mind, the more I am convinced that the intellectual anarchy which we see around us is not, as some suppose, the natural state for democracies. I think we should rather consider it as an accidental characteristic peculiar to their youth, and something that only happens during [the] transitional period (*époque de passage*). . . .

"Because the inhabitants of democracies always seem excited, uncertain, hurried, and ready to change both their minds and their situation, it has been supposed that they want immediately to abolish their laws, adopt new beliefs, and conform to new manners. It has not been noted that while equality leads men to make changes it also prompts them to have interests which require stability for their satisfaction; it both drives men on and holds them back; it goads them on and keeps their feet on the ground; it kindles their desires and limits their powers. . . .

". . . I cannot help fearing that men may reach a point where they look on every new theory as a danger, every innovation as a toilsome trouble, every social advance as a first step toward revolution, and that they may absolutely refuse to move at all for fear of being carried off their feet. . . .

"People suppose that the new societies are going to change shape daily, but my fear is that they will end up by being too unalterably fixed with the same institutions, prejudices, and mores, so that mankind will stop progressing and will dig itself in. I fear that the mind may keep folding itself up in a narrower compass forever without producing new ideas, that men will wear themselves out in trivial, lonely, futile activity, and that for all its constant agitation humanity will make no advance."[47]

This passage, in addition to a sense of foreboding and a conclusion much more pessimistic than previous ones, also offered an example of Tocqueville's use of a mental tool which would occasionally appear in the pages of the 1840 *Democracy: époque de transition* (or *de passage*). By his repeated resorts to this concept, Tocqueville underscored his assumption that France (and Europe) in the 1830s was *between* more stable periods, that the early nineteenth century was primarily an intermediate stage, an *époque de transition*, and was therefore particularly prone to a wide variety of ills too often attributed by the unthinking to *démocratie* itself. At every possible opportunity in his last two volumes, Tocqueville reminded his countrymen that France, especially, was in the midst of this painful process of *becoming* democratic (was between two worlds) and that, to a great extent, this uncomfortable state of flux, rather than *démocratie*, accounted for the severity of his nation's social, political, and moral problems. The idea of *époque de transition* thus allowed him not only partially to explain France's lamentable condition, but also to disarm certain uncompromising critics of the trend toward equality and to maintain his hope for some better, more settled future of democratic maturity.

In 1840, Tocqueville thus remained uncertain about exactly how *démocratie* would influence intellectual development. In some passages he seemed to foresee the possibility, given free institutions in times of equality, of a unique cultural flowering. Elsewhere he remained pessimistic and predicted a pervasive mental stagnation. But at least he had finally faced the dilemma which he had posed years earlier. Although Tocqueville had not dismissed the possible deleterious effects of *démocratie* on cultural progress, his attitude by 1840 was different from the one expressed in earlier, more emotional drafts. Gone were his intense fears of barbarian ascendancy and of the immediate, catastrophic collapse of civilization. After an initial delay—possibly once again caused, in part, by an unwillingness to intrude upon areas marked out by Beaumont—further thought had persuaded Tocqueville that Europe, under the onslaught of advancing equality, would not *necessarily* go the way of Rome.

CHAPTER 17

Démocratie and *Egoïsme*

Whether tracing the changes in Tocqueville's attitudes toward physical causes, his concepts of despotism, or his understandings of the tyranny of the majority, we come repeatedly to what is probably the central figure of the *Democracy*: the independent and morally responsible individual. Tocqueville envisioned an eternal tension between the individual and the society as a whole and wondered especially how *démocratie* would affect that tension. Could the dignity, strength, and self-esteem of the individual be preserved in democratic times? Or would a psychology of insignificance, helplessness, and isolation triumph? To explore this vital issue, Tocqueville embarked on a private journey. His voyage of exploration predated his visit to the New World by at least a few years and was originally undertaken with eyes toward France; but in America he made some key discoveries.

In a thoughtful letter to Charles Stoffels written about a year before leaving for America, Tocqueville set forth several ideas which would become fundamental principles as the *Democracy* developed during the next decade. The letter posited an elaborate distinction between "un peuple demi-civilisé" and "un peuple complètement éclairé" and then explored some of the consequences of these two stages of civilization. After assuming the existence of a basic struggle between what he called *la force individuelle* and *la force publique*, Tocqueville proposed that a semicivilized social state supported *la force individuelle*; there "*la force publique* is poorly organized and the struggle between it and *la force individuelle* is often unequal."[1]

Among a highly civilized people, however, "the social body has provided for everything; the individual undergoes the pain of birth; for the rest, the society takes him from his nurse, it oversees his education, opens before him the roads to fortune; it sustains him on his way, deflects dangers from his head; he advances in peace under the eyes of this second Providence; this guardian power which protected him during his life even oversees the repose of his ashes: that is the fate of civilized man. . . . The soul, asleep in this long rest, no longer knows how to awake when the opportunity occurs; individual energy (*l'énergie individuelle*) is nearly extinguished; people rely on one another when action is necessary; in all other circumstances, on the contrary, they withdraw into themselves; it is the reign of *égoïsme*."[2] But Tocqueville did mention more hopefully that in highly civilized societies the general good (*l'intérêt général*) was better understood (*mieux entendu*).[3]

Several of the ideas presented in this letter of 1830 would reappear in Tocqueville's American journey notes and in the many drafts, working manuscript, and final text of the *Democracy*. Even some of the key terminology of this epistle would resurface in the 1835 and 1840 volumes. But most important, destined to become basic themes in his book were the underlying notion of tension between each individual and the society as a whole, Tocqueville's profound concern that the dignity and vitality of each individual be maintained in the face of an increasingly strong *force publique*, and his idea that *force individuelle*, which he admired, was giving way to *égoïsme*, which he deplored.

Although Tocqueville was already thinking in 1830 about grand social developments, his thoughts were then focused on the rise of "civilization" and what that portended of mankind. His musings seemed primarily to reflect his recent attendance at and reading of François Guizot's lectures on "The History of Civilization in France." A fascination with a different force in the modern world, *démocratie*, would have to await Tocqueville's discovery of America.

Within a few weeks of his arrival in the New World, Tocqueville attempted to reconcile observed traits of the American republic with some ideas that he had previously learned from Montesquieu. The eighteenth-century theorist had proclaimed that each form of government—monarchy, republic (aristocratic or democratic), and despotism—rested on some fundamental principle. For republics, that principle was virtue (*la vertu*), which Montesquieu defined as "a renouncement of self." He had written: "This virtue can be defined: love of laws and love of country. This love, which demands the constant preference of the public interest to one's own, produces all the private virtues; they are nothing more than this preference. . . . So everything depends on establishing this love in the republic."[4]

But this principle of self-abnegation did not seem to fit the American republic, so Tocqueville soon found himself qualifying Montesquieu's argument. "The principle of the republics of antiquity was to sacrifice private interests to the general good. In that sense one could say that they were *virtuous*. The principle of this one seems to be to make private interests harmonize with the general interests. A sort of refined and intelligent selfishness (*égoïsme raffiné et intelligent*) seems to be the pivot on which the whole machine turns. These people do not trouble themselves to find out whether public virtue is good, but they do claim to prove that it is useful. If the latter point is true, as I think it is in part, this society can pass as enlightened but not as virtuous. But up to what extent can the two principles of individual well-being and the general good in fact be merged?"[5]

These speculations soon resumed in a letter to his friend Chabrol. "What serves as a tie to these diverse elements? What makes of them a people? *Interest*. That's the secret. Individual interest which sticks through at each instant, *interest* which, moreover, comes out in the open and *calls itself a social theory*. We are a long way from the ancient republics, it must be admitted, and yet this people is republican and I don't doubt will long remain so. And the Republic is for it the best of governments."[6]

So some peculiar understanding of private interest, "a sort of refined and intelligent selfishness (*égoïsme raffiné et intelligent*)," stood at the core of this society. Americans engaged in public affairs (practiced public virtue) not because of some abstract good, but because they believed such activity benefited their interests as individuals. On a presumed harmony between private and public interest, properly understood, they had boldly built a social theory and established a novel principle for their republic. Tocqueville was intrigued and almost persuaded.

In Boston several persons obligingly described for him how this American *égoïsme intelligent* operated through local self-government and associations.[7] He heard repeatedly about the widespread social and political activity and the high level of practical experience and wisdom which prevailed in the United States. As early as 20 September 1831, he summarized: "One of the happiest consequences of the absence of government . . . is the ripening of individual strength (*force individuelle*) which never fails to follow therefrom. Each man learns to think and to act for himself without counting on the support of any outside power which, however watchful it be, can never answer all the needs of man in society. The man thus used to seeking his well-being by his own efforts alone, stands the higher in his own esteem as well as in that of others: he grows both stronger and greater of soul. . . . But one must say it again, there are but few peoples who can manage like that without government. . . . For the civilized man to be able to do [so,] he must have reached that state of society in which knowledge allows a man to see clearly what is useful for him and in which his passions do not prevent him carrying it out."[8]

Here was another significant amendment to his 1830 theorizing. As a result of his experiences in America, he now realized that neither *égoïsme* (of a certain type) nor civilization were necessarily incompatible with *la force individuelle*. Civilized people could develop a sophisticated understanding of private and public interest which would actually enhance the strength of individuals. The American, for example, clearly demanded and enjoyed an unusually high degree of personal independence and responsibility.

The role played in the New World republic by informed self-interest finally led Tocqueville to another qualification of Montesquieu's premise. "Another point which America demonstrates is that virtue is not, as has long been claimed, the only thing that maintains republics, but that enlightenment (*lumières*), more than any other thing, makes this social condition easy. The Americans are scarcely more virtuous than others; but they are infinitely more enlightened (I speak of the masses) than any other people I know; I do not only want to say that there are more people there who know how to read and write (a matter to which perhaps more importance is attached than is due), but the body of people who have understanding of public affairs, knowledge of the laws and of precedents, feeling for the well-understood interests (*intérêts bien entendus*) of the nation, and the faculty to understand them, is greater than in any other place in the world."[9]

So practical intelligence allowed Americans to uphold their unique social theory. What Tocqueville had earlier called "a sort of refined and intelligent selfishness" was now on the way to becoming "well-understood" or enlightened self-interest (*intérêt bien entendu*).

In the American West certain features common to the whole society were often exaggerated. For example, Madame la Comtesse de Tocqueville, Alexis's mother, learned in a letter from Louisville, Kentucky, that in the Mississippi Valley a doubly new society was taking shape. "It is surely here that one must come to judge the most unique situation that has, without doubt, ever existed under the sun. A people absolutely without precedents, traditions, habits, or even dominant ideas, blazing without hesitation a new trail in civil, political, and criminal legislation, never looking around to examine the wisdom of other peoples and the heritage of the past; but cutting their institutions like their roads in the midst of the forests where they have just settled and where certainly no limits or obstacles are to be met; a society which does not yet have either political ties, or ties of social or religious hierarchy; where each individual stands by himself (*est soi*) because it pleases him to do so without concerning himself with his neighbor; a democracy without limits or bounds."[10]

More specifically, Tocqueville and Beaumont noticed that the pioneer of Michigan, even more than Americans elsewhere, seemed too exclusively dedicated to the pursuit of material success. "Concentrating on the single object of making his fortune, the emigrant has ended by making an altogether exceptional mode of existence. Even his feelings for his family have become merged in a vast *égoïsme*, and one cannot be sure whether he regards his wife and children as anything more than a detached part of himself."[11] The New World republic, especially in the West, was a society without any of the usual social bonds. Each individual engaged in the pursuit of fortune by himself and was forced to rely largely on his own resources. In some ways, each person stood terribly isolated and alone. Here was the potentially more somber side of the individual independence and energy which Tocqueville had earlier described.

So by the time he left the United States, Tocqueville had recognized that *démocratie* with its erosion of traditional ties had at least two possible but contrary results. On the one hand, people could fall into a narrow selfishness (*égoïsme*), purposely ignoring interests other than their own, and single-mindedly pursue their own individual destinies. This would be the opposite of Montesquieu's virtue. Or, on the other hand, people who were sufficiently enlightened could envision their individual and common interests in a way which would allow the fostering of both. They would devote themselves as necessary to private or public affairs, knowing that an ultimate harmony existed between the two. The result would thus be an intelligent selfishness (*égoïsme intelligent*) that Tocqueville eventually called enlightened self-interest (*intérêt bien entendu*). Tocqueville believed that in America, despite western excesses, the second alternative prevailed.

Even before the actual writing of the *Democracy* began, additional ideas and feelings about individual responsibility and *égoïsme* appeared in an exchange of letters between Tocqueville and Eugène Stoffels. In January 1833, Tocqueville admonished his close friend (and by implication all of his countrymen who, for whatever reasons, felt themselves above or apart from the politics of France): "I began, my dear friend, to feel seriously annoyed with you when I received your letter. . . .

"You speak to me of what you call your *political atheism* and ask if I share it. Here it is necessary to understand one another. Are you disgusted only with the parties, or also with the ideas that they exploit? In the first case, you know that such has always been my viewpoint, more or less. But in the second, I am no longer in any way your man. At the present time there is an obvious tendency to treat with indifference all ideas that can agitate society, whether they are true or false, noble or ignoble. Each person seems agreed to consider the government of his country *sicut inter alios acta.* Each person concentrates more and more on individual interest. Only men wanting power for themselves, and not strength and glory for their country, can rejoice at the sight of such a symptom. To count on tranquillity purchased at such a price, it is necessary not to know how to see very far into the future. It is not a healthy or virile calm. It is a sort of apoplectic torpor which, if it should last a long time, would lead us inescapably to great misfortunes. . . . I struggle with all my power against this bastard wisdom, this fatal indifference which in our times is sapping the energy of so many beautiful souls. I try not to make two worlds: the one moral, where I still get excited about what is beautiful and good; the other political, where to smell more comfortably the dung on which we walk, I stretch out flat on my stomach."[12]

The political withdrawal of legitimists and of others who saw themselves acting out of high moral principles profoundly disturbed the young nobleman. He saw an unfortunate tendency in France for individuals—especially the best individuals—to retreat into their private lives and to leave the political arena to the selfishly ambitious. Rising indifference and loss of energy made him uneasy for the future. So he urged men like Eugène to resist these temptations to peaceful solitude. As Tocqueville wrote his 1835 volumes, these apprehensions would never be far from his thoughts.

When Tocqueville finally undertook the composition of his work on America, he briefly sketched the characteristics of three basic social states.

Aristocratic and Monarchical System. Our Fathers.

1. Love of the King.
2. Aristocracy.
3. *Force Individuelle* against tyranny.
4. Beliefs, devotion to duty, uncivilized virtues, instincts.
5. The idea of duty.
6. Tranquillity of the people which comes because they see nothing better.
7. Monarchic immobility.
8. Strength and greatness of the State which is achieved by the constant efforts of a few persons.

Democratic and Republican System.

1. Respect for law; idea of rights.
2. Goodwill coming from the equality of rights.
3. Association.
4. *Intérêt bien entendu*; enlightenment.
5. Love of liberty.
6. Aware of its own advantages.
7. Regulated and progressive movement of Democracy.
8. [Strength and greatness of the State] by the simultaneous efforts of all.

Present Situation.

1. Fear of authority which is despised.
2. War between poor and rich; *l'égoïsme individuel sans la force.*
3. Equal weakness, without collective power (without the power of association).[13]
4. Prejudices without beliefs; ignorance without virtues; doctrine of interest

without knowledge (*la doctrine de l'intérêt sans la science*); *égoïsme imbécile.*

5. Taste for the abuse of liberty.
6. People who haven't the courage to change; the passion of old men.[14]

This analysis, tentatively made for his "Introduction,"[15] contained the seeds of much of Tocqueville's later argument about *égoïsme.* It not only described an alarming present weakness and isolation of individuals, but also disclosed his desire to move from *égoïsme individual sans la force* and *la doctrine de l'intérêt sans la science* (or *égoïsme imbécile*) to joint efforts and *l'intérêt bien entendu* (or *égoïsme intelligent*).

But most curiously, this fragment portrayed the "Democratic and Republican System" as incorporating the more positive characteristics which Tocqueville had observed in the United States; in this piece the regime of *égoïsme* was not the *système démocratique,* but the *état actuel.* As the letter to Eugène indicated, what Tocqueville had in mind was the contemporary condition of France. And here again, implicitly, was the concept *époque de transition.*

Démocratie or the movement toward equality of conditions, Tocqueville would argue in his 1835 work, broke most traditional social bonds and thus undermined the existence of independent, secondary bodies in the society.[16] While individuals grew increasingly similar, weak, and isolated, the power of the society as a whole waxed strong and irresistible.[17] *La force individuelle* was in increasing jeopardy.

"But nowadays, with all classes jumbled together and the individual increasingly disappearing in the crowd, where he is readily lost in the common obscurity, and nowadays, when monarchic honor has almost lost its sway without being replaced by virtue, and there is nothing left which raises a man above himself, who can say where the exigencies of authority and the yielding of weakness will stop? . . .

"What strength can customs have among a people whose aspect has entirely changed and is still perpetually changing, where there is already some precedent for every act of tyranny, and every crime is following some example, where nothing ancient remains which men are afraid to destroy, and where they dare to do anything new that can be conceived?

"What resistance can *moeurs* offer when they have so often been twisted before?

"What can even public opinion do when not even a *score* of people[18] are held together by any common bond, when there is no man, no family, no body, no class, and no free association which can represent public opinion and set it in motion?

"When each citizen being equally impotent, poor, and isolated cannot oppose his individual weakness to the organized force of the government?"[19]

In part because of this sense of helplessness, individuals withdrew more and more into themselves, grew indifferent to their fellows and their country, and became reluctant to engage in any public activities whatsoever. "The inhabitant in some countries shows a sort of repugnance in accepting the political rights granted to him by the law; it strikes him as a waste of time to spend it on communal interests, and he likes to shut himself up in a narrow *égoïsme*, of which four ditches with hedges on top define the precise limits."[20] A draft fragment warned of the possible consequences. "Everything is favorable in the laws [and] institutions as in the *moeurs* for preparing servitude. *Egoïsme* having replaced virtue."[21]

Taking lessons from America, Tocqueville would prescribe two basic tasks for those concerned by this pernicious democratic trend toward *égoïsme*. Efforts had to be made, first, to combine the forces of individuals who were separately powerless. "When the citizens are all more or less equal, it becomes difficult to defend their freedom from the encroachments of power. No one among them being any longer strong enough to struggle alone with success, only the combination of the forces of all is able to guarantee liberty."[22] By uniting in joint undertakings those who felt helpless apart, Tocqueville hoped to reintroduce and to encourage a sense of individual strength and independence.

Secondly, selfishness might be countered by stimulating individual participation in the public affairs of the nation. Each person would then be drawn out of his private concerns and slowly enlightened by practical political experience.

"The most powerful way, and perhaps the only remaining way, in which to interest men in their country's fate is to make them take a share in its government. In our day it seems to me that civic spirit is inseparable from the exercise of political rights, and I think that henceforward in Europe the numbers of the citizens will be found to increase or diminish in proportion to the extension of those rights.

"How is it that in the United States, where the inhabitants arrived but yesterday in the land they occupy, where, to say it in one word, the instinct of country can hardly exist—how does it come about that each man is as interested in the affairs of his township, of his canton, and of the whole state as he is in his own affairs? It is because each man in his sphere takes an active part in the government of society."[23]

A draft disclosed some of the reasoning behind this call for participation. "It is because I hear the rights of governments discussed that I think we must hasten to give rights to the governed. It is because I see Democracy triumph that I want to regulate Democracy. People tell me that, since morality has relaxed, new rights will be new arms; that, since governments are already weak, new rights will be to give new arms to their enemies; that Democracy is already too strong in society without introducing it further into government. I will answer that it is because I see morality weak that I want to put it under the safeguard of interest; it is because I see governments powerless that I would like to accustom the governed to the habit of respecting them."[24] In the margin he added: "If morality were strong enough by itself, I would not consider it so important to rely on utility. If the idea of what was just were more powerful, I would not talk so much about the idea of utility."[25]

For achieving these two general goals Tocqueville's 1835 volumes would recommend several specific institutional remedies, particularly, once again, freedom of association and local liberties.[26] Tocqueville would also endorse the concept of enlightened or well-understood self-interest as a remedy for *égoïsme*.[27] Almost all Americans, he wrote in one fragment, readily accepted the notion that "enlightened self-interest was enough to lead men to do the right thing."[28]

Returning to the problem of Montesquieu's republican principle of virtue and its relation to the United States, Tocqueville composed a brief draft of remarks entitled "Concerning Virtue in Republics" that also emphasized the crucial function of enlightened self-interest.

"The Americans are not a virtuous people and yet they are free. This does not absolutely disprove that virtue, as Montesquieu thought, is essential to the existence of republics. It is not necessary to take

Montesquieu's idea in a narrow sense. What this great man meant is that republics can survive only by the action of the society on itself. What he understood by virtue is the moral power that each individual exercises over himself and that prevents him from violating the rights of others. When this triumph of man over temptation is the result of the weakness of the temptation or of a calculation of personal interest, it does not constitute virtue in the eyes of the moralist; but it is included in the idea of Montesquieu who spoke much more of the result than of its cause. In America it is not virtue which is great, it is temptation which is small, which amounts to the same thing. It is not disinterestedness which is great, it is interest which is well-understood (*bien entendu*), which again almost amounts to the same thing. So Montesquieu was right even though he spoke of classical virtue, and what he said about the Greeks and Romans still applies to the Americans."[29]

The Americans displayed a special, calculated sort of virtue. Enlightened self-interest, though less strictly "moral," nonetheless served effectively to counteract the destructive democratic tendency toward *égoïsme.*

The tensions between selfishness and responsibility and between the individual and society as a whole profoundly influenced the type and level of citizenship which characterized each nation. In a sketch of ideas for his chapter entitled "Public Spirit in the United States,"[30] Tocqueville described the prevailing "sentiment which attaches men to their own country" during each of three separate stages of society. The first phase saw "Instinctive love of the homeland. Customs, *moeurs*, memories. Religion is not the principal passion, but gives strength to all passions. *Patrie* in the person of the King." Then came the "Intermediate epoch. *Égoïsme* without enlightenment (*lumières*). Men have no more prejudices; they do not yet have beliefs."[31] During this period civic virtues disappeared; the individual, lacking *esprit de cité,* was "a peaceful inhabitant, an honest farmer, a good head of the family." Tocqueville declared himself "ready for anything, provided that one does not force me to give him the name 'citizen.' "[32]

During that time, the people devoted themselves to "Moderation without virtue or courage; moderation which arises from faintness of heart and not from virtue, from exhaustion, from fear, from *égoïsme.*

Tranquillity which comes not from being well, but from not having the courage and the necessary energy to seek something better." They eventually became a "Mass suspended in the middle of things, inert, *égoïste*, without energy, without patriotism, sensual, sybaritic, which has only instincts, which lives from day to day, which becomes one by one the plaything of all the others."[33]

This middle stage was finally superseded by the third epoch which was marked by an "active, enlightened love [of country], . . . perhaps more reserved, more lasting, more fertile. *Égoïsme éclairé*."[34] During this period, which already existed in America, men learned to "interest themselves as much in public prosperity as in that of their families; they brought to patriotism all the energy of *égoïsme individuel*."[35] Citizens would then rise up where only inhabitants had stood before. "In order for Democracy to govern," Tocqueville insisted in another draft, "citizens are needed who take an interest in public affairs, who *have the capacity* to get involved and who *want* to do so. Capital point to which one must always return."[36]

During the making of the *Democracy*, Tocqueville repeatedly searched for ways to avoid the democratic tendency that undermined *la force individuelle* and fostered a blind and destructive selfishness. Since the "virtue" of old seemed lost, he hoped to discover new ways to interest men in public affairs and to create self-confident and self-reliant individuals. From his American journey, he learned to pose the problem in terms of moving from *égoïsme imbécile* to *égoïsme intelligent*, or, more broadly, from *égoïsme* to *intérêt bien entendu*.

What Tocqueville finally called *égoïsme* in the first two volumes of the *Democracy* appeared to have two distinct facets: first, the growing powerlessness and isolation of individuals; and secondly, the withdrawal from public life and an accelerating concentration on private affairs. So *égoïsme* meant both weakness and selfishness; perhaps the phrase *égoïsme individual sans la force* best expressed his understanding of democratic *égoïsme* in 1835. By 1840, however, Tocqueville would give yet another name to this phenomenon: *individualisme*.

CHAPTER 18

From *Egoïsme* to *Individualisme*

The word *individualisme* first appeared in the early 1820s in the writings of Joseph de Maistre and other Frenchmen; after 1825, it could be found quite regularly in the works of the Saint-Simonians.[1] René Rémond has even noted that by 1833 to 1835 certain journalists specifically applied *individualisme* to the American republic.[2] So the term was not strictly speaking one of those new words to describe new things for which Tocqueville had issued so eloquent a call. But its use was still relatively rare enough, even in 1840, to cause Tocqueville to comment: "*Individualisme* is a word recently coined to express a new idea. Our fathers only knew about *égoïsme*."[3]

Henry Reeve's translation of the 1840 *Democracy* saw the term's first appearance in English. Reeve felt obliged to add a personal note explaining his inability to offer any familiar English equivalent and apologizing for the neologism. Tocqueville's book, along with those of Michel Chevalier and Friedrich List, also introduced the word to America.[4]

Curiously, in the United States (and to a lesser degree in England) the term would have a heavily positive connotation quite at odds with the typically pejorative use of *individualisme* by Tocqueville and most other Frenchmen. To Americans, especially as the nineteenth century progressed, the word would conjure up images of extensive political and economic freedoms. Tocqueville's own diary remarks about the "fundamental social principles" in the United States of self-reliance and of individual independence and responsibility had captured some thing of what Americans would later mean by "individualism."[5] But Tocqueville's own understanding of the term would consistently be quite different.

In 1840 Tocqueville would begin his explanation by attempting carefully to distinguish *égoïsme* and *individualisme.*

"*Egoïsme* is a passionate and exaggerated love of self which leads a man to think of all things in terms of himself and to prefer himself to all.

"*Individualisme* is a calm and considered feeling which disposes each citizen to isolate himself from the mass of his fellows and withdraw into the circle of family and friends; with this little society formed to his taste, he gladly leaves the greater society to look after itself.

"*Egoïsme* springs from a blind instinct; *individualisme* is based on misguided judgment rather than depraved feeling. It is due more to inadequate understanding than to perversity of heart.

"*Egoïsme* sterilizes the seeds of every virtue; *individualisme* at first only dams the spring of public virtue, but in the long run it attacks and destroys all the others too and finally merges in *égoïsme.*

"*Egoïsme* is a vice as old as the world. It is not peculiar to one form of society more than another.

"*Individualisme* is of democratic origin and threatens to grow as conditions get more equal."[6]

Key elements in this definition were the peaceful and reflective nature of individualism and Tocqueville's insistence that, despite apparent prudence, individualism arose from short-sighted and erroneous judgments. He also stressed that individualism was new, the result of advancing *démocratie*, and that, unlike *égoïsme* which largely fixed attention on the solitary "I," individualism stimulated the creation of a narrow, sacrosanct society of family and friends which then became the exclusive concern of each person.

Two letters between Tocqueville and Royer-Collard cast additional light upon certain features of this explanation. In the summer of 1838, Alexis and Marie arrived in Normandy where the husband hoped to find solitude and quiet for his writing and the wife hoped to supervise the undertaking of badly needed renovations of the old château. Alexis's loud complaints about the noise of workmen and the incessant interruptions by visiting local dignitaries soon demonstrated the magnitude of his miscalculations. In the midst of his troubles, Tocqueville could not help reflecting on the nature of these provincial visitors. "I have again found much good will and no end of attention here. I am attached to this population, without, all the same, concealing its faults which are great. These people here are honest, intelligent, religious enough, passably moral, very steady: but they have scarcely any disinterestedness. It is true that *égoïsme* in this region does not resemble that of Paris, so violent and often so cruel. It is a mild, calm, and tenacious love of private interests, which bit by bit absorbs all other sentiments of the heart and dries up nearly all sources of enthusiasm there. They join to this *égoïsme* a certain number of private virtues and domestic qualities which, as a whole, form respectable men and poor citizens. I would pardon them all the same for not being disinterested, if they sometimes wanted to believe in disinterestedness. But they do not want to do so, and that, in the midst of all the signs of their good will, makes me feel oppressed. Unfortunately only time can help me escape an oppression of this type, and I am not patient."[7]

In reply the old Doctrinaire reminded Tocqueville that what he saw was not in any way peculiar to Normandy. "You are peeved about the country where you live; but your *Normans*, they are France, they are the world; this prudent and intelligent *égoïsme*, it is the *honnêtes gens* of our time, trait for trait."[8]

This "mild, calm, and tenacious love of private interests" which helps to form "respectable men and poor citizens," this *égoïsme* of 1838, closely paralleled Tocqueville's later description of *individualisme*. So aside from the implication that the good bourgeoisie of La Manche helped to shape Tocqueville's image of *individualisme*, these two letters raise a more significant question. Did Tocqueville's adoption by 1840 of the word *individualisme* signify that he had truly moved beyond this earlier notion of *égoïsme*? Or had he merely given a new name to a concept which he had already repeatedly defined?

Not only were many descriptions from 1835 and 1840 (and in between) similar, but also Tocqueville's 1840 list of essential remedies for *égoïsme* or *individualisme* would largely reiterate the prescriptions of 1835.[9] It is also significant that Tocqueville would liberally and apparently indiscriminately sprinkle both the terms *égoïsme* and *individualisme* throughout his final 1840 text.[10]

Yet despite great similarities and Tocqueville's habitually inexact use of key words, the *individualisme* of the 1840 *Democracy* would differ in certain significant ways from the *égoïsme* of 1835, or even 1838. In the second half of his book, Tocqueville would describe at length two additional causes of *individualisme*, would examine some new intellectual facets of the concept and, most important, would painstakingly expose its eventual political consequences.

Tocqueville had long recognized that the growth of *démocratie* and the gradual development of democratic social conditions favored the spread of selfishness and of a sense of individual helplessness in a society. But by 1840 he would also indict the *esprit révolutionnaire* as one of the forces that most exacerbated *individualisme*.[11] In a summary of essential ideas about *égoïsme*, he declared:

"*Egoïsme*. How *démocratie* tends to develop the *égoïsme* natural to the human heart. When conditions are equal, when each person is more or less sufficient unto himself and has neither the duty to give nor to receive from anyone else, it is natural that he withdraws into himself and that for him society ends where his family ends.

"Only widespread enlightenment can then teach him the indirect utility that he can gain from the prosperity of all. Here, as in many other things, only democratic institutions can partially correct the evils which the democratic social state brings forth.

"What makes democratic nations selfish is not so much the large number of independent citizens which they contain as it is the large number of citizens who are constantly arriving at independence.

"That is a principal idea.

"Feeling of independence which, for the first time, grips a multitude of individuals and exalts them. This means that *égoïsme* must appear more open and less enlightened among people who are becoming democratic than among people who have been democratic for a long time.

"Considering everything, I do not believe that there is more *égoïsme* in France than in America. The only difference is that in America it is enlightened and in France it is not. The Americans know how to sacrifice a portion of their personal interests in order to save the rest. We want to keep everything and often everything escapes us.

"Danger if conditions equalize faster than enlightenment spreads. Here perhaps a transition to the doctrine of enlightened self-interest (*intérêt bien entendu*)."[12]

This passage, probably dating from the early months of 1836, again underscored the link between *démocratie* and *égoïsme* and the importance of enlightened self-interest. It also repeated the definition of *égoïsme* as a feeling of individual detachment and exclusive concern for private interests and attempted to explain some significant differences between France and America. Tocqueville apparently believed that his own country suffered from a more virulent *égoïsme* because France had only recently undergone a democratic revolution (or was still in the midst of it); America, born in equality, had not required such an abrupt upheaval.[13]

As the composition of his work went forward, Tocqueville became increasingly aware that an important difference existed between the changes caused by advancing *démocratie* and the effects of certain revolutionary forces which he sensed were still at work in France. "Idea to express probably in the Preface. All existing democratic peoples are more or less in a state of revolution. But the state of revolution is a particular condition which produces certain effects that must not be confused and that are unique to it. The difficulty is to recognize among democratic peoples what is *revolutionary* and what is *democratic*."[14]

Elsewhere he reflected: "Idea to put well in the foreground. Effects of *démocratie*, and particularly harmful effects, that are exaggerated in the period of revolution in the midst of which the democratic social condition, *moeurs*, and laws are established . . . The great difficulty in the study of *démocratie* is to distinguish what is democratic from what is only revolutionary. This is very difficult because examples are lacking. There is no European people among which *démocratie* has completely settled in, and America is in an exceptional situation. The state of literature in France is not only democratic, but revolutionary. Public morality, the same. Religious and political opinions, the same."[15]

In the "Rubish" of the final section on the political consequences of democracy,[16] Tocqueville attempted yet another statement of the problem and a fuller definition.

"Separate with care the *esprit Démocratique* and the *esprit Révolutionnaire*. . . . Definition of the *esprit révolutionnaire:*

Taste for rapid change; use of violence to bring them about.
Esprit tyrannique.

Scorn for forms.
Scorn for established rights.
Indifference for means, considering the ends [desired].
Doctrine of the useful (*utile*).
Satisfaction given to brutal appetites.

"The *esprit révolutionnaire*, which is everywhere the greatest enemy of liberty, is so among democratic peoples above all; because there is a natural and secret link between it and *Démocratie*. A revolution can sometimes be just and necessary; it can establish liberty; but the *esprit révolutionnaire* is always detestable and can never lead anywhere except to tyranny."[17]

So the revolutionary spirit, mentality, or attitude was responsible for some of the worst abuses during times of democratic advances.[18] It was France's revolutionary heritage—rather than *démocratie* by itself—which helped to explain the severe dislocations and looming problems which so clearly faced that nation by the late 1830s. Repeatedly in the 1840 *Democracy* Tocqueville would resort to this explanation of what would otherwise have remained a baffling paradox. How did it happen that although America was the more thoroughly democratic nation, yet France more consistently witnessed the flaws and excesses of *démocratie*?

The second part of Tocqueville's book would argue that France should attempt to avoid some of the ills of *démocratie* by becoming more democratic. French political life had to be harmonized with the nation's increasingly democratic social condition; democracy had to be injected into politics. *Individualisme*, for instance, might be mitigated by local liberties and freedom of association. But his final volumes also often reminded readers of the recent and as yet incomplete nature of France's democratic revolution. That, too, helped to explain the intensity of French problems, especially the apparent epidemic of *individualisme*.[19]

In 1835 Tocqueville had devoted only a few pages to the American desire for material well-being. But by 1840 he would place much more emphasis on the *goût du bien-être* and the love of material pleasures.[20] A reason for this greater attention, in addition to his growing personal sensitivity to the materialism of the age, was probably a sharper awareness of the link between material desires and *indi-*

vidualisme; each encouraged the other. The "democratic taste for material well-being," he stated in a draft, "leads men to become absorbed in its pursuit or enjoyment." *Individualisme* "causes each person to want to be occupied only with himself."[21]

In the 1840 *Democracy*, Tocqueville exposed the preoccupation with material comfort which prevailed in democratic societies and then proceeded to explain his anxiety about such single-minded attachments. "The reproach I address to the principle of equality is not that it leads men away in the pursuit of forbidden enjoyments, but that it absorbs them wholly in quest of those which are allowed. By these means a kind of virtuous materialism may ultimately be established in the world, which would not corrupt, but enervate, the soul and noiselessly unbend its springs of action."[22]

What he feared, in part, was the gradual fixation of men on their small, private material interests and their consequent failure to contribute time and energy to wider public concerns. So democratic materialism also hastened democratic *individualisme*; and the final result might well be the loss of liberty.[23]

Tocqueville's formal definitions of *individualisme* (in manuscripts and text) usually stressed the withdrawal of individuals into petty private concerns and their indifference toward larger social issues. But his lengthy treatment in 1840 of democratic materialism added (though only implicitly) an additional feature to his definition: the relentless pursuit of physical ease for oneself and one's family. This single-minded striving for well-being diverted the talents and energies of individuals from public life as effectively as any sense of isolation or weakness. So *individualisme* actually had two faces: one passive—helplessness and withdrawal; the other active—a passion for material comfort.

In Tocqueville's broadening analysis of *individualisme*, the 1840 *Democracy* would not only disclose two major additional causes, the revolutionary spirit and materialism, but would also explore the possible intellectual results of *individualisme*. On an undated page from the 1840 "Rubish," Tocqueville remarked that "There are in *individualisme* two kinds of effects that should be well distinguished so that they can be dealt with separately. 1. *the moral effects*, hearts isolate themselves; 2. *the intellectual effects*, minds isolate themselves."[24] And in a sheet enclosed with the original working manuscript of the chapter entitled "Concerning the Philosophical Approach of the Americans," he surveyed the development of what he would call "indépendance individuelle de la pensée."[25]

"In the Middle Ages we saw that all opinions had to flow from authority; in those times philosophy itself, this natural antagonist to authority, took the form of authority; it clothed itself in the characteristics of a religion. After having created certain opinions by the free and individual force of certain minds, it imposed these opinions without discussion and compelled the [very] force that had given birth to it.

"In the eighteenth century we arrived at the opposite extreme, that is, we pretended to appeal all things only to individual reason and to drive dogmatic beliefs away entirely. And just as in the Middle Ages we gave philosophy the form and the style of a religion, so in the eighteenth century we gave religion the form and the style of philosophy.

"In our times, the movement still continues among minds of the second rank, but the others [know?] and admit that received and discovered beliefs, authority and liberty, *individualisme* and social force are all needed at the same time. The whole question is to sort out the limits of these pairs.

"It is to that [question] that I must put all my mind."[26]

In the margin, Tocqueville carefully (and luckily) penned the date: "24 April 1837."

Here is the earliest dated use by Tocqueville of the term *individualisme* that has yet been uncovered in the voluminous drafts and manuscripts of the *Democracy*.[27] But what is most intriguing about this first dated instance is Tocqueville's relatively favorable or at least neutral usage. Here he apparently grouped *individualisme* with liberty and intellectual discovery as opponents of authority and imposed belief.

Tocqueville would argue in the 1840 *Democracy* that the tendency toward *individualisme* caused men in democratic ages to abandon traditional intellectual authorities and to rely on their own powers of reason. His basic sympathy for a certain independence of mind would be evident, but he would worry first, that intellectual self-reliance might be pushed too far, and, second, that men would too quickly find a dangerous substitute for the authorities of old: the judgment of the public. The intellectual independence of individuals might thus succumb to the dictates of the mass.[28]

Perhaps Tocqueville's relatively approving use of *individualisme* in the fragment above once again reflected the depth of his anxiety about a possible loss of freedom of ideas. Of all the ways in which the mass might stifle the individual, the suppression of personal thought and opinion struck him as the most terrible. So in democratic times, a fierce intellectual self-reliance, a stubborn defense of one's own mental independence apparently did not seem as potentially dangerous to Tocqueville as did other facets of *individualisme*. Only a profoundly rooted *raison individuelle indépendante* could possibly resist the enormous pressure of society as a whole.[29]

The 1835 *Democracy* had predicted despotism as a result of the unequal struggle between "each citizen . . . equally impotent, poor, and isolated" and "the organized force of the government."[30] But the 1840 volumes would now go beyond this to offer a detailed examination of the relationships among *individualisme*, centralization, and despotism.[31]

The decline in individual energy and concern created a social and political vacuum into which the bureaucracy rushed. The "Rubish" of the large chapter entitled "How the Ideas and Feelings Suggested by Equality Influence the Political Constitution"[32] offered a succinct but revealing description of the trend. "*Individualisme*—the habit of living isolated from one's fellows, of not concerning oneself with anything that is common business, of abandoning this care to the sole, clearly visible representative of common interests, which is the government. *Chacun chez soi*; *chacun pour soi*. That is the natural instinct which can be corrected."[33]

Tocqueville also realized that, at the same time, the suffocating effects of a centralized and omnipresent government in turn further discouraged any private efforts. If unchecked, this relentless cycle of reinforcement would ultimately end in total "individual servitude,"[34] the hallmark of the New Despotism. So the final portion of his book would serve primarily to express his concern for the survival of *indépendance individuelle* in democratic times.[35] "To lay down extensive but distinct and settled limits to the action of the government; to confer certain rights on private persons, and to secure to them the undisputed enjoyment of those rights; to enable individual man to maintain whatever independence, strength, and original power he still possesses; to raise him by the side of society at large, and uphold him in that position; these appear to me the main objects of legislators in the ages upon which we are now entering."[36]

Often overlooked in Tocqueville's excellent analysis of the political effects of *démocratie* is his discussion of what he would call its liberal tendencies. His apprehensions about *individualisme*, centralization, and despotism would largely focus the last chapter of his book on the negative influences of advancing equality. His grim warnings divert attention from his praises for the encouragements which *démocratie* gave to liberty.

On an extra sheet in the working manuscript, he explicitly recognized certain redeeming democratic features:

> The liberal tendencies of equality—
> No respect.
> No immobility.
> Multitude and variety of desires.
> Mobility of the political world.[37]

In the published chapter, these ideas would first be explained and then be subsumed by the phrase "love of independence."[38] Various drafts elaborated further on this democratic encouragement of independence and revealed Tocqueville's strong approval of this influence. In one version he declared: "Begin by establishing the first tendency of equality toward individual independence and liberty. Show that this tendency can go as far as anarchy. In general it is the democratic tendency that people fear the most; and it is the one that I consider the greatest element of salvation that equality leaves us. Finish by indicating that this is not, however, the strongest and most continuous tendency that equality suggests. How through phases of anarchy (because of *individualisme*) democratic peoples tend however in a continuous manner toward the centralization of power."[39]

Another draft stated: "Two contrary tendencies, not equally sustained, not equally strong, but two tendencies. The one toward individual independence; the other toward the concentration of power. . . . As for me, I consider the taste for natural independence as the most precious gift which equality has given to men."[40]

In 1840, the text would expand upon these ideas.[41] And in his penultimate chapter Tocqueville would add: "The men who live in the democratic ages upon which we are entering have naturally a taste for independence; they are naturally impatient of regulation, and they are wearied by the permanence even of the condition they themselves prefer. They are fond of power, but they are prone to despise and hate those who wield it, and they easily elude its grasp by their own mobility and insignificance.

"These propensities will always manifest themselves, because they originate in the groundwork of society, which will undergo no change; for a long time they will prevent the establishment of any despotism, and they will furnish fresh weapons to each succeeding generation that struggles in favor of the liberty of mankind. Let us, then, look forward to the future with the salutary fear which makes men keep watch and ward for freedom, not with that faint and idle terror which depresses and enervates the heart."[42]

So strong was Tocqueville's attachment to what was, in less noble terms, the cantankerous, free individual that he once again found himself at the brink of serious contradiction. In a draft he wrote: "I have shown . . . how, as equality became greater, each man, finding himself less dependent and more separated from his fellows, felt more inclined to consider himself apart and to live in isolation." In a note immediately following, he observed: "This implies a contradiction with what precedes on the idea of centralization."[43]

In a passage in his working manuscript he declared that "during the centuries of equality, each man, living independent of all of his fellows, gets used to directing without constraint his private affairs. When these same men meet in common, they naturally have the taste and the idea of administering themselves by themselves. So equality carries men toward administrative decentralization; but at the same time it creates powerful instincts which lead them away from it."[44]

Here was an idea directly contrary to the relationship between *démocratie* and centralization which Tocqueville had posited years earlier. In the margin of this fragment he suggested: "Perhaps keep this for the place where I will speak about the liberal instincts created by equality."[45] Instead, however, he would simply strike these sentences from the final text. In 1840, the implied contradiction between the love of independence and the tendency toward centralization would remain for perceptive readers to ponder. Any explicit mention had been carefully deleted.

At the heart of Tocqueville's analysis of *égoïsme* or *individualisme* remained an abiding paradox that could be traced back at least as far as his references in 1830 to the struggle between *la force individuelle* and *la force sociale*. While condemning *individualisme*, Tocqueville consistently upheld the goal of *indépendance individuelle*. "In our times, those who fear an excess of *individualisme* are right, and those who fear the extreme dependence of the individual are also right. Idea to express somewhere *necessarily*."[46]

He believed that individuals should not occupy themselves solely with their own affairs and ignore the needs of the wider society. Yet he was also persuaded that perhaps the highest purpose of a society was the fullest possible development of the dignity and freedom of the individual. He decried the tendency in democratic times for the individual to limit his efforts to a narrowly defined circle of concern. Yet he also deeply desired a secure and independent sphere of action for each person free from any unnecessary intrusions of public power. Democratic society must not be allowed to swallow up the individual, and yet each person must be led to a higher sense of his public responsibilities and to a healthy willingness to engage in common affairs. What America had taught him was some means of reconciling these private and public interests.

A statement of the essence of this paradox appeared in yet another of Tocqueville's drafts. "To sustain the individual in the face of whatever social power, to conserve something for his independence, his force, his originality; such must be the constant effort of all the friends of humanity in democratic times. Just as in democratic times it is necessary to elevate society and lower the individual."[47]

In February 1840, a letter to Henry Reeve summarized Tocqueville's beliefs. "The great peril of democratic ages, you may be sure, is the destruction or the excessive weakening *of the parts* of the social body in the face of the *whole*. Everything that in our times raises up the idea of the individual is healthy. Everything that gives a separate existence to the species and enlarges the notion of the type is dangerous. The *esprit* of our contemporaries turns by itself in this direction. The doctrine of the realists, introduced to the political world, urges forward all the abuses of *Démocratie;* it is what facilitates despotism, centralization, contempt for individual rights, the doctrine of necessity, all the institutions and all the doctrines which permit the social body to trample men underfoot and which make the nation everything and the citizens nothing.

"That is one of my *fundamental* opinions to which many of my ideas lead. On this point I have reached an absolute conviction; and the principal object of my book has been to give this conviction to the reader."[48]

This statement to Reeve underscored an additional peculiarity of Tocqueville's attachment to *indépendance individuelle.* To combat *individualisme*, to preserve the strength and the dignity of the individual, he assigned a predominant role to "the parts of the social body," to the *corps secondaires*, principally self-governing localities and associations of all sorts. In democratic times, *la force individuelle* required new means of sustenance.[49] What Tocqueville proposed, in short, was to save the individual by encouraging the small group or the artifically created community. The individual would be buoyed up not by his own efforts or powers, but by the support of his fellows. Again we come face to face with paradox.

Concern for the integrity of the individual is one of the bedrocks of Tocqueville's book and outlook. At least as early as 1830, he had been alert to the tension between the individual and the society at large; and an acute awareness of that ancient struggle had informed the writing of his entire book. Whether Tocqueville labeled it *force individuelle* or *indépendance individuelle*, his desire for preserving the dignity of each human being remained at the core of the *Democracy*.

The fundamental solution to this ageless problem, Tocqueville argued, was to seek a deeper understanding of private and public interests and so to attempt the establishment of a new harmony between individual and social needs. This basic concept, which Tocqueville variously called *égoïsme intelligent* or *intérêt bien entendu*, had been among the many lessons of America. But it should also be noted that Tocqueville's anxiety about accelerating *individualisme*, like his interest in centralization, perhaps reflected more his concerns about the social and political conditions of France and French attitudes in the 1830s than his knowledge of American society. In fact, it might be said that on these matters, he kept forgetting America.

The 1840 volumes of the *Democracy* introduced a significant new reason for *individualisme*, the *esprit révolutionnaire*, and that cause served as yet another important analytic device throughout the last part of Tocqueville's book. It helped to explain not only the spread of *individualisme*, but also the increasing trend toward centralization, for example.

By the late 1830s, Tocqueville was increasingly persuaded that France's revolution had not ended in 1830, but was still proceeding and was perhaps even permanent.[50] So a second fundamental historical force, *esprit révolutionnaire*, came to join *démocratie* in the second part of Tocqueville's work. Indeed, his attention during the 1840s and 1850s would be drawn more and more away from *démocratie* and toward revolution. (The latter along with the persistent theme of centralization would clearly come to the fore in Tocqueville's *L'Ancien Régime et la révolution.*) Even by the late 1830s, the trend toward *démocratie* was apparently facing increasing competition for Tocqueville's attention from the concept of *esprit révolutionnaire.*

In 1840 Tocqueville also specifically acknowledged and briefly discussed the significance of a third basic development, industrialization. So by the time the last section of his masterpiece was drafted, Tocqueville was writing about the conjunction of three great forces: *démocratie*, revolution, and industrialization. The focus of his work was still on *démocratie* and its influences and possibilities; but, as Tocqueville then recognized, the future of France and, more generally, of Western civilization ultimately hinged on the interplay of these three developments. Presumably one reason for the not uncommon opinion that the last is also the best and most profound portion of the *Democracy* is Tocqueville's masterful treatment of the complex interrelation of these forces.[51] His work and thought had significantly broadened. Although that tendency presented certain well-recognized dangers of abstraction and lack of precision, it also allowed once again for great depth and insight.

So the 1840 volumes, more than the first two, presented a persistent problem of balance both for Tocqueville and his readers. Not only did he resort more frequently to double and triple comparisons of America, England, and France, but he also attempted, sometimes unsuccessfully, to distinguish clearly between what was American and what was democratic, or between what was democratic and what was revolutionary.[52] When his growing recognition of industrialization is remembered, it becomes clear that, especially by the late 1830s, Tocqueville had become a sort of ambitious and sometimes highly skilled intellectual juggler, bravely attempting to keep a large number of key concepts simultaneously in motion.

We may go beyond this observation to suggest that Tocqueville liked to think in contraries. His penchants for learning by comparison and for making distinctions sometimes led him to (or even over) the brink of contradiction. But more often his mental inclinations simply caused him to see concepts as *pairs in tension*. Our examination of the making of the *Democracy* has suggested several significant examples of this intellectual trait. *Démocratie*, he wrote at various times, exhibited opposite tendencies: toward thinking for oneself and toward not thinking at all; toward suspicion of authority and toward the concentration of power; toward individual independence and toward conformity and submission to the crowd; toward a social and political activity so intense that it spilled over into intellectual and cultural pursuits and toward a pandering of mind and soul to reigning ideas and values. The major task for responsible and thoughtful persons in democratic times was, in one sense, to "sort out the limits of these pairs." The resulting inescapable tensions (and paradoxes) were a hallmark not only of periods of advancing equality, but also of Tocqueville's masterpiece itself.

Most of the major themes treated by Tocqueville in his book are so intricately linked that to grab hold of one is inevitably to pull many others along as well. This tightly knit character is especially apparent when the triple notions of centralization, despotism, and *individualisme* are involved. Particularly in the final section of the 1840 *Democracy*, the three ideas become virtually inextricable. To the extent that Tocqueville has an identifiable "doctrine," centralization, despotism, and *individualisme* (or their opposites: pluralism, liberty, and *indépendance individuelle*) are its Trinity; and *démocratie*, its One.

Part VI

What Tocqueville Meant by *Démocratie*

CHAPTER 19

Some Meanings of *Démocratie*

Perhaps the most disconcerting feature of Tocqueville's thought has always been his failure to pinpoint the meaning of *démocratie*. Many readers have been annoyed by the varied and constantly changing ways in which he used the term, and some have even attempted to identify, count, and analyze the major definitions which appeared in his classic work.[1]

Interestingly, Tocqueville's working papers indicate that he, too, was troubled by his lack of precision and that, throughout the eight-year period of reflection and composition, he tried repeatedly to arrive at some adequate basic definition. His manuscripts provide, moreover, an intriguing and constantly expanding catalogue of the various facets of *démocratie* which he discovered between 1832 and 1840 while mentally turning and returning the concept.

In June 1831, after only a few weeks in America, Tocqueville penned a long letter to Louis de Kergolay describing his early impressions and musings. This missive contained an early definition of *démocratie* which was in many ways the most fundamental sense in which he would ever use the idea. With the United States in mind, he wrote: "*Démocratie*[2] is . . . either broadly advancing in certain states or as fully extended as imaginable in others. It is in the *moeurs*, in the laws, in the opinion of the majority." But America, he hastened to persuade Louis, was not a solitary example. "We are going . . . toward a *démocratie* without limits. . . . we are going there pushed by an irresistible force. All the efforts that people will make to stop the movement will achieve only temporary halts; . . . riches will tend more and more to become equal; the upper class, to dissolve into the middle; and the latter, to become immense and to impose its equality on all.

. . .[3] In a word, *démocratie* seems to me, from now on, a fact which a government can claim to *regulate*, but not to stop."[4]

Démocratie was thus an inescapable development, a brute fact of the modern world, one to which all intelligent men would have to accommodate themselves. More specifically, it was a pervasive tendency toward equality which affected property, *moeurs*, laws, opinions, and ultimately all other areas of society as well.[5]

Later, in drafts of the 1835 sections of his book, Tocqueville composed an apocalyptic description of this "Inevitable march of *Démocratie*." "*Démocratie!* Don't you notice that these are the waters of the Deluge? Don't you see them advance unceasingly by a slow and irresistible effort; already they cover the fields and the cities; they roll over the ruined battlements of castles and even wash against the steps of thrones. . . . Instead of wishing to raise impotent dikes, let us rather seek to build the holy guardian ark which must carry the human species on this boundless ocean."[6]

This irreversible current had obvious revolutionary implications, and Tocqueville was soon writing about yet another though closely related sense of *démocratie*: "this immense social Revolution."[7] "The social revolution I'm speaking about seems to me the great event of the modern world, the only one which is entirely new."[8]

Such uses of *démocratie* as fact, trend, or revolution were all intimately connected to a still broader and more basic definition which soon appeared in Tocqueville's rough drafts. *Démocratie* was a special social condition (*état social*) characterized by advancing equality. When writing of America, for example, he declared: "Society . . . [in the United States] is profoundly democratic in its religion, in its ideas, in its passions, in its habits as in its laws."[9] And again: "The American societies have always been democratic by their nature."[10] Even more to the point, among remarks gathered under the heading "Of the Social State of the Americans," he noted that "the outstanding feature of the *état social* of the Americans is to be democratic."[11] Such an equation of *démocratie* with a peculiar *état social* (and *égalité*) would be one of the constant themes of his 1835 volumes.[12]

Unfortunately, however, no single general definition would be reached so easily, for Tocqueville soon stumbled into a dilemma that would be one of the abiding puzzles of his work. "*Démocratie* constitutes the *état social*. The dogma of the sovereignty of the people [constitutes] the political rule. These two things are not analogous. *Démocratie* is a society's fundamental condition (*manière d'être*). Sovereignty of the people [is] a form of government."[13]

These sentences seemed merely to reinforce the idea of *démocratie* as *état social*. But the careful distinction between social conditions and political forms endured only until Tocqueville added in contradiction to his initial comments: "Note that in this chapter it is necessary never to confuse the *état social* with the political laws which proceed from it. Equality or inequality of conditions, which are facts, with *Démocratie* or aristocracy, which are laws—reexamine from this point of view."[14]

Though *démocratie* was undoubtedly related in some way to *égalité*, a stubborn riddle had now been posed: was *démocratie* "a society's fundamental condition (*manière d'être*)" (a social state tending toward equality), or certain "political laws"?[15] Tocqueville would never be able to arrive at a satisfactory resolution of this problem, and his drafts, working manuscript, and text would consequently continue to offer both meanings, sometimes emphasizing one, sometimes stressing the other.[16]

In a determined attempt to end his confusion on this matter, he undertook an investigation of the link between social and political equality. "It is incontestable that wherever social equality reaches a certain level, men will make a simultaneous effort toward equality of political rights. Wherever the people come to sense their strength and power, they will want to take part in governing the State."[17] This idea did not succeed in ending his multiple uses of *démocratie*, but at least he had now stipulated that the social connotation of the word was more fundamental than its political one. Such a judgment followed his general inclination to weigh *moeurs* more than *lois* in the destiny of mankind. Quite incidentally, he had also indicated here that *démocratie* had something to do with civic equality (and the drive toward it).

But this observation still found Tocqueville far from exhausting his analysis of the political dimensions of *démocratie*. Between 1833 and 1835, he devoted considerable mental effort to this task and succeeded in isolating several different and significant political meanings.[18] At one point, as we might have guessed, he leaned toward a definition cast in terms of an underlying principle. "*Démocratie* properly so called," he decided, meant the "*dogma* of the sovereignty of the people" and the "*principle* of the majority" (majority rule).[19] Elsewhere, however, he carefully distinguished between principle and actuality, and concluded that "the *Sovereignty* of the people and *Démocratie* are two words perfectly correlative; the one represents the theoretical idea; the other its practical realization."[20]

Finally, after considering *démocratie* in its political sense from yet another point of view, he announced that "every time that the government of a people is the sincere and permanent expression of the will of the greatest number, the government, whatever its form, is democratic."[21] In his working manuscript Tocqueville occasionally used the terms "Democratic Republics," "Democratic states," and "Democracies" interchangeably.[22]

So *démocratie*, as "political laws," was a principle (sovereignty of the people or majority rule), the actual operation of that principle (widespread political participation and legal and civic equality), and any government based on the will of the people (a democracy). We should also remember that, particularly in this last sense, *démocratie* as Tocqueville understood it had no necessary connection with liberty; as we have seen, Tocqueville was very much aware that the will of the people might well support despotism. Democracy for him, always inclined more easily toward tyranny than toward liberty.

These political meanings also had some crucial implications about who governed and eventually carried Tocqueville to yet another definition of his key word. "Democratic government, by giving an equal right to all citizens and by having all political questions decided by the majority, in reality gives the power to govern the society to the *lower classes* (*classes inférieures*) since these classes must always compose the majority. That is to say that under the rule of the Democracy (*l'empire de la Démocratie*) it is the less enlightened who lead those who are more [enlightened]."[23]

An additional draft developed the same theme: "I wish that the upper classes (*hautes classes*) and the middle classes (*classes moyennes*) of all of Europe were as persuaded as I am myself that henceforth it is no longer a matter of knowing if *the people* (*le peuple*) will attain power, but in what manner they will use their power. That is the great problem of the future. I wish that in their leisure they [the upper and middle classes] would apply themselves to inquiring into what society will become in the hands of a *restless democracy* (*une démocratie inquiète*) whose movements will not be regulated either by the situation of the country, laws, experience, or *moeurs*. . . . The great, the capital interest of the century is the organization and the education of the democracy (*la démocratie*)."[24]

Here, for the first time, Tocqueville equated *la démocratie* and *le peuple*. So democratie was not only a leveling tendency, or a social condition, or political principles and forms, but also the people themselves. But what precisely did he mean by *le peuple*?

In the "Observations critiques," one reader, perhaps Beaumont, who had seen America firsthand, wondered: "What is *le peuple* in a society where ranks, fortunes, and intelligence approach as much as possible the level of equality? Assuredly the word *peuple* in the New World has in no sense the same meaning as among us."[25]

Almost as if in anticipation of this query, Tocqueville had earlier offered a brief explanation. "*Le peuple*: [I understand] this word in the sense not of a class but of all classes of citizens, the people."[26] Rarely, however, did Tocqueville respect this broad definition; instead he continued to write of *la Démocratie* as if it were synonymous with the lower classes (*les classes inférieures*).[27] Writing of the situation in France, for example, he complained that "The most intelligent and moral portion[28] of the nation has not sought to take hold of it [the democracy] and to direct it. So *la Démocratie* has been abandoned to its savage instincts; it has grown up like those children deprived of bodily care who grow up in the streets of our cities and who know only the vices and miseries of society."[29] Elsewhere he pleaded: "If it were true that there were a way to save future races from the frightful peril[30] that menaces them, if there existed a way to raise the moral standards, to instruct, to mold the *Démocratie* and . . . to save it from itself, would it not be necessary to seize it?"[31]

In the context of this particular definition, the phrase *l'empire de la Démocratie* (quoted above) takes on considerable new significance. It should be recalled that in the summer of 1834, in the midst of these reflections about the meanings of *démocratie*, Tocqueville had actually decided to title his first two volumes *De l'empire de la Démocratie aux Etats-Unis*.[32] Perhaps this resolution indicated the full extent of his preoccupation at that time with *démocratie* as *le peuple*.

In France and the rest of Europe, democracy had long been associated with confusion and anarchy.[33] Tocqueville denied the necessity of any such connection, but while writing his masterpiece, he did develop a theory somewhat related to this popular usage. He began to link *démocratie* with activity, change, and *le mouvement*. The idea of *démocratie* as mobility (especially social and economic) initially appeared in drafts for the first part of his work (1835). When reflecting, for example, about the constantly shifting ownership of wealth and the fluidity of class lines in America, Tocqueville observed: "What is most important to *Démocratie*, is not that there are no great fortunes, but that great fortunes do not remain in the same hands. In this way, there are rich people, but they do not form a class."[34] The 1835 text, in the section entitled "Activity Prevailing in All Parts of the Political Body in the United States; The Influence Thereby Exerted on Society,"[35] would particularly stress the movement, the energy, and the bustle which seemed so integral a part of America. After describing in detail "a sort of tumult; a confused clamor" that he had discovered in the United States, he would remark that "The great political movement . . . is only an episode and a sort of extension of the universal movement, which begins in the lowest ranks of the people and thence spreads successively through all classes of citizens."[36]

Expanding this idea, he would add: "That constantly renewed agitation introduced by democratic government into political life passes, then, into civil society. . . . Democracy . . . spreads throughout the body social a restless activity, superabundant force, and energy never found elsewhere, which, however little favored by circumstances, can do wonders (*enfanter des merveilles*)."[37] So according to Tocqueville, an intimate connection did exist between such activity and energy and *démocratie*. But when his first volumes appeared, his focus still remained primarily on the United States. Only after 1835 would the concept of *démocratie* as *le mouvement* (or mobility) free itself of its American context and become a major part of his understanding of democracy.

The problem of defining *démocratie* did not end with the publication of the first portion of Tocqueville's book; between 1835 and 1840, his drafts repeated most of the meanings we have already noted. But his working papers for that period also introduced at least one almost new use of the word, offered a few final attempts at an inclusive definition of *démocratie*, and, more important, demonstrated some significant changes of emphasis in his thinking.

His almost new use of *démocratie* was somewhat related to the earlier debate over who *le peuple* was. As early as 1831, in the letter to Kergolay quoted above, Tocqueville had hinted that *démocratie* had something to do with *la classe moyenne*.[38] By 1835, however, this idea became much more specific; we have observed Tocqueville in England musing about the connection between industry and democracy and describing a particular "class apart . . . where instincts are all democratic. . . . As a people expands its commerce and its industry, this democratic class becomes more numerous and more influential; little by little its opinions pass into the *moeurs* and its ideas into the laws, until finally having become preponderant and, so to speak, unique, it takes hold of power, directs everything as it likes, and establishes democracy."[39] In the rough drafts and working manuscript of the 1840 volumes, he at least once called the English middle class "une immense Démocratie."[40] In the margin of a description of the rising power and prominence of *la classe industrielle*, or bourgeoisie, he scribbled the following phrase: "la classe Démocratique par excellence."[41] So, *démocratie*, on some occasions, could also mean *la classe moyenne*, as well as *les classes inférieures* or *le peuple*.[42]

Just after his debut in 1835 as famous author, Tocqueville patiently tried to explain some of his major ideas to a disturbed Kergolay, and in the process, he offered a significant restatement of a familiar definition: "I am as convinced as one can be of something in this world that we are carried irresistibly by our laws and by our *moeurs* toward an almost complete equality of conditions. Conditions once equal, I admit that I no longer see any intermediary between a democratic government (and by this word I understand not a republic, but a condition in the society where everyone more or less takes part in public affairs) and the government of an individual (*d'un seul*) operating without control."[43]

Tocqueville's explanation clearly distinguished once again between *démocratie* as a profound social movement and *démocratie* as particular political structures. Beyond this, however, Tocqueville here indicated his belief that political democracy did not demand republican forms, that it was not incompatible with monarchy. Politically the essential feature of a democracy was, he declared, some degree of effective participation in public affairs by the citizenry. Here was yet another specific definition of *démocratie* (in its political sense). But the focus in this letter to his friend was on *égalité des conditions* and the trend toward it. In fact, so frequently did the drafts of Tocqueville's last volumes repeat and reinforce that emphasis, that between 1836 and 1840 *égalité* or *égalité des conditions* became, more than ever, the single most important definition of *démocratie*.[44] A list of chapters under the general heading "On the Taste for Material Pleasures in Democracies" included, for example, a section labeled: "How Equality of Conditions (or Democracy) Carries Americans toward Industrial Professions."[45]

A similarly revealing choice occurred when he selected a name for the last major section of his work. The "Rubish" harbored the "great chapter entitled: How the Ideas and the Sentiments That Equality Suggests Influence the Political Constitution." But the 1840 text would call this part: "On the Influence of Democratic Ideas and Feelings on Political Society."[46]

Even the working manuscript offered numerous instances of Tocqueville's pronounced tendency between 1835 and 1840 to use *démocratie* and *égalité* (or *égalité des conditions*) interchangeably.[47] Perhaps it was his growing preoccupation with this particular sense of *démocratie* that led him once again to consider a different title for his *grande affaire*. In the fall of 1839, he had temporarily decided to call his last two volumes [*De*] *l'influence de l'égalité sur les idées et les sentiments des hommes* rather than simply *De la Démocratie en Amérique*, volumes three and four.[48]

Despite his frequent use of *démocratie* as *égalité*, Tocqueville was also fully aware that his discussions in this vein were purely theoretical. "In order to make myself well understood I am constantly obliged to portray extreme states, an aristocracy without a mixture of *Démocratie*, a *démocratie* without a mixture of aristocracy, a perfect equality, which is an imaginary state. It happens then that I attribute to one or the other of the two principles more complete effects than those that in general they produce, because in general they are not alone."[49] His use of exaggerated portraits was an increasingly important intellectual device for Tocqueville and helped him to push his thoughts forward.

Especially after 1835 he found such an analytical tool useful as he struggled to distinguish not only aristocratic and democratic features, but also American and democratic, transitional and democratic, and revolutionary and democratic. (In this technique, he was of course anticipating the common use of "models" or "types" by modern social scientists.)

Tocqueville's recognition of the dangers of dealing with "imaginary states" eventually drove him in the summer of 1838 to attempt a final, more subtle definition of *démocratie*: he returned to the concept of *démocratie* as mobility.

> Explain somewhere what I understand by centuries of democracy.[50] / equality
> It is not this chimerical time when all men are perfectly alike and equal, but (1) when a very great number of them will be . . .[51] and when an even greater number will fall sometimes below sometimes above, but not far from the common measure; (2) when there will not be permanent classification, caste, class, unbreachable barrier, or even one very difficult to breach; so that if all men are not equal, they can all aspire to the same point; . . . so that a common standard makes itself [felt][52] against which all men measure themselves in advance. This spreads the feeling of equality (*le sentiment de l'égalité*) even in the midst of unequal conditions—22 June 1838.[53]

Démocratie thus implied an open society, one without extreme or fixed distinctions,[54] and especially one that fostered the hope or belief that opportunities existed and that full equality was possible (*le sentiment de l'égalité*). In a democratic nation, people would be persuaded that, in certain respects, they were all equal and that society offered real possibilities for the achievement of individual aspirations. On the basis of such convictions, they would organize their efforts and conduct their lives. In the New World republic Tocqueville had noticed that these beliefs had become a central part of the national myth.[55] Tocqueville's recognition that democratic times would be marked by a pervasive sense or feeling of equality—despite any actual inequalities—led him to yet another significant facet of *démocratie*: its psychological dimension, the unshakable conviction of equality.

In other drafts, Tocqueville continued to pursue the idea of *démocratie* as mobility. "A democratic people, society, time do not mean a people, a society, a time when all men are equal, but a people, a society, a time when there are no more castes, fixed classes, privileges, special and exclusive rights, permanent riches, properties fixed in the hands of certain families, when all men can continuously climb and descend and mix together in all ways. When I mean this in the political sense, I say *Démocratie*. When I want to speak of the effects of equality, I say *égalité*."[56]

Here he neglected the important psychological element of democratic times, *le sentiment de l'égalité*, but presented a final attempt to separate the political and social senses of his central concept. He began by assuming a society characterized by social and economic mobility and relative legal and civic equality. When considering the political aspects of such a fluid society, he would use the word *démocratie*. When thinking of the more general (social? or economic? or cultural? or intellectual?) consequences of such a society, he would write: *égalité*. This effort, still far from satisfactory, was the closest Tocqueville ever came to solving the riddle that had troubled him since at least 1833.

If any single solution did exist, however, it probably rested with Tocqueville's recurring concept of the two levels of *démocratie*: social and political. On the one hand, democracy was an underlying social condition (characterized by advancing equality and mobility). On the other hand, democracy meant certain political laws and forms (such as widespread suffrage, freedom of association and other civil liberties, and structures for expressing the will of the citizenry). The first was especially the providential, inevitable fact with which all people would have to reckon. The second was perhaps equally inescapable (since social democracy tended to carry political democracy in its wake), but at least to some extent the impeding or furthering of political democracy depended on the efforts of men.

Most significantly, Tocqueville believed that the key to liberty in democratic times was the proper matching or balancing of these two fundamental senses of *démocratie*. One of the characteristics most attractive to Tocqueville about America was the "universal" nature of democracy in the New World republic; democracy had influenced every aspect of American life; there society and politics were in harmony. He repeatedly stressed that, in Europe, the only reasonable cure for the potential flaws of *social* democracy was the introduction of greater *political* democracy. "For there is only Democracy (by this word I understand self-government) which can lessen and make bearable the inevitable evils of a democratic social state. 5 September 1838."[57] And again: "Many people consider democratic civil laws as an evil and democratic political laws as another and greater evil; as for me, I say that the one is the only remedy that one can apply to the other. The whole idea of my politics is here."[58]

This persistent duality reflected not only the nearly insurmountable difficulty of precisely defining the "fact" of *démocratie*, but also echoed Tocqueville's earlier distinction between *moeurs* and laws (*lois*) and the power which humanity had over them. Social democracy (like *moeurs*) was more fundamental and, at the same time, less amenable to human effort. Political democracy (like *lois*) was less fundamental (though still extremely important), but could be shaped by the power of men. So human energy, Tocqueville advised, should be directed not toward any useless attempt to retard or to deflect democracy as a developing social condition. Intelligent individuals should labor to introduce political democracy and so to "educate" and "mold" the people. "Use Democracy to moderate Democracy. It is the only path to salvation that is open to us. . . . Beyond that all is foolish and imprudent."[59] Here again was the immense burden of human responsibility to which Tocqueville was always so sensitive.

Tocqueville never abandoned his plural meanings of *démocratie*. Throughout the four volumes of his work, the concept continued to conjure up a multitude of trends and conditions, laws and attitudes, political forms and social groups. Furthermore, within this cluster of definitions, he frequently shifted primary attention from one to another, from *état-social* to *lois politiques* and back again, or from *le peuple* to *l'égalité*, and then to *le sentiment de l'égalité* and *le mouvement*. But these shifts in emphasis implied neither that other uses had been forgotten nor that one particular meaning was ultimately the single most important; these changes merely reflected his desire to establish as broad and as thorough a definition as possible and his recurring tendency, while drafting his *grande affaire*, to focus on one idea to the temporary exclusion of competing ones.

Tocqueville's very failure precisely to define *démocratie* accounts, in part, for the brilliance of his observations. If he had at one time fixed definitively upon a single meaning, all of the others would have been more or less lost from sight. His vision would have been at once restricted, his message narrowed, and his audience diminished. His extraordinary ability to imagine and to consider so many different uses, to revolve the idea so continuously in his mind, led to the richness and profundity of his insights.

CHAPTER 20

Tocqueville's Return to America

Our reconstruction of Alexis de Tocqueville's long process of observation, reading, thinking, and writing the *Democracy* has offered the possibility of some new insights about Tocqueville's famous book. First of all, we have reexamined many of Tocqueville's sources and unearthed some new or almost new roots. As we have watched Tocqueville drawing in turn on his French, American, English, and then again on his French experiences, we have had a chance to reevaluate the contributions of many of his American, English, and French friends. Numerous additional specific echoes in Tocqueville's volumes of statements by such key American acquaintances as Timothy Walker, Joel Poinsett, John Latrobe, Francis Gray, and Jared Sparks have been identified. The significance of comments by such Englishmen as Dr. Bowring and John Stuart Mill and the important impact of Beaumont, Tocqueville's father, Louis de Kergolay, and other countrymen have been noted. Louis, in particular, helped immensely to shape the form and the content of the *Democracy*; especially after 1835, his influence rivaled even that of Beaumont.

Although specific connections between the *Democracy* and some of Tocqueville's more far-ranging and profound readings during the 1830s are still obscure, new traces of his printed American sources, especially the books by William Darby, Isaac Goodwin, William Rawle, Joseph Story, and others have become apparent. The thoroughness and quality of Tocqueville's research, especially in the fields of history, law, the American Constitution, and in the particular issues of the Jacksonian period, have been successfully tested once again.

Tocqueville's papers have also disclosed a surprisingly extensive use of certain essays from the *Federalist*. He listened carefully to the opinions and arguments of Alexander Hamilton and especially James

Madison, whose contributions to the *Democracy* were greater than most readers have realized. Our examination of the growth of the *Democracy* has shown Tocqueville often informed and stimulated, usually persuaded, and occasionally misled by "Publius."

In addition Tocqueville echoed Montesquieu's ideas on certain matters (like the relative nature of political institutions and the disadvantages of size) and questioned and revised his predecessor's opinions on other issues (like the role of virtue in republics). On such themes as the danger of concentrated power, the value of local liberties, the need for associations and a free press, the rise of the middle classes, and the advance of "civilization," Tocqueville also closely paralleled the writings of nineteenth-century French figures like Benjamin Constant, Pierre-Paul Royer-Collard, and François Guizot.

But the sources for Tocqueville and his book went beyond his voyages to America and England, his friends, and his readings. The *Democracy in America* also reflected the concerns of contemporary France. Many topics that appeared in Tocqueville's pages were issues debated constantly in France throughout the early nineteenth century and were therefore familiar to his countrymen. Was France overly centralized? Should the *communes* be more free to regulate their own affairs? Were associations too subversive to be allowed? Should the institution of the jury be introduced more broadly? How much independence and prerogative were appropriate for judges? Should the press be more, or less free? Was the right of suffrage too narrowly extended? Such chronic questions shaped one of the purposes of the *Democracy*: Tocqueville desired to teach France and to present a specific political program that would appeal to a segment of French opinion broad enough to lead to reform.

Other contemporary problems also captured Tocqueville's interest. After the revolution of 1830 and the disappointments of the July regime, many individuals like Kergolay or Eugène Stoffels had retreated into an internal exile, withdrawing from all public affairs. Others, like Tocqueville's own Norman constituents, seemed increasingly absorbed in self-promotion and material interests, and more and more unable to approach public issues from the viewpoint of the common good. Such developments helped to stimulate Tocqueville's thoughts about democratic materialism, *égoïsme*, and, eventually, *individualisme*. The growth of government involvement in French industry helped to alert Tocqueville to the connection between industrialization and centralization. So certain parts of the *Democracy* grew even more out of France than out of America. Sometimes, the immediacy of some of these concerns even made him almost forget about America.

French politics of the 1830s also had an effect on Tocqueville's work. His desire for a reputation which would lead to a significant political role was another of the reasons for the writing of the *Democracy*; and by the late 1830s political campaigns and legislative duties helped to delay its completion. More broadly, Tocqueville's ambivalent attitudes about the politics and politicians of his day entered into the tone of his book. His mixed feelings encouraged him to disassociate himself and his book from all particular parties or points of view and to assume a stance of lofty detachment. "I did not intend to serve or to combat any party; I have tried to see not differently but further than any party; while they are busy with tomorrow, I have wished to consider the whole future."[1]

Still another influence on Tocqueville's thinking was French history. We have noticed how knowledge of the Convention, for example, encouraged Tocqueville in 1835 to stress the dangers of legislative despotism, and how memories of Napoleon made him always suspicious about military leaders. Indeed, some events in the French past had too deep an impact on Tocqueville; they sometimes prevented him from perceiving new dangers.

Our step-by-step re-creation of the development of the *Democracy* has, in addition, disclosed many of the methods by which Tocqueville studied, wrote, and thought, including his early efforts to organize his materials and plan the task of composition and how and where he actually first set pen to page. Periodically he felt a need for the stimulation of "good instruments of conversation," usually Beaumont and Kergolay, both of whom served as invaluable critics and intellectual companions. And sometimes Tocqueville shaped and pruned the *Democracy* with an eye on the scope of the works of others like Beaumont or Michel Chevalier.

He repeatedly sought, for one particular subject or another, to grasp some basic organizing principle, the *idée-mère*, or to expose some irreducible precondition, the *point de départ*. In order to resolve certain paradoxes inherent in the French situation during the early nineteenth century, he emphasized the concepts of *époque de transition* and *esprit révolutionnaire.* The latter idea grew quickly from a convenient mental tool which helped him to get over some theoretical difficulties into an important theme of the final portion of his work. He also occasionally resorted to "models" or "types" to clarify his thinking; *démocratie* and *aristocratie* are the most famous examples of his use of this technique, but the drafts of Tocqueville's book have disclosed other instances of this method as well.

Tocqueville's interest in presenting fresh viewpoints sometimes led him to stress the originality of his insights by calling for new names. With Madison, he dubbed the unique American federal system "an incomplete national government"; he urged a "new science of politics," labeled a particular cluster of democratic traits *individualisme* (in 1840 a relatively new term which he thereafter helped to popularize), and warned against a new despotism.

Still another methodological trait vividly demonstrated by the successive drafts of the *Democracy* is Tocqueville's sensitivity to style. For him, form could emphatically not be detached from content. He labored toward a high ideal of literary craftsmanship (and quite probably took Montesquieu as his standard); the qualities which he sought were clarity, directness, a sparseness or economy of language, and a certain detachment, in short, a style marked by elegant and precise restraint. To achieve this goal he solicited oral and written critiques from friends and family and relentlessly reworked his words, sentences, paragraphs, and chapters looking for the best possible use of words and order of ideas. It was this effort which produced his many memorable phrases as well.

With the attainment of a certain style in mind, he also took pains to excise passionate or exaggerated passages from his drafts and working manuscript. Much of the cool detachment of the *Democracy* arose rather naturally from the author's own personality, but some also resulted from his determined efforts, on more than one occasion, to suppress the dogmatism and emotionalism which sometimes broke forth when he was immersed in the excitement of composition. His working papers reveal, for example, a softening of his strong pronouncements about Jefferson's political legacy and the "certain" future of the Union, a calming of his excited alarms about the abilities of *le peuple* and the survival of European civilization, and a lightening of his dark pessimism about the future of liberty.

But Tocqueville's compulsion to revision arose from more than stylistic considerations. He was extremely self-conscious about his book. The drafts and manuscripts of the *Democracy* are everywhere sprinkled with Tocqueville's comments to himself. The margins abound with his own curious criticisms, questions, warnings, and especially with reminders to himself about major themes and larger purposes. As his book developed, there was a striking running attempt to keep fundamental motifs in view, and a constant measuring of what he wrote against the basic tasks he hoped to accomplish. A major difficulty was the multiplicity of his objectives. Was he attempting to describe the American republic to his countrymen? To trace the advance of *démocratie* and its effects? To save France by suggesting possible ways to reconcile liberty and equality? To publish a work which would assure a prominent future for Alexis de Tocqueville? The fact that he usually had several purposes simultaneously in view only complicated his efforts to pare away what might be irrelevant or harmful to his goals.

Even more fundamental than his striving for literary excellence is the characteristic style of logic or pattern of thought which emerges from our story of Tocqueville's second voyage. Tocqueville repeatedly clarified and deepened his thought by means of comparisons and distinctions. He set, for example, Ohio against Kentucky, Quebec against New Orleans, and—most important—France against both America and England. He separated sudden from gradual death of the Union; governmental from administrative centralization; one variety of despotism from another; the specific (political and legal) from the general (moral and intellectual) tyranny of the majority; the cultural vulnerability of semicivilized peoples from the deeply rooted civilization of modern Europeans; the *égoïsme* of old from the *individualisme* of today; and *démocratie* defined politically from *démocratie* defined socially.

Such frequent use of comparisons and distinctions is related to a more general trait: Tocqueville's tendency to think in terms of contraries or pairs in tension. In his analyses of the results of *démocratie* and of the relationship between the individual and society, for example, he was grappling with near paradoxes, with almost opposites. And occasionally he moved too boldly and fell into true contradiction. Sometimes he extricated himself; at other times he apparently failed even to recognize his predicament. So the making of the *Democracy* seems to reveal a mind marked by superb analytical powers and, beyond that, by a rarer facility for original insights and bold theoretical leaps. If this sometimes led Tocqueville into errors or caused him to overshoot the factual basis for some of his ideas, readers must consider whether his brilliant contributions to our understanding of society do not more than balance these flaws.

Yet another major feature of Tocqueville's pattern of thought should be considered. The author of the *Democracy* never ceased turning and returning his ideas; his work is built out of a long accumulation of information, opinions, insights, and second thoughts. This unending process of reconsideration was not only in the mind but also on the page. Time itself became an important ingredient in the making of the *Democracy*. This gradual but relentless building up of ideas produced a book far longer and far wider in scope than Tocqueville had originally conceived.

Tocqueville's commitment to ongoing reconsideration occasionally suggested a method of postponement when he was wrestling with particularly stubborn issues. He assumed that he would come back to such puzzles later; time would presumably produce the needed fresh insights. Sometimes this strategy had its rewards. But a few problems, like the definitions of *circonstances* or *démocratie*, proved insoluble even after long periods of rumination. In these instances, postponement lengthened into a kind of abandonment.

Tocqueville's constant revolving of ideas (and the sheer passage of time) also help to explain many of his ambiguities and confusions. While concentrating on a newly perceived facet of some complex concept (like *démocratie*), Tocqueville could hardly fail, at times, to forget what he had previously discovered. It was almost impossible to keep so many notions in mind simultaneously.

So his determination to analyze each notion from as many viewpoints as possible, to discover all possible dimensions, was a vital part of his second journey. If this constant reconsideration must bear some blame for his recognized inability adequately to define some of his key concepts, it must also be credited with producing some of Tocqueville's most perceptive ideas. Above all, his instinct for thoroughness should make us sufficiently wary of attempting to impose too much consistency on his thought. Such a straining after unity would also obscure the chronological dimensions of his ideas, and neither the slow maturation, nor the false starts, rapid reversals, and forgotten paths should be overlooked. So we must abandon any searches for the coherent system of a philosopher and concentrate instead on capturing the pluralism and diversity of Tocqueville's mind. These are some of the essential qualities which continuously attract thoughtful people to his work.

The diverse and sometimes strange ways in which Tocqueville's concepts developed have also been illuminated by our study of the *Democracy*. One or two of his ideas were never quite born (the impact of *démocratie* on education). Some withered early (the role of physical environment; the importance of internal improvements), and others matured late. Among the late bloomers, some had appeared (at least in germ) in the 1835 *Democracy*, but by 1840 had assumed far greater importance: the New Despotism; *égoïsme/individualisme*; the democratic threat to freedom of thought; the crowd or mass; and *démocratie* defined as *le mouvement*. Others had belatedly made first appearances in the working papers of the 1840 volumes, but had grown rapidly from then on: for example, the mutual reinforcement of *démocratie* and industry; and Tocqueville's mental encounter with that powerful trio of forces, *démocratie*, industrialization, and revolution.

Some concepts slowly faded after an early blossoming in 1835 (legislative despotism; the image of a reborn tyranny of the Caesars; *démocratie* as *le peuple*), and others flourished increasingly throughout all stages of the making of the *Democracy* (the role of *moeurs*; the value of associations and other means to link the ideas and unite the actions of isolated citizens; and *démocratie* as equality of conditions). A few ideas were so fundamental that for nearly a decade they were almost unchanging: the inevitable advance of *démocratie* itself; the tendency toward centralization; the tension between the individual and the society as a whole; and Tocqueville's concern for the freedom and dignity of each person.

Some notions were lost, among others: the personal repudiation of racial theories which Tocqueville developed during the 1830s; his condemnation of Jefferson's administration; his stated preference for democratic monarchy; and especially his belief that industrialization ranked with *démocratie* as the two great features of modern Western history. Still others, first appearing before 1835 and then not reemerging until 1840, were lost temporarily: the rise of a new industrial aristocracy; and the troublesome problem of the influence of *démocratie* on civilization, for instance.

Although some preconceptions were uprooted (the influence of *géographie*; and the identity of the American pioneer), certain beliefs were too deeply imbedded to be shaken by any contradictory experience or testimony (the benefits of the jury; the advantages of independent localities; and the distrust of size).

Confusions and unresolved dilemmas also sometimes mark the *Democracy*. Was the republic an indivisible Union or a compact of states? Were the states more villains or benefactors for the American future? What about the ambiguities left by Tocqueville's attempts to distinguish two centralizations and to identify various despotisms? How were his readers to reconcile his disclaimer that the majority actually abused its power in America and his declaration that intellectual liberty did not exist there? If *démocratie* encouraged a love of independence and a distrust of authority, how did it also lead so easily to the concentration of power? What finally did he mean by *circonstances,* or *majorité,* or *individualisme,* or *démocratie*?

Nor should we overlook the many paradoxes of his thought, some that Tocqueville recognized and presented for his readers to ponder, others that he never saw. He visited America, but thought of France. He disliked politics, but offered an agenda of reform and became an important political figure. He proposed to escape the evils of democracy by introducing more democracy and hoped to strengthen *indépendance individuelle* by combating *individualisme*.

His concept of *démocratie* caught him in yet another paradox which perhaps he never resolved. He spoke about the providential fact of democracy's advance and seemed to understand the increasing equality of conditions as a divine and therefore inescapable necessity. Yet he also repeatedly denounced the fatalists, the prophets of necessity, the people like Gobineau who bound humanity to iron laws.[2] He always insisted with some vehemence that human beings were free and therefore had the responsibility for moral choices. For him, humankind could never be merely a pawn to the fates, to the forces of environment, race, climate or whatever, or even to God. Perhaps the closest he ever came to reconciling this dilemma of inevitable equality and human choice was the final passage of the 1840 *Democracy*. "Providence did not make mankind entirely free or completely enslaved. Providence has, in truth, drawn a predestined circle around each man beyond which he cannot pass; but within those vast limits man is strong and free, and so are peoples."[3] Whether this resolved or simply sidestepped the issue each reader must judge for himself.

There is a common impression that Tocqueville was basically uninterested in and unacquainted with economic and technological matters. He is often criticized for missing perhaps the major developments of the nineteenth and twentieth centuries. Clearly his primary intellectual interests were elsewhere; his mind, like Montesquieu's, inclined toward political theory as it related to broader social, cultural, intellectual, and moral questions. He conceived of the *Democracy* as primarily "un ouvrage philosophico-politique." This did not mean, however, that he ignored or remained misinformed about economic developments. In the New World he was very much aware of many of the important economic and technological changes occurring around him. He grasped the scope and the significance of the physical transformation that Jacksonian America was undergoing. He put his finger on two crucial features of the American economy then just taking shape: the rise of the corporation and the development of a complex, pluralistic approach to economic activities that blended public (federal, state, and local) and private (individual and corporate) efforts in an amazing variety of ways. He also noticed the rage of Americans for the latest improvement and their peculiar philosophy of planned obsolescence. And if, in 1831 and 1832, he failed to appreciate the future importance of manufacturing in the United States, he did not by the late 1830s continue to make quite the same mistake (at least for Europe). By 1838 he was persuaded that industrialization and increasing equality were the two great forces of the times. He worried, as early as 1833 or 1834, about the rise of an industrial aristocracy, wrestled with the connection between decentralization and economic prosperity, and by the late 1830s, recognized and explored the ways in which industry, centralization, and *démocratie* strengthened one another and moved relentlessly ahead together.

The drafts, working manuscript, and "Rubish" as well as the published text of the *Democracy* thus demonstrate in many places that Tocqueville was aware of the various ways in which economic attitudes, institutions, and changes influenced society. So the *Democracy's* relative lack of attention to economics and technology should not be exaggerated. Nor should it be primarily attributed to either gaps in knowledge or failures of insight. Tocqueville's choices of emphasis arose from his determination to keep his book focused on his major subject, from his personal interests, from his beliefs about where he could make the most original contributions, and most important, from his moral assumptions about which areas of human activity were most truly fundamental.[4]

For some readers, Tocqueville's warnings against an omnipresent central government and his unforgettable prophecies about the regime of the New Despotism unfortunately obscure his profound attachment to what he admired most about *démocratie*: its "liberal instincts." The perennial lack of submissiveness, the anti-authoritarian bias, and the unquenchable discontent which democracy bred were delights for Tocqueville. He knew that a free society would not necessarily be one of order and tranquillity and observed in the 1840 *Democracy* that "I cannot forget that all nations have been enslaved by being kept in good order. . . . A nation that asks nothing of its government but the maintenance of order is already a slave at heart."[5] Liberty almost always had its loose ends, its confusions, its storms and upheavals.

To nurture these "liberal instincts" and thus to preserve freedom in democratic times, he championed greater freedom of assembly, association, speech, and press (as well as wider suffrage). In the context of his age he was something of a civil libertarian staunchly protecting the individual in the face of the pressures of the wider society. "Everything that in our times raises up the idea of the individual is healthy. . . . The doctrine of the realists, introduced to the political world . . . is what facilitates despotism, centralization, contempt for individual rights, the doctrine of necessity, all the institutions and the doctrines which permit the social body to trample men underfoot and which make the nation everything and the citizens nothing."[6] If Tocqueville can be taken for some neoconservative carping about an active government, he can also be read as a civil libertarian rushing in wherever the individual seems in danger. But either view distorts a position that was at once original and highly complex.

One of the most intriguing characteristics of the *Democracy*, despite the extended period of its growth, is the essential harmony of the whole. Despite some errors which Tocqueville hoped to correct and some opinions which he wanted to revise, almost all significant changes in ideas between 1835 and 1840 resulted from the gradual maturation of Tocqueville's thinking. During the 1830s he did not so much reverse judgments as flesh out earlier ideas. The number of times that a chapter or whole group of chapters from the last half of the *Democracy* may be traced directly back to germs in a sentence or paragraph of the first two volumes is remarkable.[7] We should not exaggerate the concept of two *Democracies*, suggestive though it is in certain respects.[8]

This is not to deny that some of the differences between the first and second parts of Tocqueville's book are significant. A process of broadening out, of always expanding dimensions, was crucial to the making of the *Democracy*. After 1835, Tocqueville's readings were drawn from a much wider range of time and place. America faded more and more into the background. In 1835 Tocqueville's journey was still fresh; his reflections were more or less grounded in specific conversations, experiences, impressions, and information. He was right when he described his first effort as somehow more tangible, more solid. But by 1840, the whole American experience had become something of a recollection; by then it was intimately intermingled with new lessons of all sorts, and much of the immediacy was gone. Deeper knowledge of England as well as greater direct involvement in contemporary French public affairs also led him to ever more frequent consideration of those two nations. His comparisons became more often three-cornered. His attention was increasingly captured by developments other than the advance of *démocratie*. So his work not only became less American and more democratic, but it also outgrew the limits of one or even two nations and moved beyond *démocratie* to consider other major social forces as well. The second half of the *Democracy*, as Tocqueville himself suspected, turned out to be far more abstract, theoretical, and demanding.

Tocqueville's tendency to wander over an ever-wider mental range, to move always farther from the specific, helped to produce both the strengths and weaknesses of the 1840 volumes. If the last part of the *Democracy* sometimes presented long and occasionally dubious series of deductions, if many readers felt terribly far from the reality of America, if generalizations sometimes overreached prudence, still the second portion of Tocqueville's book displayed a thorough, profound, and marvelously stimulating analysis of his subject matter. His ambitious movement into ever wider spheres took him in some ways far from his 1835 work, but the rewards were worth the risks.

Our retelling of Tocqueville's second voyage also makes clear his fascination with what he usually labeled "spirit" and what we might call the psychology, or the fundamental attitude or approach of people. Again and again, when he sought to penetrate to the core of an idea or issue, he thought and wrote about the "spirit" of locality, or liberty, or religion, or trade, or revolution; the *sentiment de l'égalité*, one fundamental meaning of *démocratie,* was another closely related example. This readily observable tendency is part of a more basic inclination. Whenever Tocqueville searched for the most profound causes, meanings, or influences, he went not to physical, economic, legal, or even to intellectual features, but to the elements of what he called *moeurs*: customs, attitudes, values, ways of life.[9] It was almost always to the intangible motivations of human belief and behavior that he ultimately resorted. One of the lasting contributions of his book was the importance bestowed on *moeurs*; the *Democracy* was one of the earliest extended statements of their crucial role in society.

This sensitivity to "spirit" and more broadly to *moeurs* reflects the way in which Tocqueville's personal moral beliefs also helped to shape the *Democracy*. Whether weighing the significance of race, or choosing between *moeurs* or *lois*; whether calculating the chances for a future of liberty, or deciding which sense of *démocratie* (social or political) was more basic, he fell back again and again to moral convictions. It was in the majority's moral authority that he placed the ultimate power of the many; and it was also in moral limits that he found the best barrier to abuse of that power. When he considered the influence of some idea or institution, it was the potential moral benefit or harm which he usually weighed most heavily. Thus local liberties were praised especially for their moral advantages, and despotism condemned most harshly for the way it undermined self-esteem and brought men to despise themselves.

A strong case may therefore be made that Tocqueville's most essential concern was the moral condition of mankind. He valued, above all, the freedom and dignity of the individual. What *démocratie* did to enhance these he applauded; what it did to endanger them he feared. As he wrote the *Democracy*, he remained always aware that to spur men to significant achievement it was necessary to allow them a circle of meaningful action, to think highly of their capacities, and to expect a great deal.

But was Tocqueville primarily concerned with moral issues or did he instead look most essentially to what would work? In democratic times, did he favor whatever would be useful for warding off the worst dangers? Was he a type of utilitarian rather than a type of moralist? Closely related to this question is the ambiguity of Tocqueville's attitude toward *démocratie*. Did he secretly admire *démocratie*, sympathize with its advance, and even hope to hasten it by his own political program? Or did he go along with *démocratie* only out of necessity, resigned to making the best of a bad—or at least a dangerous—situation? Again, was he mostly thinking practically rather than morally?

We can offer a possible answer to this old puzzle. Tocqueville believed that, for more and more of his contemporaries, appeals to morality were no longer effective, no longer powerful enough to persuade or to change actions. Those still sensitive to moral considerations would hear and heed them, but for all the others, appeals would now have to be cast in terms of utility or self-interest. Tocqueville would at times have to argue from points of view which were increasingly amoral if he hoped at all to engage most of his contemporaries.[10]

So what Tocqueville resurrected in new form in the *Democracy* was the famous wager of Pascal, with whom (at least for some periods during the mid-1830s) he had lived a bit every day. Some of Tocqueville's most powerful arguments to open the eyes of his readers to the possible benefits and pitfalls of democracy and to move them toward securing the first and avoiding the second were, like the wager, part of a final effort to persuade especially the sophisticated, the knowledgeable, the intelligent, the "best"; to appeal effectively to their own self-interest; to argue convincingly on their own terms. Tocqueville hoped to bring these people, above all, to accept *démocratie*, not because it was good, but because all the alternatives were worse. Reasonable, dispassionate people, Tocqueville argued, should take a chance on making the best of *démocratie*. To work for that at least brought hope; to refuse would lead only to certain disaster. Tocqueville, like Pascal, had deeply moral sensibilities, yet understood his contemporaries well enough to cast a net beautifully appropriate to his age—and ours.

Notes

Selected Bibliography

Index

Notes

Preface

1. I am indebted to George Wilson Pierson for both the phrase and the concept "second voyage." Consult his provocative essay, "Le 'second voyage' de Tocqueville en Amerique" (hereafter cited as Pierson, "Second voyage") in the commemorative collection entitled *Alexis de Tocqueville: Livre du centenaire, 1859–1959*, pp. 71–85 (hereafter cited as *Tocqueville: centenaire*). In addition, Pierson has written a superb and thorough account of Tocqueville's first journey and a brief description of some episodes of the second in *Tocqueville and Beaumont in America* (hereafter cited as Pierson, *Toc. and Bt.*). His work is also available in an abridged edition prepared by Dudley C. Lunt in both paper and hardback versions, Pierson, *Tocqueville in America*.

2. The largest depository of Tocqueville papers is located in Paris under the supervision of the Commission nationale pour l'édition des oeuvres d'Alexis de Tocqueville. But for this study, the Yale Tocqueville Manuscripts Collection, which includes either originals or copies of almost all materials relating to the *Democracy*, is fully adequate when used in conjunction with published materials. The appearance and importance of many of the Yale manuscripts are described more fully in chapters 1 and 2 below.

3. See the excellent book by Doris Goldstein, *Trial of Faith: Religion and Politics in Tocqueville's Thought.*

4. *Oeuvres, papiers et correspondances d'Alexis de Tocqueville*, Edition définitive sous la direction de J.-P. Mayer, sous le patronage de la commission nationale pour l'édition des oeuvres d'Alexis de Tocqueville; hereafter cited as *O.C.* (Mayer).

5. *Journey to America,* hereafter cited as Mayer, *Journey*, is a translation of pertinent parts of *Voyages en Sicile et aux Etats-Unis*, also edited by J. P. Mayer, *O.C.* (Mayer), vol. 5.

6. *Democracy in America*; hereafter cited as *Democracy* (Mayer). The hard-cover version, jointly edited by J. P. Mayer and Max Lerner, first appeared in 1966.

7. *Democracy in America*, edited by Phillips Bradley, based on the Henry Reeve translation as revised by Francis Bowen, 2 vols.; hereafter cited as *Democracy* (Bradley).

1. The Writing of the First Part of the *Democracy*

1. Toc. to Eugène Stoffels, Paris, 21 February 1831, from the volume entitled *Correspondance et oeuvres posthumes* of the *Oeuvres complètes* edited by Gustave de Beaumont, 5:411–12; hereafter cited as *O.C.* (Bt.).

2. All omissions are mine unless otherwise noted.

3. Bt. to his father, aboard the *Havre*, 25 April 1831, copy, Beaumont Letters Home: 1831–32, Yale Tocqueville Mss. Collection, BIb2; hereafter cited as Bt. letters, Yale, BIb2. These letters have recently been edited and published by André Jardin and George Wilson Pierson, *Lettres d'Amérique, 1831–1832* (hereafter cited as Bt. *Lettres*). For this item, see Bt. *Lettres*, p. 28.

4. Bt. to his brother Jules, New York, 26 May 1831, copy, Bt. letters, Yale, BIb2. See Bt. *Lettres*, p. 48.

5. Toc. to Edouard (brother), New York, 20 June 1831, copy, Tocqueville's Letters Home: 1831–32, Yale Toc. Mss., BIa; hereafter cited as Toc. letters, Yale, BIa.

6. The date of the decision to write separate works remains a point of controversy. See André Jardin's discussion of the problem in his "Introduction," pp. 17–20, in *Correspondance d'Alexis de Tocqueville et de Gustave de Beaumont*, ed. Jardin, 3 vols. *O.C.* (Mayer), tome 8, vol. 1. This meticulous and invaluable work is hereafter cited as *O.C.* (Mayer), Jardin, 8. His verdict, based largely on numerous letters which the two friends wrote to family and friends at home, is that at some time between July and November 1831, the previously projected single book became two. Cf. a similar view in Pierson, *Toc. and Bt.*, pp. 31–33 and 511–23, where Beaumont's awakening, during October and November 1831, to the problems of race in America is presented as the single most important catalyst for the eventual appearance of two separate works. But also see *Tocqueville and Beaumont on Social Reform*, ed. and trans. Seymour Drescher, pp. 210–11 (hereafter cited as Drescher, *Social Reform*), for a different opinion. It may also have been between June and September when the two friends first decided that Beaumont would concentrate on American *moeurs* and Tocqueville on the republic's laws and institutions. By late September, both men began to write of "*my*" work. See pertinent letters home.

7. Toc. to Bt., Paris, 4 April 1832, *O.C.* (Mayer), Jardin, 8:1, pp. 111–14.

8. Toc. to Bt., Saint-Germain, 10 April 1832, ibid., pp. 114–16.

9. Tocqueville was in Toulon in May and in June visited the prisons of Lausanne and Geneva. It should also be noted that he did contribute statistics and appendices for the report.

10. Bt. to Toc., Paris, 17 May [1832], *O.C.* (Mayer), Jardin, 8:1, pp. 116–18. Beaumont's concern for the future was compounded by his abrupt dismissal from his post with the government. Tocqueville responded by submitting his own resignation, so the unhappy affair at least left both men free to concentrate all their energies on their official and personal American works.

11. Bt. to Lieber, Paris, 16 November 1832, Photostats of Lieber Correspondence (from the Huntington Library), Yale Toc. Mss., BVa. Lieber was to be the American translator of the prison report.

12. In 1833, the book won the Prix Monthyon of the Académie française.

13. For more detail, consult Pierson, *Toc. and Bt.*, pp. 685–87.

14. Bt. to Toc., Paris, 7 August 1833, *O.C.* (Mayer), Jardin, 8:1, pp. 119–23.

15. For a full account of this voyage (and for the later journey in 1835), see Seymour Drescher's excellent *Tocqueville and England* and Pierson, *Toc. and Bt.*, pp. 688–92. Also indispensable are Tocqueville's own travel notebooks, edited by J.-P. Mayer and published in English as *Journeys to England and Ireland*; hereafter cited as Mayer, *Journeys to England.*

16. Toc. to Bt., Paris, 1 November 1833, *O.C.* (Mayer), Jardin, 8:1, pp. 136–38.

17. Concerning the methods for observing and recording that the two travelers followed, consult Pierson, *Toc. and Bt.*, pp. 46–47 and 77–80.

18. The bulk of his travel *cahiers* were simply in chronological order. See American Trip, Diaries and Notes: 1831–32, copies, Yale Toc. Mss., BIIa,b; hereafter cited as American Diaries, Yale, BIIa,b. These copies should always be checked against the definitive fifth tome of the *Oeuvres complètes, Voyages en Sicile et aux Etats-Unis*, edited by J.-P. Mayer; hereafter cited as *O.C.* (Mayer), 5. Also see the convenient English edition, Mayer, *Journey.* (Note that for this book I have relied primarily on the Mayer editions rather than on the Yale copies of the diaries.)

19. I am not certain that these activities occupied Tocqueville during October 1833. It is quite possible that he had tackled some of these preliminary chores during brief periods of calm that presumably occurred at scattered intervals between November 1832 and October 1833.

20. "Sources manuscrites," copy, Yale Toc. Mss., CIIc; hereafter cited as "Sources manuscrites," Yale, CIIc.

21. Tocqueville's Reading Lists, copy, Yale Toc. Mss., CIIa; hereafter cited as Reading Lists, Yale, CIIa. There is also, in Beaumont's hand, an additional bibliography labeled "Ouvrages littéraires," which lists 27 titles; see Toc. Reading List, copy, Yale Toc. Mss., CIIb. Also consult Pierson, *Toc. and Bt.*, pp. 728–30.

22. We should recall that the *Democracy in America* would ultimately appear in two parts, 1835 and 1840, and that each part would be divided into two volumes.

23. Manuscript Drafts for the *Democracy*, Yale Toc. Mss., CVh, Paquet 3, cahier 1, p. 23; hereafter cited as Drafts, Yale, CVh. Many early notes, outlines, fragments, and other papers for the *Democracy* (both 1835 and 1840) were once copied for the Yale Toc. Mss. Collection. Since that time, most of the originals have been lost, so that only the Yale versions, divided in various *paquets* and labeled a–m, now exist. (The sole exception is Paquet 9, CVg, for which there are two boxes of original papers in addition to the copies; Alexis called these materials his "Rubish.") It should be noted that while translating all previously unpublished excerpts drawn from the drafts, or from the Original Working Manuscript of the *Democracy*, Yale Toc. Mss., CVIa, I have often supplied necessary punctuation. In addition, since Tocqueville's handwriting is frequently difficult to read, I have indicated all doubtful readings. All emphases within quotations are Tocqueville's, unless otherwise noted.

24. *Democracy* (Mayer), pp. 31–49.

25. This is the opening chapter of Tocqueville's book; *Democracy* (Mayer), pp. 23–30. For further discussion of Tocqueville's evolving attitudes toward the American environment, see chapter 3 below.

26. What happened to *société religieuse?* Perhaps Tocqueville had surrendered this topic to Beaumont when they had decided to divide the burden of America. Both the text and the extensive notes of Beaumont's *Marie, ou l'esclavage aux Etats-Unis* would contain lengthy discussions of religion and religious sects in America. Although Tocqueville did not award a totally separate *partie* of his 1835 book to religion, he did devote to the subject three sections of a chapter from the second volume of the 1835 *Democracy* entitled "The Main Causes Tending to Maintain a Democratic Republic in the United States." See the subheadings: "Religion Considered as a Political Institution . . ."; "Indirect Influence of Religious Beliefs upon Political Society in the United States"; "The Main Causes That Make Religion Powerful in America." See *Democracy* (Mayer), pp. 287–301. For an excellent discussion of this matter, consult Goldstein, *Trial of Faith*. Also see Goldstein's article, "The Religious Beliefs of Alexis de Tocqueville."

27. Compare the last chapter of the first half of the 1835 *Democracy*, "The Federal Constitution," *Democracy* (Mayer), pp. 112–70.

28. Copyist's note: illegible word.

29. Compare the final table of contents for the first part of the 1835 *Democracy*, especially chapters 4–8.

30. See Tocqueville's fourth chapter, "The Principle of the Sovereignty of the People in America," *Democracy* (Mayer), pp. 58–60.

31. Drafts, Yale, CVh, Paquet 3, cahier 1, pp. 20–22.

32. Consult Pierson, *Toc. and Bt.*, pp. 407–13. Also see Herbert B. Adams, "Jared Sparks and Alexis de Tocqueville."

33. Compare *Democracy* (Mayer), "Freedom of the Press in the United States," pp. 180–88; "Political Association in the United States," pp. 189–95; and the section from "What Tempers the Tyranny of the Majority in the United States" entitled "The Jury in the United States Considered as a Political Institution," pp. 270–76.

34. Drafts, Yale, CVh, Paquet 3, cahier 1, p. 22.

35. Ibid., pp. 18–20. For the "Introduction," see *Democracy* (Mayer), pp. 9–20.

36. Drafts, Yale, CVh, Paquet 3, cahier 1, pp. 27–28 and 64–67. The full title of the chapter, Tocqueville's second, was "Concerning Their Point of Departure and Its Importance for the Future of the Anglo-Americans," *Democracy* (Mayer), pp. 31–49. Pierson has also noted and praised Tocqueville's concern for history; consult Pierson, "Second voyage," *Tocqueville: centenaire*, pp. 73–76.

37. Tocqueville to Kergolay, Paris, 13(?) November 1833, vol. 1, p. 344, *Correspondance d'Alexis de Tocqueville et de Louis de Kergolay*, text established by André Jardin, introduced and annotated by Jean-Alain Lesourd, 2 vols., *O.C.* (Mayer), tome 13; hereafter cited as *O.C.* (Mayer), Jardin and Lesourd, 13.

38. Toc. to Bt., Paris, 1 November 1833, *O.C.* (Mayer), Jardin, 8:1, pp. 136–38.

39. This description applies both to two boxes of original fragments, Drafts, Yale, CVg, "Rubish," and to four boxes of the Original Working Manuscript of the *Democracy*, Yale Toc. Mss., CVIa. The final reading in the latter document usually differs in only minor ways from the text as it would appear in 1835 and 1840. But as a record of the last stages of Tocqueville's thinking and writing process, the working manuscript is invaluable.

40. This was the third chapter of the first volume of the 1835 *Democracy*. See "Social State of the Anglo-Americans," *Democracy* (Mayer), pp. 50–57.

41. Original Working Ms., Yale, CVIa, tome 1. The reader's identity is unknown. Cf. the opening paragraphs of the chapter on *état social*; *Democracy* (Mayer), p. 50.

42. Chapter on *état social,* Original Working Ms., Yale, CVIa, tome 1.

43. The reader's comment is in pencil and does not seem to be in Alexis's hand; the author remains unknown. For further discussion of some meanings of *démocratie*, see chapter 19 below.

44. This advertisement, undated, is found among copies of Tocqueville's drafts. Drafts, Yale, CVh, Paquet 3, cahier 2, p. 85

45. For the following account of the aid given by Sedgwick and Lippitt, I have relied heavily upon Pierson's more complete discussion; see Pierson, *Toc. and Bt.*, pp. 731–34 and notes. Also compare an article about Lippitt's contributions by Daniel C. Gilman, "Alexis de Tocqueville and His Book on America—Sixty Years After."

46. Reading Lists, Yale, CIIa.

47. For elaboration, see chapter 7 below.

48. Toc. to Senior, 24 March 1834, from a work edited by M. C. M. Simpson, entitled *Correspondence and Conversations of Alexis de Tocqueville with Nassau William Senior from 1834 to 1859*, 2 vols., 1:1–2; hereafter cited as Simpson, *Correspondence with Senior.* Tocqueville had already announced this scheme to Beaumont in November 1833; see *O.C.* (Mayer), Jardin, 8:1, pp. 136–38.

49. Drafts, Yale, CVh, Paquet 3, cahier 5, pp. 12–13 Tocqueville ultimately divided the last title into two chapters. Compare this list with the contents of the second part of the 1835 *Democracy*.

50. "Some Considerations concerning the Present State and Probable Future of the Three Races That Inhabit the Territory of the United States," *Democracy* (Mayer), pp. 316–407.

51. See, for example, the observations made by Rev. Benedict Gaston Songy, O.S.B., "Alexis de Tocqueville and Slavery: Judgments and Predictions," p. 88; hereafter cited as Songy, "Toc. and Slavery."

52. Toc. to Bt., Paris, 5 July 1834, *O.C.* (Mayer), Jardin, 8:1, pp. 139–40.

53. According to André Jardin, Gosselin apparently had a not-quite-unblemished reputation as a businessman; consult *O.C.* (Mayer), Jardin, 8:1, p. 139 note.

54. The proposed title had changed by January 1835, but no one has been able to discover exactly why or when the transformation took place. Compare the following notice found among the drafts for the 1835 *Democracy:* "M. de Tocqueville . . . is preparing to publish in the coming month of October a work in two volumes which has . . . America for its subject. This book will be titled: *De l'empire de la Démocratie en Amérique.*" This

brief announcement, perhaps drawn up after a July meeting with Gosselin, indicated yet a different title and also an intention to publish the 1835 *Democracy* in October 1834; Drafts, Yale, CVh, Paquet 3, cahier 3, p. 101. For a summary of the changing name of Tocqueville's American work, see chapter 2, note 69, below.

55. Toc. to Bt., Paris, 14 July 1834, *O.C.* (Mayer), Jardin, 8:1, pp. 140–43.

56. Perhaps the very papers carried to Beaumont in August are those preserved as the Original Working Ms., Yale, CVIa.

57. The original of the "Observations critiques . . ." has evidently been lost, but a copy is preserved in the Yale Toc. Mss. Collection; see "Observations critiques," Yale, CIIIb, cahiers 1–3. Unfortunately, the authorship of the various comments is now difficult if not impossible to establish, for the best clue, handwriting, disappeared with the original. Remarks by Kergolay concerning Tocqueville's "Introduction" were also included in the document. The "Observations" were largely stylistic, but some suggestions did challenge the content of Alexis' book. His ideas were occasionally criticized as unclear, contradictory, mistaken, or politically unwise, and alternative readings, sometimes extensive, were frequently provided for the author to consider and, perhaps, to include. I have treated the "Observations" as though they were compiled during the last half of 1834. It is also possible that Tocqueville's manuscript of the first part of the 1835 *Democracy* had been copied and circulated as early as the spring of 1834.

58. The 1835 *Democracy* (vols. 1 and 2) won the Prix Monthyon in June 1836 and in 1838 secured for Tocqueville a seat in the Académie des sciences morales et politiques.

2. An Expanding Task Resumed

1. Toc. to P.-P. Royer-Collard, Baugy, 6 December 1836, from André Jardin, ed., *Correspondance d'Alexis de Tocqueville avec P.-P. Royer-Collard et avec J.-J. Ampère, O.C.* (Mayer), 11:28–30; hereafter cited as *O.C.* (Mayer), Jardin, 11.

2. Toc. to Beaumont, "Monday morning" [12 January 1835], *O.C.* (Mayer), Jardin, 8:1, pp. 149–50.

3. Tocqueville and Marie would marry on 26 October 1835.

4. What if the 1835 *Democracy* had been less noticed and less hailed? Here Tocqueville hinted that a poor reception would have meant the end of his writings on America.

5. This seems to be the old distinction between *société politique* and *société civile* in a new guise.

6. Toc. to Molé, Paris, August 1835, *O.C.* (Bt.), 7:133–36. Molé was a distant relative and a leading political figure during the July Monarchy.

7. Date uncertain, but some time between the fall of 1835, when Tocqueville began the 1840 *Democracy*, and the summer of 1836, when he completed the first section of the 1840 *Democracy*.

8. Drafts, Yale, CVa, Paquet 8, pp. 2–3.

9. The chapter cover, with title and comment, and containing only the note quoted above, is found among Tocqueville's original drafts of the 1840 volumes; Drafts, Yale, CVg, "Rubish," tome 3.

10. *Democracy* (Mayer), pp. 590–92.

11. For example, see Pierson, *Toc and Bt.*, p. 448 note and p. 766.

12. Drafts, Yale, CVa, Paquet 8, p. 45, and CVk, Paquet 7, cahier 2, p. 50.

13. Drafts, Yale, CVa, Paquet 8, p. 6. Most of the material in this notebook is dated 1836.

14. Toc. to John Stuart Mill, Paris, 10 February 1836, from J.-P. Mayer and Gustave Rudler, editors, *Correspondance d'Alexis de Tocqueville avec Henry Reeve et John Stuart Mill*, pp. 306–7, tome 6, vol. 1 of the Mayer edition; hereafter cited as *Correspondance anglaise, O.C.* (Mayer), 6:1.

15. Toc. to Mill, Paris, 10 April 1836, *O.C.* (Mayer), 6:1, pp. 308–9. An early outline, dated "17 May [1836?]," of the section of the *Democracy* concerning *les moeurs* also disclosed Tocqueville's decision to write two additional volumes; Drafts, Yale, CVa, Paquet 8, pp. 28–31.

16. Toc. to Reeve, Baugy, 5 June 1836, *O.C.* (Mayer), 6:1, pp. 33–34. A comment dated "5 February 1838" and found in one of Tocqueville's drafts also mentioned this idea of coordinating all four volumes of the *Democracy:* "recast the whole thing later." See Drafts, Yale, CVk, Paquet 7, cahier 1, p. 50.

17. Toc. to Reeve, Cherbourg, 17 April 1836, *O.C.* (Mayer), 6:1, pp. 29–30.

18. Toc. to M. Bouchitté, Baugy, 26 May 1836, *O.C.* (Bt.), 7:149.

19. Ibid.

20. The time in Switzerland had not been entirely wasted. While there, Tocqueville had read Plato and Machiavelli and had written several pages of miscellaneous ideas, some of which eventually found their way into the *Democracy.*

21. Toc. to Beaumont, Baugy, 16 October 1836, *O.C.* (Mayer), Jardin, 8:1, pp. 168–72.

22. The 1840 *Democracy* would contain four sections. The first two would make up volume three of the complete work; the second two, volume four. The chapters on ideas would constitute the first section: "Influence of Democracy on the Intellectual Movements in the United States." The section of *les sentiments* would be the second: "Influence of Democracy on the Sentiments of the Americans."

23. Toc. to Reeve, Baugy, 21 November 1836, *O.C.* (Mayer), 6:1, pp. 35–36.

24. Ibid.

25. Toc. to Beaumont, Baugy, 22 November 1836, *O.C.* (Mayer), Jardin, 8:1, pp. 172–75. For another illustration of the kind of help provided by Beaumont and Kergolay, see Bt. to Toc., "Friday" [13 January 1837], *O.C.* (Mayer), Jardin, 8:1, p. 178.

26. Jean-Jacques Ampère (1800–1864) and Claude François de Corcelle (1802–1892) would also read (or hear) and criticize drafts of the 1840 *Democracy.* Tocqueville and Ampère had first met in 1832 and had soon

become good friends. In the summer of 1839, Ampère would visit Tocqueville in Normandy and would subsequently become a frequent guest. Corcelle would also become a close friend. Both he and Tocqueville would be elected to the Chamber of Deputies in 1839 and would remain active in French politics until Louis-Napoleon's coup-d'état and the end of the Second Republic.

27. Kergolay did not emerge from private life until 1871, when he became a member of the National Assembly.

28. "Tocqueville never wrote anything without submitting his work to Louis de Kergolay," wrote Gustave de Beaumont in his "Notice sur Alexis de Tocqueville," *O.C.* (Bt.), 5:99–100.

29. Toc. to Kergolay, Baugy, 10 November 1836, *O.C.* (Mayer), Jardin and Lesourd, 13:1, pp. 415–18. It should be noted that various commentators have examined the influence of Pascal, Montesquieu, and Rousseau on Tocqueville's style. See for example, Pierson, *Toc. and Bt.*, pp. 742–45. These three writers may also have helped to shape some of Tocqueville's ideas. Consult a controversial thesis concerning Rousseau's influence in Marvin Zetterbaum, *Tocqueville and the Problem of Democracy.* Concerning Montesquieu, see especially chapter 9 below.

30. Toc. to Senior, Paris, 11 January 1837, Simpson, *Correspondence with Senior*, vol. 1. Compare the later letter to Reeve, Paris, 22 March 1837, in which Tocqueville said that his two volumes would not be ready for the printer before December 1837; *O.C.* (Mayer), 6:1, pp. 37–39.

31. One of his political activities in 1837 would be the writing of two articles. After the success of the prison report in 1833 and of the *Democracy* in 1835, Tocqueville had realized that publication was an effective instrument for advancing his political ambitions, and in 1835, he had delivered a paper on pauperism; see "Memoir on Pauperism" in Drescher, *Social Reform*, pp. 1–27. The two articles of 1837 concerned Algeria; see "Deux lettres sur Algérie," André Jardin, ed., *Ecrits et discours politiques, O.C.* (Mayer), 3:1, pp. 129–53. For additional commentary, see A. Jardin, "Tocqueville et l'Algérie."

32. Toc. to M. le Baron de Tocqueville (Edouard), Tocqueville, 13 June 1837, *O.C.* (Bt.), 7:152. Compare another admission to Beaumont: Toc. to Bt., Tocqueville, 9 July 1837, *O.C.* (Mayer), Jardin, 8:1, pp. 205–8.

33. Toc. to Mill, Tocqueville, 24 June 1837, *O.C.* (Mayer), 6:1, pp. 324–26. Compare a subsequent letter to Reeve, Tocqueville, 24 July [1837], in which Tocqueville stated that his book would not be published until March 1838 at the earliest; *O.C.* (Mayer), 6:1, pp. 39–40.

34. Beaumont and his wife stayed at the château during the last two weeks of August. M. and Mme. de Corcelle also arrived in Normandy at the end of July and remained until the middle of August. Both Gustave and Corcelle must have read or heard parts of Tocqueville's manuscript and discussed it with him. Concerning the visits of both men, see Toc. to Bt., Tocqueville, 9 July 1837, and Cherbourg, 18 July 1837; and Bt. to Toc., Dublin, 27 July 1837, and Paris, 3 September 1837; *O.C.* (Mayer), Jardin, 8:1.

35. See the Toc.-Bt. correspondence of September, October, and November 1837; *O.C.* (Mayer), Jardin, 8:1; also Toc. to Beaumont, Paris, 26 May 1837, ibid., pp. 191–96.

36. Toc. to Bt., Tocqueville, 12 November 1837, *O.C.* (Mayer), Jardin, 8:1, pp. 262–64.

37. Toc. to Bt., Paris, 11 December 1837, *O.C.* (Mayer), Jardin, 8:1, pp. 269–72.

38. Toc. to Bt., Baugy, 18 January 1838, *O.C.* (Mayer), Jardin, 8:1, pp. 277–79. Tocqueville also wrote of "the feeling of imperfection" in a letter to Royer-Collard; Toc. to Royer-Collard, Baugy, 6 April 1838, *O.C.* (Mayer), Jardin, 11:59–61.

39. The chapters on *les moeurs* are the third section of the 1840 *Democracy* (vol. 4), "Influence of Democracy on Mores Properly So Called." During January and February 1838, Tocqueville drafted several chapters from that section.

40. This fragment is part of a larger note labeled "Préface" and dated "5 February 1838"; Drafts, Yale, CVk, Pacquet 7, cahier 1, p. 50.

41. "Note relative à la préface de mon grand ouvrage." Drafts, Yale, CVk, Pacquet 7, cahier 1, p. 39. The date of this note is unknown. I have included it here because several of the preliminary drafts for Tocqueville's preface are dated in the early months of 1838, and this fragment is included among them. Also, concerning Negroes and ultrademocratic tendencies, compare a letter from Tocqueville to John Quincy Adams, 4 December 1837, photocopy, Toc. and Bt. Relations with Americans, 1832–40, Yale Toc. Mss., CId; hereafter cited as Relations with Americans, 1832–40, Yale, CId.

42. Drafts, Yale, CVk, Paquet 7, cahier 1, p. 39, undated. Drescher has also cited Tocqueville's decision to "admit my error" (Drescher, *Tocqueville and England*, p. 78), but implies, mistakenly I believe, that Tocqueville had in mind a repudiation of some of his earlier comments about the relationship between *démocratie* and centralization. For elaboration on this matter, see the chapters below on the nature and future of the Union and on centralization.

43. Drafts, Yale, CVk, Paquet 7, cahier 1, p. 53.

44. The fourth and last section of the 1840 *Democracy* is entitled: "On the Influence of Democratic Ideas and Feelings on Political Society." Tocqueville originally intended the fourth section to be one large chapter (see Original Working Ms., Yale, CVIa, tome 4), and, although his letters do not indicate it, he began sketches of this last section as early as March 1838. Various pages of drafts concerning despotism are dated "7 March 1838" and others on centralization and administrative despotism are dated "23 March." See the final large chapter, Drafts, Yale, CVg, "Rubish," tome 4. Tocqueville insisted that this fourth section was the most important as well as the last. See, for example, Toc. to Royer-Collard, Tocqueville, 15 August 1838, *O.C.* (Mayer), Jardin, 11:66–68. For further discussion of this section, see the chapters below on centralization and despotism.

45. Toc. to Reeve, Baugy, 2 March 1838, *O.C.* (Mayer), 6:1, pp. 41–42.

46. Toc. to Beaumont, Baugy, 21 March 1838; and Bt. to Toc., La Grange, 23 March [1838]; *O.C.* (Mayer), Jardin, 8:1, pp. 283–90. Beaumont lectured Tocqueville on his carelessness and prescribed various measures. In April, Tocqueville finally admitted that his health had been unsteady for weeks; see Toc. to Beaumont, Baugy, 22 April 1838, ibid., pp. 290–94.

47. Toc. to Beaumont, Tocqueville, 15 June 1838, ibid., pp. 303–5. The persons involved were "useful" for political reasons.

48. Toc. to Royer-Collard, Tocqueville, 23 June 1838, *O.C.* (Mayer), Jardin, 11:63–65.

49. Toc. to Beaumont, Tocqueville, 19 October 1838, *O.C.* (Mayer), Jardin, 8:1, pp. 318–21.

50. The two chapters involved are "Concerning the Philosophical Approach of the Americans" and "Concerning the Principal Source of Beliefs among Democratic Peoples." See Toc. to Beaumont, Tocqueville, 5 November 1838 and 5 December 1839 [1838], *O.C.* (Mayer), Jardin, 8:1, pp. 325–30.

51. Ibid., p. 329.

52. The chapters on ideas refer to the first section of the 1840 *Democracy:* "Influence of Democracy on the Intellectual Movements in the United States." The chapters on *individualisme* and *jouissances matérielles* are from the second section: "The Influence of Democracy on the Sentiments of the Americans."

53. Drafts, Yale, CVk, Paquet 7, cahier 1, pp. 11–12; dated "December 1838." The chapter on method is the very first chapter of the 1840 *Democracy.*

54. The chapter appeared neither in the Original Working Ms., Yale, CVIa, nor in a late list of all chapters to be included in the 1840 *Democracy* (see Drafts, Yale, CVf, Paquet 4), but only as a draft chapter, Drafts, Yale, CVg, "Rubish," tome 3. It then reappeared in the 1840 printed text.

55. Drafts, Yale, CVk, Paquet 7, cahier 2, pp. 1–2.

56. In the 1840 text, this chapter is titled "Why Democratic Nations Show a More Ardent and Enduring Love for Equality Than for Liberty." See *Democracy* (Mayer), pp. 503–6.

57. Toc. to Beaumont, Tocqueville, 6 January 1839, and Baugy, 21 March 1838 ["mon cher aristarque"], *O.C.* (Mayer), Jardin, 8:1, pp. 283–85 and 330–33.

58. Toc. to Beaumont, Nacqueville, 30 September 1838, *O.C.* (Mayer), Jardin, 8:1, pp. 315–18.

59. Drafts, Yale, CVk, Paquet 7, cahier 2, pp. 35–36. The chapter here mentioned may be found in *Democracy* (Mayer), pp. 572–80.

60. Compare, for instance, some of Tocqueville's opinions about domestic servants in America, *Democracy* (Mayer), p. 578, and Beaumont's comments on the same subject, "Appendix I: Note on Equality in American Society," Gustave de Beaumont, *Marie, or Slavery in the United States*, p. 227; hereafter cited as Bt. *Marie* (Chapman).

61. There are four chapters directly concerning sociability. See *Democracy* (Mayer), pp. 561–72.

62. The chapters on sociability, Drafts, Yale, CVg, "Rubish," tome 4. Also consult CVg, copy, Paquet 9, cahier 1, p. 99. In 1835, Beaumont had also written about American sociability; see "Appendix G," Bt. *Marie* (Chapman), pp. 223–25.

63. *Democracy* (Mayer), pp. 690–95, especially p. 692.

64. "What Sort of Despotism Democratic Nations Have to Fear," Drafts, Yale, CVg, "Rubish," tome 4; also consult CVg, copy, Paquet 9, cahier 2, p. 98.

65. See the January letters of Tocqueville to Beaumont.

66. Beaumont, however, was defeated for a second time. Tocqueville's

report consumed much of June and July; see "Rapport . . . relative aux esclaves des colonies," *O.C.* (Mayer), 3:1, pp. 41–78. For a highly enlightening account of the American reaction to the paper, consult Drescher, *Social Reform*, pp. 98–99, notes. Also see Songy, "Toc. and Slavery," pp. 140–42 and 185–205.

67. Toc. to Reeve, Tocqueville, 12 September 1839, *O.C.* (Mayer), 6:1, pp. 45–46.

68. See Toc. to Ampère, Tocqueville, 17 September 1839, and 2 November 1839, O.C. (Mayer), Jardin, 11:128–30 and 134.

69. Toc. to Mill, Paris, 14 November 1839, *O.C.* (Mayer), 6:1, pp. 326–27. This letter seems to indicate a different title for the 1840 *Democracy*. If this is the case, then the title of Tocqueville's book underwent the following changes: (1) In August 1833, Jared Sparks told Tocqueville that he hoped "to see the work which you promise, on the Institutions and Manners of the Americans" (cited and quoted by Pierson, "Second voyage," *Toc.: centenaire*, pp. 80–81 note); (2) in the spring of 1834, the first of the 1835 volumes was to be published separately as *American Institutions*; (3) in the summer of 1834, the 1835 *Democracy* (2 vols.) was to be titled *De l'empire de la Démocratie aux Etats-Unis*; (4) in January 1835, these first two volumes of the book appeared as *De la Démocratie en Amérique*; (5) in the fall of 1839, the last two volumes were to be titled *L'Influence de l'égalité sur les idées et les sentiments des hommes*; (6) in April 1840, the 1840 *Democracy* was published as *De la Démocratie en Amérique*, vols. 3 and 4.

70. Toc. to Beaumont, Tocqueville, 23 October 1839, *O.C.* (Mayer), Jardin, 8:1, pp. 389–90.

71. Toc. to Beaumont [2 November 1839], *O.C.* (Mayer), Jardin, 8:1, pp. 395–96. Kergolay was unavailable at the time; see Jardin's note, p. 396. Politics almost robbed Tocqueville of Beaumont's services. Beaumont learned in November that a special election would be held in December to elect a new deputy from Mamers. He threw himself into the campaign and, on 15 December 1839, was elected. The unexpected development delayed his reading of Tocqueville's manuscript and, at times, threatened to prevent it altogether. See Bt. to Toc., La Grange, 10 November 1839, *O.C.* (Mayer), Jardin, 8:1, pp. 397–99.

72. Concerning the first of these three chapters: "Read this chapter to men of quality *(des hommes du monde)* and study their impressions"; Original Working Ms., Yale, CVIa, tome 3. This chapter may be found in *Democracy* (Mayer), pp. 477–82. Concerning the second: "Consult L. and B."; Original Working Ms., Yale, CVIa, tome 3. On this lost chapter also see my chapter below. Concerning the third: "Have these two versions copied and submit them to my friends" (dated "October 1839"); Drafts, Yale, CVk, Paquet 7, cahier 2, p. 14. The chapter may be found in *Democracy* (Mayer), pp. 600–03.

73. Original Working Ms., Yale, CVIa, tome 3. Also see *Democracy* (Mayer), pp. 534–35.

74. Toc. to Reeve, Paris, 15 November 1839, *O.C.* (Mayer), 6:1, pp. 47–48.

3. An Hypothesis Weighed and Rejected

1. C. F. Volney, *Tableau du climat et du sol des Etats-Unis*, 2 vols.; hereafter cited as Volney, *Tableau*. Tocqueville read Volney's volumes, but only after returning to France in 1832.

2. *North American Review* 36 (January 1833): 273.

3. Toc. to Chabrol, New York, 18 May 1831; Toc. letters, Yale BIa2.

4. Toc. to Beaumont, Gray, 25 October 1829, *O.C.* (Mayer), Jardin, 8:1, pp. 93–94. This letter was written before the idea of going to the United States occurred to the two friends; thus no speculation about America and its *position géographique* was hidden behind Tocqueville's words.

5. Toc. to his mother, aboard the *Havre*, 26 April 1831, from the section dated "9 May"; Toc. letters, Yale, BIa2.

6. Ibid., from the section dated "14 May."

7. Toc. to E. Stoffels, New York, 28 June 1831; Toc. letters, Yale, BIa2.

8. "Physical Configuration of North America," *Democracy* (Mayer), pp. 25–26. Of course, Tocqueville's readings also strongly reinforced this early impression. See his footnotes and appendices to the first chapter of the *Democracy*. Also consult his major printed sources on the *situation physique* (see chapter 6 below).

9. Toc. to his mother, aboard the *Havre*, 26 April 1831, from the section dated "Sunday 15 [May]"; Toc. letters, Yale, BIa2.

10. Ibid., from the section dated "14 May."

11. For further information about the stay in New York, consult Pierson, *Toc. and Bt.*, pp. 67–92.

12. Consult Pierson, *Toc. and Bt.*, p. 76.

13. "Public Education," Sing Sing, 1 June 1831, Alphabetic Notebook 1, Mayer, *Journey*, p. 196. Here Tocqueville implied that the republic's *situation physique* actually stimulated mental efforts. But compare a somewhat contrary comment made to Mr. Livingston on 7 June 1831, ibid., p. 19: "It seems to me that American society suffers from taking too little account of intellectual questions." Also note a related statement to Tocqueville's father: "Nature here offers a sustenance so immense to human industry that the class of theoretical speculators is absolutely unknown"; from Pierson, *Toc. and Bt.*, pp. 115–16. The latter idea would briefly appear in the 1835 work, *Democracy* (Mayer), pp. 301–5, especially p. 301; and would have a more important place in the first part of the 1840 text, ibid., pp. 437–41 and 459–65. For elaboration, see chapter 16 below.

14. Quoted from Pierson, *Toc. and Bt.*, pp. 115–16. A copy of the letter, from Toc. to M. le Comte de Tocqueville (father), Sing Sing, 3 June 1831, is included in Toc. letters, Yale, BIa1, Paquet 5, pp. 5–6.

15. Drafts, Yale, CVh, Paquet 3, cahier 3, p. 96. Compare the following comment: "That governments have relative value. When Montesquieu [says that (?)] I admire him. But when he describes the English constitution as the model of perfection, it seems to me that for the first time I see the limits of his genius"; ibid., cahier 4, p. 91.

16. Compare comments under the heading "General questions," Sing Sing,

29 May 1831, Alphabetic Notebook 1, Mayer, *Journey*, p. 211.

17. Compare the 1835 *Democracy:* "The Americans have no neighbors and consequently no great wars, financial crises, invasions, or conquests to fear; they need neither heavy taxes nor a numerous army nor great generals; they have also hardly anything to fear from something else which is a greater scourge for democratic republics than all these others put together, namely, military glory"; *Democracy* (Mayer), p. 278.

18. Emphasis added. The 1835 *Democracy* would remark: "The physical state of the country offers such an immense scope to industry that man has only to be left to himself to work marvels"; *Democracy* (Mayer), p. 177.

19. The 1835 *Democracy* would note: "The present-day American republics are like companies of merchants formed to exploit the empty lands of the New World, and prosperous commerce is their occupation. The passions that stir the Americans most deeply are commercial"; *Democracy* (Mayer), p. 285. Also see p. 283.

20. Emphasis added; quoted from Pierson, *Toc. and Bt.*, pp. 129–30. A copy of the letter from Toc. to Chabrol, New York, 9 June 1831, may be found in Toc. letters, Yale, BIa2.

21. As one example, see Tocqueville's conversation with Mr. Latrobe, Baltimore, 3 November 1831, Non-Alphabetic Notebooks 2 and 3, Mayer, *Journey*, p. 85

22. One of the Frenchman's most penetrating insights was his recognition that the weakness of the American presidency resulted more from circumstances than from law. From this awareness came a remarkable prophecy: "If executive power is weaker in America than in France, the reason for this lies perhaps more in circumstances than in the laws. It is generally in its relations with foreign powers that the executive power of a nation has the chance to display skill and strength. If the Union's existence were constantly menaced, and if its great interests were continually interwoven with those of other powerful nations, one would see the prestige of the executive growing, because of what was expected from it and of what it did"; *Democracy* (Mayer), pp. 125–26.

23. For Tocqueville's own discussions of these matters, see the following pages from *Democracy* (Mayer): on decentralization and the federal principle, pp. 167–70; on the presidency, pp. 125–26 and 131–32; on the armed forces, pp. 219 and 278; on America's unusual privilege to make mistakes, pp. 223–24, 224–25, 232–33. Note also the following striking passages from the 1835 work: pp. 169–70 and p. 232.

24. Quoted from Pierson, *Toc. and Bt.*, p. 76. Compare Edward Livingston's remarks of 7 June, Mayer, *Journey*, p. 20.

25. Toc. to Madame la Comtesse de Grancey, New York, 10 October 1831, Toc. letters, Yale, BIa1, Paquet 15, p. 35.

26. Compare these phrases from the letter of 9 June 1831 to Chabrol (quoted above) to the following sentence from the 1840 text: "[In the United States] Immutable Nature herself seems on the move, so greatly is she daily transformed by the works of man"; *Democracy* (Mayer), p. 614.

27. Quoted from Pierson, *Toc. and Bt.*, p. 119. For further commentary on this and the other long excerpts quoted above, consult Pierson's book, pp.

120–31. Compare the above fragment to one from the chapter entitled "Why the Americans Are Often So Restless in the Midst of Their Prosperity" (1840 text), *Democracy* (Mayer), p. 536.

28. Toc. to E. Stoffels, New York, 28 June [July] 1831, Toc. letters, Yale, BIa2. Tocqueville was more specific in a letter to his mother, written aboard the *Havre*, 26 April 1831, in the section dated "Sunday 15 [May]," Toc. letters, Yale, BIa2: "Each year brings nearly 15 to 20 thousand European Catholics who spread over the western wilderness."

29. Toc. to his mother, New York, 19 June 1831, Toc. letters, Yale, BIa2.

30. Ibid.

31. For the story of how Gustave and Alexis missed their chance to see West Point, consult Pierson, *Toc. and Bt.*, pp. 171–73.

32. Toc. to his mother, Auburn, 17 July 1831, Toc. letters, Yale, BIa1, Paquet 15, pp. 14–15.

33. Ibid.

34. Tocqueville's own title for his narrative, written in August 1831, of the travelers' frontier experiences. Two translations have been made, Pierson, *Toc. and Bt.*, pp. 229–89, and Mayer, *Journey*, pp. 328–76. I have followed Pierson's version below.

35. There is another striking description in Pocket Notebook Number 2, 21 July, Mayer, *Journey*, pp. 133–34.

36. George W. Pierson has pointed out that these ideas about "stages of history" were drawn from an old European tradition, one which came into American historiography with the writings of Frederick Jackson Turner, who was in turn influenced by Achille Loria. On the background for these ideas and the connection between Turner and Loria, see the first section of Lee Benson, *Turner and Beard: American Historical Writing Reconsidered.*

37. Quoted from Pierson, *Toc. and Bt.*, pp. 235–37.

38. Tocqueville's own phrase. Quoted in Pierson, *Toc. and Bt.*, p. 287. For further discussion of this idea, consult Pierson.

39. *Democracy* (Mayer), p. 55.

40. Toc. to his mother, Louisville, 6 December 1831, Toc. letters, Yale, BIa1.

41. Remarks about the Mississippi are quoted from Pierson, *Toc. and Bt.*, p. 76; compare a letter from Toc. to Kergolay, 18 May 1831, *O.C.* (Mayer), Jardin and Lesourd, 13:1, p. 224. Remarks about Lake Huron are from Toc. to M. le Comte de Tocqueville, on Lake Huron, 14 August 1831, Toc. letters, Yale, BIa1, Paquet 15, p. 19.

42. From a "Fortnight in the Wilderness," quoted in Pierson, *Toc. and Bt.*, p. 232.

43. Quoted in Pierson, *Toc. and Bt.*, p. 239. This recognition of what inspired an American would disappear from Tocqueville's writings until 1840; compare a passage from a chapter of the second part of the *Democracy* entitled "On Some Sources of Poetic Inspiration in Democracies," *Democracy* (Mayer), p. 485. Also see Beaumont's comments of 1835, *Marie* (Chapman), pp. 115–16.

44. From a "Fortnight in the Wilderness," quoted in Pierson, *Toc. and Bt.*, pp. 278–79.

45. From a "Fortnight in the Wilds," Mayer, *Journey*, p. 345. See also pp. 343–45 and comments under "Virgin lands," 22 and 25 July 1831, Alphabetic Notebook 1, Mayer, *Journey*, pp. 209–10.

46. Toc. to Chabrol, Buffalo, 17 August 1831, Toc. letters, Yale, BIa2.

47. *Democracy* (Mayer), p. 281.

48. Toc. to Chabrol, Buffalo, 17 August 1831, Toc. letters, Yale, BIa2.

4. Further Considerations of Environment

1. For elaboration, consult Pierson, *Toc. and Bt.*, pp. 349–425, and Mayer, *Journey*, especially Non-Alphabetic Notebooks 2 and 3, pp. 49–66.

2. Conversation with Mr. Clay, 18 September 1831, Non-Alphabetic Notebooks 2 and 3, Mayer, *Journey*, p. 49.

3. Interview with Mr. Adams, 1 October 1831, ibid., p. 61. Tocqueville also knew of the southern Italian climate firsthand; he had visited Sicily in 1827.

4. Ibid., p. 62.

5. Several diary comments illustrated Tocqueville's awareness of the American fear of metropolitan centers. See, for example, "Reasons for the social state and present government in America," Alphabetic Notebook 1, and "Centralization," 25 October 1831, Alph. Notebook 2, Mayer, *Journey*, p. 181 and p. 216.

6. Again, Tocqueville anticipated Frederick Jackson Turner.

7. Visit with Charles Carroll, 5 November 1831, Non-Alph. Notebooks 2 and 3, Mayer, *Journey*, p. 86.

8. *Democracy* (Mayer), p. 284. Also related to this idea would be Tocqueville's remarks concerning the lack of great issues in America and the resulting difficulties involved in the building of political parties; see ibid., p. 177.

9. Conversations with Mr. Everett and Mr. Sparks, 29 September 1831, Non-Alph. Notebooks 2 and 3, Mayer, *Journey*, pp. 57–59. The term, *point de départ*, assumed an important place in Tocqueville's thinking.

10. For further illustrations and commentary, see Pierson, *Toc. and Bt.*, pp. 120–25.

11. Conversation with Mr. Quincy, 20 September 1831, Non-Alph. Notebooks 2 and 3, Mayer, *Journey*, p. 51.

12. "Reasons for the social state and present government in America," undated, Alph. Notebook 1, Mayer, *Journey*, p. 181. Another somewhat different translation by Pierson, *Toc. and Bt.*, p. 453, departs once or twice from the original as found in *Voyages, O.C.* (Mayer), 5:207. Pierson did, however, place the composition of this list in early October 1831. See *Toc. and Bt.*, pp. 450–54.

13. Conversation with Mr. Latrobe, Baltimore, 30 October 1831, Non-Alph.

Notebooks 2 and 3, Mayer, *Journey*, pp. 76–77. For a detailed discussion of the ideas of both Tocqueville and Beaumont on slavery, in general, and the connection between that institution and climate, in particular, consult the pertinent sections of Songy, "Toc. and Slavery."

14. For detailed accounts of their adventures, see Pierson, *Toc. and Bt.*, pp. 543–616.

15. Undated conversation, Pocket Notebook Number 3, Mayer, *Journey*, p. 161.

16. Tocqueville's first two volumes would identify four separate migrations important to the United States: (1) Europeans, across the Atlantic Ocean; (2) White or Anglo-Americans, toward the interior; (3) Negroes, toward the South as the zone of slavery retreated—see *Democracy* (Mayer), pp. 350–51, 353, 354–55; and (4) Indians, westward always ahead of the American line of march.

17. *Democracy* (Mayer), p. 283.

18. "Ohio," 2 December 1831, Notebook E, Mayer, *Journey*, p. 263. Also consult "Second conversation with Mr. Walker," 3 December 1831, and "Conversation with Mr. MacIlvaine," 9 December 1831, Non-Alph. Notebooks 2 and 3, Mayer, *Journey*, pp. 97–99.

19. Ibid., p. 264. Note the contrast between this remark and Tocqueville's position in May: "Up to now all I have seen doesn't enchant me, because I attribute it more to accidental circumstance than to the will of man." (See chapter 3 above.)

20. "Second conversation with Mr. Walker," 3 December 1831, Non-Alph. Notebooks 2 and 3, Mayer, *Journey*, pp. 95–96.

21. "Conversation with Mr. Guillemin," 1 January 1832, ibid., p. 104.

22. Joseph Story, *Commentaries on the Constitution of the United States,* one volume abridgment, pp. 474–75. For further discussion of Tocqueville's use of this work, see chapter 7 below.

23. William Darby, *View of the United States*, pp. 443–44. For additional information about Darby's volume, see chapter 6 below.

24. Drafts, Yale, CVh, Paquet 3, cahier 1, p. 63. Also see *Democracy* (Mayer), p. 380.

25. *Democracy* (Mayer), p. 25 and p. 26. Other similar comments would be found on pp. 24–25 and p. 30.

26. Ibid., p. 380.

27. Conversation with Mr. Mazureau, New Orleans, 1 January 1832, Non-Alph. Notebooks 2 and 3, Mayer, *Journey*, p. 102.

28. Conversations with Mr. Poinsett, 12–17 January 1832, ibid., p. 115.

29. Toc. to Chabrol, From Chesapeake Bay, 16 January 1832, Toc. letters, Yale, BIa2.

30. Ibid., pp. 352–53. Compare Beaumont's opinion with his friend's treatment; see Bt. *Marie* (Chapman), pp. 204–6.

31. *Democracy* (Mayer), p. 352. Note Tocqueville's qualifications of these statements; see his footnotes, ibid., p. 352.

32. (Note the resemblance between this passage and the *North American Review* article quoted in chapter 3 above.) Reflections dated "14 January 1832," Notebook E, Mayer, *Journey*, pp. 234–35. Also see a somewhat different

version, Pocket Notebooks Number 4 and 5, ibid., p. 179. These remarks would serve as the skeleton for a section of the 1835 *Democracy*; compare "The Laws Contribute More to the Maintenance of the Democratic Republic Than Do the Physical Circumstances of the Country, and Mores *(moeurs)* Do More Than the Laws," *Democracy* (Mayer), pp. 305–8. See especially page 306, where Tocqueville would declare: "Therefore physical causes do not influence the destiny of nations as much as is supposed."

33. The only possible general exception to this sanguine view involved the life of the mind, which benefited only insofar as activity encouraged by the continent's gifts spilled over into intellectual and cultural efforts. Concerning this matter, see chapter 16 below.

34. Drafts, Yale, CVh, Paquet 3, cahier 4, p. 48.

35. "Sources manuscrites," Yale, CIIc. Other relevant titles were "What permits the republic in the United States" and some of the specific possible causes: *moeurs, point de départ,* federal organization, etc.

36. Drafts, Yale, CVh, Paquet 3, cahier 4, p. 46.

37. Drafts, Yale, CVj, Paquet 2, cahier 2, pp. 20–21.

38. "The origin of the Americans is the first [accidental] cause of their prosperity and their grandeur. The second is the place that they inhabit." "Accidental or Providential Causes . . . ," Original Working Manuscript, CVIa, tome 2.

39. *Democracy* (Mayer), p. 279.

40. Ibid. See also pp. 279–80, 305–8, and especially 308.

41. Drafts, Yale, CVh, Paquet 3, cahier 4, p. 18. Also see Drafts, Yale, CVj, Paquet 2, cahier 2, p. 19. Compare the fragment quoted above with the 1835 text, *Democracy* (Mayer), p. 277.

42. *Democracy* (Mayer), pp. 286–87.

43. Consult Tocqueville's own definitions, *Democracy* (Mayer), p. 287 and p. 305 note. Also compare the following attempt found in a draft of the 1835 *Democracy*: "By *moeurs* I understand all of the dispositions which man brings to the government of society. *Moeurs*, strictly speaking, enlightenment, habits, sciences"; Drafts, Yale, CVh, Paquet 3, cahier 3, p. 58.

44. Compare Tocqueville's remarks of January 1832 (quoted above). Also consult the following drafts of the 1835 *Democracy*: Drafts, Yale, CVe, Paquet 17, p. 52; CVh, Paquet 3, cahier 4, pp. 46–47; and CVj, Paquet 2, cahier 2, p. 19. See in addition the section from the 1835 work entitled "The Laws Contribute More to the Maintenance of the Democratic Republic in the United States Than Do the Physical Circumstances of the Country, and Mores *(moeurs)* Do More Than the Laws," *Democracy* (Mayer), pp. 305–8, especially page 308. Note that in his emphasis on *moeurs*, Tocqueville anticipated the interpretation of human societies later offered by William Graham Sumner, who stressed the role of *mores*. See particularly Sumner's *Folkways: A Study of the Sociological Importance of Usages, Manners, Customs, Mores, and Morals.*

45. *Democracy* (Mayer), pp. 277–315.

46. Drafts, Yale, CVh, Paquet 3, cahier 4, p. 19.

47. Written above "permanent" is the word "durable." Neither is crossed out.

48. "So therefore" written above "Not only." Neither crossed out.

49. Originally written "exercise little," but "little" is crossed out and "no" substituted.

50. Originally written "possesses nearly none," but "nearly" is deleted and "so to speak" substituted.

51. Drafts, Yale, CVh, Paquet 3, cahier 4, pp. 19–20.

52. Ibid., p. 19.

53. Toc. to Beaumont, Baugy, "22 April 1838," *O.C.* (Mayer), Jardin, 8:1, p. 292.

54. Drafts, Yale, CVh, Paquet 3, cahier 4, p. 49.

55. Ibid.; compare this assertion with the *Democracy* (Mayer), p. 308.

5. Was Race a Sufficient Explanation of the American Character?

1. This and passages below from a "Fortnight in the Wilderness," quoted in Pierson, *Toc. and Bt.*, pp. 270–75. Another translation may be found in Mayer, *Journey*, pp. 364–69.

2. For a brief but suggestive discussion of the problems and possibilities surrounding the much-abused term *national character*, consult "The Study of National Character," David M. Potter, *People of Plenty: Economic Abundance and the American Character*, pp. 3–72.

3. See Pierson, *Toc. and Bt.*, p. 49.

4. Ibid., p. 54. Also note Beaumont's impressions of the town and its people, pp. 54–55.

5. "General Questions," Sing Sing, 29 May 1831, Alphabetic Notebook 1, Mayer, *Journey*, p. 211. (Compare these comments with the letter of 9 June 1831, to Chabrol, quoted above, chapter 3.)

6. From the passage on Saginaw, "Fortnight in the Wilderness," quoted in Pierson, *Toc. and Bt.*, pp. 270–75.

7. 21–25 November 1831, Pocket Notebook 3, Mayer, *Journey*, pp. 161–62.

8. Toc. to M. l'Abbé Lesueur, Albany, 7 September 1831, Toc. letters, Yale, BIa1, Paquet 15, p. 28.

9. "Morals," undated, Alphabetic Notebook 2, Mayer, *Journey*, pp. 222–23. Pierson has dated this note 21 September 1831.

10. "Reasons for the social state and present government in America," Alphabetic Notebook 1, Mayer, *Journey*, p. 181.

11. 21–25 November 1831, Pocket Notebook 3, Mayer, *Journey*, pp. 161–62.

12. Conversation with Mr. Poinsett, Philadelphia, 20 November 1831, Non-Alphabetic Notebooks 2 and 3, Mayer, *Journey*, p. 89.

13. See conversation with J. Q. Adams, Boston, 1 October 1831, Non-Alphabetic Notebooks 2 and 3, Mayer, *Journey*, pp. 60–61; second conversation with Mr. Walker, Cincinnati, 3 December 1831, ibid., pp. 97–98; and comments about "Ohio," 2 December 1831, Notebook E, ibid., p. 263.

14. A general comparison of North and South also apparently helped to focus Tocqueville's mind on *moeurs*: "Influence of *moeurs* proved by the very differences which exist between the North and the South of the Union.

. . . It is not blood which makes the difference; it is not the laws, nor the social position"; Drafts, Yale, CVj, Paquet 2, cahier 2, p. 19.

15. A final—but by now unnecessary—blow to any possible racial theory came on New Year's Day 1832, when Tocqueville and Beaumont arrived in New Orleans and once again found large numbers of fellow Frenchmen. But how these citizens of Louisiana differed from the inhabitants of Montreal and Quebec! Biology obviously did not overcome the effects of dissimilar environmental and institutional settings. (See chapter 4 above.)

16. 26 December 1831, Pocket Notebook 3, Mayer, *Journey*, p. 163. Note the striking change since the Saginaw experience. No longer were the Americans simply transplanted Englishmen.

17. Reflections of 14 January 1832, Notebook E, Mayer, *Journey*, pp. 234–35. Also see Pocket Notebooks 4 and 5, ibid., p. 179.

18. In a draft fragment dated January 1838, Tocqueville wrote: "Many particular causes like climate, race, religion influence the ideas and the feelings of men independently of the social state. The principle aim of this book is not to deny these influences, but to put in relief the particular cause of the social state (*l'état social*)"; Drafts, Yale, CVk, Paquet 7, cahier 1, pp. 47–48. But by 1840 his list would change, and *origin* would apparently subsume *race*; see *Democracy* (Mayer), p. 417.

19. Vagueness about the relation between race and national character was typical of European thought in the early nineteenth century. As an illustration of Tocqueville's overlapping definitions, compare the various meanings of *moeurs* (cited above, chapter 4) with the following explanation of national character: "The cast (*tournure*) of the ideas and the tastes of a people. A hidden force which struggles against time and revolutions. This intellectual physiognomy of nations that is called the character is apparent across the centuries of their history and in the midst of the innumerable changes which take place in the social state, the beliefs, and the laws"; Drafts, Yale, CVj, Paquet 2, cahier 2, p. 22.

20. See the "Foreword," Bt., *Marie* (Chapman), pp. 4–5. Also consult Tocqueville's note, *Democracy* (Mayer), p. 340.

21. See the long chapter entitled "Some Considerations concerning the Present State and Probable Future of the Three Races That Inhabit the Territory of the United States," *Democracy* (Mayer), pp. 316–407, especially pp. 316–63.

22. Ibid., pp. 316–17.

23. Consult the chapter from the 1835 *Democracy* cited above. Also see Songy, "Tocqueville and Slavery," pp. 17–73, especially p. 28, and pp. 88–110. For a contrary analysis in which Tocqueville's views are labeled "neoracist," see Richard W. Resh, "Alexis de Tocqueville and the Negro: *Democracy in America* Reconsidered."

24. See, for instance, the 1840 volumes of the *Democracy* (Mayer), p. 417 and pp. 493–96, "Some Characteristics Peculiar to Historians in Democratic Centuries."

25. Tocqueville to Corcelle, Berne, 27 July 1836, *O.C.* (Bt.), 6:62–63.

26. See *Democracy* (Mayer), pp. 565–67.

27. "How Democracy Leads to Ease and Simplicity . . . ," Drafts, Yale,

CVh, "Rubish," tome 4. Also see Bonnel's copy, CVg, Paquet 9, cahier 1, pp. 98–99. Cf. Tocqueville's remarks about historians in democratic times, *Democracy* (Mayer), pp. 493–96.

28. Cf. the 1840 text, *Democracy* (Mayer), pp. 566–67.

29. Tocqueville's "Report on Abolition" of July 1839 would read: "It has sometimes been assumed that Negro slavery had its foundation and justification in nature itself. It has been declared that the slave trade was beneficial to its unfortunate victims, and that the slave was happier in the tranquillity of bondage than in the agitation and the struggles that accompany independence. Thank God, the Commission has no such false and odious doctrines to refute. Europe has long since discarded them." Quoted from Drescher, *Social Reform*, p. 99. Cf. Beaumont's opinions as found in Bt., *Marie* (Chapman), pp. 202–4 and pp. 214–16.

30. Undated; Drafts, Yale, CVk, Paquet 7, cahier 1, p. 37; emphasis added.

31. "12 March 1838," Drafts, Yale, CVg, "Rubish," tome 3. Also see Bonnel's copy, CVg, Paquet 9, cahier 1, pp. 143–44.

32. *Democracy* (Mayer), p. 705. For an interesting discussion of the complexities and paradoxes of Tocqueville's thoughts on determinism, consult Richard Herr, *Tocqueville and the Old Regime*, pp. 91–95, especially p. 92.

33. Arthur de Gobineau, *Essai sur l'inégalité des races humaines,* 4 vols. (Paris 1853 and 1855). Tocqueville and Gobineau had been closely associated since at least 1843, when they first began to correspond with each other. For further discussion of their personal and official relationships, see Jean-Jacques Chevallier's introduction to *O.C.* (Mayer), vol. 9, *Correspondance d'Alexis de Tocqueville et d'Arthur de Gobineau*, edited by Maurice Degros; hereafter cited as *O.C.* (Mayer), 9. Also consult John Lukacs, editor and translator, *Alexis de Tocqueville: The European Revolution and Correspondence with Gobineau;* hereafter cited as Lukacs, *Toc.: Gobineau.*

34. This and following excerpts from Toc. to Gobineau, Saint-Cyr, 11 October 1853, *O.C.* (Mayer), 9:199–201.

35. Tocqueville was even more blunt in a letter written to Beaumont shortly after receiving Gobineau's treatise: "He endeavors to prove that everything that takes place in the world may be explained by differences of race. I do not believe a word of it, and yet I think that there is in every nation, whether in consequence of race or of an education which has lasted for centuries, some peculiarity, tenacious if not permanent, which combines with all the events that befall it, and is seen both in good and in bad fortune, in every period of its history." Quoted from Lukacs, *Toc.: Gobineau*, p. 16. For the original, consult Toc. to Beaumont, 3 November 1853, *O.C.* (Mayer), Jardin, 8:3, pp. 163–65.

36. Cf. the following undated fragment: "Idea of *necessity*, of fatality. Explain how my system differs essentially from that of Mignet and company. . . . Explain how my system is perfectly compatible with human freedom. Apply these general ideas to Democracy. That is a very beautiful piece to put either at the head or the tail of the work." Drafts, Yale, CVa, Paquet 8, cahier unique, pp. 58–59. François-Auguste Mignet (1796–1884), historian, close associate of Guizot and Thiers, perpetual secretary of the Académie des

sciences morales et politiques after 1837, was not infrequently a valuable aid to Tocqueville's career.

37. This and following excerpts from Toc. to Gobineau, Saint-Cyr, 17 November 1853, *O.C.* (Mayer), 9:201–4.

38. Toc. to Gobineau, Saint-Cyr, 20 December 1853, ibid., pp. 205–6.

39. For a perceptive account of some of the contradictions in Tocqueville's thinking on the matters of race and biological determinism, see Seymour Drescher, *Dilemmas of Democracy: Tocqueville and Modernization*, pp. 274–76.

40. Original Working Manuscript, Yale, CVIa, tome 1.

41. Toc. to Reeve, Baugy, 21 November 1836, *O.C.* (Mayer), 6:1, pp. 35–36; quoted above in chapter 2.

6. The Transformation of a Continent

1. Chevalier and Guillaume-Tell Poussin, among others, are frequently mentioned as travelers who recognized the American technological revolution and understood its implications for the republic. Among those commentators who have chastised Tocqueville for his oversight are René Rémond, *Etats-Unis*, 1:384–85, and John William Ward, who edited Michel Chevalier, *Society, Manners, and Politics in the United States*, pp. viii–xi. Pierson also conceded, perhaps too easily, to the arguments of Tocqueville's critics on this point; consult *Toc. and Bt.*, pp. 762–63 and pp. 761–65. (But also see pp. 174–75.)

2. Only Beaumont described the Albany-Schenectady Railroad; Tocqueville, who presumably inspected the railroad with his companion, failed even to mention it in his letters home. References to railroads in Tocqueville's travel diaries, letters and drafts are relatively few. I have found only one in his letters home, Toc. to Le Peletier d'Aunay (?), Philadelphia, 8 November 1831, Toc. letters, Yale, BIa2. Concerning Lowell, see Pierson, *Toc. and Bt.*, p. 393. Again it was Beaumont who referred in his letters to the manufacturing city.

3. In 1831 the first true American railroad was scarcely a year old, and the second was still under construction. For a fuller discussion, see George R. Taylor, *The Transportation Revolution, 1815–1860*, pp. 77–78.

4. For details of these accidents, consult Pierson, *Toc. and Bt.*, pp. 545–48, 574–77, 599–601, 619–20.

5. In December 1831, as he headed down the Mississippi aboard the *Louisville*, Tocqueville questioned the captain about the expenses for building and maintaining such a steamboat; Notebook E, Mayer, *Journey*, p. 257. This conversation also introduced him to an American concept that he would mention in his 1840 text: planned obsolescence; *Democracy* (Mayer), pp. 453–54. In 1840 Tocqueville would also note several other significant features of American industry, including mass production (pp. 465–68), division of labor (pp. 555–56), periodic business cycles (p. 554), and a possible industrial aristocracy (pp. 555–58).

6. Conversation with Mr. Howard, Baltimore, 4 November 1831, Pocket

Notebook Number 3, Mayer, *Journey*, pp. 158–59. From Mr. Howard he learned about American efforts to join the Great Lakes to the Mississippi by canal.

7. Conversation with Mr. Chase, Cincinnati, 2 December 1831, Non-Alphabetic Notebooks 2 and 3, Mayer, *Journey*, p. 92. See also "Ohio—canals," 2 December 1831, Notebook E, ibid., p. 265; also Tocqueville's comments about the projected canal linking Pittsburgh with Erie, Pennsylvania, 20 July 1831, Pocket Notebook 2, and "A Fortnight in the Wilds," ibid., p. 133 and p. 334.

8. "Questions left by MM. Beaumont and Tocqueville," 1 October 1831, from Correspondence and Relations with Americans, 1831–32, Yale Toc. Mss., BIc; hereafter cited as Relations with Americans, 1831–32, Yale, BIc.

9. Letter from B. W. Richards to Beaumont, Philadelphia, 2 February 1832, Relations with Americans, 1831–32, Yale, BIc.

10. See Tocqueville's treatment of this question in the 1835 *Democracy* (Mayer), p. 387.

11. Conversation with Mr. Poinsett, 13–15 January 1832, Pocket Notebooks 4 and 5, Mayer, *Journey*, p. 178.

12. "Associations," Notebook E, Mayer, *Journey*, p. 252.

13. Notes on Kent and "Associations," Notebook E, Mayer, *Journey*, pp. 232–33 and p. 253. For further discussion of Kent, his work, and his influence on Tocqueville, see chapters 7 and 8 below.

14. Kentucky-Tennessee, Notebook E, Mayer, *Journey*, p. 268.

15. Means of Increasing Public Prosperity, Notebook E, Mayer, *Journey*, p. 270. Also consult Pierson's discussion of Tocqueville, the post, and prosperity, *Toc. and Bt.*, pp. 588–92.

16. Means of Increasing Public Prosperity, Notebook E, Mayer, *Journey*, pp. 270–73. This long passage is also quoted in Pierson, *Toc. and Bt.*, pp. 588–92.

17. See several pages from the section entitled "What Are the Chances That the American Union Will Last? What Dangers Threaten It?" *Democracy* (Mayer), pp. 384–86.

18. The 1816 edition of Pitkin contained no information on internal improvements and almost nothing on manufacturing. By the early 1830s, Pitkin realized the inadequacies of his work, and in 1835, when the first two volumes of the *Democracy* appeared, he published an enlarged and updated edition. This 1835 version, which was too late for Tocqueville to use, did include extensive information on internal improvements, manufacturing, and even the factories at Lowell.

19. All of Tocqueville's citations of Warden are from the first volume of Warden's five.

20. A partial list of Tocqueville's sources on American transportation and communication, other than the volumes cited above, would include: various legislative and executive documents (see Drafts, Yale, CVh, Paquet 3, cahier 1, pp. 6–13); the *American Almanac*, 1831, 1832, 1834; the *National Calendar*, 1833; and *Niles Weekly Register*. Also consult Pierson's extensive list of sources, *Toc. and Bt.*, pp. 727–30 note.

21. In 1836 Poussin also wrote *Chemins de fer américains . . . .*

22. Mathew Carey (1760–1839), author, publisher, nationalist, economist, and champion of industry and internal improvements, produced many articles

and essays. Perhaps *The Crisis* (Philadelphia 1823) and a *Brief View of the System of Internal Improvements of Pennsylvania* (Philadelphia 1831) would have been of special interest to Tocqueville. Note that he did know and would cite Carey's *Letters on the Colonization Society* (Philadelphia 1832); see *Democracy* (Mayer), pp. 353–54 note and p. 359 note.

23. "Statistiques et généralités," Reading Lists, Yale, CIIa.

24. "Livres à demander à M. King," Reading Lists, Yale, CIIa. James Gore King, prominent New York financier, had entertained the companions several times while they were in America.

25. Darby and Dwight, *A New Gazetteer*, p. 257. (A second edition of the volume appeared in 1835.)

26. Consult the next-to-last section of the 1835 *Democracy*, entitled "Some Considerations concerning the Causes of the Commercial Greatness of the United States," *Democracy* (Mayer), pp. 400–407.

27. Le Peletier d'Aunay, a cousin to Tocqueville, was an influential political figure during the July Monarchy.

28. M. le Comte [Edouard] Roger [du Nord] (1802–1881), political figure and close associate of Thiers, was a deputy (or representative) under the July Monarchy, the Second Republic, and even the Third Republic.

29. Livingston to Toc., Paris, 24 March 1834, Relations with Americans, 1832–40, Yale, CId. (Edward Livingston, Senator, Jackson's Secretary of State, and Minister to Paris, 1833–35, was of great aid to Tocqueville both in America and in France.) In the margin of the working manuscript, next to his discussion of the constitutional dispute over internal improvements (see *Democracy* [Mayer], p. 387), Tocqueville wrote: "Examine here the series of Messages of the various Presidents who have successively held office during the past forty years"; Original Working Ms., Yale, CVIa, tome 2.

30. "Livres à demander à M. King," Reading Lists, Yale, CIIa. On the subject of corporations, Tocqueville also read various collections of state laws. He copied, in particular, from *Revised Statutes of New York*; see Drafts, Yale, CVh, Paquet 3, cahier 1, p. 103. Even after the publication of the 1835 *Democracy*, Tocqueville watched for information about internal improvements in the New World. See, for example, Drafts, Yale, CVa, Paquet 8, pp. 15–22.

31. One word is illegible; comment by the copyist, Bonnel.

32. Drafts, Yale, CVh, Paquet 3, cahier 1, p. 1.

33. Emphasis added. Ibid., pp. 7–8.

34. In the manuscript, this sentence is crossed out. Original Working Ms., Yale, CVIa, tome 1. "Here" refers to *Democracy* (Mayer), pp. 54–55.

35. "How an Aristocracy May Be Created by Industry," *Democracy* (Mayer), pp. 555–58. Beaumont advanced this thesis, in brief form, in his *Marie* (1835); see *Marie* (Chapman), p. 106.

36. Consult the discussion with Vaux, 27 October 1831, Non-Alphabetic Notebooks 2 and 3, Mayer, *Journey*, pp. 68–69.

37. Alban de Villeneuve-Bargemont, *Economie politique chrêtienne*. Seymour Drescher first demonstrated Tocqueville's use of this multi-volume work, but apparently did not realize the full possible importance of Villeneuve-Bargemont's influence. Drescher also did not know that Tocqueville's ideas about a manufacturing aristocracy had originally appeared in pre-1835 drafts. Consequently he overemphasized the effect of the English voyages on this matter. Consult

Drescher, *Toc. and England*, pp. 66 and 136; and Drescher, *Social Reform*, p. 3.

38. Villeneuve-Bargemont, *Economie politique chrétienne*, 1:389.

39. Consult Albert Schatz, *L'Individualisme économique et social: ses origines—son évolution—ses formes contemporaines*, pp. 304–5.

40. *Democracy* (Mayer), pp. 189–90.

41. Original Working Ms., Yale, CVIa, tome 3. Another copy appears in the Drafts, Yale, CVg, "Rubish," tome 4. It should be noted that this small chapter is not one of those concerning associations which do appear in the 1840 volumes; *Democracy* (Mayer), pp. 513–24.

42. The reading of "interesting" is uncertain.

43. Title page of the deleted chapter on civil associations; Drafts, Yale, CVg, "Rubish," tome 4.

44. Ernest de Blosseville, friend of both Tocqueville and Beaumont.

45. Toc. to Bt., Baugy, 4 November [3 December] 1836, *O.C.* (Mayer), Jardin, 8:1, p. 176. Another letter also implied that Beaumont kept his friend informed about recent writings by travelers to America; see Bt. to Toc., Dublin, 2 July 1836, wherein he described Harriet Martineau's book; ibid., pp. 202–3.

46. In the summer of 1838, Beaumont even met Michel Chevalier. See Bt. to Toc., Paris, 10 June 1838, ibid., pp. 301–2.

7. The Bond between the States and the Central Government

1. In this and the following chapter, I have attempted to indicate some specific origins for certain of Tocqueville's ideas about American federalism. In some cases, his travel notebooks, drafts, or working manuscript of the *Democracy* offer precise references not contained in the published text of 1835, thus making new links between sources and ideas clear and incontrovertible. At other times, I have quoted materials not specifically cited by Tocqueville, but contained, nevertheless, in works which he consulted. In the latter cases, any connection between sources and ideas is, admittedly, only probable. Too often those searching for the origins of ideas forget that an author's citation of one work does not exclude the possibility of his reliance on others. I have tried to avoid this error and, by drawing attention to certain of Tocqueville's sources, have not intended to imply that he did not use others as well.

2. Tocqueville to Ernest de Chabrol, New York, 20 June 1831, Toc. letters, Yale, BIa2. Also see another letter to Chabrol, New York, 9 June 1831, ibid.

3. Other Americans often described to Tocqueville and Beaumont the advantages and dangers of federalism, but rarely detailed the mechanics of the interrelation of state and nation. For the conversation with Mr. Clay, see 2 October 1831, Non-Alphabetic Notebooks 2 and 3, Mayer, *Journey*, pp. 65–66. For Mr. Walker, consult second conversation, which Tocqueville labeled *important*, 3 December 1831, Non-Alphabetic Notebooks 2 and 3, Mayer, *Journey*, p. 96. According to Elizabeth Kelley Bauer, Walker had been a student of Justice Joseph Story and actively disseminated Story's gospel to

the West; see Bauer's *Commentaries on the Constitution, 1790–1860*, pp. 162–67; hereafter cited as Bauer, *Commentaries*.

4. See Tocqueville's compliment to the authors of the *Federalist*; *Democracy* (Mayer), p. 115 note.

5. See for example, quotations in the travel diaries, Notebook E, Mayer, *Journey*, p. 247, p. 249, pp. 249–50; also in the various stages of the *Democracy*, Drafts, Yale, CVh, Paquet 3, cahier 1, p. 48 and p. 49; and pertinent chapters in the Original Working Ms., Yale, CVIa, tome 1. ("Publius" is the pseudonym of Alexander Hamilton, James Madison, and John Jay, each of whom wrote parts of the *Federalist*.)

6. Samples may be found in the pertinent chapters of Tocqueville's Original Working Ms., Yale, CVIa, tome 1; these translations might also have been made by Francis Lippitt.

7. For information about these editions, consult Paul Leicester Ford, *A List of Editions of the Federalist*.

8. "Union: Central Government" and "Sovereignty of the People," 27–29 December 1831, Notebook E, Mayer, *Journey*, pp. 245–50. Some of Tocqueville's comments (pp. 246–47) strongly hint that he also read numbers 16 and 17, even though he did not mention them. There is also an undated reference to Number 83 in his diaries; see Notebook F, ibid., p. 289 note.

9. For two excellent discussions of the authorship of the *Federalist* and the differences in emphasis between the papers by Hamilton and those by Madison, see Alpheus Thomas Mason, "The Federalist—A Split Personality," pp. 625–43; and Douglass Adair, "The Authorship of the Disputed Federalist Papers," pp. 97–122 and 235–64.

10. *Federalist* Papers 15–22. For convenience, I have drawn all of my citations to the *Federalist* from the widely available Mentor edition, which contains an introduction, elaborate table of contents, and index of ideas by Clinton Rossiter; hereafter cited as *Federalist* (Mentor).

11. See "Union: Central Government," 28 December 1831, Notebook E, Mayer, *Journey*, p. 245. This idea was presented most forcefully in Number 15, which Tocqueville cited in his travel notebooks. In 1835, he would declare: "This Constitution . . . rests on an entirely new theory, a theory that should be hailed as one of the great discoveries of political science in our age"; *Democracy* (Mayer), p. 156.

12. Number 23, *Federalist* (Mentor), p. 155. This passage was quoted somewhat inaccurately by Tocqueville in his travel diaries: "Union: Central Government," 28 December 1831, Notebook E, Mayer, *Journey*, p. 247.

13. "Union: Central Government," 29 December 1831, Notebook E, Mayer, *Journey*, p. 248. Tocqueville's emphasis. These remarks are particularly reminiscent of conversations and lessons in Boston. See especially "General Comments," Boston, 18 September 1831, Non-Alphabetic Notebook 1, Mayer, *Journey*, p. 48; and conversations with Mr. Quincy, 20 September 1831, and Mr. Sparks, [29 September 1831], Non-Alph. Notebooks 2 and 3, ibid., pp. 50–52 and 58–59.

14. "Union: Central Government," 28 December 1831, Notebook E, Mayer, *Journey*, p. 247.

15. *Democracy* (Mayer), p. 61; also p. 162. In the basic organization of

the 1835 *Democracy* we have already encountered an earlier echo of these ideas which resulted from the many lessons about America's local and state government that the visitors had learned during the first months of their American journey. It was also a message carried in Jared Sparks's essay "On the Government of Towns in Massachusetts," which the historian wrote for Tocqueville and Beaumont. See as well Sparks's remarks about the "spirit of locality," 29 September 1831, Non-Alphabetic Notebooks 2 and 3, Mayer, *Journey*, pp. 58–59. Also consult Pierson's discussion of Sparks's influence, *Toc. and Bt.*, pp. 397–416.

16. See Tocqueville's remarks of 18 September 1831, Non-Alphabetic Notebook 1, and his undated "Reflection," Non-Alphabetic Notebooks 2 and 3, Mayer, *Journey*, pp. 48 and 56–57 respectively. Also consult George Pierson's account of the Boston experience, *Toc. and Bt.*, pp. 355–425.

17. Conservations with Mr. Poinsett, 12–17 January 1832, Non-Alphabetic Notebooks 2 and 3, Mayer, *Journey*, p. 118.

18. *Democracy* (Mayer), pp. 164–65.

19. Pierson, *Toc. and Bt.*, p. 136.

20. "Sources. Nature des livres où je puis puiser—Livres de droit," Reading Lists, Yale, CIIa. Tocqueville devoted a separate travel diary to his notes and observations on Kent's *Commentaries*: "Notes on Kent," undated, Mayer, *Journey*, pp. 228–33. Also see his comments on Kent's work under various headings in Notebook E, 27 and 29 December 1831, ibid., p. 245, pp. 249–57; and in Notebook F, 31 December 1831, ibid., pp. 297–302.

21. Conversation with Gallatin, 10 June 1831, and with Spencer, Canadaigua, 17–18 July 1831, Non-Alphabetic Notebook 1, Mayer, *Journey*, pp. 21 and 28–29. Also consult conversations with Mr. Gray, Boston, 21 September 1831; with Jared Sparks, 29 September 1831; and with Mr. Chase, 2 December 1831; Non-Alph. Notebooks 2 and 3, ibid., pp. 53, 59, and 93 respectively. Cf. Tocqueville's own comments of 30 September 1831, Pocket Notebook 3, ibid., p. 149.

22. 16 October 1831, Notebook F, Mayer, *Journey*, p. 313.

23. "Reflection," undated, Notes on Kent, Mayer, *Journey*, pp. 229–30. Compare this to "Judicial Power in the United States and Its Effect on Political Society," *Democracy* (Mayer), pp. 102–3.

24. Hereafter cited as Conseil, *Mélanges.*

25. Hereafter cited as Story, *Commentaries.* The complete edition (3 vols.) also appeared in 1833. Pierson, *Toc. and Bt.*, p. 729, mistakenly cited the larger edition as the one which Tocqueville used, but the Frenchman's own page references are drawn from the abridgement. Tocqueville also used Story's *The Public and General Statutes Passed by the Congress of the United States of America from 1789–1827*; hereafter cited as Story, *Laws.* (Two additional volumes of this work appeared in 1837 and 1847.)

26. In 1848, in the twelfth edition of the *Democracy*, Tocqueville would add translations of the Federal and New York state constitutions drawn from Conseil's work and would also at that time include the praises quoted above; see *Démocratie*, 12th ed., 1:307.

27. Number 15, *Federalist* (Mentor), p. 111.

28. Number 17, ibid., p. 120.

29. Ibid., p. 119; cf. Number 45, pp. 295–300.

30. *Democracy* (Mayer), pp. 112–70.

31. The chapter on the federal constitution, Original Working Ms., Yale, CVIa, tome 1.

32. See *Democracy* (Mayer), p. 166.

33. Number 17, *Federalist* (Mentor), pp. 119–20.

34. Number 46, ibid., pp. 294–95; cf. Number 45, pp. 290–93.

35. See *Democracy* (Mayer), p. 167; also pp. 365–67.

36. The chapter on the federal constitution, Original Working Ms., Yale, CVIa, tome 1.

37. Number 39, *Federalist* (Mentor), p. 246.

38. Alternative written above "confederation": "federal government." Neither is effaced.

39. The chapter on the federal constitution, Original Working Ms., Yale, CVIa, tome 1. Contrast this and other statements about the nature of the Union to a criticism that Tocqueville, in his description of the structure of the American government, failed to distinguish between "la forme fédérale" and "la forme confédérale," Paul Bastid, "Tocqueville et la doctrine constitutionnelle," *Toc.: centenaire*, p. 46.

40. *Democracy* (Mayer), p. 157. Here is an additional instance of Tocqueville's inclination to give names to new phenomena.

41. On the subjects of the importance of the federal courts and of the necessity for a strong and independent judiciary, the *Commentaries* of the two jurists are strikingly similar. The drafts of the *Democracy* indicate that, between 1832 and 1835, Tocqueville relied more heavily on Story than on Kent.

42. Drafts, Yale, CVh, Paquet 3, cahier 1, pp. 39–40.

43. Number 22, *Federalist* (Mentor), pp. 150–51.

44. Drafts, Yale, CVh, Paquet 3, cahier 1, pp. 39–40. Tocqueville's own emphasis.

45. Number 39, *Federalist* (Mentor), pp. 245–46. Compare Tocqueville's paragraph from the 1835 text, *Democracy* (Mayer), p. 115.

46. "The Federal Courts," *Democracy* (Mayer), p. 140.

47. "Means of Determining the Competence of the Federal Courts," ibid., pp. 142–43. Nowhere in his sections on the American judiciary would Tocqueville cite either Number 22 or Number 39 of the *Federalist.*

48. See various descriptions of those complexities in the 1835 volumes. *Democracy* (Mayer), p. 61, pp. 114–15, pp. 155–58, pp. 164–65.

49. Compare passages containing the phrases "one single people" or "one and the same people" (*Democracy* [Mayer], p. 140, p. 145) with others that mention "twenty-four little sovereign nations" or "an assemblage of confederated republics" or "the association of several peoples" or "a society of nations," ibid., pp. 61, 117, 364, 376.

50. Number 45, *Federalist* (Mentor), pp. 292–93; this passage would be included in the 1835 *Democracy* as a footnote, *Democracy* (Mayer), p. 115 note.

51. Story, *Commentaries*, p. 192.

52. Jefferson to Major John Cartwright, Monticello, 5 June 1824, Conseil,

Mélanges, 2:404–12. For the English version, see A. A. Lipscomb and A. E. Bergh, eds., *The Writings of Thomas Jefferson*, 16:47; hereafter cited as *Jefferson*, Memorial Ed.

53. *Democracy* (Mayer), p. 61; the second instance occurs on page 115.

54. Ibid., p. 246 note.

55. In a challenging essay entitled "Tocqueville on American Federalism," Robert C. Hartnett, S.J., described the author of the *Democracy* as hopelessly confused about the nature of the Union. The piece is found in William J. Schlaerth, S.J., ed., *A Symposium on Alexis de Tocqueville's Democracy in America*, pp. 22–30.

56. The obligations demonstrated above concern the relationship between the states and the Union, but Tocqueville's drafts and working manuscript reveal several additional borrowings in other areas treated in the *Democracy*, such as the threat of legislative tyranny, the necessity of an independent judiciary, the powers of the President, and the dangers of frequent elections.

57. See Pierson's discussion, *Toc. and Bt.*, pp. 730–35.

58. The chapter on the federal constitution, Original Working Ms., Yale, CVIa, tome 1. Nowhere in his published chapter on the federal Constitution did Tocqueville use the term *contract* to describe the Union; consult *Democracy* (Mayer), pp. 112–70. The word *contract* appears elsewhere in the 1835 text, however; see ibid., p. 369.

59. *Democracy* (Mayer), p. 369 (my emphasis); cf. pp. 367–68, 369–70, and 383–84. Elsewhere in the *Democracy*, however, by implication at least, Tocqueville would contradict this position. Compare the statement quoted immediately above to his repudiation of John C. Calhoun's nullification doctrine, ibid., pp. 390–91.

60. Hereafter cited as Rawle, *View*. According to Bauer, *Commentaries*, p. 27 and p. 63, Rawle's work was the first textbook on the Constitution designed for use on the college and law school levels and was highly popular.

61. Conseil, *Mélanges*, 1:127–28 note.

62. Ibid., 1:129–30 note; cf. Rawle, *View*, pp. 25–26.

63. For a complete account of Lippitt's memories, see Daniel C. Gilman, "Alexis de Tocqueville and His Book on America—Sixty Years After." Also consult Pierson's description in his *Toc. and Bt.*, pp. 732–34 and notes.

64. Rawle, *View*, p. 290; cf. pp. 288–90 and 295–301. Pierson indicated that Tocqueville had been exposed to Rawle through Lippitt, but stated incorrectly that Rawle was merely a further translation of Story, Kent, and the *Federalist*, Pierson, *Toc. and Bt.*, pp. 733–34 and notes.

65. For a description of Rawle's work and its reception, see Bauer, *Commentaries*, pp. 58–65.

66. Rémond, *Etats-Unis*, 1:382; Rémond's work contains a particularly perceptive discussion of Tocqueville's originality, ibid., 1:377–90.

67. For elaboration on this idea, consult Paul C. Nagel, *One Nation Indivisible: The Union in American Thought, 1776–1861*.

8. A Prophet in Error

1. Hereafter cited as Scheffer, *Histoire*. This history is the only one

published in Paris during the few years previous to Tocqueville's journey to America and also cited by him in his lists of sources. See Pierson, *Toc. and Bt.*, p. 46.

2. Scheffer, *Histoire*, p. 284; my translation. In the *Commentaries*, p. 718, Story expressed a similar opinion. Compare Tocqueville's own text, *Democracy* (Mayer), p. 364.

3. In the 1835 *Democracy* Tocqueville would carefully distinguish between the future of the Union as a nation and its future as a republic; *Democracy* (Mayer), pp. 395–400. This chapter considers only the first of these two questions. (For an identical distinction between federal and republican destinies, see Conseil's introductory essay to the *Mélanges*, 1:112–14. Did Tocqueville borrow this concept from Conseil's volume?)

4. "Division de l'empire américaine," April 1831, Shipboard Conversations, Yale, BIIb. Translated by Pierson and quoted from his *Toc. and Bt.*, pp. 49–50. (Consult Pierson's account of the conversation.) Neither the original French nor the English translation of the *O.C.* (Mayer) edition of Tocqueville's travel diaries contains any of his shipboard notes.

5. Conversation with John Quincy Adams, Boston, 1 October 1831, Non-Alphabetic Notebooks 2 and 3, Mayer, *Journey*, pp. 60–63.

6. Second conversation with Mr. Walker, 3 December 1831, Non-Alphabetic Notebooks 2 and 3, ibid., p. 96.

7. Conversation with Mr. Poinsett, 12–17 January 1832, Non-Alphabetic Notebooks 2 and 3, ibid., pp. 113–15. Compare *Democracy* (Mayer), p. 381.

8. Conversation with Mr. Clay, 2 October 1831, Non-Alphabetic Notebooks 2 and 3, Mayer, *Journey*, pp. 65–66.

9. "Centralization," 25 October 1831, Alphabetic Notebook 2, ibid., p. 216.

10. Drafts, Yale, CVh, Paquet 3, cahier 2, pp. 48–49. Compare *Democracy* (Mayer), p. 384.

11. 31 January 1832, Notebook E, Mayer, *Journey*, pp. 235–36.

12. Number 15, *Federalist* (Mentor), p. 111.

13. Number 45, ibid., pp. 289–90.

14. Drafts, Yale, CVh, Paquet 3, cahier 1, p. 76.

15. In this exposition, Tocqueville once again displayed his eagerness to discover and employ a *point de départ*, one of his favorite mental tools.

16. Drafts, Yale, CVh, Paquet 3, cahier 1, p. 78. Cf. *Democracy* (Mayer), pp. 364–66.

17. See *Democracy* (Mayer), pp. 368–70 and 383–84.

18. *Democracy* (Mayer), pp. 370–74 and 384–86. Tocqueville would cite as material interests: various geographic circumstances, the presence of the slaves in the South, and the bonds of commerce, transportation, and communication. As nonmaterial factors, he would include: common opinions, beliefs, and sentiments, and a growing sense of nationhood.

19. Ibid., pp. 374–83. According to the 1835 text, the most important of these contrary forces would be the one we have already noted, the shifting balance of wealth and influence among the states and sections as the Union expanded. But Tocqueville would also mention the incompatible passions and character traits created by slavery.

20. The following brief excerpts are from the section entitled "What Are

the Chances that the American Union Will Last," Original Working Ms., Yale, CVIa, tome 2. Initially the sentence ended: "of all of its parts." But Tocqueville deleted "all" and substituted the word "some."

21. Original Working Ms., Yale, CVIa, tome 2.

22. Ibid. Compare these phrases with the *Democracy* (Mayer), p. 383.

23. Original Working Ms., Yale, CVIa, tome 2; my emphasis.

24. Consult the section of the 1835 *Democracy* entitled "What Are the Chances that the American Union Will Last? What Dangers Threaten It?" *Democracy* (Mayer), pp. 363–95. (Also consult pp. 166–70.) Only once, significantly while discussing the results of the Union's growth, would Tocqueville approach so direct a statement; see ibid., p. 378.

25. Drafts, Yale, CVh, Paquet 3, cahier 1, pp. 80–81. Compare *Democracy* (Mayer), pp. 383–84.

26. Hereafter cited as Blunt, *Historical Sketch.*

27. Hereafter cited as Duer, *Outlines.*

28. Second revised edition; hereafter cited as Sergeant, *Constitutional Law.*

29. "Sources. Nature des livres où je puis puiser—Livres de droit." Reading Lists, Yale, CIIa.

30. Bauer, *Commentaries*, pp. 27, 39, and notes.

31. Sergeant, *Constitutional Law*, pp. 324–28 and notes. Compare Tocqueville's discussion of the issue, *Democracy* (Mayer), pp. 386–87.

32. Sergeant, *Constitutional Law*, pp. 353–54. Concerning the debate on the bank, Tocqueville also cited in his drafts two issues of the *National Intelligencer*, "6 February 1834" and "5 [*sic:* 4] March 1834." The first contained a speech by Daniel Webster; the second, one by Henry Clay. See Drafts, Yale, CVh, Paquet 3, cahier 5, pp. 10–12. Also consult the *Democracy* (Mayer), pp. 388–89.

33. Blunt, *Historical Sketch*, pp. 5–6. Compare Tocqueville's analysis of the controversy over the Indians, *Democracy* (Mayer), pp. 387–88, and over the public lands, p. 388.

34. Bauer, *Commentaries*, p. 101; also Pierson, *Toc. and Bt.*, p. 729 note.

35. Duer specifically disagreed, however, with what he called Rawle's "restricted views" on "the perpetual obligation of the Federal Constitution."

36. Duer, *Outlines*, preface, pp. v-xviii. According to Bauer, *Commentaries,* p. 28, Duer wrote his book as a reply to nullification doctrines.

37. According to the copyist, Bonnel, the first word in this phrase was illegible.

38. Drafts, Yale, CVh, Paquet 3, cahier 2, pp. 61–64. The governor during the crisis was Robert Y. Hayne. Perhaps Tocqueville was thinking of James Hamilton, Jr., a prominent nullifier. Consult the footnotes in the *Democracy* (Mayer), pp. 389–92, where other documents are cited, especially the compromise tariff of 1833. Note that nowhere did Tocqueville indicate that he had read President Jackson's Proclamation of December 1832.

39. Drafts, Yale, CVh, Paquet 3, cahier 2, p. 52.

40. Bonnel indicated that the word following "its" was illegible, but similar passages in the draft make possible the educated guess: "power."

41. Drafts, Yale, Paquet 3, cahier 2, p. 66.

42. Drafts, Yale, CVh, Paquet 3, cahier 2, pp. 80–81.

43. Drafts, Yale, CVh, Paquet 3, cahier 2, pp. 52–53.

44. *Democracy* (Mayer), p. 386; see also pp. 384–85 and pp. 394–95. Note Tocqueville's recognition of several circumstances which could reverse the decline of the federal government: "a change of opinion, an internal crisis, or a war could all at once restore the vigor it needs" (p. 394).

45. Drafts, Yale, CVh, Paquet 3, cahier 1, p. 76.

46. Bauer, *Commentaries*, pp. 21 and 28.

47. Story, *Commentaries*, p. 193; not specifically cited by Tocqueville. Compare *Democracy* (Mayer), pp. 394–95.

48. Drafts, Yale, CVh, Paquet 3, cahier 2, pp. 48–49. For the softened version, see *Democracy* (Mayer), p. 384.

49. Conseil, *Mélanges*, 1:84–85, 232–34; 2:310–16, 420–21. Tocqueville's papers give no indication that he noticed any of these letters.

50. Conseil, *Mélanges*, 2:420–21. For the original English version, see Jefferson to William B. Giles, Monticello, 26 December 1825, *Jefferson*, Memorial Ed., 16:146–47.

51. *Democracy* (Mayer), p. 386.

52. Drafts, Yale, CVh, Paquet 3, cahier 1, p. 25.

53. This and the following excerpt are from the section "What Are the Chances That the American Union Will Last," Original Working Ms., Yale, CVIa, tome 2; this sentence is crossed out.

54. Original Working Ms., Yale, CVIa, tome 2; the final three sentences in this paragraph are crossed out in the manuscript. Compare this timetable to Arnold Scheffer's, *Histoire*, p. 246; see also pp. 251 and 252.

55. Cf. *Democracy* (Mayer), p. 387.

56. Ibid., p. 395.

57. Letter from Sparks to Tocqueville, Boston, 30 August 1833, Relations with Americans, 1832–40, Yale, CId; Bonnel copy.

58. Letter from H. D. Gilpin to Tocqueville, Philadelphia, 24 September 1833, Relations with Americans, 1832–40, Yale, CId; original from Madame de Larminat.

59. For elaboration, see chapter 2 above.

60. It should be emphasized that his description also obviously had its optimistic elements: the nation's dominance of North America, its future commercial greatness, its apparently boundless wealth, and others.

9. How Large Might a Republic Be?

1. Second conversation with Mr. Walker, 3 December 1831, Non-Alphabetic Notebooks 2 and 3, Mayer, *Journey*, pp. 95–96.

2. Conversation with Mr. Mazureau, New Orleans, 1 January 1832, Non-Alphabetic Notebooks 2 and 3, ibid., pp. 101–2. Mazureau's remark was clearly an echo of Montesquieu (see below).

3. See the section entitled: "Advantages of the Federal System in General and Its Special Usefulness in America," *Democracy* (Mayer), pp. 158–63.

4. From the section "Advantages of the Federal System . . . ," Original Working Ms., Yale, CVIa, tome 1.

5. Justice Story argued from a more empirical point of view. See his *Commentaries*, pp. 169–70.

6. Conversation with Mr. MacLean, 2 December, Non-Alphabetic Notebooks 2 and 3, Mayer, *Journey*, p. 93. See Tocqueville's remarks of 14 January 1832, Notebook E, ibid., pp. 234–35. In 1835, Tocqueville would reproduce the essence of MacLean's comment; see *Democracy* (Mayer), p. 163.

7. "Union: Central Government," 29 December 1831, Notebook E, Mayer, *Journey*, p. 248.

8. Conversations with Mr. Poinsett, 12–17 January 1832, Non-Alphabetic Notebooks 2 and 3, Mayer, *Journey*, p. 118. Poinsett prefaced this remark by citing the example of South America; and in 1835, Tocqueville would repeat his illustration, *Democracy* (Mayer), p. 162.

9. *De l'esprit des lois*, edited by Gonzague Truc. The selections quoted are from "Propriétés distinctives de la république," 1:131–32 and "Comment les républiques pourvoient à leur sureté," 1:137–38; my translations.

10. Number 9, *Federalist* (Mentor), pp. 71–76.

11. Madison's brilliant thesis is developed primarily in papers 10 and 51 (also see Number 14) and still stands as one of America's most creative contributions to political theory. For analysis, consult two articles by Neal Riemer, "The Republicanism of James Madison" and "James Madison's Theory of the Self-Destructive Features of Republican Government"; also two articles by Douglass Adair, "The Tenth *Federalist* Revisited" and "That Politics May Be Reduced to a Science," in which Adair discloses Madison's debt to David Hume. Two more recent examinations are Paul F. Bourke, "The Pluralist Reading of James Madison's Tenth *Federalist*," and Robert Morgan, "Madison's Theory of Representation in the Tenth *Federalist*." Also pertinent is the study by Robert A. Dahl and Edward R. Tufte, *Size and Democracy*, especially pp. 34–40. Concerning Madison's creativity, see Edmund S. Morgan, "The American Revolution Considered as an Intellectual Movement."

12. Concerning the possible application of Madison's theory to Tocqueville's fears about the danger of tyranny of the majority, see chapter 15 below.

13. Perhaps Tocqueville skimmed Number 10 during December 1831, but if he did so, he left no indication in his travel notebooks.

14. Drafts, Yale, CVb, Paquet 13, p. 25 (where two citations occur) and p. 26; CVh, Paquet 3, cahier 1, p. 48. Tocqueville referred only to pages of the *Federalist*, not to papers, but a glance at his edition reveals that the essay which he repeatedly mentioned was Number 51; nowhere in the drafts or manuscript of the *Democracy* did he cite Number 10. (In 1835 he would quote a passage from Number 51; without any indication, however, he would delete from the excerpt the essence of Madison's argument about size; (*Democracy* [Mayer], p. 260).

15. Drafts, Yale, CVb, Paquet 13, p. 26.

16. Number 51, *Federalist* (Mentor), pp. 324–25.

17. Drafts, Yale, CVh, Paquet 3, cahier 5, p. 2. He cited an epistle from "Jefferson à Devernois [*sic*] 6 février 1795," but did not indicate that the letter appeared in Conseil, *Mélanges*, 1:407–8. For the original English version, see letter to M. D'Ivernois, 6 February 1795, *Jefferson*, Memorial Ed., 9:299–300.

18. Tocqueville's draft contained all except the last sentence of this

passage. Note that Jefferson had evidently not learned anything from Hamilton about Montesquieu's complete opinions concerning large republics.

19. See "Influence of the Laws upon the Maintenance of a Democratic Republic," Original Working Ms., Yale, CVIa, tome 1; and *Democracy* (Mayer), p. 287 (also pp. 161–62). Pierson, *Toc. and Bt.*, pp. 768–69, wrote that the resemblance between Tocqueville and Montesquieu was primarily outward. This is true in many ways, but on the question of the size of a republic the similarity is far more than superficial; the ideas of the two men are strikingly parallel. Compare Tocqueville's comments in the *Democracy* (Mayer), pp. 158–63, with Montesquieu's remarks in the sections from *De l'esprit des lois* cited above. For further discussion of similarities between Tocqueville and Montesquieu, see Melvin Richter's stimulating essay, "The Uses of Theory: Tocqueville's Adaptation of Montesquieu."

20. *Democracy* (Bradley), 1:170. Note the contrast between this idea and Tocqueville's usual low opinion of the states and their selfish striving for power.

21. *Democracy* (Mayer), p. 263; also see p. 287.

22. Ibid., pp. 377–78. See also pp. 376–77 and compare p. 381, where Tocqueville would state that a large federation could exist if none of the component parts had contradictory interests.

23. Ibid., p. 159.

24. Ibid., p. 160. Tocqueville seemed to define *la majorité* as underlying support within a society for the form and operation of its government, that is, as something essential to the continued orderly existence of a nation.

25. See, for example, *Democracy* (Mayer), pp. 262–63.

26. See chapter 15 below on Tocqueville's concept of the majority.

10. Centralization and Local Liberties

1. For elaboration, consult the standard works by Felix Ponteil, *Les Institutions de la France de 1814 à 1870*, hereafter cited as Ponteil, *Institutions*; F. Ponteil, *La Monarchie parlementaire: 1815–1848*, hereafter cited as Ponteil, *Monarchie parlementaire*; and Dominique Bagge, *Le Conflit des idées politiques en France sous la Restauration*, hereafter cited as Bagge, *Idées politiques*. Also see an old but still valuable work, Edouard Laboulaye, *L'Etat et ses limites*, the essay entitled "Alexis de Tocqueville," pp. 138–201, especially pp. 160–71 where Laboulaye discusses the originality of Tocqueville's ideas on centralization; hereafter cited as Laboulaye, *L'Etat*.

2. Le Peletier d'Aunay to Tocqueville, August 1831, copy, Letters from French Friends: 1831–32, Yale Toc. Ms., BId.

3. Toc. to M. le Comte de Tocqueville, Sing-Sing, 3 June 1831, Toc. letters, Yale, BIa1, Paquet 15, pp. 2–3. Also see Tocqueville's letter to Ernest de Chabrol, New York, 20 June 1831, Toc. letters, Yale, BIa2. And compare the 1835 text: *Democracy* (Mayer), p. 72.

4. Toc. to Ernest de Chabrol, Auburn, 16 July 1831, Toc. letters, Yale, BIa1. Also see a similar comment by Beaumont, Beaumont to his father, New York, 16 May 1831, Bt. *Lettres*, pp. 39–46.

5. "Note" to a conversation with Mr. Quincy, 20 September 1831, Non-Alphabetic Notebooks 2 and 3, Mayer, *Journey*, pp. 51–52. See in the 1835 *Democracy* an almost exact reproduction of these remarks, *Democracy* (Mayer), p. 95. Also compare a conversation with Mr. Lieber, 22 September 1831, Non-Alph. Notebooks 2 and 3, Mayer, *Journey*, pp. 51–52 and its echo in the 1835 *Democracy*, *Democracy* (Mayer), p. 189.

6. Conversation with Mr. Gray, 21 September 1831, Non-Alph. Notebooks 2 and 3, Mayer, *Journey*, p. 52.

7. 28 September 1831, ibid., p. 57. Compare the 1835 volumes, *Democracy* (Mayer), p. 189.

8. 29 September 1831 (date in Yale copy), Mayer, *Journey*, p. 59. Cf. the 1835 portion of Tocqueville's book, *Democracy* (Mayer), p. 67 and pp. 68–70.

9. 30 September 1831, Pocket Notebook 3, Mayer, *Journey*, p. 149.

10. [1 October 1831], ibid., p. 150. Cf. 1835 volumes, *Democracy* (Mayer), p. 96.

11. During discussion of the 1848 Constitution, for example, Tocqueville would again call for greater local liberties; consult Edward Gargan, *Alexis de Tocqueville: The Critical Years, 1848–1851*, pp. 98–99; hereafter cited as Gargan, *Critical Years*.

12. "Centralization," 27 September 1831, Alphabetic Notebook 2, Mayer, *Journey*, p. 213.

13. "Questions left by MM. Beaumont and Tocqueville," 1 October 1831, Relations with Americans, 1831–32, Yale, BIc.

14. Quoted from Herbert Baxter Adams, "Jared Sparks and Alexis de Tocqueville," p. 570.

15. Toc. to his father, Hartford, 7 October 1831, Toc. letters, Yale, BIa2. Also see inquiries to Chabrol, Hartford, 7 October 1831, and to Blosseville, New York, 10 October 1831, Toc. letters, Yale, BIa2.

16. For example, see Pierson, *Toc. and Bt.*, pp. 397–416; and André Jardin, "Tocqueville et la décentralisation," pp. 91–92; hereafter cited as Jardin, "Décentralisation."

17. Toc. to Louis de Kergolay, Yonkers, 29 June 1831, *O.C.* (Mayer), Jardin and Lesourd, 13:1, pp. 233–34.

18. Philadelphia, 25 October 1831, Pocket Notebook 3, Mayer, *Journey*, pp. 155–56. Cf. the 1835 volumes, *Democracy* (Mayer), pp. 92–93.

19. Conversation with Mr. Guillemin, New Orleans, 1 January 1832, Non-Alph. Notebooks 2 and 3, Mayer, *Journey*, pp. 104–5; also see "*Coup d'oeil* of New Orleans," ibid., pp. 381–83.

20. 4 January 1832, Pocket Notebook 3, ibid., p. 166.

21. "Means of Increasing Public Prosperity," Notebook E, ibid., p. 272.

22. [1 October 1831], Pocket Notebook 3, ibid., p. 150. An additional American attitude should also be noted here. Repeatedly Tocqueville and Beaumont noticed a deep American fear of centralized power and especially of great cities or political capitals. For elaboration see chapter 8 above.

23. Toc. to M. le Comte de Tocqueville (father), Washington, 24 January 1832, Toc. letters, Yale, BIa1, Paquet 15, pp. 72–73.

24. This and following passages from "Coup d'oeil sur l'administration

française," Essays by Father, Chabrol, and Blosseville, Yale Toc. Ms., CIIIa, Paquet 16, pp. 23–47.

25. Letter-essay from Chabrol, Yale, CIIIa, Paquet 16, pp. 57–58. The complete contributions from Chabrol and Blosseville are found on pp. 48–59 and pp. 59–69 respectively.

26. *On the Penitentiary System in the United States and Its Application in France*, pp. 125 and 128; hereafter cited as *Penitentiary System*. This is another excellent illustration of how closely Tocqueville and Beaumont worked as an intellectual team.

27. My emphasis; "Centralization," 24 August 1833, Mayer, *Journeys to England*, pp. 61–62. Also see Conversation with Lord Radnor, Longford Castle, 1 September 1833, ibid., p. 58.

28. "Uniformity," undated, ibid., pp. 65–66. Compare these remarks to the 1835 volumes, *Democracy* (Mayer), pp. 91–92 and 161–63.

29. At one time he planned a single large chapter entitled "Du gouvernement et de l'administration aux Etats-Unis." See Drafts, Yale, CVb, Paquet 13.

30. For his study of the states, see Drafts, Yale, CVh, Paquet 3, cahier 1, pp. 27–28, where he listed various titles of state histories, and pp. 97–114, where he discussed some other sources and ideas on administration. For his decision about five models, consult pp. 85 and 91. This choice had obvious dangers; it was unbalanced in terms of old/new, east/west, and north/south. Only one of the five was not among the original thirteen states, yet eleven new states had joined the Union. And Tocqueville included no state from the deep South or from the Southwest. In the 1835 work, Tocqueville would particularly single out Massachusetts, see *Democracy* (Mayer), p. 63.

31. Nos. 1 and 2, drafts, Yale, CVb, Paquet 13, pp. 1–2.

32. Nos. 3 and 4, ibid., pp. 16–17. Compare *Democracy* (Mayer), p. 72 and p. 69.

33. Drafts, Yale, CVb, Paquet 13, p. 15; also see p. 12. Cf. *Democracy* (Mayer), pp. 71 and 72.

34. Drafts, Yale, CVb, Paquet 13, p. 15.

35. Ibid., p. 24.

36. Drafts, Yale, CVc, Paquet 17, pp. 57–58. Cf. in the 1835 volumes, *Democracy* (Mayer), p. 87.

37. Drafts, Yale, CVb, Paquet 13, pp. 11–12; compare in the 1835 work, *Democracy* (Mayer), pp. 87–88.

38. Drafts, Yale, CVh, Paquet 3, cahier 1, pp. 78–79. Cf. *Democracy* (Mayer), pp. 363–68, especially 364–65.

39. *Democracy* (Mayer), p. 87.

40. Ponteil, *Institutions*, pp. 159–64, demonstrates the particularly high level of interest, during the early and mid-1830s, in the issue of decentralization and notes that by the middle of the decade several participants in the literary debate were writing about two types of centralization, administrative and governmental. Whether Tocqueville's 1835 *Democracy* influenced these theorists or whether the distinction was already fairly common among French political thinkers (and merely borrowed by Tocqueville) is not entirely clear.

41. See, for example, Jardin's criticism about how Tocqueville's distinction

remains imprecise, Jardin, "Décentralisation," p. 105 note and pp. 105–6.

42. Drafts, Yale, CVb, Paquet 13, pp. 11–12. Compare *Democracy* (Mayer), pp. 87–89.

43. "Political Effects of Administrative Decentralization," Original Working Ms., Yale, CVIa, tome 1. See *Democracy* (Mayer), pp. 88–89. Also compare p. 97 and pp. 723–24.

44. Later Laboulaye would describe Tocqueville's call for greater freedom for the French *commune* as utopian for the year 1835; see Laboulaye, *L'Etat*, pp. 166–70.

45. *Democracy* (Mayer), pp. 62–63.

46. Ibid., pp. 68–69.

47. Ibid., p. 88.

48. *Democracy* (Bradley), 1:310.

49. Drafts, Yale, CVh, Paquet 3, cahier 1, p. 24; also see pp. 23–26.

50. Drafts, Yale, CVe, Paquet 17, p. 60.

51. Drafts, Yale, CVb, Paquet 13, p. 26.

52. *Democracy* (Mayer), pp. 96–97. Also consult Drafts, Yale, CVh, Paquet 3, cahier 1, p. 77, and cahier 2, pp. 48–49.

53. For a different opinion on this question, see Seymour Drescher, *Tocqueville and England*, p. 78, and "Tocqueville's Two *Démocraties*."

54. On the originality of Tocqueville's views, consult particularly J.-J. Chevallier, "De la Distinction des sociétés aristocratiques et des sociétés démocratiques," p. 18. Also see Laboulaye, *L'Etat*, pp. 160–71.

11. Where Would Power Accumulate?

1. 12 January [1832], Mayer, *Journey*, Pocket Notebooks 4 and 5, p. 176.

2. Tocqueville to Reeve, Tocqueville par St. Pierre Eglise, 24 July [1837], *Correspondance anglaise*, *O.C.* (Mayer), 6:1, p. 40.

3. For elaboration, see particularly Bagge, *Idées politiques*, and Ponteil, *Institutions*.

4. Tocqueville to Hippolyte (?), Cincinnati, 4 December 1831, Toc. letters, Yale, BIa2.

5. "Public Officials," 1 June 1831, Alphabetic Notebook 1, Mayer, *Journey*, p. 195. Also see "American Mores," Notebook E, ibid., p. 273; and "Public Officials," Auburn, 12 July 1831, Alphabetic Notebook 1, ibid., p. 195.

6. New York: "Public Officials," Auburn, 12 July 1831, ibid.; Massachusetts: conversation with Mr. Sparks, Non-Alphabetic Notebooks 2 and 3, ibid., p. 58; Ohio: Second conversation with Mr. Walker: *important*, 3 December 1831, Non-Alphabetic Notebooks 2 and 3, ibid., p. 94.

7. 14 October 1831, Pocket Notebook 3, Mayer, *Journey*, pp. 154–55. Cf. *Democracy* (Mayer), pp. 253–54.

8. Conversations with Mr. Poinsett, Mayer, *Journey*, pp. 118 and 178. In the 1835 volumes, see especially "The Executive Power," *Democracy* (Mayer), pp. 121–22; various sections on the presidency, ibid., pp. 122–38; and a brief comparison of executive power on the state and federal levels, ibid., p. 154.

9. Conversation with Mr. Storer, Cincinnati, 2 December 1831, Non-Alph. Notebooks 2 and 3, Mayer, *Journey*, p. 90; conversation with Mr. Walker, 2 December 1831, ibid., p. 90.

10. Conversation with Mr. Storer, Cincinnati, 2 December 1831, ibid., p. 90; and conversation with Mr. Chase, 2 December 1831, ibid., p. 93.

11. Second Conversation with Mr. Walker: *important*, 3 December 1831, ibid., pp. 94–95.

12. Conversation with a lawyer from Montgomery, Alabama, 6 January 1832, ibid., p. 108.

13. Concerning mandates, see remarks of 27 December 1831, Notebook E, Mayer, *Journey*, p. 255; also consult chapter 14 below on tyranny of the majority.

14. Drafts, Yale, CVb, Paquet 13, p. 25; cf. ibid., p. 26.

15. *Federalist* (Mentor), pp. 308–9. Also consult Papers 47 and 49 which treat the same subject.

16. Ibid., pp. 310–11. Cf. a similar opinion by Tocqueville in his 1840 volumes, *Democracy* (Mayer), p. 436.

17. *Federalist* (Mentor), pp. 322–23. Cf. the 1835 volumes, *Democracy* (Mayer), p. 260, where Tocqueville quotes other excerpts from Number 51.

18. See for example, Drafts, Yale, CVh, Paquet 3, cahier 4, pp. 81–82.

19. *Democracy* (Mayer), pp. 154–55. Cf. ibid., pp. 121–22.

20. Ibid., pp. 89–90. For further mention of possible legislative tyranny, see ibid., pp. 104, 110–11, 137.

21. "Political Effects of Administrative Decentralization," Original Working Ms., Yale, CVIa, tome 1.

22. *Democracy* (Mayer), pp. 260–61.

23. See chapters 14 and 15 below.

24. Consult Drafts, Yale, CVb, Paquet 13, p. 25. Also cf. *Democracy* (Mayer), pp. 88–89 and pp. 96–97.

25. Drafts, Yale, CVh, Paquet 3, cahier 1, p. 82. Cf. Tocqueville's 1835 chapter on associations, *Democracy* (Mayer), pp. 189–95.

26. Drafts, Yale, CVb, p. 1. Cf. *Democracy* (Mayer), pp. 93–94.

27. For elaboration, see chapters 17 and 18 below on *individualisme.*

28. This concept of the need for intermediate groupings is a striking echo of some of the ideas of Royer-Collard, who called for the recognition of *libertés-résistances* (including individual liberties, freedom of the press, freedom of education, and separation of religion and politics) and especially advocated the reconstitution of *corps intermédiaires*, specifically local liberties and associations, as buffers for the individual in face of the state. The many close parallels as well as the numerous important differences between the ideas of Royer-Collard and Tocqueville are intriguing. A thorough comparative analysis of the two theorists would be well worthwhile.

29. Drafts, Yale, CVh, Paquet 3, cahier 1, p. 78. Cf. the chapters above on the nature and future of the American Union where this phrase is already quoted.

30. *Democracy* (Mayer), p. 93. Also see pp. 90–98.

31. Ibid., p. 87.

32. "On the Influence of Democratic Ideas and Feelings on Political Society," ibid., pp. 665–705.

33. Ibid., p. 315.

34. Drafts, Yale, CVb, Paquet 13, p. 28. Concerning this choice between

despotism or a republic, also see remarks of 30 November 1831, Notebook E, Mayer, *Journey*, p. 258.

35. *Democracy* (Mayer), pp. 56–57. Cf. in the 1840 work the chapter entitled "Why Democratic Nations Show a More Ardent and Enduring Love for Equality Than for Liberty," pp. 503–6; and the final eloquent passage, p. 705.

36. See the following examples from Mayer, *Journey*: conversation with Mr. Sparks, 19 September 1831, Non-Alphabetic Notebooks 2 and 3, p. 50; "Public Functions," *Daily New York Advertiser*, 30 June 1830 (?), Alphabetic Notebook 1, pp. 194–95; "Second Conversation with Mr. Walker: *important*," 3 December 1831, Non-Alphabetic Notebooks 2 and 3, pp. 96–97; and *Vincennes Gazette*, 12 November 1831, Pocket Notebook 3, p. 161.

37. Conversation with Mr. Sparks, 19 September 1831, Non-Alphabetic Notebooks 2 and 3, Mayer, *Journey*, p. 50. Cf. remarks dated 25 October 1831, Pocket Notebook 3, ibid., p. 156; and conversation with Mr. Biddle, Philadelphia, 18 November 1831, Non-Alphabetic Notebooks 2 and 3, ibid., pp. 88–89.

38. Concerning the encounter with Jackson, consult Pierson, *Toc. and Bt.*, pp. 663–66.

39. Remarks of 1 November 1831, Pocket Notebook 3, Mayer, *Journey*, pp. 157–58. Also see some miscellaneous ideas dated 14 January [1832], Pocket Notebooks 4 and 5, ibid., pp. 179–80.

40. *Democracy* (Mayer), p. 278.

41. "Accidental or Providential Causes Helping to Maintain a Democratic Republic," Original Working Ms., Yale, CVIa, tome 2. Cf. *Democracy* (Mayer), p. 278.

42. See Gargan, *Critical Years*, p. 81 note and pp. 198–99, 215, 218–19.

43. *Democracy* (Mayer), pp. 314–15.

44. Toc. to Kergolay, undated letter, *O.C.* (Mayer), Jardin and Lesourd, 13:1, p. 373. Compare an outline from the working manuscript:

> Today.
> Liberty with its storms.
> Despotism with its rigors.
> No middle ground.
> Something like the Roman empire.
> So there is only one path to salvation. To seek to regulate liberty, to moralize the Democracy.
> For me, I believe that the undertaking is possible.
> I do not say that it is necessary to do as America. I do not say that the Americans have done the best.
> Is there only one type of Republic? Only one type of Royalty? Likewise there is more than one way to make the Democracy reign.
> ("Elsewhere Than in America, Would Laws and Mores Be Enough . . . ?" Original Working Ms., Yale, CVIa, tome 2.)

Also compare: "To delude ourselves that we could stop the march of democracy would be folly. May God grant us some more time to direct it and to prevent it from leading us to despotism, that is, to the most detestable form of government that the human mind has ever imagined" (Drafts, Yale, CVb, Paquet 13, p. 29). Also: "I believe that tyranny is the greatest of evils; liberty, the greatest of goods. But as for knowing what is best for preventing the one and bringing about the other among peoples, and whether all peoples are made to escape from tyrants, there is where doubt begins" (Drafts, Yale, CVh, Paquet 3, cahier 3, p. 97).

45. My emphasis. Drafts, Yale, CVh, Paquet 3, cahier 4, pp. 10–11. Other examples of Tocqueville's sensitivity to "new" things include his discussion of *individualisme* (see the chapters below), his desire for a new science of politics, his claim to be a liberal of a new type, and his sense that society in the early nineteenth century was new.

46. My emphasis; *Democracy* (Mayer), p. 312.

47. Ibid., p. 314. Cf. p. 263.

48. Consult the 1835 work, *Democracy* (Mayer), p. 312.

49. During the early nineteenth century the memory of the Convention and its excesses amounted almost to a fixation with many French political theorists; consult, for example, Bagge, *Idées politiques*, pp. 141–44. Gargan has remarked specifically on Tocqueville's deep fear of legislative tyranny in 1848 when he served on the committee charged with drawing up a new constitution for France; Gargan, *Critical Years*, pp. 100–101.

12. Administrative Centralization and Some Remedies

1. For further discussion of this visit, consult Drescher, *Tocqueville and England* and Mayer, *Journeys to England*, especially Mayer's "Introduction," pp. 13–19.

2. The reader will recall that at this time Tocqueville planned only one additional volume for the second half of his work. Conversation with Reeve, 11 May 1835, Mayer, *Journeys to England*, pp. 77–78.

3. "Same subject [centralization]. Conversation with John Stuart Mill," 26 May 1835, ibid., pp. 81–82. Concerning the question of the relationship between democracy and centralization, consult Mill's reviews of the 1835 and 1840 portions of Tocqueville's book which appeared in the *London Review*, October 1835, and the *Edinburgh Review*, October 1840, respectively. For a stimulating essay comparing and contrasting many of the ideas of Tocqueville and Mill, see Joseph Hamburger, "Mill and Tocqueville on Liberty."

4. Cf. Tocqueville's own note here: "I must *re-examine* the Americans in the light of this question. Analogous principle *perhaps* more simple and more rational."

5. "Ideas concerning centralization . . . ," "Deduction of Ideas," Birmingham, 29 June 1835, Mayer, *Journeys to England*, pp. 95–98.

6. See *Democracy* (Mayer), pp. 674–79.

7. "Centralization," Manchester, 3 July 1835, Mayer, *Journeys to England*, pp. 109–10.

8. "Liberty. Trade." Dublin, 7 July 1835, Mayer, *Journeys to England*, pp. 115–16; also see pp. 114–15.

9. *Democracy* (Mayer), p. 539.

10. See especially, *Democracy* (Mayer), "How the Americans Combat the

Effects of Individualism by Free Institutions," pp. 509–13; "On the Use Which the Americans Make of Associations in Civil Life," pp. 513–17; and "On the Connection between Associations and Newspapers," pp. 517–20.

11. For this section, see *Democracy* (Mayer), pp. 665–705.

12. Beaumont's edition has the obviously incorrect reading "construction."

13. Tocqueville to Baron Edouard de Tocqueville, "Tocqueville, 10 July 1838," *O.C.* (Bt.), 7:166–68.

14. The long chapter was to have been most of the final portion of the book, *Democracy* (Mayer), pp. 665–705; for the summary, see "General Survey of the Subject," pp. 702–5.

15. Drafts, Yale, CVk, Paquet 7, cahier 1, pp. 73–74.

16. Drafts, Yale, CVk, Paquet 7, cahier 2, pp. 50–52.

17. Cf. the eloquent, final passage of the 1840 text, *Democracy* (Mayer), p. 705.

18. My translation; Tocqueville to Royer-Collard, "Tocqueville, 15 August 1838," *O.C.* (Mayer), Jardin, 11:67. Also see De Lanzac de Laborie, "L'Amitié de Tocqueville et de Royer-Collard: D'après une correspondance inédite," pp. 885–86.

19. Original Working Ms., Yale, CVIa, tome 4. Cf. Drafts, Yale, CVg, Paquet 9, cahier 2, pp. 68–69.

20. *Democracy* (Mayer), p. 155. Cf. chapter 10 above.

21. The last section of Tocqueville's 1840 volumes would be replete with references to the "public administration" and the "State." For examples, see *Democracy* (Mayer), pp. 675–76, 682, 688, 693, and 694, and pp. 671, 673, 677, 680, 682, 683, 684, 686, and 696, respectively.

22. Consult *Democracy* (Mayer), pp. 674–89; on industrialization, see especially pp. 684–87.

23. Ibid., p. 539. Cf. pp. 514–15.

24. Drafts, Yale, CVj, Paquet 2, cahier 2, pp. 16–17.

25. Drafts, Yale, CVd, Paquet 5, p. 30; also see p. 15.

26. Drafts, Yale, CVg, Paquet 9, cahier 2, p. 124; for further discussion of ideas suggested by the mining issue, consult pp. 122–25. Also see *Democracy* (Mayer), p. 685, footnote 5.

27. Tocqueville to Royer-Collard, "Baugy, this 6 April 1838," *O.C.* (Mayer), Jardin, 11:60.

28. "*Rubish* of the chapter: that centralization is the greatest peril of the democratic nations of Europe," Original Working Ms., Yale, CVIa, tome 4; cf. Drafts, CVg, Paquet 9, cahier 2, p. 145. In the 1840 volumes this chapter would be titled: "How the Sovereign Power Is Increasing among the European Nations of Our Time, Although the Sovereigns Are Less Stable," *Democracy* (Mayer), pp. 679–89.

29. "How the Sovereign Power Is Increasing Among the European Nations," Original Working Ms., Yale, CVIa, tome 4. Cf. *Democracy* (Mayer), p. 687.

30. *Democracy* (Mayer), pp. 684, 687.

31. "Continuation of the Preceding Chapters," ibid., pp. 695–702.

32. Original Working Ms., Yale, CVIa, tome 4.

33. Drafts, Yale, CVk, Paquet 7, cahier 2, pp. 42–43.

34. Drafts, Yale, CVg, Paquet 9, cahier 2, p. 139.

35. "Continuation of the Preceding Chapters," Original Working Ms., Yale, CVIa, tome 4. Cf. *Democracy* (Mayer), pp. 695–96.

36. Drafts, Yale, CVg, Paquet 9, cahier 2, p. 139.

37. *Democracy* (Mayer), p. 697. Also see the 1835 portion, ibid., p. 192.

38. In 1828 Martignac proposed some limited reorganization of administration on the local level (certain local officials were to be elected rather than appointed). After prolonged debate the proposals, which would have slightly lessened French administrative centralization, were defeated in 1829. For further details consult Ponteil, *Monarchie parlementaire*; Ponteil, *Institutions*; and J.-J. Chevallier, *Histoire des institutions des régimes politiques de la France moderne, 1789–1958.*

13. Tocqueville's Changing Visions of Democratic Despotism

1. "*Rubish* of section 4 entitled: 'What [Sort] of Despotism Democratic Nations Have to Fear,' " Drafts, Yale, CVg, "Rubish," tome 4; cf. CVg, copy, Paquet 9, cahier 2, p. 79.

2. See *Democracy* (Mayer), pp. 697–98.

3. "Why the Ideas of Democratic Peoples About Government Naturally Favor the Concentration of Power," Original Working Ms., Yale, CVIa, tome 4. Cf. *Democracy* (Mayer), p. 669.

4. Also, in France during the late 1830s any legislative despotism was a remote possibility; what Tocqueville and others worried about was, instead, the threat of personal rule by Louis-Philippe.

5. For elaboration, consult the two chapters on tyranny of the majority below.

6. *Democracy* (Mayer), p. 503.

7. Drafts, Yale, CVd, Paquet 5, p. 4. Cf. *Democracy* (Mayer), pp. 649–50; also see, in the 1835 volumes, ibid., p. 168.

8. Drafts, Yale, CVd, Paquet 5, pp. 14–15.

9. Concerning Tocqueville's advice to Kergolay and especially his suggestion that Louis pay particular attention to local and provincial government in Prussia, see a letter from Alexis to Louis, Nacqueville, 10 October 1836, *O.C.* (Mayer), Jardin and Lesourd, 13:1, pp. 407–12.

10. Kergolay to Tocqueville, undated letter, *O.C.* (Mayer), Jardin and Lesourd, 13:1, pp. 426–27.

11. Drafts, Yale, CVa, cahier unique, p. 50; cf. *Democracy* (Mayer), p. 735. Tocqueville worked on his chapters on war and armies in democratic nations during late 1837 or early 1838.

12. Drafts, Yale, CVd, Paquet 5, p. 4. Cf. Tocqueville's own notes, *Democracy* (Mayer), p. 681 and p. 735. In addition to "aristocracies" of soldiers and bureaucrats, of course, Tocqueville would also predict an aristocracy of captains of industry; see his famous chapter, "How an Aristocracy May Be Created by Industry," ibid., pp. 555–58.

13. Drafts, Yale, CVd, Paquet 5, pp. 1–3.

14. *Democracy* (Mayer), pp. 649–51 and 677.

15. Part IV, entitled "On the Influence of Democratic Ideas and Feelings on Political Society," ibid., pp. 665–705.

16. At first, Tocqueville had planned to make his final section a single, long chapter.

17. Drafts, Yale, CVd, Paquet 5, pp. 1–3.

18. *Democracy* (Mayer), p. 690.

19. Ibid., pp. 665–74.

20. Ibid., pp. 674–79.

21. Ibid., p. 691.

22. Ibid., p. 688; compare pp. 688–89.

23. Ibid., pp. 691–92; cf. in chapter 11 above, Tocqueville's earlier 1835 description of administrative despotism.

24. Final long section on political society, Original Working Ms., Yale, CVIa, tome 4; cf. *Democracy* (Mayer), pp. 694–95.

25. Final long section on political society, Original Working Ms., Yale, CVIa, tome 4; cf. *Democracy* (Mayer), pp. 687–89.

26. Final long section on political society, Original Working Ms., Yale, CVIa, tome 4; cf. *Democracy* (Mayer), p. 702.

27. Final long section on political society, Original Working Ms., Yale, CVIa, tome 4.

28. See *Democracy* (Mayer), pp. 693–95; also pp. 687–89.

29. Final long section on political society, Original Working Ms., Yale, CVIa, tome 4; cf. *Democracy* (Mayer), p. 670.

30. *Democracy* (Mayer), p. 693.

31. Ibid., p. 222; cf. also from the 1835 volumes, pp. 253–54 and p. 396.

32. Final long section on political society, Original Working Ms., Yale, CVIa, tome 4. Cf. *Democracy* (Mayer), pp. 690–95.

33. "Political Effects of Administrative Decentralization," Original Working Ms., Yale, CVIa, tome 1; cf. *Democracy* (Mayer), pp. 88–89.

34. Final long section on political society, Original Working Ms., Yale, CVIa, tome 4; cf. *Democracy* (Mayer), p. 693.

35. Drafts, Yale, CVc, Paquet 6, p. 60.

36. *Democracy* (Mayer), pp. 678–79.

37. Drafts, Yale, CVk, Paquet 7, cahier 2, p. 56.

38. Ibid., CVc, Paquet 6, p. 58; compare *Democracy* (Mayer), pp. 673–74.

39. Final long section on political society, Original Working Ms., Yale, CVIa, tome 4.

40. In Tocqueville's draft, "self-government" appears in English.

41. Drafts, Yale, CVk, Paquet 7, cahier 2, pp. 53–54.

42. Ibid., pp. 55–56. Cf. *Democracy* (Mayer), pp. 700–705.

43. Drafts, Yale, CVk, Paquet 7, cahier 2, p. 52.

44. See in the 1835 work, *Democracy* (Mayer), p. 252.

45. In the 1835 portion, consult ibid., pp. 314–15; for 1840, pp. 695–702 (especially p. 701) and pp. 702–5.

46. For 1835, see, for example, ibid., pp. 311–15; for 1840, pp. 693–95 and p. 735. Another major safeguard was, of course, religion. For an excellent discussion of the importance of religion in Tocqueville's thinking, consult Doris Goldstein, *Trial of Faith*.

47. See Tocqueville's comment: "As for me, . . . I tremble for tomorrow's freedom." Drafts, Yale, CVh, Paquet 3, cahier 3, p. 29.

48. Consult Tocqueville's famous concluding passage, *Democracy* (Mayer), p. 705. On the issue of Tocqueville's optimism or pessimism, also compare the viewpoint of Cushing Strout, who asserts that Tocqueville made an essentially "optimistic assessment" of America's future, but an essentially "pessimistic assessment" of Europe's; see Cushing Strout, "Tocqueville's Duality: Describing America and Thinking of Europe."

49. Drafts, Yale, CVc, Paquet 6, p. 55. Cf. *Democracy* (Mayer), p. 705.

14. The Tyranny of the Majority

1. Conversation with Mr. Gallatin, New York, 10 June 1831, Non-Alphabetic Notebook 1, Mayer, *Journey*, p. 21.

2. Conversation with Mr. Spencer, Canandaigua, 17–18 July 1831, ibid., pp. 28–29.

3. My emphasis. Conversation with Mr. Sparks, 29 September 1831, Non-Alph. Notebooks 2 and 3, ibid., p. 59. Sparks also mentioned two preventive devices: the governor's veto and the power of judges to declare laws unconstitutional.

4. My emphasis, except for *even in America*; 30 September 1831, Pocket Notebook 3, ibid., p. 149.

5. 25 October 1831, ibid., p. 156. See the 1835 work where the first of these conversations is recounted: *Democracy* (Mayer), p. 225. Also compare a conversation with Mr. Roberts Vaux in which the majority's occasional desire for "disorder and injustice" was discussed: 27 October 1831, Non-Alph. Notebooks 2 and 3, Mayer, *Journey*, pp. 68–69. It should be noted further that Tocqueville's brief comments about the "dogma of the republic" are yet another echo of Royer-Collard. Also compare the ideas of Benjamin Constant.

6. From the section entitled "American Democracy's Power of Self-Control," *Democracy* (Mayer), p. 224. The other examples cited would be American bankruptcy laws and the not-uncommon resort, in certain areas, to murder and dueling as ways to settle disputes. For a discussion with a somewhat different emphasis, consult the section entitled "Respect for Law in the United States," ibid., pp. 240–41.

7. My emphasis; conversation with Mr. Stewart, Baltimore, 1 November 1831, Non-Alph. Notebooks 2 and 3, Mayer, *Journey*, p. 80. Cf. in the 1835 volumes the section "The Power Exercised by the Majority in America over Thought," *Democracy* (Mayer), pp. 254–56, especially p. 256.

8. Conversation with Mr. Cruse, Baltimore, 4 November 1831, Pocket Notebook 3, Mayer, *Journey*, pp. 159–60.

9. 11 October 1831, ibid., p. 153. Also compare some later remarks where Tocqueville would note that under certain circumstances, such as when a powerful aristocracy makes itself master of the juries, "the jury is the most terrible weapon of which tyranny could make use" (12 January 1832, Pocket Notebooks 4 and 5, ibid., pp. 174–75).

10. Second conversation with Mr. Walker: *important*, 3 December 1831, Non-Alph. Notebooks 2 and 3, ibid., p. 95.

11. Consult especially the conversations with Storer, Chase, and Walker, 2 and 3 December 1831, ibid., pp. 89–95.

12. Conversation with Mr. Chase, Cincinnati, 2 December 1831, ibid., pp. 92–93.

13. Notes on Kent, ibid., pp. 228–29.

14. On the Mississippi, 27 December 1831, Notebook E, Mayer, *Journey*, p. 255; also see other remarks on mandates, 12 January 1832, Pocket Notebooks 4 and 5, ibid., p. 173. The broader analysis of this issue which Tocqueville would later present in the 1835 *Democracy* would have a strong impact on the thinking of John Stuart Mill, who would subsequently heavily emphasize the distinction between direct and representative democracy; consult especially Mill's reviews of the 1835 and 1840 *Democracy*; also Iris W. Mueller, *John Stuart Mill and French Thought*.

15. Conversation with a lawyer from Montgomery, Alabama, 6 January 1832, Non-Alph. Notebooks 2 and 3, Mayer, *Journey*, p. 108.

16. On 8 September 1834, the *Journal des débats* carried lengthy news about the riots which had occurred in Philadelphia, New York, and Charlestown during the preceding summer. If Tocqueville read or heard of these ugly events, his fear of the use of violence against minorities would certainly have been heightened; cf. Rémond, *Etats-Unis*, 2:699–700 and notes.

17. Tocqueville's emphasis; "Sources manuscrites," Yale, CIIc.

18. In the draft, "the absence of ranks" is crossed out.

19. Drafts, Yale, CVh, Paquet 3, cahier 4, pp. 15–17. In the 1835 volumes Tocqueville would discuss various institutional barriers, including bicameralism, indirect elections, parties and other associations, the press, and especially the jury system, the legal and judicial establishments, and decentralization and federalism. See the pertinent chapters, but particularly "What Tempers the Tyranny of the Majority in the United States," *Democracy* (Mayer), pp. 262–76.

20. Drafts, Yale, CVh, Paquet 3, cahier 5, p. 21.

21. Drafts, Yale, CVb, Paquet 13, p. 15. Cf. in the 1835 volumes, *Democracy* (Mayer), "The Executive Power of the State," p. 86; also p. 154 and pp. 246–47.

22. The phrase "establishment of the judges" means various things to Tocqueville, but it stood especially for the generally "conservative" influence of lawyers and judges in the society, the power of judges to declare laws unconstitutional, and the institution of the jury. See especially the sections "The Temper of the American Legal Profession and How It Serves to Counterbalance Democracy" and "The Jury in the United States Considered as a Political Institution," *Democracy* (Mayer), pp. 263–76.

23. Drafts, Yale, CVh, Paquet 3, cahier 4, pp. 15–17. Cf. ibid., cahier 5, p. 40: "Judicial power—The most original part, and the most difficult to understand, of all the American Constitution. Elsewhere there have been confederations, a representative system, a democracy; but no where a judicial power organized like that of the Union."

24. Ibid., cahier 1, pp. 14–15.

25. Ibid., CVe, Paquet 17, p. 64.

26. *Federalist* (Mentor), pp. 464–72; the quote is from pp. 465–66.

27. Drafts, Yale, CVh, Paquet 3, cahier 3, pp. 9–10. Cf. in the 1835 work, *Democracy* (Mayer), p. 269.

28. Drafts, Yale, CVh, Paquet 3, cahier 5, p. 17. Compare especially *Democracy* (Mayer), pp. 269–70.

29. Kent and Story particularly stressed the tendencies in the states toward mandates and the popular election of judges.

30. Drafts, Yale, CVh, Paquet 3, cahier 5, p. 14. Compare *Democracy* (Mayer), p. 246 and footnote 1; also pp. 154–55.

31. My emphasis; Drafts, Yale, CVh, Paquet 3, cahier 3, pp. 53–54. See in the 1835 volumes, *Democracy* (Mayer), p. 271, note 7, and pp. 262–63.

32. *Democracy* (Mayer), p. 262.

33. Ibid., p. 260, note 7.

34. Consult particularly the section "The Superiority of the Federal Constitution over That of the States," ibid., pp. 151–55. Tocqueville also recognized the possibility that, through the Senate, a minority might effectively frustrate the will of the majority; ibid., p. 119.

35. Ibid., p. 248.

36. Ibid., pp. 254–55; also see the entire section entitled "The Power Exercised by the Majority in America over Thought," pp. 254–56. A remark similar to this last sentence is found in the drafts: "All things considered, the Americans still make up the people of the world where there is the greatest number of men of the same opinion"; Drafts, Yale, CVh, Paquet 3, cahier 4, pp. 35–36.

37. *Democracy* (Mayer), pp. 255–56.

38. Drafts, Yale, CVh, Paquet 3, cahier 3, p. 59.

39. Original Working Ms. Yale, CVIa, tome 2, additional paragraphs at the conclusion of the chapter on liberty of the press. Compare "Freedom of the Press in the United States," *Democracy* (Mayer), pp. 180–88.

40. My own translation. Cf. *Démocratie, O.C.* (Mayer), 1:1, p. 267.

41. See James Bryce, *The American Commonwealth*, 2:335–53, the chapters entitled "The Tyranny of the Majority" and "The Fatalism of the Multitude."

42. Drafts, Yale, CVh, Paquet 3, cahier 2, pp. 68–69; compare *Democracy* (Mayer), pp. 395–96. Cf. Royer-Collard's idea of *la souveraineté de la raison.*

43. *Democracy* (Mayer), pp. 250–51.

44. Original Working Ms., Yale, CVIa, tome 2; the sketch may be found next to the opening page of the second volume of the 1835 *Democracy.*

45. Consult the chapters entitled "What Tempers the Tyranny of the Majority in the United States" and "The Main Causes Tending to Maintain a Democratic Republic in the United States," *Democracy* (Mayer), pp. 262–76 and pp. 277–315 respectively.

46. *Democracy* (Bradley), 1:264. For Tocqueville's full discussion, see his chapters "The Omnipotence of the Majority in the United States and Its Effects" and "What Tempers the Tyranny of the Majority in the United States," *Democracy* (Mayer), pp. 246–61 and pp. 262–76 respectively.

47. *Democracy* (Mayer), p. 247.

48. Ibid., p. 247; also see pp. 250–53.

49. Ibid., p. 252.

50. Ibid.

51. Ibid., p. 253.

52. For some examples, see the 1840 volumes, *Democracy* (Mayer), pp. 516, 669, 704; or *Démocratie*, *O.C.* (Mayer), 1:2, pp. 115–16, 298, 337.

53. *Democracy* (Mayer), p. 520.

54. Ibid., pp. 433–36; the quote is from p. 433.

55. Ibid., p. 435; cf. pp. 643–44.

56. Cf. ibid., p. 436; and pp. 643–44.

57. Ibid., p. 436; cf. pp. 515–17.

58. See the 1840 chapter "Concerning the Principal Source of Beliefs among Democratic Peoples," ibid., pp. 433–36.

59. Copyist indicated an illegible word.

60. Copyist indicated another illegible word.

61. This paragraph is written in the margin.

62. This paragraph is written in the margin.

63. Compare *Democracy* (Mayer), p. 436.

64. In 1848, as a member of the committee charged with drafting a new constitution, Tocqueville would indeed have his opportunity as lawmaker. For discussion of his views and contributions at that time, consult Gargan, *Critical Years*, pp. 97–113 and Ponteil, *Institutions*, pp. 269–76.

65. Drafts, Yale, CVj, Paquet 2, cahier 1, pp. 33–42. I have quoted excerpts.

66. Consult chapter 16 below: "Would *Démocratie* Usher in a New Dark Ages?"

15. The Tyranny of the Majority: Some Paradoxes

1. "The Jury in the United States Considered as a Political Institution," *Democracy* (Mayer), pp. 270–76; especially pp. 274–75.

2. For elaboration on the American sources of these ideas, especially the influence of Charles Curtis and Henry Gilpin, see Pierson, *Toc. and Bt.*, pp. 384–89 and pp. 529–30.

3. 11 October 1831, Pocket Notebook 3, Mayer, *Journey*, p. 153.

4. Conversation with Mr. Cruse, Baltimore, 4 November 1831, Pocket Notebook 3, Mayer, *Journey*, pp. 159–60.

5. Conversation with a lawyer from Montgomery, Alabama, 6 January 1832, Non-Alph. Notebooks 2 and 3, Mayer, *Journey*, pp. 107–10.

6. Tocqueville and Beaumont attended trials in five different cities; see Pierson, *Toc. and Bt.*, pp. 723–24.

7. Bt., *Marie* (Chapman), pp. 74–75.

8. *Democracy* (Mayer), p. 252.

9. Drafts, Yale, CVh, Paquet 3, cahier 5, p. 23.

10. *Democracy* (Mayer), pp. 31–49; especially pp. 42–43.

11. Ibid., pp. 158–59.

12. Consult ibid., pp. 253–54 and pp. 728–29, Appendix 1, R.

13. Letters from Tocqueville to Sparks, Cincinnati, 2 December 1831, and from Sparks to Tocqueville, Boston, 2 February 1832, quoted in Herbert

Baxter Adams, "Jared Sparks and Alexis de Tocqueville," pp. 571–75 and pp. 577–83 respectively.

14. On this entire issue consult especially Robert A. Dahl and Edward R. Tufte, *Size and Democracy.*

15. See Jardin, "Décentralisation," pp. 106–8; also Charles Pouthas, "Alexis de Tocqueville: Représentant de la Manche (1837–1851)," *Tocqueville: centenaire*, pp. 17–32.

16. See in the 1835 volumes, the pertinent chapters on the omnipotence and tyranny of the majority; and in the 1840 volumes, a discussion of the need for common beliefs in any society, *Democracy* (Mayer), pp. 433–34.

17. Consult chapter 9 above on the size of a republic.

18. Sparks to Major Poussin, 1 February 1841; and Sparks to Prof. William Smyth, 13 October 1841. Quoted from Herbert Baxter Adams, "Jared Sparks and Alexis de Tocqueville," pp. 605–606.

19. Consult the following additional, critical discussions: David Spitz, "On Tocqueville and the 'Tyranny' of Public Sentiment"; Irving Zeitlin, *Liberty, Equality and Revolution in Alexis de Tocqueville*; and concerning the unreality of Tocqueville's theory, Hugh Brogan, *Tocqueville*, especially pp. 39, 40–45, 47, 59–60. In addition, see a good comparison of Tocqueville's and Madison's views of the "majority" and an astute analysis of Tocqueville's concept of the tyranny of the majority, Morton Horwitz, "Tocqueville and the Tyranny of the Majority." Also compare works by James Fenimore Cooper, *The American Democrat, or Hints on the Social and Civic Relations of the United States of America* (1838), which discusses at length possible tyranny of the "publick" and "publick opinion"; and James Bryce, *The American Commonwealth*, which presents Bryce's theory of the "fatalism of the multitude."

20. Consult Mayer, *Journey*, pp. 77, 98, 156, and 224–26. Also, from the 1835 chapter on the "Three Races," see *Democracy* (Mayer), pp. 342–43.

21. "Negroes," 27 September 1831, Alph. Notebook 2, Mayer, *Journey*, p. 224.

22. Conversation with Mr. Latrobe, Baltimore, 30 October 1831, Non-Alph. Notebooks 2 and 3, ibid., p. 77; and "Negroes," 4 November 1831, Alph. Notebook 2, ibid., pp. 225–26.

23. Second Conversation with Mr. Walker: *important*, 3 December 1831, Non-Alph. Notebooks 2 and 3, ibid., p. 98.

24. *Democracy* (Mayer), p. 343. Cf., in the 1840 work, another interesting discussion, ibid., pp. 561–65. A case could be made that Tocqueville saw the racial situation in America as a holdover of aristocratic relationships. Negroes and whites (and other racial groups) were rigidly defined groups in a society otherwise marked by the lack of fixed classes.

25. Bt. *Marie* (Chapman), p. 74.

26. Drafts, Yale, CVj, Paquet 2, cahier 2, pp. 2–3.

27. *Democracy* (Mayer), pp. 259–60.

28. From the 1840 work, *Democracy* (Bradley), 2:270.

29. See *Democracy* (Mayer), p. 248; also p. 174 and pp. 177–78.

30. This concern was repeatedly demonstrated by Tocqueville's interest in the right of association and liberty of the press and the uses which Americans made of these instruments of opinion.

31. See especially two thought-provoking works: Henry Steele Commager, *Majority Rule and Minority Rights*, particularly pp. 65–67, 81; and Michael Wallace, "The Uses of Violence in American History," particularly pp. 96–102. Also consult the excellent anthology edited by Norman A. Graebner, *Freedom in America: A 200-Year Perspective*, especially the essays by Henry Abraham, Paul Conkin, Hans Morgenthau, and Gordon Wood.

32. Pierson, for example, pointed out this oversight; see Pierson, *Toc. and Bt.*, pp. 766–67 and note. It should be remembered, however, that Tocqueville did worry about a new aristocracy of captains of industry (which would constitute a type of tyranny of the minority). Often overlooked in addition is a passage from the 1840 volumes in which Tocqueville warned about the consequences of *individualisme* and too great an attachment to physical pleasures. "The despotism of a faction is as much to be feared as that of a man. When the great mass of citizens does not want to bother about anything but private business, even the smallest party need not give up hope of becoming master of public affairs"; *Democracy* (Mayer), pp. 540–41.

33. Mayer, *Journeys to England*, Appendices, "On Bribery at Elections," from testimony given by Tocqueville before a select committee of the House of Commons on 22 June 1835, pp. 210–32; the quote is from p. 231.

16. Would *Démocratie* Usher in a New Dark Ages?

1. For examples of the former, see *Democracy* (Mayer), p. 314 [1835] and p. 694 [1840]; for an example of the latter, ibid., p. 705 [1840].

2. 6 November 1831, Pocket Notebook 3, Mayer, *Journey*, p. 160. Also consult Tocqueville's reflections after speaking with Charles Carroll, 5 November 1831, Non-Alph. Notebooks 2 and 3, ibid., pp. 86–87. Compare with Tocqueville's musings of 1831 the following questions from Beaumont's *Marie* (1835): "Is the world of the spirit subject to the same laws as physical nature? That great minds appear, is it necessary that the masses be ignorant to serve as their shadow? Do not great personalities shine above the vulgar as high mountains, their crests glittering with snow and light, tower over dark precipices?" (Bt. *Marie* [Chapman], p. 105).

3. Rémond, *Etats-Unis*, 1:266 and 283–305, especially pp. 301–305. Note that proponents of this view often cited the American republic as proof of their contention.

4. Drafts, Yale, CVb, Paquet 13, p. 32. In the 1835 *Democracy*, Tocqueville would not include any chapter on this idea; only when he drafted the second part of his project (1840) would he develop it.

5. Alternative written above "this invasion": "the fall of Rome." Neither phrase is crossed out (Drafts, Yale, CVh, Paquet 3, cahier 3, p. 28).

6. The copyist noted that one word was illegible; possibly "awaits."

7. Drafts, Yale, CVh, Paquet 3, cahier 3, p. 28.

8. Drafts, Yale, CVb, Paquet 13, pp. 28–29.

9. *Democracy* (Mayer), pp. 55–56 and 301–305.

10. Ibid., pp. 254–56.

11. Ibid., p. 208. A related statement, one which says a great deal about

Tocqueville's personal attitudes toward *démocratie*, appeared in the working manuscript: "Democratic government [is] the *chef-d'oeuvre* of civilization and knowledge"; "Administrative Instability in the United States," Original Working Ms., Yale, CVIa, tome 2.

12. "Administrative Instability in the United States," Original Working Ms., Yale, CVIa, tome 2.

13. *Democracy* (Mayer), pp. 301–5.

14. Tocqueville purposely devoted his first two volumes primarily to America rather than to *démocratie* in general.

15. Bt., *Marie* (Chapman), pp. 105–16; also see p. 95.

16. Rémond, *Etats-Unis*, 1:286–87 and 300–301.

17. See Beaumont's treatment of these and other figures in *Marie* (Chapman), p. 95, pp. 111–12 note, and pp. 115–16. Also consult Pierson's discussion of efforts by the companions to see a lesser known American writer, Catherine Maria Sedgwick, Pierson, *Toc. and Bt.*, pp. 349–50 and notes.

18. Particularly significant would have been the rise of the Transcendentalists from 1836 forward. In 1841 a still-valuable work written in defense of American cultural and literary vitality did indeed appear in France: Eugène Vail, *De la littérature et des hommes de lettres des Etats-Unis d'Amérique.*

19. Cf. Bt., *Marie* (Chapman), pp. 111–12 note.

20. *Democracy* (Mayer), p. 455; also see pp. 454–58.

21. Copyist's note: "on leaf forming [the] jacket." The chapters alluded to may be found in the first book of the 1840 volumes, "Influence of Democracy on the Intellectual Movements in the United States," chapters 9–11 and 13–15; see especially chapter 9, "Why the Example of the Americans Does Not Prove That a Democratic People Can Have No Aptitude or Taste for Science, Literature, or the Arts," *Democracy* (Mayer), pp. 454–58.

22. Alternative crossed out: "It is necessary for men to make a prodigious effort by themselves in order to take the first step."

23. Alternative crossed out: "I think that it is more difficult for a savage."

24. Alternatives for "interests": "needs," "works," and "cares." All crossed out.

25. Alternative deleted: "of physical nature."

26. Alternative deleted: "equality of conditions."

27. Alternative crossed out: "mind."

28. Alternative not crossed out: "enlightenment" (*lumières*).

29. Alternative not crossed out: "over his peers."

30. Alternative deleted: "societies."

31. Alternative for the remainder of this sentence, deleted: "and I think that it is by losing their liberty that men have acquired the means to reconquer it."

32. Drafts, Yale, CVk, Paquet 7, cahier 1, pp. 18–20. Cf. *Democracy* (Mayer), pp. 456–57.

33. "Why the Example of the Americans Does Not Prove that a Democratic People Can Have No Aptitude or Taste for Science, Literature or the Arts," Original Working Ms., Yale, CVIa, tome 3. This sentence is written in the margin and is not crossed out.

34. Ibid.; this sentence is written on an extra sheet of paper enclosed within the manuscript.

35. Cf. *Democracy* (Mayer), pp. 433–36 and especially pp. 454–58.

36. Drafts, Yale, CVa, Paquet 8, cahier unique, p. 8.

37. Tocqueville's own omission; Drafts, Yale, CVk, Paquet 7, cahier 1, p. 5.

38. Ibid.

39. For elaboration of this idea, see the following two chapters.

40. Page partially destroyed by water and mildew.

41. "On the Use Which the Americans Make of Associations in Civil Life," Drafts, Yale, CVg, "Rubish," tome 3. Cf. *Democracy* (Mayer), pp. 513–17.

42. See the chapter entitled "On the Use Which the Americans Make of Associations in Civil Life," *Democracy* (Mayer), pp. 513–17; especially pp. 514 and 517.

43. ". . . Aptitude or Taste for Science, Literature, or the Arts," Original Working Ms., Yale, CVIa, tome 3. Cf. *Democracy* (Mayer), p. 458. Note however that in 1840 Tocqueville would also insist that the intellectual and cultural fruits of a democracy, though abundant, would be different from those of an aristocracy. And if equality reigned without liberty, Tocqueville foresaw probable intellectual and cultural disaster; see for example, ibid., p. 436.

44. Drafts, Yale, CVa, Paquet 8, cahier unique, pp. 47–48, dated June 1838. In the margin of this remark, Tocqueville wrote "good to develop," and in 1840 he would expand upon the idea, but neglect to indicate how it had been inspired.

45. Drafts, Yale, CVk, Paquet 7, cahier 1, p. 20. Note in these remarks Tocqueville's interchangeable use of the terms "democracy," "free institutions," and "equality of conditions."

46. Consult *Democracy* (Mayer), pp. 640–45.

47. Ibid.

17. *Démocratie* and *Egoïsme*

1. These ideas seem to reflect the influence of François Guizot's lectures on "The General History of Civilization in Europe" (1828) and especially his lectures on "The History of Civilization in France," given between April 1829 and May 1830; Tocqueville attended many of these sessions. For a convenient, modern edition in English, see François Guizot, *Historical Essays and Lectures*.

2. Compare Tocqueville's later concept and descriptions of the New Despotism; see chapters 11 and 13 above.

3. Tocqueville to Charles Stoffels, Versailles, 21 April 1830, Tocqueville and Beaumont Correspondence, 1830-April 1831, Yale, A VII.

4. My translation; *De l'esprit des lois*, 1:39.

5. "General Questions," Sing-Sing, 29 May 1831, Alph. Notebook 1, Mayer, *Journey*, pp. 210–11; cf. Pierson's translation, *Toc. and Bt.*, p. 113.

Tocqueville's viewpoint was quite unusual for the time. According to René Rémond, there was—up to the early 1830s—a widespread belief among French admirers of the United States that America did stand for virtue in the classic sense; see Rémond, *Etats-Unis*, 2:556–57.

6. Quoted from Pierson, *Toc. and Bt.*, pp. 129–30; see Tocqueville to Chabrol, New York, 9 June 1831, Toc. letters, Yale, BIa2.

7. See especially the conversations with Quincy and Lieber, 20 and 22 September 1831, respectively, Non-Alph. Notebooks 2 and 3, Mayer, *Journey*, pp. 50–52 and 54–56.

8. Tocqueville's own "Note" to the conversation with Quincy, 20 September 1831, Non-Alph. Notebooks 2 and 3, Mayer, *Journey*, pp. 51–52.

9. 30 November 1831, Notebook E, ibid., p. 258; this passage contains the first use of the phrase "intérêts bien entendus" which I have found in Tocqueville's American papers. Cf., in the 1835 work, "Public Spirit in the United States," *Democracy* (Mayer), pp. 235–37.

10. Toc. to Madame la Comtesse de Tocqueville, Louisville, 6 December 1831, Toc. Letters Home, Yale, BIa1. Compare *Democracy* (Mayer), pp. 55–56 and p. 283.

11. "Fortnight in the Wilds," Written on the Steamboat *Superior*, Begun on 1 August 1831, Mayer, *Journey*, p. 339.

12. Toc. to Eugène Stoffels, Paris, 12 January 1833, *O.C.* (Bt.), 1:424–6. This letter not only demonstrates Tocqueville's disapproval of the behavior of those, like his other friend, Louis, who met the final fall of the Bourbons by withdrawal into an internal exile, but also his deep aversion to the July régime, especially its political life. The letter makes clear as well, however, that—despite his disgust—Tocqueville was unable to keep out of politics.

13. "The power of association" is an alternative, deleted, for the preceding phrase, "the collective power."

14. Drafts, Yale, CVh, Paquet 3, cahier 3, pp. 110–11.

15. See *Democracy* (Mayer), pp. 9–20; especially pp. 12–16.

16. Cf. ibid., pp. 53–54, 96–97, 313–14.

17. Cf. ibid., p. 57; also pp. 87–88.

18. Tocqueville's mention of a *score* in this passage is not accidental. In April 1834 the July regime, in an effort to end organized political opposition by the republicans or other groups, instituted a new law severely restricting associational activities. The law applied to any association of over twenty persons, even if divided into sections of fewer than twenty; see Paul Bastid, *Les Institutions politiques de la monarchie parlementaire française, 1814–1848*, pp. 385–88. This measure effectively turned all political groups into secret societies; yet despite such official efforts at discouragement, the period from 1830 to 1848 was a time of intense activity by associations.

19. *Democracy* (Mayer), pp. 313–14.

20. Ibid., p. 243.

21. Drafts, Yale, CVh, Paquet 3, cahier 1, p. 14.

22. *Democracy* (Mayer), p. 57.

23. Ibid., pp. 236–37.

24. Drafts, Yale, CVh, Paquet 3, cahier 4, p. 30.

25. Ibid. Concerning the idea of utility and any possible early links

between Tocqueville and utilitarian theory, consult the brief but thoughtful discussion by Doris Goldstein, "Alexis de Tocqueville's Concept of Citizenship," pp. 39–53, especially p. 42.

26. For elaboration, see the chapters above on centralization. Also consult especially the chapter on "Political Association in the United States," *Democracy* (Mayer), pp. 189–95. For Tocqueville, liberty of the press was closely related to the right of association; see "Freedom of the Press in the United States," ibid., pp. 180–88 and particularly p. 191. In the 1835 work, Tocqueville also urged the use of the jury system to combat *égoïsme individuelle* which he called the "rust" of societies; ibid., p. 274.

27. In the 1835 volumes, the specific term *intérêt bien-entendu* seldom appeared. (It did however appear in the American diaries and the drafts of the 1835 *Democracy.*) In the work itself Tocqueville usually wrote more generally about how, in the United States, enlightenment (*lumières*) countered *égoïsme* and about the American idea of harmony between private and public interests. By 1840 the phrase *intérêt bien-entendu* would be more frequently used.

28. Drafts, Yale, CVh, Paquet 3, cahier 2, pp. 78–79.

29. In the margin of this passage, Tocqueville wrote: "concerning *l'intérêt bien entendu*"; Drafts, Yale, CVe, Paquet 17, pp. 66–67.

30. *Democracy* (Mayer), pp. 235–37; also compare p. 95.

31. Drafts, Yale, CVh, Paquet 3, cahier 3, p. 3. Cf., again, the idea of *époque de transition.*

32. Ibid., cahier 1, pp. 2–4; cf. cahier 3, p. 17. On Tocqueville's ideas about what made a citizen, see Doris Goldstein, "Alexis de Tocqueville's Concept of Citizenship."

33. Drafts, Yale, CVh, Paquet 3, cahier 3, pp. 36–37; cf. in the 1835 work, *Democracy* (Mayer), pp. 87–98, especially pp. 89–94. These descriptions seem once again to reflect Tocqueville's observations of France during the 1830s and his dislike of what he saw: a society marked by shortsightedness, materialism, boredom, and the ideal of "middlingness" or the *juste milieu.* On the last, consult Vincent E. Starzinger, *Middlingness, "Juste Milieu" Political Theory in France and England, 1815–1848.*

34. Drafts, Yale, CVh, Paquet 3, cahier 3, p. 3. Cf. *Democracy* (Mayer), pp. 235–37.

35. Drafts, Yale, CVh, Paquet 3, cahier 3, p. 6.

36. Tocqueville's emphasis: Drafts, Yale, CVe, Paquet 17, p. 65. Compare a passage from the 1835 "Introduction": *Democracy* (Mayer), pp. 14–15.

18. From *Egoïsme* to *Individualisme*

1. On the history and meanings of the words *individualisme* and individualism, consult the following articles: Steven Lukes, "The Meanings of 'Individualism' " and "Types of Individualism"; Léo Moulin, "On the Evolution of the Meaning of the Word 'Individualism' "; Koenraad W. Swart, "Individualism in the Mid-Nineteenth Century (1826–1860)." See also two books: Albert Shatz, *L'Individualisme économique et social: ses origins—son évolution—ses formes contemporaines*; and the more recent fine study of Tocqueville's

ideas on individualisme, Jean-Claude Lamberti, *La Notion d'individualisme chez Tocqueville.*

2. Rémond, *Etats-Unis,* 2:670.

3. *Democracy* (Mayer), p. 506.

4. See Steven Lukes, "The Meaning of 'Individualism,'" pp. 58–63.

5. See Tocqueville's remarks dated 30 September 1831, Pocket Notebook 3, Mayer, *Journey,* p. 149.

6. "Of Individualism in Democracies," *Democracy* (Mayer), pp. 506–7. In the "Rubish" of this chapter Tocqueville wrote: "*Individualisme,* isn't it simply the disposition which men have to set themselves apart?" Drafts, Yale, "Rubish," CVg, tome 3.

7. Tocqueville to Royer-Collard, Tocqueville par Saint-Pierre-Eglise, 23 June 1838, *O.C.* (Mayer), Jardin, 11:64; my translation.

8. Royer-Collard to Tocqueville, Châteauvieux, 21 July 1838, ibid., p. 66; my translation.

9. See *Democracy* (Mayer), pp. 509–13.

10. For examples, see *Democracy* (Mayer), pp. 508–9 and pp. 509–10.

11. Consult, for example, "How Individualism Is More Pronounced at the End of a Democratic Revolution Than at Any Other Time," ibid., pp. 508–9.

12. Drafts, Yale, CVa, Paquet 8, cahier unique, pp. 7–8.

13. Cf. Louis Hartz's famous thesis built on Tocqueville's observation: Louis Hartz, *The Liberal Tradition in America.*

14. Drafts, Yale, CVk, Paquet 7, cahier 2, p. 42.

15. Ibid., cahier 1, pp. 51–53.

16. The fourth part of the 1840 volumes, "On the Influence of Democratic Ideas and Feelings on Political Society," *Democracy* (Mayer), pp. 665–705.

17. Drafts, Yale, "Rubish," CVg, tome 4, for the chapter entitled "Continuation of the Preceding Chapters," *Democracy* (Mayer), pp. 695–705.

18. The *esprit révolutionnaire* fostered not only *individualisme,* but also centralization; it therefore greatly increased the chances for despotism. For elaboration of possible results of the revolutionary spirit, see in the 1835 volumes, *Democracy* (Mayer), p. 59 and p. 97; and in the 1840 volumes, ibid., pp. 432–33, 460–61, 505–6, 508–9, 548, 578–79, 632–33, 634–45, 669–70, 674–79, 688–89, 699–700. Also related to Tocqueville's efforts to explain this paradox would be his concept of *époque de transition*; see the chapter on the possible new Dark Ages above.

19. See *Democracy* (Mayer), pp. 508–9.

20. See, in the 1835 work, ibid., pp. 283–86 and 375–76; for 1840, consult especially the second part of the 1840 volumes, "The Influence of Democracy on the Sentiments of the Americans," chapters 10–16, ibid., pp. 530–47.

21. Drafts, Yale, CVd, Paquet 5, p. 2.

22. *Democracy* (Bradley), 2:141. Cf. the entire chapter, "Particular Effects of the Love of Physical Pleasures in Democratic Times," *Democracy* (Mayer), pp. 532–34, especially p. 533.

23. For elaboration, see a remarkable passage, *Democracy* (Mayer), pp. 540–41.

24. "On the Use Which the Americans Make of Associations in Civil

Life," Drafts, Yale, "Rubish," CVg, tome 3. Cf. *Democracy* (Mayer), pp. 509–13 and 515–16.

25. For the chapter which opens the 1840 work, see *Democracy* (Mayer), pp. 429–33.

26. Original Working Ms., Yale, CVIa, tome 3.

27. Most other dated pages with the word *individualisme* were written in 1838; see, for example, Drafts, Yale, CVd, Paquet 5, p. 1, 28 July 1838. An undated instance of Tocqueville's shift in usage from *égoïsme* to *individualisme* may be found in one of his drafts; Drafts, Yale, CVa, Paquet 8, pp. 28–32, especially p. 29.

28. Consult "Concerning the Philosophical Approach of the Americans," *Democracy* (Mayer), pp. 429–33; also see "Concerning the Principal Source of Beliefs among Democratic Peoples," pp. 433–36.

29. Cf. chapters 14 and 16 above.

30. *Democracy* (Mayer), p. 314; already quoted above.

31. For elaboration, consult especially the final portion of the 1840 work, "On the Influence of Democratic Ideas and Feelings on Political Society," ibid., pp. 665–705.

32. This is an earlier title for the fourth book or final portion of the 1840 *Democracy.* Tocqueville at first planned a single, long chapter.

33. Drafts, Yale, "Rubish," CVg, tome 4. Cf. Drafts, Yale, CVg, Paquet 9, cahier 2, p. 35.

34. *Democracy* (Mayer), p. 676 and p. 679.

35. Tocqueville frequently used *indépendance individuelle* and similar terms; see especially ibid., pp. 679, 681, 688, 691–92, 695–96, 699-700, 701–2, 703–4.

36. *Democracy* (Bradley), 2:347.

37. "Equality Naturally Gives Men the Taste for Free Institutions," Original Working Ms., Yale, CVIa, tome 4.

38. See the chapter entitled "Equality Naturally Gives Men the Taste for Free Institutions," *Democracy* (Mayer), pp. 667–68.

39. Drafts, Yale, CVk, Paquet 7, cahier 2, p. 44. Cf. *Democracy* (Mayer), pp. 667–68, 687–89, 701–2.

40. Drafts, Yale, CVk, Paquet 7, cahier 2, pp. 45–46.

41. See, for example, *Democracy* (Mayer), p. 667; also *Democracy* (Bradley), 2:305.

42. *Democracy* (Bradley), 2:348.

43. Drafts, Yale, CVd, Paquet 5, pp. 9–10.

44. "Continuation of the Preceding Chapters," Original Working Ms., Yale, CVIa, tome 4. Cf. *Democracy* (Mayer), pp. 701–2.

45. *Democracy* (Mayer), pp. 701–2.

46. Drafts, Yale, CVg, Paquet 9, cahier 2, p. 151.

47. Drafts, Yale, CVk, Paquet 7, cahier 2, p. 41.

48. Tocqueville to Henry Reeve, Paris, 3 February 1840, *Correspondance anglaise, O.C.* (Mayer), 6:1, pp. 52–53.

49. See *Democracy* (Mayer), p. 696.

50. After his experiences of 1848 and 1849, Tocqueville would be persuaded that the revolution was, unfortunately, a permanent state for France; see Gargan, *Critical Years*, p. 181 and p. 188.

51. This final section is entitled "On the Influence of Democratic Ideas and Feelings on Political Society."

52. In addition, Tocqueville repeatedly contrasted models of "aristocratic" and "democratic" societies.

19. Some Meanings of *Démocratie*

1. Consult, in particular, the efforts of Pierson, *Toc. and Bt.*, pp. 6–7 note, 158–59 and note, 165–66 and 757–58; and Jack Lively, *The Social and Political Thought of Alexis de Tocqueville*, pp. 49–50. Both men identify over a half-dozen major senses in which Tocqueville used the term *démocratie*, and even then, their lists do not entirely overlap. Also see the briefer but valuable discussions of this question by Phillips Bradley, *Democracy* (Bradley), 2:407–8 note; Marvin Zetterbaum, *Tocqueville and the Problem of Democracy*, pp. 53–54, 55–56, and 69; and Seymour Drescher, *Dilemmas of Democracy: Tocqueville and Modernization*, pp. 14 note, 30–31, and especially 30–31 note.

2. Almost always, from very early correspondence, through early and later drafts, and even to the original working manuscript of the last volumes of his work, Tocqueville capitalized the term *démocratie*. Only in the final published text did this idiosyncrasy disappear.

3. Here Tocqueville echoed Guizot's theme of the rise of the middle classes.

4. Toc. to Louis de Kergolay, Yonkers, 29 June 1831, *O.C.* (Mayer), Jardin and Lesourd, 13:1, pp. 232–34

5. Cf. the famous "Introduction" to the 1835 volumes, especially *Democracy* (Mayer), pp. 9 and 12–13.

6. Drafts, Yale, CVh, Paquet 3, cahier 3, pp. 27–28. Compare the emotion of this excerpt to that found in passages on the threat of barbarism (quoted in chapter 16).

7. Drafts, Yale, CVh, Paquet 3, cahier 3, p. 28.

8. Ibid., CVh, Paquet 3, cahier 4, p. 1.

9. Ibid., CVb, Paquet 13, p. 14.

10. Ibid., CVe, Paquet 17, p. 61. Here Tocqueville presumably had particularly in mind the historical preconditions of the United States, i.e., a rough social and economic equality.

11. Ibid., CVh, Paquet 3, cahier 5, pp. 8–9.

12. See especially *Democracy* (Mayer), "Author's Introduction," pp. 7–20.

13. Chapter on *état social*, Original Working Ms., Yale, CVIa, tome 1. These sentences are also quoted above in chapter 1; see that chapter for elaboration.

14. Chapter on *état social*, Original Working Ms., Yale, CVIa, tome 1. See above chapter 1, for elaboration.

15. The question might also be put another way: Why was *démocratie* not synonymous with *égalité* (or *égalité des conditions*)?

16. Note that Tocqueville's indecision about whether to stress *démocratie* as a particular *état social* or as a political form somehow related to *la souveraineté du peuple* would also be reflected in the 1835 text. Consult his two chapters entitled "Social State of the Anglo-Americans" and "The Principle

of the Sovereignty of the People in America"; *Democracy* (Mayer), pp. 50–57 and 58–60.

17. Drafts, Yale, CVh, Paquet 3, cahier 3, p. 32.

18. The letter to Kergolay cited above (Yonkers, 29 June 1831) had also briefly hinted at possible political definitions of *démocratie*. Several times in the epistle, Tocqueville had referred to a "democratic government," and once he had actually identified such a government as "the government of the multitude."

19. Drafts, Yale, CVh, Paquet 3, cahier 5, pp. 7–8.

20. Ibid., CVh, Paquet 3, cahier 1, p. 22. Cf. Tocqueville's previous attempts (quoted above) to distinguish between *démocratie* and *souveraineté du peuple*.

21. Ibid., CVh, Paquet 3, cahier 3, pp. 38–39. Compare with this remark the following pages from the 1835 text: *Democracy* (Mayer), pp. 231–35.

22. For examples, see Original Working Ms., Yale, CVIa, tome 1, section entitled "How the Federal Constitution Is Superior to the State Constitutions," and ibid., tome 2, section entitled "Activity Which Reigns in All Parts of the Political Body of the United States."

23. Drafts, Yale, CVh, Paquet 3, cahier 4, pp. 84–85. In the copy, the final sentence is incomplete. Emphasis added.

24. Ibid., CVh, Paquet 3, cahier 3, pp. 30–33; emphasis added. Also consult ibid., cahier 3, p. 107; and cahier 4, pp. 42–43 and 54–57.

25. "Observations critiques," Yale, CIIIb, cahier 2, p. 90.

26. Drafts, Yale, CVh, Paquet 3, cahier 1, p. 82.

27. For example, in the Original Working Ms., Yale, CVIa, tome 2, see the section entitled: "On the Legal Mind (*esprit*) in the United States and How It Serves as a Counterweight to the Democracy."

28. Alternative to "portion": "class."

29. Drafts, Yale, CVh, Paquet 3, cahier 3, p. 107.

30. Alternative to "peril": "fate."

31. Drafts, Yale, CVh, Paquet 3, cahier 4, p. 57.

32. See above, chapters 1 and 2.

33. Tocqueville referred to this tradition in a letter to Eugène Stoffels, Paris, 21 February 1835, *O.C.* (Bt.), 5:425–27.

34. Drafts, Yale, CVe, Paquet 17, pp. 60–61.

35. *Democracy* (Mayer), pp. 241–45.

36. Ibid., p. 243.

37. Ibid., pp. 243–44.

38. Also in 1831, he had discussed the American and French middle classes in his American travel diaries; see, for example, comments dated 30 November 1831, Notebook E, Mayer, *Journey*, pp. 257–58.

39. Drafts, Yale, CVj, Paquet 2, cahier 2, pp. 16–17. Already quoted in chapter 12 above.

40. Drafts, Yale, CVg, Paquet 9, cahier 1, p. 171. Also quoted in Drescher, *Tocqueville and England*, p. 126 note.

41. Original Working Ms., Yale, CVIa, tome 4, from the section entitled: "That among European Nations of Today the Sovereign Power Increases Even Though Sovereigns Are Less Stable."

42. Cf. an ambiguous but related classification which had appeared in the 1835 text, *Democracy* (Mayer), p. 34.

43. Toc. to Kergolay, undated letter, *O.C.* (Mayer), Jardin and Lesourd, 13:1, p. 373.

44. As should be clear from remarks above, this is not meant to imply that *démocratie* as *égalité* had been unimportant in 1835. I am only pointing out a shift in emphasis among several basic definitions.

45. Drafts, Yale, "Rubish," tome 3. (For Bonnel's copy, see ibid., CVg, Paquet 9, cahier 1, pp. 186–87.) Compare this title to the one which would appear in the 1840 text: "What Gives Almost All Americans a Preference for Industrial Callings." *Democracy* (Mayer), pp. 551–54.

46. Drafts, Yale, CVg, "Rubish," tome 4; and *Democracy* (Mayer), pp. 665–705.

47. For examples, see Original Working Ms., Yale, CVIa, tome 3, the section entitled: "On Some Sources of Poetry within Democratic Nations"; and ibid., tome 4, the title page of "Ch. [Chapter] 47."

48. See above, chapter 2.

49. Drafts, Yale, CVk, Paquet 7, cahier 1, p. 51. Cf. Jack Lively's comment about Tocqueville's use of "models"; Lively, *Social and Political Thought*, pp. 49–50.

50. Note the significantly unresolved choice.

51. Copyist's comment: two illegible words.

52. Copyist's comment: one illegible word; "felt" is an educated guess on my part.

53. Drafts, Yale, CVk, Paquet 7, cahier 1, pp. 45–46.

54. Drescher has already drawn attention to this aspect of Tocqueville's thought; see Drescher, *Dilemmas of Democracy*, pp. 30–31 and notes, and his full discussion of Tocqueville's use of the contrast between aristocratic and democratic societies, pp. 25–31.

55. See the conversation with Mr. Duponceau, 27 October 1831, Non-Alph. Notebooks 2 and 3, Mayer, *Journey*, pp. 69–70, in which the Philadelphian mentioned that "there is no one but believes in his power to succeed in [growing rich and rising in the world]."

56. Drafts, Yale, CVk, Paquet 7, cahier 1, pp. 50–51. Another version of this passage is quoted in Drescher, *Dilemmas of Democracy*, pp. 30–31 note. For echoes of this idea in the 1840 text, see especially *Democracy* (Mayer), pp. 429–30, 440, 452–54, 465–66, 485–86, 537–38, and 548.

57. Drafts, Yale, CVk, Paquet 7, cahier 2, pp. 53–54; quoted above, chapter 13.

58. Ibid.

59. Ibid., p. 52.

20. Tocqueville's Return to America

1. *Democracy* (Mayer), "Author's Introduction," p. 20.

2. See, for example, Tocqueville's chapter entitled "Some Characteristics Peculiar to Historians in Democratic Centuries," ibid., pp. 493–99.

3. Ibid., p. 705.

4. On this matter, also see Robert Nisbet, "Many Tocquevilles."

5. *Democracy* (Bradley), 2:150.

6. Tocqueville to Henry Reeve, Paris, 3 February 1840, *Correspondance anglaise, O.C.* (Mayer), 6:1, pp. 52–53; already quoted above, chapter 18.

7. We have already noted significant examples of this phenomenon in our discussions of Tocqueville's portraits of administrative despotism and his rising concern for the intellectual effects of majoritarian tyranny. Other important instances become evident after a comparison of the chapter from the 1840 portion entitled "Why Democratic Nations Show a More Ardent and Enduring Love for Equality Than for Liberty," with passages from the 1835 work, *Democracy* (Mayer), p. 57; also the 1840 chapters on the love of well-being and its effects, with several pages from 1835, ibid., pp. 283–87.

8. Compare Seymour Drescher, "Tocqueville's Two *Démocraties*."

9. See chapter 4 above for other definitions.

10. Compare the following, already quoted above: "If morality were strong enough by itself, I would not consider it so important to rely on utility. If the idea of what was just were more powerful, I would not talk so much about the idea of utility"; Drafts, Yale, CVh, Paquet 3, cahier 4, p. 30.

Selected Bibliography

Primary Materials

The largest collection of materials relating to the American experiences and writings of Alexis de Tocqueville and Gustave de Beaumont is the Yale Tocqueville Manuscripts Collection, begun by Paul Lambert White and J. M. S. Allison, sustained and enlarged since the 1930s by the energies of George Wilson Pierson, and presently housed in the Beinecke Rare Book and Manuscript Library at Yale University.

The Yale collection—based on the premise that the lives of Tocqueville and Beaumont are inseparable—contains materials on the backgrounds, educations, and careers of both men, as well as numerous manuscripts relating to their joint endeavor, *Du système pénitentiaire*, and to Beaumont's two books, *Marie* and *L'Irelande*. But most important—from the viewpoint of this study—are Yale's holdings of letters, travel notes, drafts, working manuscript, and other papers concerning the genesis and growth of the *Democracy*.

"Appendix E: Bibliography" in George Wilson Pierson's *Tocqueville and Beaumont in America* provides a good history of the Yale collection. Pierson has updated this account in the "Bibliographical Note" of the abridged edition of his work, *Tocqueville in America*, 1959. Also consult the "Yale Tocqueville Manuscripts Catalogue—Revised" (1974), compiled by George Wilson Pierson. A copy is kept at the Beinecke Library with the collection.

For additional detailed descriptions of some of the specific papers, see chapters 1 and 2 above. Concerning, in particular, the Original Working Manuscript of the *Democracy*, also see George Wilson Pierson, "The Manuscript of Tocqueville's *De la Démocratie en Amérique*," *Yale University Library Gazette* 29 (January 1955): 115–25.

The greatest single depository of Tocqueville materials, presently at the Bibliothèque de l'Institut in Paris, is under the supervision of the Commission nationale pour l'édition des oeuvres d'Alexis de Tocqueville. Many of the papers which have been inventoried by André Jardin, Secretary of the Commission, are gradually being published as work progresses on the *Oeuvres, papiers et correspondances d'Alexis de Tocqueville* [*Oeuvres complètes*], Edition définitive sous la direction de J.-P. Mayer et sous le patronage de la Commission nationale.

Concerning the publication plans of the Commission nationale, see Charles Pouthas, "Plan et programme des 'Oeuvres, papiers, et correspondances d'Alexis de Tocqueville,'" from *Alexis de Tocqueville: Livre du centenaire, 1859–1959*, Paris: Editions du Centre nationale de la recherche scientifique, 1960. The following volumes of the *Oeuvres complètes* have appeared to date:

Tome I. *De la Démocratie en Amérique*. With an introduction by Harold Laski. 2 vols. Paris: Gallimard, 1951.

Tome II. vol. I. *L'Ancien Régime et la Révolution*. Introduction by Georges Lefebvre. Paris: Gallimard, 1953.
vol. II. *L'Ancien Régime et la Révolution: Fragments et notes inédites sur la Révolution*. Edited and annotated by André Jardin. Paris: Gallimard, 1953.

Tome III. *Ecrits et discours politiques*. Introduction by Jean-Jacques Chevallier and André Jardin. Paris: Gallimard, 1962.
(A second volume is planned.)

Tome V. vol. I. *Voyages en Sicile et aux Etats-Unis*. Introduced, edited, and annotated by J.-P. Mayer. Paris: Gallimard, 1957.
vol. II. *Voyages en Angleterre, Irelande, Suisse et Algérie*. Edited and annotated by J.-P. Mayer and André Jardin. Paris: Gallimard, 1958.

Tome VI. *Correspondance anglaise: Correspondance d'Alexis de Tocqueville avec Henry Reeve et John Stuart Mill*. Introduction by J.-P. Mayer. Edited and annotated by J.-P. Mayer and Gustave Rudler. Paris: Gallimard, 1954.
(A second volume is planned.)

Tome VIII. *Correspondance d'Alexis de Tocqueville et de Gustave de Beaumont*. Introduced, edited, and annotated by André Jardin. 3 vols. Paris: Gallimard, 1967.

Tome IX. *Correspondance d'Alexis de Tocqueville et d'Arthur de Gobineau*. Introduction by J.-J. Chevallier. Edited and annotated by Maurice Degros. Paris: Gallimard, 1959.

Tome XI. *Correspondance d'Alexis de Tocqueville avec P.-P. Royer-Collard et avec J.-J. Ampère*. Introduced, edited, and annotated by André Jardin. Paris: Gallimard, 1970.

Tome XII. *Souvenirs*. Introduced, edited, and annotated by Luc Monnier. Paris: Gallimard, 1964.

Tome XIII. *Correspondance d'Alexis de Tocqueville et de Louis de Kergolay.* 2 vols. Text established by André Jardin. Introduced and annotated by Jean-Alain Lesourd. Paris: Gallimard, 1977.

Several volumes of the *Edition définitive* have been translated and are now available in English:

Democracy in America. Translated by George Lawrence and edited by J.-P. Mayer and Max Lerner. New York: Harper and Row, 1966. (A paperback edition of this work, somewhat revised, has also been published: Anchor Books, Garden City, New York: Doubleday, 1969.)

Journey to America. Translated by George Lawrence and edited by J.-P. Mayer. New Haven: Yale University Press, 1960.

Journeys to England and Ireland. Translated by George Lawrence and J.-P. Mayer and edited by J.-P. Mayer. London: Faber and Faber, and New Haven: Yale University Press, 1958. (Also available in paper: Anchor Books, Garden City, New York: Doubleday, 1968).

Recollections. Translated by George Lawrence and edited by J.-P. Mayer and A. P. Kerr. Garden City, New York: Doubleday, 1970. (Also available in paper: Anchor Books, Garden City, New York: Doubleday, 1971.)

The *Edition définitive* will ultimately largely supersede the older *Oeuvres complètes d'Alexis de Tocqueville*, 9 vols., Paris: Michel Lévy, 1861–66, edited by Gustave de Beaumont. Beaumont, as editor, took considerable liberties with Tocqueville's papers. Even so, his final tribute to the thought and career of his friend, when read with a healthy skepticism and when checked, as possible, against the new *Edition définitive* of the Commission nationale, still remains immensely valuable.

Of the following additional published works by Tocqueville and Beaumont, several have been superseded by the new *Edition définitive.*

Tocqueville

Adams, Herbert Baxter. "Jared Sparks and Alexis de Tocqueville." Johns Hopkins University *Studies in Historical and Political Science* 16 (December 1898):563–611. Presents Sparks's essay on town government in New England and correspondence between the two men.

Engel-Janosi, Friedrich. "New Tocqueville Material from the Johns Hopkins University Collections." Johns Hopkins University *Studies in Historical and Political Science* 71 (1955):121–42.

Hawkins, R. L. "Unpublished Letters of Alexis de Tocqueville." *Romantic Review* 19 (July-September 1928):192–217; and 20 (October-December 1929):351–56.

Lanzac de Laborie, L. de. "L'Amitié de Tocqueville et de Royer-Collard: D'après une correspondance inédite." *Revue des deux mondes* 58 (15 August 1930):876–911. Contains extracts from correspondence with commentary.

Lukacs, John. *The European Revolution and Correspondence with Gobineau.* Translations of parts of the *Ancien régime* and of the Tocqueville-Gobineau correspondence. New York: Doubleday, 1959.

Mayer, J.-P. "Alexis de Tocqueville: Sur la démocratie en Amérique. Fragments inédites." *Nouvelle revue française* 76 (April 1959):761–68.

———. "De Tocqueville: Unpublished Fragments." *Encounter* 12 (April 1959):17–22.

———. "Sur la démocratie en Amérique." *Revue internationale de philosophie* 13 (1959):300–12.

Pierson, George Wilson. "Alexis de Tocqueville in New Orleans, January 1–3, 1832." *Franco-American Review* 1 (June 1936):25–42.

Schleifer, James T. "Alexis de Tocqueville Describes the American Character: Two Previously Unpublished Portraits." *The South Atlantic Quarterly* 74 (Spring 1975):244–58.

———. "How Democracy Influences Preaching: A Previously Unpublished Fragment from Tocqueville's *Democracy in America.*" *The Yale University Library Gazette* 52 (October 1977):75–79.

Simpson, M. C. M. *Correspondence and Conversations of Alexis de Tocqueville with Nassau William Senior.* 2 vols. London: Henry S. King, 1872.

Tocqueville, Alexis de. *Democracy in America.* Edited by Phillips Bradley. Based on the Henry Reeve translation as revised by Francis Bowen. 2 vols. New York: Alfred A. Knopf, 1945. The standard English translation until the recent publication of the Lawrence-Mayer edition. Bradley's notes and bibliography are especially informative; see, for example, his list of editions of the *Democracy.* (A paperback version is available: Vintage Books, New York: Random House, 1945.)

———. *Democracy in America.* With an introduction by Daniel C. Gilman. The Henry Reeve translation as revised by Francis Bowen. 2 vols. New York: Century, 1898. Gilman's excellent introduction and his extensive index to the *Democracy* distinguish this edition.

———. *De la Démocratie en Amérique.* 4 vols. Paris: Gosselin, 1835–40. The first edition.

———. *The Old Regime and the French Revolution.* Translated by Stuart Gilbert. Anchor Books. Garden City, New York: Doubleday, 1955.

———. "Political and Social Condition of France." *London and Westminster Review* 3 and 25 (April 1836):137–69.

Beaumont

Beaumont, Gustave de. *L'Irelande sociale, politique et religieuse.* 2 vols. Paris: Gosselin, 1839.

———. *Lettres d'Amérique: 1831–1832.* Text established and annotated by A. Jardin and G. W. Pierson. Paris: Presses Universitaires de France, 1973.

———. *Marie, ou l'esclavage aux Etats-Unis: Tableau des moeurs américaines.* 2 vols. Paris: Gosselin, 1835.

———. *Marie, or Slavery in the United States: A Novel of Jacksonian*

America. Translated by Barbara Chapman. Introduced by Alvis Tinnin. Stanford: Stanford University Press, 1958.

Joint Works

Drescher, Seymour, translator and editor. *Tocqueville and Beaumont on Social Reform.* Harper Torchbooks. New York: Harper and Row, 1968. A selection of writings on social questions. Note especially Drescher's appendix: "Tocqueville and Beaumont: A Rationale for Collective Study."

Tocqueville, Alexis de, and Gustave de Beaumont. *On the Penitentiary System in the United States and Its Application in France.* Introduction by Thorsten Sellin. Foreword by Herman R. Lantz. [Translated by Francis Lieber.] Carbondale and Edwardsville, Illinois: Southern Illinois University Press, 1964.

Tocqueville's Own Printed Sources

For an extensive catalogue of books consulted by Tocqueville (based upon notes in the *Democracy*, Reading Lists in the Yale collection, and Alexis's own library), see pages 727–30 of Pierson's *Tocqueville and Beaumont in America.* Pierson lists approximately one hundred entries under the following headings: Description, Indians, History, Legal Commentary, Documents Legal and Political, Other Documents and Statistics, and Miscellaneous.

For the themes presented in this book, each of the following of Tocqueville's own printed sources has been closely examined. (For further commentary on certain works, consult descriptions in relevant chapters above.)

The American's Guide: Comprising the Declaration of Independence; the Articles of Confederation; the Constitution of the United States, and the Constitutions of the Several States Composing the Union. Philadelphia: Towar and Hogan, 1830. On the spine this work is called *American Constitutions*, and that is the title which appears in Tocqueville's notes.

Blunt, Joseph. *A Historical Sketch of the Formation of the Confederacy, Particularly with Reference to the Provincial Limits and the Jurisdiction of the General Government over the Indian Tribes and the Public Territory.* New York: George and Charles Carvill, 1825.

Conseil, L. P. *Mélanges politiques et philosophiques extraits des mémoires et de la correspondance de Thomas Jefferson.* 2 vols. Paris: Paulin, 1833.

Darby, William, and Theodore Dwight, Jr. *A New Gazetteer of the United States.* Hartford: E. Hopkins, 1833. Not used by Tocqueville; a missed opportunity.

Darby, William. *View of the United States Historical, Geographical, and Statistical. . . .* Philadelphia: H. S. Tanner, 1828.

Duer, William Alexander. *Outlines of the Constitutional Jurisprudence of the United States.* New York: Collins and Hannay, 1833.

Force, Peter, comp. *National Calendar and Annals of the United States.* Vols. 10, 11, and 12. Washington, D.C., 1832, 1833, and 1834.

Goodwin, Isaac. *Town Officer; Or, Laws of Massachusetts Relating to the Duties of Municipal Officers.* Worcester: Dorr and Howland, 1825. A second revised edition appeared in 1829.

Guizot, François. *Cours d'histoire moderne: Histoire de la civilisation en France depuis la chute de l'empire romain jusqu'en 1789.* 5 vols. Paris: Pichon et Didier, 1829–32. Contains the lectures attended by Tocqueville and Beaumont in 1829 and 1830.

Hamilton, Alexander, James Madison, and John Jay. *The Federalist on the Constitution Written in the Year 1788.* Washington, D.C.: Thompson and Homans, 1831. The edition which Tocqueville read and used in the writing of the *Democracy.*

———. *The Federalist Papers.* With an introduction, table of contents, and index of ideas by Clinton Rossiter. A Mentor Book. New York: The New American Library, 1961.

James, Edwin. *Account of an Expedition from Pittsburgh to the Rocky Mountains.* [Under the command of Major Stephen H. Long.] 2 vols. Philadelphia: H. C. Carey and I. Lea, 1823.

Jefferson, Thomas. *Notes on the State of Virginia.* Introduced by Thomas Perkins Abernethy. Harper Torchbooks. New York: Harper and Row, 1964.

Keating, William H. *Narrative of an Expedition to the Source of St. Peter's River.* [Under the command of Major Stephen H. Long.] 2 vols. Philadelphia: H. C. Carey and I. Lea, 1824.

Malte-Brun, Conrad, ed. *Annales de voyages, de la géographie et de l'histoire. . . .* 24 vols. Paris: Brunet, 1808–14.

Montesquieu, Charles-Louis de Secondat, Baron de. *De l'esprit des lois.* Edited and introduced by Gonzague Truc. 2 vols. Paris: Garnier, 1961.

Pitkin, Timothy. *A Political and Civil History of the United States of America, 1763–1797.* 2 vols. New Haven: H. Howe, Durrie, and Peck, 1828.

———. *A Statistical View of the Commerce of the United States.* Hartford: C. Hosmer, 1816.

Randolph, Thomas Jefferson, ed. *Memoir, Correspondence, and Miscellanies from the Papers of Thomas Jefferson.* 4 vols. Charlottesville: F. Carr, 1829.

Rawle, William. *A View of the Constitution of the United States of America.* Philadelphia: H. C. Carey and I. Lea, 1825.

Scheffer, Arnold. *Histoire des Etats-Unis de l'Amérique septentrionale.* Paris: Raymond, 1825.

Sergeant, Thomas. *Constitutional Law; Being a View of the Practice and Jurisdiction of the Courts of the United States and of the Constitutional Points Decided.* Second revised edition. Philadelphia: P. H. Nicklin and T. Johnson, 1830.

Story, Joseph. *Commentaries on the Constitution of the United States.* One-volume abridgment. Boston: Hilliard, Gray; Cambridge, Mass.: Brown, Shattuck, 1833. (A complete three-volume work was published at the same time, but Tocqueville used the shorter version.)

———. *The Public and General Statutes Passed by the Congress of the United States of America from 1789–1827 Inclusive.* 3 vols. Boston: Wells and Lilly, 1828. (Two additional volumes were published in 1837 and 1847.)

Villeneuve-Bargemont, Alban de. *Economie politique chrétienne, ou recherches sur la nature et les causes du paupérisme en France et en Europe.* 3 vols. Paris: Paulin, 1834.

Volney, C. F. *Tableau du climat et du sol des Etats-Unis d'Amérique.* 2 vols. Paris: Courcier, 1803.

Warden, D. B. *Description statistique, historique et politiques des Etats-Unis de l'Amérique septentrionale.* 5 vols. Paris: Rey et Gravier, 1820.

Worcester, J. E., comp. *American Almanac.* Boston: Gray and Bowen, 1831, 1832, and 1834.

Also the following newspapers and journals:

National Intelligencer, 1832–34.

Niles Weekly Register, 1833–34.

North American Review, 1830–35. Not used by Tocqueville, but valuable nonetheless.

The following three works also proved particularly helpful in unraveling some of the problems posed by Tocqueville's printed sources on America:

Bauer, Elizabeth Kelly. *Commentaries on the Constitution, 1790–1860.* New York: Columbia University Press, 1952.

Ford, Paul Leicester. *A List of Editions of the Federalist.* Brooklyn, 1886.

Lipscomb, A. A., and A. E. Bergh, eds. *The Writings of Thomas Jefferson.* 20 vols. Under the auspices of the Thomas Jefferson Memorial Association. Washington, D.C., 1904. This Memorial Edition will, of course, eventually be entirely superseded by *The Papers of Thomas Jefferson.* Julian P. Boyd, editor; Lyman H. Butterfield and Mina R. Bryan, associate editors. 19 vols. (to date). Princeton, N.J.: Princeton University Press, 1950– . This new edition has not yet reached the materials that I have quoted, so I have relied on the earlier work.

Secondary Materials

In recent years the number of books and essays on Tocqueville's work and thought has grown rapidly; the renaissance of interest that began in the 1930s continues unabated. The following is a selection of works that have been of particular value in the preparation of this volume.

Alexis de Tocqueville: Livre du Centenaire, 1859–1959. Paris: Editions du Centre national de la recherche scientifique, 1960.

Aron, Raymond. *Les Etapes de la pensée sociologique. Montesquieu. Comte. Marx. Tocqueville. Durkheim. Pareto. Weber.* Paris: Gallimard, 1967.

Artz, Frederick B. *France under the Bourbon Restoration, 1814–1830.* Cambridge, Mass.: Harvard University Press, 1931.

Bagge, Dominique. *Le Conflit des idées politiques en France sous la Restauration.* Paris, 1952.

Barth, Niklas Peter. *Die Idee der Freiheit und der Demokratie bei Alexis de Tocqueville.* Aarau: Eugen Kaller, 1953.

Bastid, Paul. *Les Institutions politiques de la monarchie parlementaire française (1814–1848).* Paris: Editions du recueil Sirey, 1954.

Benson, Lee. *Turner and Beard: American Historical Writing Reconsidered.* Glencoe, Illinois: Free Press, 1960.

Blau, Joseph L., ed. *Social Theories of Jacksonian America.* New York: Liberal Arts Press, 1954.

Blumenthal, Henry. *American and French Culture, 1800–1900: Interchanges in Art, Science, Literature and Society.* Baton Rouge: Louisiana State University Press, 1975.

Brinton, Crane. *English Political Thought in the Nineteenth Century.* Harper Torchbooks. New York: Harper and Row, 1962.

Brogan, Hugh. *Tocqueville.* Fontana: Collins, 1973.

Brunius, Teddy. *Alexis de Tocqueville: The Sociological Aesthetician.* Uppsala, 1960.

Bryce, James. *The American Commonwealth.* 2 vols. 3rd edition revised. New York: Macmillan, 1894.

Charléty, S. *La Monarchie de juillet, 1830–1848.* Vol. 5 of *Histoire de France contemporaine depuis la révolution jusqu'à la paix de 1919.* Edited by Ernest Lavisse. 10 vols. Paris: Hachette, 1921.

———. *La Restauration, 1815–1830.* Vol. 4 of *Histoire de France contemporaine. . . .* Edited by Ernest Lavisse. 10 vols. Paris: Hachette, 1921.

Chevalier, Michel. *Society, Manners, and Politics in the United States.* Edited by John William Ward. Ithaca, New York: Cornell University Press, 1961.

Chevallier, J. J. *Histoire des institutions et des régimes politiques de la France moderne, 1789–1958.* 3rd revised edition. Paris: Librairie Dalloz, 1967.

———. *Les Grandes Oeuvres politiques de Machiavel à nos jours.* Paris: Armand Colin, 1949.

Chinard, Gilbert. *Saint Beuve: Thomas Jefferson et Tocqueville, avec une introduction.* Institut français de Washington. Princeton: Princeton University Press, 1943.

Cobban, Alfred. *A History of Modern France.* Vol. 2: *From the First Empire to the Second Empire, 1799–1871.* 2nd edition. Pelican. Harmondsworth, Middlesex, England: Penguin Books, 1965.

Commager, Henry Steele. *Majority Rule and Minority Rights.* New York: Oxford University Press, 1943.

Conkin, Paul K. *Self-Evident Truths: Being a Discourse on the Origins and Development of the First Principles of American Government—Popular*

Sovereignty, Natural Rights and Balance and Separation of Powers. Bloomington: Indiana University Press, 1974.

Cooper, James Fenimore. *The American Democrat, or Hints on the Social and Civic Relations of the United States of America.* New York: Vintage, 1956.

Dahl, Robert A. *A Preface to Democratic Theory.* Chicago: The University of Chicago Press, 1956.

——— and Edward R. Tufte. *Size and Democracy.* Stanford: Stanford University Press, 1973.

Drescher, Seymour. *Dilemmas of Democracy: Tocqueville and Modernization.* Pittsburgh: University of Pittsburgh Press, 1968.

———. *Tocqueville and England.* Cambridge, Mass.: Harvard University Press, 1964.

Eichtal, E. d'. *Alexis de Tocqueville et la démocratie libérale.* Paris: C. Lévy, 1897.

Fabian, Bernhard. *Alexis de Tocquevilles Amerikabild.* Heidelberg: Carl Winter, 1957.

Freehling, William W., ed. *The Nullification Era: A Documentary Record.* Harper Torchbooks. New York: Harper and Row, 1967.

Gargan, Edward T. *Alexis de Tocqueville: The Critical Years, 1848–1851.* Washington, D.C.: Catholic University of America Press, 1955.

———. *De Tocqueville.* New York: Hillary House, 1965.

Gobineau, Arthur de. *Essai sur l'inégalité des races humaines.* Paris: P. Belfond, 1967.

Goldstein, Doris. *Trial of Faith. Religion and Politics in Tocqueville's Thought.* New York: Elsevier, 1975.

Graebner, Norman A., ed. *Freedom in America: A 200-Year Perspective.* University Park: The Pennsylvania State University Press, 1977.

Grund, Francis J. *Aristocracy in America: From the Sketch-Book of a German Nobleman.* Introduced by George E. Probst. Harper Torchbooks. New York: Harper and Row, 1959.

Guizot, François. *Historical Essays and Lectures.* Edited and introduced by Stanley Mellon. Chicago: University of Chicago Press, 1972.

Hartz, Louis. *The Liberal Tradition in America.* New York: Harcourt, Brace and Co., 1955.

Herr, Richard. *Tocqueville and the Old Regime.* Princeton: Princeton University Press, 1962.

Laboulaye, Edouard. *L'Etat et ses limites.* Paris: Charpentier, 1863.

Lamberti, Jean-Claude. *La Notion d'individualisme chez Tocqueville.* Preface by Jean-Jacques Chevallier. Paris: Presses Universitaires de France, 1970.

Laski, Harold J. *The Rise of European Liberalism: An Essay in Interpretation.* London: Allen and Unwin, 1936.

Lawlor, Sister Mary. *Alexis de Tocqueville in the Chamber of Deputies: His Views on Foreign and Colonial Policy.* Washington, D.C.: Catholic University of America Press, 1959.

Lerner, Max. *Tocqueville and American Civilization.* Harper Colophon Books. New York: Harper and Row, 1969. Originally published as the "Introduction" to the new George Lawrence translation of *Democracy in America*, edited by J. P. Mayer and Max Lerner.

Leroy, Maxime. *Histoire des idées sociales en France*. Vol. 2: *De Babeuf à Tocqueville*. Paris: Gallimard, 1962.

Lively, Jack. *The Social and Political Thought of Alexis de Tocqueville*. Oxford: Clarendon Press, 1962.

Mahieu, Robert G. *Les Enquêteurs français aux Etats-Unis de 1830 à 1837. L'Influence américaine sur l'évolution démocratique en France*. Paris: Honoré Champion, 1934.

Marcel, R. Pierre. *Essai politique sur Alexis de Tocqueville avec un grand nombre de documents inédits*. Paris: Félix Alcan, 1910.

Mayer, J.-P. *Political Thought in France from the Revolution to the Fourth Republic*. Revised edition. London: Routledge and Paul, 1949.

———. *Prophet of the Mass Age: A Study of Alexis de Tocqueville*. London: J. M. Dent and Sons, 1939. The American edition carried a different title: *Alexis de Tocqueville: A Biographical Essay in Political Science*. New York: Viking Press, 1940. (The latter was revised as a new edition with a new essay, "Tocqueville after a Century," Harper Torchbooks. New York: Harper and Row, 1960.)

Mellon, Stanley. *The Political Uses of History: A Study of Historians in the French Restoration*. Stanford: Stanford University Press, 1958.

Merriman, John M., ed. *1830 in France*. New York: New Viewpoints, 1975.

Meyers, Marvin. *The Jacksonian Persuasion: Politics and Belief*. Stanford: Stanford University Press, 1957.

Miller, Perry, ed. *The Legal Mind in America: From Independence to the Civil War*. Anchor Books. Garden City, New York: Doubleday, 1962.

———. *The Life of the Mind in America: From the Revolution to the Civil War*. New York: Harcourt, Brace and World, 1965.

Mueller, Iris W. *John Stuart Mill and French Thought*. Urbana, Illinois: University of Illinois Press, 1956.

Nagel, Paul C. *One Nation Indivisible, the Union in American Thought, 1776–1861*. New York: Oxford University Press, 1964.

Nantet, Jacques. *Tocqueville*. Paris: Seghers, 1971.

Pessen, Edward. *Jacksonian America: Society, Personality and Politics*. Homewood, Ill.: Dorsey Press, 1969.

———. *Riches, Class, and Power before the Civil War*. Lexington, Mass.: D. C. Heath and Co., 1973.

———, ed. *Three Centuries of Social Mobility in America*. Lexington, Mass.: D. C. Heath and Co., 1974.

Pierson, George Wilson. *Tocqueville and Beaumont in America*. New York: Oxford University Press, 1938. An abridged edition, entitled *Tocqueville in America*, was prepared by Dudley C. Lunt in paper and hardback versions; paper: Anchor Books, New York: Doubleday, 1959; cloth: Gloucester, Mass.: Peter Smith, 1969.

Pinkney, David H. *The French Revolution of 1830*. Princeton: Princeton University Press, 1972.

Pole, J. R. *The Pursuit of Equality in American History*. Berkeley: University of California Press, 1978.

Ponteil, Félix. *Les Institutions de la France de 1814 à 1870.* Paris: Presses Universitaires de France, 1966.

———. *La Monarchie parlementaire: 1815–1848.* 3rd edition revised. Paris: Armand Colin, 1949.

Potter, David M. *People of Plenty: Economic Abundance and the American Character.* Chicago: University of Chicago Press, 1954.

Poussin, Guillaume-Tell. *Chemins de fer américains.* Paris: Carilian-Goeury, 1836.

Probst, George E., ed. *The Happy Republic: A Reader in Tocqueville's America.* Harper Torchbooks. New York: Harper and Brothers, 1962.

Redier, Antoine. *Comme disait M. de Tocqueville. . . .* Paris: Perrin, 1925.

Remini, Robert V. *Andrew Jackson.* New York: Harper and Row, 1969.

Rémond, René. *Les Etats-Unis devant l'opinion française, 1815–1852.* 2 vols. Paris: Armand Colin, 1962.

———. *The Right Wing in France from 1815 to de Gaulle.* Translated by James M. Laux. 2nd revised edition. Philadelphia: University of Pennsylvania Press, 1966.

Rozwenc, Edwin C., ed. *Ideology and Power in the Age of Jackson.* Anchor Books. Garden City, New York: Doubleday, 1964.

Ruggiero, Guido de. *History of European Liberalism.* Translated by R. G. Collingwood. Beacon Paperback. Boston: Beacon Press, 1959.

Sauvigny, Guillaume de Bertier de. *The Bourbon Restoration.* Translated by Lynn M. Case. Philadelphia: University of Pennsylvania Press, 1966.

Schatz, Albert. *L'Individualisme économique et social: ses origines—son évolution—ses formes contemporaines.* Paris: Armand Colin, 1907.

Schlaerth, William J., S.J., ed. *A Symposium on Alexis de Tocqueville's Democracy in America.* Burke Society Series. New York: Fordham University Press, 1945.

Schlesinger, Arthur M., Jr. *The Age of Jackson.* Boston: Little, Brown, 1945.

Soltau, Roger. *French Political Thought in the Nineteenth Century.* New Haven: Yale University Press, 1931.

Songy, Benedict Gaston, O.S.B. "Alexis de Tocqueville and Slavery: Judgments and Predictions." Ph.D. dissertation, St. Louis University, 1969. Available from University Microfilms, Ann Arbor, Michigan.

Starzinger, Vincent E. *Middlingness, Juste Milieu Political Theory in France and England, 1815–1848.* Charlottesville: University Press of Virginia, 1965.

Sumner, William Graham. *Folkways: A Study of the Sociological Importance of Usages, Manners, Customs, Mores, and Morals.* Boston: Ginn & Co., 1907.

Taylor, George R. *The Transportation Revolution: 1815–1860.* Vol. 4 of *The Economic History of the United States.* 10 vols. Edited by Henry David et al. Harper Torchbooks. New York: Harper and Row, 1968.

Vail, Eugène. *De la littérature et des hommes de lettres des Etats-Unis d'Amérique.* Paris, 1841.

Van Deusen, Glyndon G. *The Jacksonian Era, 1828–1848.* Harper Torchbooks. New York: Harper and Row, 1963.

Ward, John William. *Red, White and Blue: Men, Books, and Ideas in American Culture*. New York: Oxford University Press, 1969.

White, Leonard D. *The Jacksonians: A Study in Administrative History, 1829–1861*. New York: Macmillan, 1954.

Zeitlin, Irving M. *Liberty, Equality and Revolution in Alexis de Tocqueville*. Boston: Little, Brown, 1971.

Zetterbaum, Marvin. *Tocqueville and the Problem of Democracy*. Stanford: Stanford University Press, 1967.

Articles

Adair, Douglass. "The Authorship of the Disputed *Federalist Papers*." *William and Mary Quarterly* 3rd ser. 1 (1944):97–122 and 235–64.

———. "That Politics May be Reduced to a Science." *Huntington Library Quarterly* 20 (August 1957):343–60.

———. "The Tenth *Federalist* Revisited." *William and Mary Quarterly* 3rd ser. 8 (January 1951):48–67.

Aron, Raymond. "Idées politiques et vision historique de Tocqueville." *Revue française de science politique* 10 (September 1960):509–26.

Boisdettre, P. de. "Tocqueville et Gobineau." *Revue de Paris* 66 (August 1959):138–42.

Bourke, Paul F. "The Pluralist Reading of James Madison's Tenth *Federalist*." *Perspectives in American History* 9 (1975):271–95.

Bryce, James. "The Predictions of Hamilton and De Tocqueville." Johns Hopkins University *Studies in Historical and Political Science* 5 (September 1887):329–81.

———. "The United States Constitution as Seen in the Past." *Studies in History and Jurisprudence* 1 (1901):311–58.

Chevallier, Jean-Jacques. "De la distinction des sociétés aristocratiques et des sociétés démocratiques, en tant que fondement de la pensée politique d'Alexis de Tocqueville." Communication à l'Académie des sciences morales et politiques. 1955.

Colwell, James L. " 'The Calamities Which They Apprehend': Tocqueville on Race in America." *Western Humanities Review* 21 (Spring 1967):93–100.

Diamond, Martin. "The Ends of Federalism." *Publius: The Journal of Federalism* 3 (Fall 1973):129–52.

Drescher, Seymour. "Tocqueville's Two *Démocraties*." *Journal of the History of Ideas* 25 (April-June 1964):201–16.

Gargan, Edward T. "The Formation of Tocqueville's Historical Thought." *Review of Politics* 24 (January 1962):48–61.

———. "Some Problems in Tocqueville Scholarship." *Mid-America* 41 (January 1959):3–26.

———. "Tocqueville and the Problem of Historical Prognosis." *American Historical Review* 68 (January 1963):332–45.

George, W. H. "Montesquieu and de Tocqueville and Corporative Individualism." *American Political Science Review* 16 (February 1922):10–21.

Gershman, Sally. "Alexis de Tocqueville and Slavery." *French Historical Studies* 9 (Spring 1976):467–83.

Gilman, Daniel C. "Alexis de Tocqueville and His Book on America—Sixty Years After." *The Century Illustrated Monthly Magazine* 56 (May–October 1898):703–15.

Goldstein, Doris S. "Alexis de Tocqueville's Concept of Citizenship." *American Philosophical Society Proceedings* 108 (February 1964):39–53.

———. "The Religious Beliefs of Alexis de Tocqueville." *French Historical Studies* 1 (Fall 1960):379–93.

Hamburger, Joseph. "Mill and Tocqueville on Liberty." From John M. Robson and M. Laine, eds., *James and John Stuart Mill. Papers of the Centenary Conference.* Toronto: University of Toronto Press, 1976.

Heilprin, M. "De Tocqueville in the United States." *Nation* 1 (24 August 1865):247–49.

Horwitz, J. Morton. "Tocqueville and the Tyranny of the Majority." *The Review of Politics* 28 (July 1966):293–307.

Jardin, André. "Tocqueville et l'Algérie." *Revue des travaux de l'Académie des sciences morales et politiques* 115 (1962):61–74.

———. "Tocqueville et la décentralisation." "La Décentralisation": Sixth colloquium on history organized by the faculty of letters and human sciences of Aix-en-Provence, 1 and 2 December 1961. *Publications des Annales*, la Faculté des Lettres, Aix-en-Provence, undated.

Laski, Harold J. "Alexis de Tocqueville and Democracy." From F. J. C. Hearnshaw, ed., *The Social and Political Ideas of Some Representative Thinkers of the Victorian Age.* London: G. G. Harrap, 1933.

Lukes, Steven. "The Meanings of 'Individualism.'" *Journal of the History of Ideas* 32 (January-March 1971):45–66.

———."Types of Individualism." *Dictionary of the History of Ideas: Studies in Selected Pivotal Ideas.* Philip P. Wiener, Editor in Chief. 4 vols. New York: Charles Scribner's Sons, 1973. 2:593–604.

Mason, Alpheus Thomas. "The *Federalist*—A Split Personality." *American Historical Review* 57 (1952):625–43.

Mayer, J.-P. "Alexis de Tocqueville: A Commentated Bibliography." *Revue internationale de philosophie* 13 (1959):313–19.

———. "Tocqueville's Influence." *History* 3 (1960):87–103.

———. "Tocqueville's Travel Diaries." *Encounter* 54 (March 1958):54–60.

Mill, John Stuart. "Democracy in America." *Edinburgh Review* 72 (October 1840):1–48.

———. "De Tocqueville on Democracy in America." *London Review* 2 (October 1835):85–129.

Morgan, Edmund S. "The American Revolution Considered as an Intellectual Movement." From Arthur M. Schlesinger, Jr., and Morton White, eds., *Paths of American Thought.* Boston: Houghton Mifflin, 1963.

Morgan, Robert. "Madison's Theory of Representation in the Tenth *Federalist.*" *Journal of Politics* 36 (1974):852–85.

Moulin, Léo. "On the Evolution of the Meaning of the Word 'Individualism.'" *International Social Science Bulletin* 7 (1955):181–85.

Nef, John. "Truth, Belief and Civilization: Tocqueville and Gobineau." *Review of Politics* 25 (October 1963):460–82.

Nisbet, Robert. "Many Tocquevilles." *The American Scholar* 46 (Winter 1976–77):59–75.

Pappé, H. O. "Mill and Tocqueville." *Journal of the History of Ideas* 25 (April-June 1964):217–34.

Pessen, Edward. "The Egalitarian Myth and the American Social Reality:

Wealth, Mobility, and Equality in the 'Era of the Common Man.'" *The American Historical Review* 76 (October 1971):989–1034.

Pierson, George Wilson. "Gustave de Beaumont: Liberal." *Franco-American Review* 1 (June 1936):307–16.

———. "Tocqueville's Visions of Democracy." *The Yale University Library Gazette* 51 (July 1976):4–17.

Resh, Richard. "Alexis de Tocqueville and the Negro: *Democracy in America* Reconsidered." *Journal of Negro History* 48 (October 1963):251–59.

Richter, Melvin. "Debate on Race: Tocqueville-Gobineau Correspondence." *Commentary* 25 (February 1958):151–60.

———. "Tocqueville on Algeria." *Review of Politics* 25 (July 1963):362–98.

———. "The Uses of Theory: Tocqueville's Adaptation of Montesquieu." From Melvin Richter, ed., *Essays in Theory and History: An Approach to the Social Sciences*. Cambridge, Mass.; Harvard University Press, 1970.

Riemer, Neal. "James Madison's Theory of the Self-Destructive Features of Republican Government." *Ethics* 65 (1954):34–43.

———. "The Republicanism of James Madison." *Political Science Quarterly* 69 (March 1954):45–64.

Salomon, Albert. "Tocqueville's Philosophy of Freedom." *Review of Politics* 1 (October 1939):400–31.

Schleifer, James T. "Images of America after the Revolution: Alexis de Tocqueville and Gustave de Beaumont Visit the Early Republic." *The Yale University Library Gazette* 51 (January 1977):125–44.

Spitz, David. "On Tocqueville and the 'Tyranny' of Public Sentiment." *Political Science* 9 (September 1957):3–13.

Strout, Cushing. "Tocqueville's Duality: Describing America and Thinking of Europe." *American Quarterly* 21 (Spring 1969):87–99.

Suter, Jean François. "Tocqueville et le problème de démocratie." *Revue internationale de philosophie* 13 (1959):330–40.

Swart, Koenraad W. "Individualism in the Mid-Nineteenth Century (1826–1860)." *Journal of the History of Ideas* 23 (January-March 1962):77–90.

Wallace, Michael. "The Uses of Violence in American History." *The American Scholar* 40 (Winter 1970–1971):81–102.

White, Paul Lambert. "American Manners in 1830: de Tocqueville's Letters and Diary." *Yale Review* 12 (October 1922):118–31.

Index